T0209715

A Case for Latter-day Christianity

Evidences for the restoration of the
New Testament's "Mere" Christian Church

Robert Starling

BALBOA.
PRESS
A DIVISION OF HAY HOUSE

Balboa Press books may be ordered through booksellers or by contacting:

Balboa Press
A Division of Hay House
Liberty Drive
Bloomington, IN 47403
www.balboapress.com
(877) 407-4847

Because of the dynamic nature of the Internet, any web addresses or links contained in this book may have changed since publication and may no longer be valid. The views expressed in this work are solely those of the author and do not necessarily reflect the views of the publisher, and the publisher hereby disclaims any responsibility for them.

The author of this book does not dispense medical advice or prescribe the use of any technique as a form of treatment for physical, emotional, or medical problems without the advice of a physician, either directly or indirectly. The intent of the author is only to offer information of a general nature to help you in your quest for emotional and spiritual well-being. In the event you use any of the information in this book for yourself, which is your constitutional right, the author and the publisher assume no responsibility for your actions.

Any people depicted in stock imagery provided by Getty Images are models,
and such images are being used for illustrative purposes only.
Certain stock imagery © Getty Images.

KJV: Scripture taken from the King James Version of the Bible.

Print information available on the last page.

ISBN: 978-1-9822-3204-7 (sc)
ISBN: 978-1-9822-3202-3 (e)

Library of Congress Control Number: 2019910354

Balboa Press rev. date: 08/23/2019

CONTENTS

DEDICATION

For Wendy

— that you may know my heart

ABOUT THE AUTHOR

Hi, I'm Robert Starling. Since we'll be spending some time together in this book, let me tell you a little about myself. I hope we can become good friends.

I was born and raised in Columbus, Georgia, in the heart of the Bible Belt. As you might imagine, religion is a serious matter in that part of the world. You can't drive down Georgia back roads for more and a mile without seeing one or more little country churches, usually of some Baptist variety.

My uncle Rudolph was a Methodist pastor, and I attended Baptist vacation bible school with my friends, but I was raised as a member of The Church of Jesus Christ of Latter-day Saints. Lots of folks call us "Mormons". My parents became members of that church when they were teenagers, so I was born into the faith.

All my life I've gotten along fine with people of other religions. I had lots of friends in high school and they even put me in the yearbook as the "Most Representative" student even though I was one of only seven Latter-day Saints in a school population of 2,500. I love to share my beliefs and to answer questions, and sometimes there are a lot of them. That's one of the reasons I wrote this book.

After two years of studying Chemistry at Georgia Tech in Atlanta, I served as a Spanish-speaking missionary for another two years in California and Arizona. After that I attended Brigham Young University in Utah where I got a degree in Broadcasting. I've worked in film and television production for over 40 years as a writer, producer, and director. I wrote and helped produced one film called *"In Search of Historic Jesus"* that you might have seen on NBC or in theaters. There were others too, but that one is most pertinent to this book.

My wife, four kids and I spent 13 years in the Los Angeles area before we escaped the rat race there. I've lived for the last 25 years in Utah, where I worked for nine years as a producer in the media production department of The Church of Jesus Christ of Latter-day Saints.

The apostle Peter admonished every Christian to "*be* ready always to *give* an answer to every man that asketh you a reason of the hope that is in you" (1 Peter 3:15). That's what this book is all about. Ya'll can read more about that in the Introduction. Don't skip it, okay? Enjoy.

INTRODUCTION

This is going to be a personal book about my faith. I'm a member of The Church of Jesus Christ of latter-day Saints (sometimes called "Mormons"), and I'm a Christian. If you are interested in how that works, I'm willing (and hopefully able) to "bring forth my strong reasons" for my beliefs and share them with you. I'll use reason, scripture, the teachings of the early Church Fathers (some of the earliest Christians), and quotes from some of the most respected Catholic and Protestant scholars, pastors and theologians in history.

I'm not a Baptist Christian nor a Methodist Christian nor a Presbyterian Christian nor a Lutheran Christian, nor do I claim to be. I'm not a Protestant Christian, an Evangelical Christian or a Catholic Christian. Therefore I am not a "traditional" or "historic" or "orthodox" or "reformed" Christian. But I <u>AM</u> a "Biblical" and a "New Testament" Christian.

I often refer to myself as a "pre-Catholic" or a "pre-Nicene" or "latter-day" Christian.

Why am I writing this? Perhaps this story will make it a bit clearer:

> When the Mormon candidate announced his intention to run for the office of President of the United States, there were many who felt he was well qualified for the job. He was handsome, charismatic, a proven leader, and he had already been elected to a substantial political office.
>
> However, despite his qualifications and the support of a large number of sympathetic voters in at least one western state, many political pundits felt his candidacy was doomed from the start because of the man's affiliation with a religion that was considered strange and mysterious to many, and to some people even dangerous.

In an attempt to alleviate some of the misunderstandings about his faith, the candidate wrote a letter to a major publisher that was considered a well-formed position paper, explaining the salient points of his beliefs and those of other members of his church.

Unfortunately the major media did not help to publicize the explanation of the candidate's beliefs, and tragic miscarriages of justice arose. Even government entities violated numerous Constitutional rights of the candidate and his followers. At one point an official order was given to exterminate them if they did not leave the state where their majority population resided.

Eventually corrupt local officials arrested the candidate on trumped-up charges and placed him in a jail where a terroristic mob of thugs broke in and assassinated him and his brother.

Denied government protection from roving mobs of armed men, tens of thousands of members of this Presidential candidate's faith were dragged from their beautiful homes at gunpoint. Their lands and businesses were confiscated and they were forced to leave the boundaries of the United States to find a place where they eventually could live their religion in peace.

Does this sound like a fantastic fictional story? In point of fact it is actually horribly true. It happened in "the land of the free and the home of the brave." The year was 1844. The candidate was Joseph Smith, the first president of The Church of Jesus Christ of Latter-day Saints, commonly known as the "Mormons."

The purpose of this book is to try to illuminate (and hopefully eliminate) some of the kinds of misunderstandings that led to those tragic events of a century and a half ago. Sadly, many of those misconceptions about members of the "LDS" church are still in evidence today.

As an example: A volunteer campaign worker for Senator John McCain said during the run-up to the 2008 Presidential campaign that "Mormons gave money to Hamas terrorists and treat women like the Taliban." [1]

I'M NOT TRYING TO CONVERT ANYONE

This book's purpose is not to engage in contention or debate, nor to preach nor to proselytize, nor to convert people away from their own beliefs to join my church. Nor it is to be an official pronouncement of The Church of Jesus Christ of Latter-day Saints. As I said, it is my personal confession of faith, and an attempt to "bring forth my strong reasons" (Isaiah 41:21) for my beliefs, and "to give an answer to every man... a reason for the hope that is in me." (1 Peter 3:15) "Having a good conscience," I feel a need to follow the Apostle Peter's admonition to speak out and share my beliefs with any and all interested parties.

Before I go too far down this road, let me admit up front that I don't have a string of letters like Ph.D. or Th.D. or L.L.D., or Doctor of Divinity after my name. (Although I have an uncle who does — he's retired now after a long and happy career as a United Methodist pastor.) I'm just a good ol' boy from Georgia, but I can read Scripture just like anyone else, and there are some things that seem to be pretty self-evident to me. I'll leave it to you to decide if it makes sense to you.

WHY DO I CALL MY BOOK *A CASE FOR LATTER-DAY CHRISTIANITY?*
My first edition of this book was published under the title *Really Inside Mormonism*. I had not orignally planned to include "Really" in the title, but I found that a Catholic priest named Isaiah Bennett had renounced Catholicism and was baptized into the LDS church, then he left "Mormonism" after a year or two. Both he and his wife (yes, he got married) participated in that alleged conversion/de-conversion experience. He then wrote a book called *"Inside Mormonism: What Mormons Really Believe."* So I needed to make my title different.

I happened to get a chance to hear "Brother" Bennett speak to an LDS audience during the time he claimed to be a Latter-day Saint, and I thought he gave a pretty convincing talk about how he became a member of my faith. I'm not going to accuse him of a "conversion of convenience" so that he could write an expose' book, but I can see where some folks might think his situation looks kinda fishy.

He was only a "Mormon" for a few years, whereas I've been a member of the Church of Jesus Christ all my life (65 years in 2019, since my baptism at age eight). My father served on the first High Council in the first LDS stake (regional organization) organized in Georgia. I served two years as a full-time Spanish-speaking missionary in California and Arizona. I received my BA from Brigham Young University where I attended college for three years.

I've held almost every Church office at the local level except Bishop, and I've had several Stake and Area callings including Stake Mission President. I worked professionally at LDS Church Headquarters in Salt Lake City as a writer/producer/ director for nine years in the media production department. For the last 25 years I've lived in the Salt Lake Valley, in the "epicenter" of Mormondom. So I've "really" been "inside Mormonism" for a lifetime. That's where the "really" in the original title cames from. Really.

THE CASE FOR CHRIST – AND FOR LATTER-DAY CHRISTIANITY

So why did I change the title for this second edition? First, the President of our church requested that we avoid the term "Mormon" whenever possible in favor of the complete name of the church. Second, I was impressed with investigative reporter Lee Strobel's book (and movie) *The Case for Christ*. Third, I was also impressed with Tad Callister's book *A Case for the Book of Mormon*. I liked those titles so I wanted to echo them in mine. (I recommend those books too.) As I "bring forth my strong reasons" or evidences, I think I can make a case that The Church of Jesus Christ of Latter-day Saints is indeed a latter-day restoration of the Biblical Christian church.

WHAT IS A "MERE" CHRISTIAN?

Since I began writing this book I've also revised my original working title to include the word "mere." I did this after reading C.S. Lewis's "Mere Christianity" and I did it in homage to the great wisdom and eloquence of that wonderful Christian writer and apologist. C. S. Lewis has become one of my heroes. He defined "mere" disciples or Christians as *"those who accepted the teachings of the apostles"* (Acts 11:26). He said that *"if we once allow people to start spiritualizing and refining or as they might say 'deepening' the word Christian, it ... will speedily become a useless word."*

He described "mere" Christianity as being like a large hallway in a building, out of which doors open into several rooms (or denominations). His goal was simply to bring people into the hall, not to convince them which door to open. He said,

"Even in the hall you must begin trying to obey the rules which are common to the whole house. And above all you must be asking which door is the true one; not which one pleases you best by its paint and paneling." He says the "mere" Christian must ask of a "door" he might plan to enter; "Are these doctrines true? Is holiness here? Does my conscience move me towards this?" Then finally he adds, *"When you have reached your own room, be kind to those who have chosen different doors and to those who are still in the hall. If they are wrong they need your prayers all the more; and if they are your enemies, then you are under orders to pray for them. That is one of the rules common to the whole house."*

After reading Lewis's book I believe that in the eyes of my Christian brothers and sisters I should at least be considered a "mere" Christian, for I do indeed accept the teachings and essential beliefs of the apostles as found in the New Testament. The founder of my own chosen "room" Joseph Smith once said, *"The fundamental principles of our religion are the testimony of the Apostles and* Prophets, concerning Jesus Christ, that He died, was buried, and rose again the third day, and ascended into heaven: and all other things which pertain to our religion are only appendages to it. "[2]

Even the most ardent critics of The Church of Jesus Christ of Latter-day Saints seem to focus mostly on the "appendages" of our faith to find differences from their own beliefs, since our "fundamental principles" of Christ, his death and resurrection are nearly identical with those of other "mere" Christians.

I believe in a Christianity that was established by Jesus himself hundreds of years before the religion that became "historic" or "traditional" Christianity existed. This original Christianity was lost after the deaths of the original apostles, but it was restored to the earth in these "latter days" in its fullness as part of the "restitution of all things" the Bible says must take place before the Second Coming of Christ (Acts 3:21). Therefore I also call myself a "latter-day Christian."

This "restitution" or restoration was necessary because of the "falling away" from the original teachings of Christ and His apostles that Paul lamented in his second letter to the Thessalonians (chapter 2 verse 3). The "falling away" or "apostasy" became even more pronounced during the centuries of the "dark ages" of human history that have been well-documented and that were foreseen by the prophet Amos as a time when there would be a "famine" of the word of God and men would *"run to and fro, seeking the word of the Lord, but shall not find it."* (Amos 8:11-12)

The great Reformers like Martin Luther and others recognized that the "faith once delivered to the saints" had been corrupted almost beyond recognition by the time they were born. Luther wrote: *"I simply say that Christianity has ceased to exist among those who should have preserved it – the bishops and scholars."*[3]

Although he and other brave men did their best to <u>reform</u> the Christian faith as they knew it, our Savior said that new wine in old bottles or new patches on old clothes were not enough. The Protestant Reformation did however bring about some measure of religious freedom that paved the way eventually for the "restitution of all things" — the <u>restoration</u> of Christ's original New Testament church to the earth.

THE TERM "LATTER-DAY SAINTS"

I am a follower of Jesus Christ. My predecessors in New Testament times called themselves "saints." Outsiders used the term "Christian" to describe them with derision. That name stuck and gradually became a generic term, synonymous with that of "Saint". In a return to Biblical practice and combined with the recognition that we're living in what the scriptures refer to as the last days, or "the latter times," I and fellow members of my faith call ourselves "Latter-day Saints." Like our spiritual forefathers who "were first called Christians at Antioch", we too are known by a term coined and used initially with disrespect by outsiders. We're often called "Mormons." And like the "former-day" Saints of the New Testament Church, we too have acquiesced to the terminology and have (at least passively) accepted the name "Mormons".

But to be a bit more precise as I begin this book I've decided also to call myself a "Latter-day Christian" to clearly emphasize my faith as a follower of Jesus Christ. As I attempt to "bring forth my strong reasons" for thus believing, I invite the curious reader to come along on a journey that I guarantee will be enlightening and definitely NOT boring.

CAN YOU HANDLE THIS BOOK?

Maybe it comes from my Southern roots in Georgia, but I guess I'm a bit of what some might call a Christian Rebel. Not that I rebel against Christ. I love and adore Him as my Lord and my Savior. But I do like to stir things up a bit among my fellow Christians. Especially the ones Amy Grant refers to in her song *Fat Baby*. You know… the ones who love their "bottle" of Christian "milk", but whose comfort zone doesn't extend much farther than that. Amy says they've "*sampled solid food once or twice, but <u>doctrine</u> leaves them cold as ice.*"[4]

Paul expressed the same concerns about some Christians in his day when he said:
"*ye have need that one teach you again … the first principles of the oracles of God; and are become such as have need of <u>milk</u>, and not of strong <u>meat</u>.*" (Heb. 5:12-14) *Getting back to those "Fat Baby" Christians: Amy sings, "I know a man, maybe you know him, too. You never can tell, he might even be you…."*

These are the folks I'm reminded of by a scene in the movie *A Few Good Men*, when Tom Cruise tells Jack Nicholson, "I want the truth!", and Jack yells back, "You can't handle the truth!"

Well, buckle your seat belts and get out your forks and steak knives, brothers and sisters. It's time to try a little high protein diet! You can handle the truth, right?

ENDNOTES FOR INTRODUCTION

1   *Boston Globe*, June 21, 2007
2   *Teachings of the Prophet Joseph Smith, p. 121*
3   Tyler, John Murray. *Martin Luther, a Biographical Study,* Westminster, MD: Newman Press, 1964
4   Amy Grant *Fat Baby*, album *Age to Age*, Universal Music - Brentwood Benson Publ.

EVIDENCE 1

Jesus Christ is my personal Savior

(If you haven't read my Introduction, it would be good to go back
and do that now so that this will make more sense.)

MY PERSONAL FAITH IN JESUS CHRIST

The Bible says that before the Final Judgment, *"every knee shall bow... and every tongue shall confess that Jesus Christ is Lord."*[1] I consider myself no exception, so let me begin by gladly confessing my own witness that Jesus is indeed the Christ, the divine Son of God. From the time I was a small child I have loved and honored him, worshiped him, sung his praises, and prayed to my Heavenly Father in his holy name.

Jesus is my friend, my Savior, my King, my Lord, and my God. He is my advocate with the Father, and under the Father's direction Christ created this earth and the other planets, moons and stars – the entire physical universe as we know it. (John 1:1-3)

Although he is God, Jesus took upon himself a physical body and came into mortality as a babe in Bethlehem so that he might experience all things and set the ideal example for me to follow. He endured all things and ultimately suffered and died for me. He suffered both in Gethsemane and on the cross of Calvary. Then after three days he overcame death and hell and was resurrected in a glorified physical body. Today He lives and reigns in the heavens at the right hand of the Father in that same glorious physical body of flesh and bone that he showed to Thomas and the other apostles in the Upper Room. (John 20: 19-28)

As a follower of Jesus Christ and as his adopted child, my greatest desire is to someday be able to kneel before him and wash his feet with my tears of love and gratitude for all he has done for me. I long to have him lift me up, call my name, and clasp me to his bosom in his embracing arms. I have no greater wish or desire for my life than this.

Obviously anyone's testimony of the importance of Christ in his or her life is intensely personal. I know that for me there is nothing I consider more sacred. So in sharing my confession of faith with you the reader, I'm extending to you my friendship, and my trust. A novelist named Dinah Maria Craik wrote in 1859:

> But oh! the blessing it is to have a friend to whom one can speak fearlessly on any subject; with whom one's deepest as well as one's most foolish thoughts come out simply and safely.

> Oh, the comfort — the inexpressible comfort of feeling safe with a person — having neither to weigh thoughts nor measure words, but pouring them all right out, just as they are, chaff and grain together; certain that a faithful hand will take and sift them, keep what is worth keeping, and then with the breath of kindness blow the rest away. [2]

In that respect, at least, I hope you can be my friend. And I hope that you can feel in your heart the truth of what I'm going to share with you.

As with any Christian, it's hard for me to find the right words to fully express what Jesus Christ really means to me in my life. And like many "cradle Christians" I find it hard to pinpoint a specific time in my life when I came to know the Lord as my personal Savior. Suffice it to say that it was at an early age. It seems as though a simple faith was always there. When I was a small boy attending Primary in the little Mormon chapel in Columbus, Georgia I sang with child-like simplicity the old Protestant song:

"Jesus loves me, this I know,
for the Bible tells me so,
Little ones to him belong,
we are weak but he is strong.
Yes Jesus loves me, yes Jesus loves me,
Yes Jesus loves me, for the Bible tells me so."
        (1862, public domain)

(I sang the same song when I attended summer Vacation Bible School with childhood friends at Northside Baptist Church in Columbus, so I'm sure it's familiar to most of my readers.)

Jesus Christ IS my Lord, and he IS the king of my life. I know that it is only through his name and through his precious blood that I am saved. I love him with all my heart. I have no greater desire in life than to serve him and strive to keep his commandments. And I know there is nothing I can ever do that can even begin to repay what he's done for me. There is one of our LDS hymns I often sing that comes pretty close to explaining my feelings about the Lord. May I share a part of it with you? It may also be familiar to you, as other Christians use it also:

"I stand all amazed at the love Jesus offers me,
Confused at the grace that so fully He proffers me.
I tremble to know that for me He was crucified,
That for me, a sinner, He suffered, he bled, and died.
Oh it is wonderful, that He should care for me, enough to die for me!
Oh it is wonderful, wonderful to me!"[3]

MY EARLY YEARS AS A LATTER-DAY SAINT

Like the prophet Nephi in *The Book of Mormon*, I was "born of goodly parents". Both my mother and my father were converted to The Church of Jesus Christ of Latter-day Saints in their youth, so I was born and reared in a Latter-day Saint home.

Thus from my earliest years I was taught in The Church of Jesus Christ of Latter-day Saints who Jesus was. I was taught that He was indeed my Savior and Redeemer - that He died for my sins and was bodily resurrected. I learned that he is the Only Begotten Son of God. His deity and his Lordship were so much a part of the fabric of my life that it was simply taken for granted.

MY PERSONAL CONVERSION TO CHRIST

But like all Christians, (even "cradle" Christians!) there came a time when my faith was tested, and I had to find out for myself whether the beliefs I'd been taught all my life were true. For me, the "conversion experience" came in 1967 when I was serving in the fourth month of my two years as a Spanish-speaking LDS missionary in Phoenix, Arizona. I'd been concerned for some time that my intellect-based testimony of Christ wasn't enough. I had been teaching people that God would answer their prayers and give them a witness of the truth through the Holy Spirit, and I felt like a hypocrite because I didn't feel that I had had that kind of experience myself.

During a period of fasting and intense prayer I was in a church meeting one day when the speaker began to talk about a particular appearance of the resurrected Savior in modern times. It was the description found in the *Doctrine and Covenants*, where Jesus was seen in vision by Joseph Smith and Oliver Cowdery in the Kirtland (Ohio) LDS Temple on April 3, 1836:

> The veil was taken from our minds, and the eyes of our understanding were opened. We saw the Lord standing upon the breastwork of the pulpit, before us; and under his feet was a paved work of pure gold, in color like amber. His eyes were as a flame of fire; the hair of his head was white like the pure snow; his countenance shone above the brightness of the sun; and his voice was as the rushing of great waters, even the voice of Jehovah, saying: I am the first and the last; I am he who liveth, I am he who was slain; I am your advocate with the Father.
>
> —(D&C 110:1-4)

As I listened to this account, suddenly I was "pricked in the heart" as were those who heard Peter preach on the day of Pentecost about the risen Savior (Acts 2:37). Like John Wesley, the founder of the Methodist church writing in his journal of his own conversion, *"I felt my heart strangely warmed"*. With a rush, the Holy Spirit enveloped me and I <u>knew</u> without a doubt that Jesus was <u>real</u>, and that he is my Lord and Savior. With tears in my eyes as I sat in that little chapel in Arizona I silently thanked my Heavenly Father for that sweet answer to prayer. I had gained a <u>personal</u> witness of the Lordship of Christ and of his divinity. —And my life has never been the same.

The funny thing is … I then realized that I had felt this testimony of the Holy Spirit to my soul many times before, but I had not recognized what it was. I wonder if perhaps you have also had a similar experience? Have you sought for and received a sweet personal witness of the Spirit that Jesus is indeed our Lord and Savior? If not, I invite you to do so. Your life too will never be the same.

INSIDE LATTER-DAY CHRISTIANITY

Now you know how <u>I</u> feel about Jesus. But what do <u>other</u> Latter-day Saints think of Christ? As a born-again Christian, do I feel at home as a member of my church? Yes, very much so. Let me explain why...

First of all, many people overlook the fact that the very <u>name</u> of the so-called "Mormon" church is actually <u>The Church of Jesus Christ of Latter-day Saints</u>. And the subtitle to the *Book of Mormon* is <u>*Another Testament of Jesus Christ*</u>. It's hard to see how Jesus could be more central to our faith.

THE PLACE OF JESUS CHRIST IN OUR CHURCH

As I mentioned in my introduction to this book, Joseph Smith, the first President of The Church of Jesus Christ of Latter-day Saints summed it up this way:

The fundamental principles of our religion are the testimony of the Apostles and Prophets concerning Jesus Christ, that He died, was buried, and rose again the third day and ascended into heaven: and all other things which pertain to our religion are only appendages to it. [4]

The Latter-day Saints believe quite literally what the Bible says about Jesus, his life and his mission. And if I may be permitted, let me share with you also some pertinent statements from our own LDS scriptures, and from the writings and sermons of our church leaders: In *The Book of Mormon* we read:

And we talk of Christ, we rejoice in Christ, we preach of Christ, we prophesy of Christ, and we write according to our prophecies, that our children may know to what source they may look for a remission of their sins.

– (2 Nephi 25:26)

Joseph Smith wrote:

And now, after the many testimonies which have been given of him, this is the testimony, last of all, which we give of him: That he Lives! For we saw him, even on the right hand of God; and we hear the voice bearing record that he is the Only Begotten of the Father— That by him, and through him and of him, the worlds are and were created, and the inhabitants thereof are begotten sons and daughters unto God.

—(Joseph Smith in *Doctrine and Covenants* 76:22-24)

Some of our modern-day Apostles have said:

"I am one of [Jesus Christ's] witnesses, and in a coming day I shall feel the nail marks in his hands and in his feet and shall wet his feet with my tears. But I shall not know any better then than I know now that he is God's Almighty Son, that he is our Savior and Redeemer, and that salvation comes in and through his atoning blood and in no other way."

— LDS Apostle Bruce R. McConkie, *Ensign*, May 1985, p 9

"Jesus Christ was and is the Lord God Omnipotent. He was chosen before he was born. He was the all-powerful Creator of the heavens and the earth. He is the source of life and light

to all things. His word is the law by which all things are governed in the universe. All things created and made by Him are subject to His infinite power."

— *Teachings of Ezra Taft Benson* (An LDS Apostle and church President)

With this great love for the Lord so evident among the Latter-day Saints, can you see why it's like a dagger piercing my heart when a dear Christian brother or sister wants to put me in a pigeonhole and label me a "non-Christian cultist"? How would <u>you</u> feel?

OUTSIDE LATTER-DAY CHRISTIANITY - - A DIFFERENT JESUS?

I know that there are critics outside my faith (I've had personal contact with many of them) who say that as a Latter-day Saint I worship a "different Jesus". In doing this they quote *2nd Corinthians 3:5*. Here's one example of the criticisms so often made of my faith:

> The Christ of Mormonism is not the same Christ of the Bible. 2 Cor.11:3-5 tells us that there will be those who would teach a different Christ. Paul says of them, *"For such men are false apostles, deceitful workmen, masquerading as apostles of Christ"*. So there is a Biblical warning about those who would bring the doctrine of another Jesus...
>
> —Ed Decker, President, Saints Alive in Jesus

There was one anti-Mormon article which went so far as to describe a man on a hippie commune in New Mexico who <u>called</u> himself Jesus Christ, and then the writer compared the LDS belief in the Savior to the followers of that "different Jesus". For the record, I believe in Jesus of <u>Nazareth</u> as my Lord, not the so-called "Jesus" of New Mexico or any other "Jesus"! And no, I <u>don't</u> have a "different Jesus" from the Bible.

But if I <u>seem</u> to have a "different Jesus" from that of some other Christians, I hope they will read the <u>rest</u> of Paul's admonition in 2nd Corinthians (we'll talk about Bible context later) He says:

"Would to God ye could <u>bear with me a little in my folly</u>: and indeed bear with me."

I hope they'll accept Paul's admonition and "bear with me" a bit until we can "reason together"

—(Isaiah 1:18).

A "DIFFERENT JESUS" FOR EVERYONE?

I guess in some respects <u>everyone</u> worships a "different Jesus" from the person next to them in the pew. Each person's mental picture of the Savior is a little different. In a way, it's kind of like this: I used to work at the Osmond TV Studio in Orem, Utah right across the hall from Donny Osmond's office. I didn't know Donny very well, but I knew him better than the average person on the street, so I guess in one sense I was acquainted with a "different" Donny Osmond from those fans who knew him only from what they read in the pulp magazines. Not that there was anything different about the Donny I knew, but there was a difference in <u>perception</u>.

ESSENTIAL VS. NON-ESSENTIAL DIFFERENCES

This "different Jesus" topic can be taken to the extreme. For instance some predominately black churches have even claimed that "their" Jesus is black! But is He "different" in the <u>essentials</u>? The <u>important</u> thing is this; Did He die on the cross for our sins, and was he bodily resurrected on the third day? <u>These</u> are the things on which our salvation is based. These are the things that <u>matter</u>.

Whenever I hear these accusations that as a Latter-day Saint I allegedly worship a "different Jesus", I ask myself, <u>how</u> is the "Mormon Jesus" supposed to be different? Is He <u>physically</u> different? If we're talking about the weak, pale, effeminate character that I see portrayed in some artists' paintings of Christ, then yes I worship a different Jesus from what I see there.

<u>My</u> Jesus is a strong, vibrant individual. The Son of God was no physical weakling.

If we're talking about a Jesus who is somehow not an <u>individual person</u> himself, but mystically some sort of modular part of God the Father and the Holy Ghost, then <u>yes</u> I worship a different Jesus. (But that gets into the whole "mystery of the Trinity", which I'll discuss in a following chapter.)

INSIDE MERE LATTER-DAY CHRISTIANITY
SOME OF THE BELIEFS WE SHARE ABOUT JESUS WITH OTHER CHRISTIANS

Let me tell you about the Jesus that I worship, and you can determine for yourself if He is "different" from "your" Jesus in any <u>essential</u> ways...

JESUS IS GOD INCARNATE

I'd like to put to rest some of the claims out there that we as Latter-day Saints don't believe in the deity of Christ. In the Bible (KJV) John 1 begins;

"In the beginning was the Word, and the Word was with God, and the Word was God. The same was in the beginning with God."

7

Then later in verse 14, John says;

"And the Word was made flesh, and dwelt among us, (and we beheld his glory, the glory as of the only begotten of the Father,) full of grace and truth."

These Biblical references to the deity of Jesus Christ are exactly what we as Latter-day Saints believe! For example, the following is from an official proclamation by the First Presidency and the Quorum of the Twelve Apostles of The Church of Jesus Christ of Latter-day Saints:

> We solemnly testify that His life, which is central to all human history, neither began in Bethlehem nor concluded on Calvary. He was the Firstborn of the Father, the Only Begotten Son in the flesh, the Redeemer of the world. ... We bear testimony, as His duly ordained Apostles—that Jesus is the Living Christ, the immortal Son of God. He is the great King Immanuel, who stands today on the right hand of His Father. He is the light, the life, and the hope of the world. His way is the path that leads to happiness in this life and eternal life in the world to come. God be thanked for the matchless gift of His divine Son.[5]

So is the "Mormon Jesus" divine? Is he Diety? Of course! Is he what my Protestant and Catholic friends would call "God incarnate"? Well here's the funny thing - many of my LDS brothers and sisters might answer "No" and immediately the anti-Mormons would pounce upon them with glee and shout, "Heretic!" But not so fast...

Me? I would say a wholehearted "Yes"! I do indeed believe that Jesus is "God incarnate". Does that mean that I'm the heretic from the LDS point of view? No, but this is a good example of how LDS and other Christians get mixed up in definitions. Actually, we're just understanding the question differently.

You see, Latter-day Saints will usually assume that they're being asked if God the Father is being "made flesh" or become "incarnate", which of course He is not. Jesus is God the Son "incarnate". For Trinitarians that's not an important distinction, but for Latter-day Saints it is. (More about that later in the chapter on the Trinity).

JESUS IS THE CREATOR
To continue in John 1:3, we read:

"All things were made by him; and without him was not any thing made that was made."

Under our Heavenly Father's direction, my Jesus created the heavens and the earth. Again, we find more detail on this process in some of our Latter-day Saint scriptures (emphasis mine):

"And he shall be called Jesus Christ, the Son of God, the Father of heaven and earth, the <u>Creator of all things from the beginning</u>; and his mother shall be called Mary."
> —Mosiah 3:8 The Book of Mormon, Another Testament of Jesus Christ

"And also that ye might know of the coming of Jesus Christ, the Son of God, the Father of heaven and of earth, the <u>Creator of all things from the beginning</u>; and that ye might know of the signs of his coming, to the intent that ye might believe on his name."
> —Helaman 14:12 The Book of Mormon, Another Testament of Jesus Christ

"Behold, I am Jesus Christ, the Son of the living God,<u> who created the heavens and the earth</u>, a light which cannot be hid in darkness"
> — Doctrine and Covenants 14:9

JESUS, THE "JEHOVAH" OF THE OLD TESTAMENT

The Jesus whom I worship was not only <u>prophesied</u> of throughout the Old Testament, but he was indeed the God of Israel, the God of Abraham, Isaac and Jacob. Prior to His birth into mortality, he was known in Scripture by his pre-mortal name/title of YHWH, or Jehovah.

—It was Jesus (Jehovah) who spoke to Moses from a fiery bush.[6]
—It was Jesus (Jehovah) who was the "spiritual rock" that followed the children of Israel through the wilderness. [7]
—It was Jesus who said, "Before Abraham was, I AM."[8]

JESUS MY ELDER BROTHER

The Jesus of Latter-day Christianity is not only our Lord and our God, but He is also our elder brother. Just as we have <u>earthly</u> fathers who are the fathers of our <u>physical</u> <u>bodies</u>, we also have a <u>Heavenly</u> Father who is the father of our <u>spirits</u>.[9] We lived with our Father in Heaven before the foundations of this earth were laid, and we "shouted with joy" when we learned that Jesus would pay for our sins with His blood so we could be forgiven.[10]

You see, our brother Jesus Christ was there too. According to the New Testament, He was the <u>Firstborn</u> of all our Heavenly Father's children in the <u>spirit</u>.[11] He was the first among many "brethren" (and sisters), which includes you and me![12] But because he was also the Only Begotten son of God in the flesh [13], he is divine and we're not.

Latter-day Saints are not the only Christians who understand this concept. R.C. Sproul writes in the teachings of his Ligonier Ministries about the parable Jesus told of the prodigal son: *The one who told the story (Jesus) was our elder brother, who left His Father's house to bring home His lost brothers. Jesus left His Father's house and went to seek the lost for His Father.*[14]

IS JESUS ALSO THE BROTHER OF LUCIFER?
As the sons and daughters of God, we also had another spirit brother. His name was Lucifer, and he was another child of our Heavenly Father [15]. (After his "fall" from heaven, he became known as "The Adversary", or in Hebrew "Satan".) But Jesus is the brother of Lucifer only in the sense that Adolph Hitler and Mother Teresa are siblings. That is, they both are children of the same Heavenly Father.

They are the exact opposites of each other in every possible way. Lucifer wanted to enslave our Father's children, whereas Jesus wants to set us free. Lucifer rebelled against our Father and took a third part of our spirit brothers and sisters with him.[16] They were cast out of Heaven and they lost their chance to come to earth in mortality and gain physical bodies.

My friend Allen Richardson puts it this way:

Is Jesus the spirit brother of Lucifer? The critics have intentionally calculated this wording to appear sensational and inflammatory. They readily admit that a bad brother is no reflection on a good brother.

Why have they not asked if the Mormons believe that Jesus was the spirit brother of Abraham, Moses, or Paul? Surely, they realize that Lucifer has long since lost his Heavenly status (Isa.14:12). He and all those in rebellion against God have become "bastards and not sons" (Hebrews 12:8), to use Paul's wording. So to answer the question, no, they are not (currently) brothers.

All theatrics aside, the real issue is whether or not Jesus had any brothers at all. The critics believe Jesus was not created, but was the creator. The critics would not care to hear anyone using the same type of wording in accusing them of believing that Jesus is the *Creator* of

Lucifer, or of Hitler, or the Creator of murderers, rapists, or child molesters — even though the critics do believe he is.

Latter-day Saints believe that Jesus has lived for all eternity as an "intelligence," but that at one point, he was born as a spirit before his mortal birth. Indeed, the Bible states that Jesus was the "firstborn" among many brethren (Rom. 8:29), the "firstborn" of every creature (Col. 1:14), and that he was the "beginning" of the creations of God (Rev. 3:14).

Apparently, the critics are oblivious to the fact that the early Christians believed that Jesus and Lucifer were created as brothers. One of the early Christian fathers, Lactantius, said that before God "commenced this business" of creating the world:

"...*He produced a spirit like unto Himself...then He made another being*, in whom the disposition of the divine origin did not remain. Therefore, he [the second being] was infected with his own envy as with poison, and passed from good to evil... for he envied his predecessor, who through his steadfastness is acceptable and dear to God the Father. This being, who from good became evil by his own act, is called by the Greeks Diabolus..." [17]

This is another historical fact that puts the Latter-day Saints closer to original Christianity than their critics.

IS LUCIFER A "CREATED BEING"?

I'm aware that those who oppose this truth say that Lucifer was a created being, and since Jesus created "all things in heaven and earth" (see John 1:1) he couldn't be a "brother" to his own creation.

The fallacy here is that it is God the Father who is the "father of spirits"[18], not God the Son. While it is true that Jesus created the physical universe in which we live, we've already seen that the spirits of the "sons of God" were in existence long before the foundations of "all things in heaven and earth" were laid.[19] And that included our "black sheep" spirit brother, Lucifer and the third part of Father's spirit children who followed him.[20] (For more information on this topic, see Chapter 13.)

JESUS THE BABE OF BETHLEHEM AND THE MAN OF NAZARETH

The Jesus whom I worship was born in a manger in Bethlehem and wrapped in swaddling clothes. He grew into manhood in Nazareth. After he was baptized by John in the river Jordan he began his ministry in Palestine, teaching his gospel to His "sheep" there. He performed many wondrous miracles. He chose twelve apostles and ordained them to be the foundation of his church, with himself as the chief cornerstone.[21]

I accept as truth the account given in the four Gospels about the mortal ministry of our Savior.

I believe Jesus died on the cross to pay for my sins. And more importantly, I believe in his bodily resurrection from the grave in victory over death. Is this a "different" Jesus from the one you worship?

JESUS THE SON OF GOD
Jesus is the literal Son of God with all the usual characteristics that a son inherits from a father. The Jesus whom I worship was begotten in the flesh by God the Father, according to the Bible.[22] He is the only one of our Heavenly Father's children to have one parent who was mortal and one who was Deity, to create his physical body. The rest of humanity was born in the flesh of two mortal parents although we are spirit children of God the Father. This belief raises another "sticking point" between the Latter-day Saints and other Christians although it seems quite "orthodox" to me.

WHO IS THE FATHER OF JESUS?
There's been a lot of sensationalism used by anti-Mormons surrounding the conception of Jesus. It is said by critics that Latter-day Saints believe our Savior was conceived through *"incestuous sexual relations between the Mormon God Elohim and Mary"* [23]. These misunderstandings stem primarily from statements made by some LDS church leaders that emphasize the Savior's role as the Only Begotten Son of God the Father:

Latter-day Saints recognize Jesus as literally the Only Begotten Son of God the Father in the flesh (John 3:16; D&C 93:11; Moses 6:52). This title signifies that Jesus' physical body was the offspring of a mortal mother and of God the Eternal Father ("Luke 1:35, 1 Ne. 11:18).
—*Daniel Ludlow – Encyclopedia of Mormonism* p. 729

That Child to be born of Mary was begotten of Elohim, the Eternal Father, not in violation of natural law but in accordance with a higher manifestation thereof; and the offspring from that association of supreme sanctity, celestial Sire-ship, and pure though mortal maternity, was of right to be called the "Son of the Highest." In His nature would be combined the powers of Godhood with the capacity and possibilities of mortality; and this through the ordinary operation of the fundamental law of heredity, declared of God, demonstrated by science, and admitted by philosophy, that living beings shall propagate after their kind.

The Child Jesus was to inherit the physical, mental, and spiritual traits, tendencies, and powers that characterized His parents — one immortal and glorified — God, the other human — woman.

—James E. Talmadge (LDS Apostle) *Jesus the Christ* p. 77

Christ is called in scripture the "Only Begotten", the "Only Begotten Son", and the "Only Begotten of the Father". These name-titles all signify that our Lord is the only Son of the Father in the flesh. Each of the words is to be understood literally. Only means only; Begotten means begotten; and Son means son. Christ was begotten by an Immortal Father in the same way that mortal men are begotten by mortal fathers.

—Bruce R. McConkie, *Mormon Doctrine*, p. 546

Only begotten in the flesh ... in mortality. This designation of our Lord signifies that He was begotten by Man of Holiness as literally as any mortal father begets a son. The natural processes of procreation were involved; Jesus was begotten by His Father as literally as He was conceived by his mother.

—Daniel Ludlow, *Companion to Your Study of the Doctrine and Covenants, vol 2 p. 265*

We believe that Mary was the literal mother of Jesus Christ in the flesh and that God was his father. In testifying of Christ, we do not use language in a deceptive or metaphorical sense. Our scripture declares Christ to be the Son of God "after the manner of the flesh" ("1 Ne. 11:181 Nephi 11:18).

President Ezra Taft Benson explained:

"The Church of Jesus Christ of Latter-day Saints proclaims that Jesus Christ is the Son of God in the most literal sense. The body in which He performed His mission in the flesh was sired by that same Holy Being we worship as God, our Eternal Father. Jesus was not the son of Joseph nor was He begotten by the Holy Ghost. He is the Son of the Eternal Father!"

—Joseph Fielding McConkie, *Here We Stand*, p. 166-167

Latter-day saints aren't as concerned about exactly <u>how</u> Jesus was "begotten", as we are about making sure we understand exactly <u>who</u> did the "begetting". (The sexual hangups all come from the anti-Mormon literature!) Regarding the conception of Jesus, the account of Luke (the physician – possibly an OB/GYN who would understand these things) clearly indicates that on that wondrous occasion two things happened: (1) *"the Holy Ghost came upon her"* (Mary) and (2) *"the power of the Highest overshadowed her."*

—(Luke 1:35)

There seems to be a lot of confusion about this in traditional Christianity, because many Catholics and Protestants advocate the position that Jesus is the son of the <u>Holy Ghost</u>. To those who are laboring under that "misconception" (pun definitely intended), I would have to confess that I <u>do</u> worship a different Jesus than they do.[24] For me, the scriptures clearly indicate that of the three separate and distinct persons of the Godhead, it is God the Father ("the Highest") who is the divine parent of Jesus, <u>not</u> God the Holy Ghost (the third, and positional subordinate member of the Godhead). The reason the Holy Ghost "came upon her" was to enable her to endure the presence of "the Highest" (God the Father) and not be consumed by His power and glory. The Scriptures tell us that without the presence of the Holy Ghost, "no man (or woman) can see God and live".[25]

SAME JESUS, DIFFERING OPINIONS

There are some other things the Latter-day Saints believe about Jesus that differ from the thoughts of other Christians. Let's look at a few:

JESUS' MINISTRY TO HIS "OTHER SHEEP" IN ANCIENT AMERICA

According to the Bible, The Jesus whom I worship remained on earth for 40 days after his resurrection and taught the apostles "many things pertaining to the kingdom of Heaven" which are not found in the canonical record.[26] He then ascended into heaven, and angels foretold that he would some day return in a "like manner".[27]

But during His ministry in the Holy Land, Jesus had spoken of <u>other sheep</u> *"which are not of this fold and they shall hear my voice."*[28] The Jesus in whom I believe <u>did</u> teach his "other sheep" and they <u>did</u> hear his voice. According to the account found in the 3rd book of Nephi in *The Book of Mormon*, he descended from heaven shortly after his resurrection and appeared to a group of Israelites that were living in ancient America. He told them:

"<u>ye are they</u> of whom I said, 'other sheep I have which are not of this fold and they shall hear my voice'. But they misunderstood and supposed that I was speaking of the Gentiles, but they did not understand that <u>the Gentiles would not at any time hear my voice</u>, but ye have both heard my voice and seen me."[29]

Jesus taught his gospel —the <u>same</u> gospel— to those "other sheep" in ancient America who had long awaited his coming. He also chose twelve more disciples in that land as special witnesses and established his church among the people. He taught them the Sermon on the Mount, almost verbatim.

And he commanded that they keep records of His teachings. Unlike the nation of Israel in Palestine who rejected their Messiah, these people in ancient America accepted Jesus and worshiped him, and he performed great miracles among them. After a length of time he left them and ascended again into heaven, but before doing so he called a number of their children before him and blessed them in a marvelous and touching scene.

"And it came to pass that He commanded that their little children should be brought. So they brought their little children and set them down upon the ground round about him, and Jesus stood in the midst, and the multitude gave way till they had all been brought unto him. ... and he took their little children one by one, and blessed them, and prayed unto the Father for them. Behold they cast their eyes towards heaven, and they saw the heavens open, and they saw angels descending out of heaven as it were in the midst of fire; and they came down and encircled those little ones about, and they were encircled about with fire, and the angels did minister unto them. And the multitude did see and hear and bear record; and they know that their record is true..."[30]

Before he left the Americas, Jesus also explained that he was going to visit still <u>others</u> of our Heavenly Father's children who lived upon the "isles of the sea" and also the Ten Tribes in the north (the lost ten tribes of Israel). The account of Christ's visit to ancient America, is found in 3rd Nephi in *The Book of Mormon*. There are also many references in the oral histories of the indigenous peoples of the western hemisphere to the coming of a great white and bearded God who visited the Americas. These visits occurred in 33 AD at precisely the time of Christ's resurrection, according to the Maya and Aztec calendars, which are well known for their accuracy. He was known by many names among the different peoples, such as Quetzalcoatl, Viracocha, Itzamna, and Kulkulkan, but the descriptions of the appearance and teachings of this person in these native histories are identical with the New Testament characteristics of Jesus. We'll talk more about this in Chapter 7.

LITTLE KNOWN ASPECTS ABOUT THE MORTAL LIFE OF JESUS

There are a few other things about the life of Jesus (the Jesus in whom I believe) that may differ from other Christians and in fact may differ from the beliefs of some other Latter-day Saints as well!

THE EIGHTEEN MISSING YEARS OF JESUS'S LIFE

One of the differences deals with a little known-theory that during the eighteen missing years of Jesus's life not mentioned in the New Testament (between the ages of twelve and thirty) that the boy Jesus may have traveled to other lands. During my research for writing the documentary motion picture *"In Search of Historic Jesus"* I learned that in the folklore of England there is an account of Joseph of Arimathea taking the boy Jesus with him to what was referred to as "the blessed isles of Great Britain." (In the old Latin Vulgate translation of the Bible, Joseph of Arimathea is referred to as a "Decurian" or Roman officer and metal merchant, and the British Isles were the chief source of lead and tin in the Roman Empire at that time.) In fact the alternate national anthem of England (somewhat similar to our "America the Beautiful") is known as "The Jerusalem Hymn" and in this anthem the lyrics say:

And did those feet in ancient time
Walk upon England's mountains green?
And was the Holy Lamb of God
On England's pleasant pastures seen?
And did the countenance divine
Shine forth upon our clouded hills? "[31]

This story of the travels of the boy Jesus to foreign lands is not necessarily relevant to my salvation or to any one else's, nor does it change or detract from the Biblical account of the Savior's life. In fact, I'm not even sure that it really happened. However, unlike many other Christians who might take a narrower view, I do believe it <u>could</u> have happened. To me, it's merely a point of interest that may add another dimension to our study of the life of Christ.

SUMMARY

Well there you have it. My "confession" of Jesus Christ. I hope you'll agree that although "my" Jesus may differ in some respects from that of other Christians, in the <u>essentials</u> he is not "another Jesus". He is definitely the Jesus of the Bible, although he may not be the Jesus of some theologians.

But this I know beyond a shadow of a doubt... When I see him I will fall at his feet and wash them with my tears of gratitude, and thank him will all my soul for His marvelous gift of salvation to me.

ENDNOTES FOR CHAPTER 1

1   Philippians 2:10-11
2   from Dinah Craik's novel, *A Life for a Life.* Chapter 16 (1859). Also published in a collection of poems under the title, "Friendship" (this poem is often attributed incorrectly to George Eliot)
3   LDS Hymnbook, "I Stand All Amazed", Hymn #193, Text and music by Charles H. Gabriel, 1856-1932
4   *Teachings of the Prophet Joseph Smith p. 121*
5   https://lds.org/study/living-christ?cid=email-shared&lang=eng
6   Exodus 3:4-6
7   1 Cor. 10:4 "the spiritual rock that followed them was Christ"
8   John 8:58
9   Heb. 12:9 "shall we not rather be in subjection to the Father of spirits, and live?" Num. 16:22; Deut. 14:1; Job 32:8; Ps. 82:6; Eccl. 12:7; Hosea 1:10; Acts 17:29; Rom. 8:16; Eph. 4:6
10 Job 38:7
11 Ps 89:27; Isa 49:4; Rom 8:29; Col 1:15; Heb 1:6
12 Rom 8:29; Heb 2:11 &17
13 John 1:14,18; John 3:16; 1 John 4:9
14 http://www.ligonier.org/learn/articles/the-story-of-two-older-brothers/
15 Lucifer was in heaven before he "fell" (Isa 14:12), and he walked among the "sons" of God (Job 1:6 See also Rev. 12:4,7-9.)
16 Isa 14:12; Rev 12:4,7-9; Jude 1:6
17 "Divine Institutions," Book 2, chap. 9, *The AnteNicene Fathers*, 7 Grand Rapids: Wm. B.Eerdmans Publishers, (1978) p.52
18 Heb. 12:9
19 Job 38:7 "all the sons of God shouted for joy" Jer. 1:5 "Before I formed thee in the belly I knew thee" Eph. 1:4 "chosen us in him before the foundation of the world"
20 Jude 1:6 the "angels which kept not their first estate"
21 Ephesians 2:19-20 "And are built upon the foundation of the apostles and prophets, Jesus Christ Himself being the chief cornerstone."
22 John 1:14,18; John 3:16; 1 John 4:9
23 Anti-Mormons often refer to what they call "the Mormon God Elohim". "Elohim" is not "the Mormon God". It is simply the Hebrew name/title used in the Bible for God the Father. (Strong's Exhaustive Concordance of the Bible, Hebrew & Chaldee Dictionary, p. 12.)
24 I suspect that some of the Protestant thinking re: the conception of Jesus has been influenced (whether they realize it or not) by the teachings of "Mariology", which reached its zenith in the "Immaculate Conception" doctrine, first defined officially in Roman Catholic theology by Pope Pius IX in 1854.
25 compare Exodus 33:20 and John 1:18 with Gen. 32:30 and Exodus 33:11.
26 Acts 1:3; John 20:30; 21:35
27 Acts 1:9-11

Robert Starling

28 John 10:16
29 3 Nephi 15:21-24
30 3 Nephi 17:11-25
31 First printed in a poem by William Blake in 1808 and incorporated into a hymn by Sir Hubert Parry in 1916. "Jerusalem" is sung before rugby matches and other sporting events and in churches.

EVIDENCE 2

TRINITY OR GODHEAD?

I confess that in some respects I believe in a "different Jesus" from that of many of my dear friends who are part of the Protestant and Catholic "flavors" of Christianity. If their Jesus is one of the "three incomprehensibles yet one incomprehensible" described in some of the so-called Apostolic Creeds that define the traditional Trinity, then my Jesus is indeed different. My Jesus is firmly rooted in the New Testament, not in the creeds of the 4th and 5th centuries.

Now I'm sure there are those who will undoubtedly take the above statement out of context for their own purposes. But I would remind them of the words of the renowned evangelical scholar D.A. Carson who often quoted his father as saying that *"a text without a context becomes a pretext for a proof text."* [1]

So let me explain what I mean:

First of all, Latter-day Christians are not alone in our belief that the traditional "trinity" is not taught in the Bible: **Harper's Bible Dictionary** records that *"the formal <u>doctrine of the Trinity</u> as it was defined by the great church councils of the fourth and fifth centuries <u>is not to be found in the [New Testament]</u>."* [2]

How important is it to know the true nature of God? Many Christians are okay with accepting that the "trinity" is a "mystery", and letting it go at that. But what did Jesus say?

"this is <u>life eternal</u>, that they might <u>know</u> thee the only true God, and Jesus Christ, whom thou hast sent"

—John 17:3

If our "life eternal" is at stake, is it okay to just leave the nature of God and Jesus a "mystery"? Not for me!

I believe in the Biblical <u>godhead</u>. As a Latter-day Saint I've been taught all my life to believe in God the Father, God the Son Jesus Christ and God the Holy Ghost. However, I must say that I do NOT believe in the man-made **"<u>trinity</u>"** that was formulated by the Hellenizers of Christianity hundreds of years after the close of the New Testament. This definition-of-God-by-councils became crystallized in the Nicene Creed (and revisions that followed it) and confused forever the persons of the Father, the Son and the Holy Ghost. As my friend Scott Giles summed it up:

Joseph Smith's First Vision when he saw God the Father and God the Son did more damage to the "orthodox" doctrine of the Trinity than anything else since Stephen's vision in the New Testament.

—Scott Giles

Look at both statements and judge for yourself:

"but he (Stephen), being full of the Holy Ghost, looked up steadfastly into heaven, and saw the glory of God, and <u>Jesus standing on the right hand of God</u>. And said, behold I see the heavens opened, and the <u>Son of man standing on the right hand of God</u>"

— Acts. 7:55-56 31 A.D.

When the light rested upon me <u>I saw two Personages</u> whose brightness and glory defy all description, standing above me in the air. One of them spake unto me, calling me by name and said, pointing to the other – "This is My Beloved Son, hear Him."

—Joseph Smith History 1832 A.D.

Okay, here's one of the biggies. Perhaps THE biggest problem many folks have in admitting Mormons into their "Christian" club. This is despite the wise comment once made by Rich Buhler, host of the nationally syndicated Christian talk show "Table Talk" when he said,

"I find it difficult to withhold Christian fellowship from another person just because his fuzzy understanding of the Trinity is different from my fuzzy understanding of it."[3]

My personal belief in the Godhead is most clearly summed up in the first Article of Faith of the Church of Jesus Christ of Latter-day Saints, which reads:

We believe in God the Eternal Father, and in His son Jesus Christ, and in the Holy Ghost.
—First LDS Article of Faith

Now that sounds pretty "orthodox", doesn't it? Just like the New Testament Saints, Latter-day Christians believe that the Father is God, the Son is God, and the Holy Ghost is God. In fact when I was baptized at the age of eight in the little LDS chapel in Columbus, Georgia, my baptism was performed *"in the name of the Father, and of the Son, and of the Holy Ghost."* The same was said when I was married in the Salt Lake Temple to my beautiful bride. That's three persons in the Godhead, right?

And yet like the apostle Paul, we as Latter-day Saints *"worship the One God, the Father of our Lord Jesus Christ"* (1 Cor. 8:6). So then why all the fuss? One God, three Persons. Don't the LDS believe in the Trinity then, just like other Christians?

Well, not exactly... Here's the official position (beyond what is stated above) of The Church of Jesus Christ of Latter-day Saints.

INSIDE LATTER-DAY CHRISTIANITY
The Father has body of flesh and bones as tangible as man's; The Son also; But the Holy Ghost has not a body of flesh and bones, but is a personage of Spirit. Were it not so, the Holy Ghost could not dwell in us.
—Doctrine and Covenants 130:22

(note that it says the Father and the Son have bodies of flesh and <u>bones</u>, not flesh and <u>blood</u> – blood is an earthly element. We'll get into the physical body thing later.)

THREE SEPARATE PERSONS - EACH IS GOD
As stated above, the Latter-day Saints believe like other Christians that there are three persons in the Godhead, God the Father, God the Son, and God the Holy Ghost. Also, like other Christians, we believe that each of the three persons is equally God, and equally divine. In addition, like other Christians (although there is some confusion on this point

among various faiths), we believe that God the Father is "positionally superior" to the other two members of the Godhead.

Here are a couple of authoritative statements by modern apostles and prophets:

They are distinct beings, but they are one in purpose and effort. They are united as one in bringing to pass the grand, divine plan for the salvation and exaltation of the children of God.
—Gordon B. Hinckley, *Ensign*, March 1998

"We declare it is self evident from the scriptures that the Father, the Son, and the Holy Ghost are separate persons, three divine beings, noting such unequivocal illustrations as the Savior's great Intercessory Prayer, His baptism at the hands of John, the experience on the Mount of Transfiguration, and the martyrdom of Stephen— to name just four.

We believe these three divine persons constituting a single Godhead are united in purpose, in manner, in testimony, in mission. ... I think it is accurate to say we believe They are one in every significant and eternal aspect imaginable except believing them to be three persons combined in one substance, a Trinitarian notion never set forth in the scriptures because it is not true."
—Jeffrey R. Holland, Ensign, Nov. 2007, p. 40

The trinity is three separate Gods: The Father, the Son, and the Holy Ghost. "That these three are separate individuals, physically distinct from each other, is demonstrated by the accepted records of divine dealings with man,"
—James Talmage, *Articles of Faith*, p. 35

"Many men say there is one God; the Father, the Son and the Holy Ghost are only one God. I say that is a strange God [anyhow].— three in one and one in three... It is curious organization... All are crammed into one God according to sectarianism. It would make the biggest God in all the world. He would be a wonderfully big God—he would be a giant or a monster,"
—Joseph Smith, *Teachings*, p. 372

OUTSIDE LATTER-DAY CHRISTIANITY
Now let's see what the critics say outside The Church of Jesus Christ of Latter-day Saints who delight in calling us a "non- Christian cult" because we don't accept the exact "three-in-one" concept of the Godhead that is promulgated in the major creeds of historical

Christendom. The Trinitarian formula seems to be their favorite "litmus test" to see who fits their definition of a Christian.

Here is a comment from Dr. R. Albert Mohler, Jr. President of The Southern Baptist Theological Seminary: (emphasis mine)

The orthodox consensus of the Christian church is defined in terms of its historic <u>creeds</u> and doctrinal affirmations. <u>... the church has used these definitional doctrines as the standard for identifying true Christianity</u>.

The Mormon doctrine of God does not correspond to the Christian doctrine of the Trinity. Mormonism rejects the central logic of this doctrine (one God in three eternal persons) and develops its own doctrine of God - a doctrine that bears practically no resemblance to Trinitarian theology. <u>...Normative Christianity is defined by the Apostles Creed</u>, the Nicene Creed, and the other formulas of the doctrinal consensus.[4]

I would argue that "normative Christianity" should be defined by the Bible, not the creeds. This "normative Christianity" is still arguing over what the Trinity really means after almost two thousand years! Even the above-mentioned creeds have been debated and revised time after time over the centuries by one church council after another. The so-called "central logic" of the doctrine of the Trinity is not logic at all, but a blind acceptance of the fuzzy thinking by religious philosophers that originated back before medieval doctors used leeches to treat sicknesses.

Matt Slick at the website of the Christian Apologetics Research Ministry (CARM – an anti-Mormon organization) rightly draws a distinction between his Trinitarian view of the Godhead and Mormon doctrine, but then on another page he admits that his fuzzy understanding of the subject is inadequate (emphasis is mine):

So, when we view descriptions and attributes of God manifested in the Father, the Son, and the Holy Spirit, we discover that <u>a completely comprehensible and understandable explanation of God's essence and nature is not possible</u>. What we have done, however, is <u>derive</u> from the Scripture the truths that we can grasp and <u>combine</u> them into the doctrine we call The Trinity. The Trinity is, to a large extent, a mystery. After all, we are dealing with God Himself.[5]

I could quote lots of other Bible teachers and theologians who say the same thing – that their view of the godhead is a "mystery". But you already know that, so why bother?

THE TRINITY IS NOT FOUND IN THE BIBLE

Where does the doctrine of the "Trinity" come from, anyway? We know the word "Trinity" is not in the Bible. It seems to have been first used in the Latin form "trinitas" by the lawyer-turned-theologian Tertullian around 211 A.D, over 100 years after the deaths of the Apostles. But even Tertullian's teachings came under fire –like the Latter-day Saints- by the "orthodox" Christianity of his time and later. *The New Catholic Encyclopedia* has commented:

"In not a few areas of theology, Tertullian's views are, of course, completely unacceptable. Thus, for example, his teaching on the Trinity reveals a subordination of Son to Father that in the later crass form of Arianism the Church rejected as heretical." [6]

(Trust it to the lawyers to mess things up – with apologies to my son-in-law-the-lawyer.) The same source indicates that a solid Trinitarian doctrine was not "derived" and "combined" into "orthodoxy" by the whole Catholic church until at least another hundred years:

"the formulation of "one God in three Persons' was not solidly established, certainly not fully assimilated into Christian life and its profession of faith, prior to the end of the 4th century...

Among the Apostolic Fathers, there had been nothing even remotely approaching such a mentality or perspective." [7]

Other Christian sources agree:

On the other hand, we must honestly admit that the doctrine of the Trinity did NOT form part of the early Christian-New Testament message. Certainly, it cannot be denied that not only the word "Trinity," but even the EXPLICIT IDEA of the Trinity is absent from the apostolic witness of the faith.. The doctrine of the Trinity itself, ... is NOT a Biblical Doctrine..." [8]

Some of the crucial concepts employed by these creeds, such as "substance," "person," and "in two natures" are postbiblical novelties. If these particular notions are essential, the doctrines of these creeds are clearly conditional, dependent on the late Hellenistic milieu." [9]

I could list a lot more comments like these, but why bore you?

Okay, I'll put them in an appendix…

WHAT DO THE CREEDS ACTUALLY SAY?
The "Trinity" as most Christians understand it today is defined primarily by the three "creeds" quoted below. I won't quote the entirety of each creed here (maybe I'll also put them in an appendix – does anybody read those?), but instead I'll excerpt some lines and emphasize only the parts I <u>disagree</u> with. Will it surprise you how little I find to be incorrect? But there are some crucial errors.

The Nicene Creed 325 A.D.
This creed was formulated and signed by 272 bishops at the Council of Nicea under the direction of the Emperor Constantine in 325 A.D.

(note that some of them signed the agreement under protest – they didn't believe it)

We believe in one Lord, Jesus Christ, the only Son of God, eternally begotten of the Father, God from God, Light from Light, true God from true God, begotten, not made, <u>of one being with the Father.</u> … We believe in the Holy Spirit, the Lord, the giver of life, <u>who proceeds from the Father and the Son,</u>

(note that this last line was hotly debated and required the convening of another council at Constantinople in 381 AD. These "orthodox" creeds were re-negotiated several times.)

The Apostles' Creed 390 A.D.
This creed is relatively short and I really only have a problem with one or two lines: *I believe in God the Father Almighty, Maker of heaven and earth: And in Jesus Christ his only Son, our Lord; who was <u>conceived by the Holy Ghost</u>, born of the virgin Mary,* … (since Jesus Christ is the Only Begotten Son of God the <u>Father</u>, he can't really be conceived by the Holy Ghost or he would be the son of the Holy Ghost, right? Earlier versions of this creed said Christ was conceived by the <u>power</u> of the Holy Ghost, to which I agree. More on this later.)

Athanasian Creed 450-570 A.D.
This creed has been widely quoted and used by almost all the Western Christian churches but it doesn't appear in the records of any ecumenical church councils. Why it's been accepted

as doctrine is a bit of a mystery. It seems to have been written in the sixth century at least a hundred years after the death of Athanasius even though it bears his name.

The Athanasian Creed is so long and rambling and so full of contradictions and "anathemas" or curses that it is no wonder Jesus told Joseph Smith that it was an "abomination". Here some excerpts, with the errors underlined:

We worship one God in three persons and three persons in one God, without mixing the persons or dividing the divine being.

For each person — the Father, the Son, and the Holy Spirit — is distinct, but the deity of Father, Son, and Holy Spirit is one, _yet they are not three who are eternal, but there is one who is eternal, just as they are not three who are uncreated, nor three who are infinite, but there is one who is uncreated and one who is infinite. yet they are not three who are almighty, but there is one who is almighty._

So the Father is God, the Son is God, the Holy Spirit is God; yet they are not three Gods, but one God. So the Father is Lord, the Son is Lord, the Holy Spirit is Lord; yet they are not three Lords, but one Lord.

For just as Christian truth compels us to confess each person individually to be God and Lord, so the true Christian faith forbids us to speak of three Gods or three Lords.

The Holy Spirit is neither made nor created nor begotten, but proceeds from the Father and the Son. as stated before, all three persons are to be worshiped as one God and one God worshiped as three persons. Whoever wishes to be saved must have this conviction of the Trinity. [10]

SO WHERE DO THE CREEDS LEAVE MODERN CHRISTIANS?
Many of my Christian friends have a favorite saying, which seems to be a nice "pat answer" to the problem. They simply say "In the three persons is the one God". Unfortunately that cute little phrase is more litany than logic. And while it may satisfy some of them, it's not enough for me.

MODALISM – AN ANCIENT HERESY
From the conversations I've had, it seems that a lot of Christians resolve the "mystery" of the Trinity in their own minds by falling into the old heresy of Sabellianism, also known as

"Modalism" – the notion that there is really only one being called God who is manifested at different times in the "mode" of either the Father, the Son, or the Holy Ghost.

Sabellius was a theologian and priest from the third century who taught that God put on three different "faces" or "masks" (Latin "personae") to appear to mortals at times as different members of the Godhead. I've found that many (most?) everyday Christians who don't understand the finer theological and philosophical arguments for the Trinitarian creeds are left with a Modalistic view of God. A comment on one early example of this heresy was made by an early Bishop named Hippolytus (170-235 A.D.)

"Some others are secretly introducing another doctrine, who have become disciples of one Noetus,... He alleged that Christ was the Father Himself, and that the Father Himself was born, and suffered, and died... But the case stands not thus; for the Scriptures do not set forth the matter in this manner... the Scriptures themselves confute their senselessness, and attest the truth... The Scriptures speak what is right"[11]

DOES GOD HAVE A BODY?

Most of this whole Trinitarian issue becomes clear when we understand what the true "nature" of God actually is. Latter-day Saints get a lot of criticism from other Christians over our belief that God has a physical body. Most Protestants and Catholics believe in the portion of The Westminster Confession of Faith (formulated in 1646 after a bloody religious war in England) that says God is:

"a most pure spirit, invisible, without body, parts, or passions"

In contrast, as I've already quoted above, Latter-day Saints believe that: *The Father has body of flesh and bones as tangible as man's; The Son also; But the Holy Ghost has not a body of flesh and bones, but is a personage of Spirit. Were it not so, the Holy Ghost could not dwell in us.*

— Doctrine and Covenants 130:22

(Again let me state this caveat that the Father and the Son have bodies of flesh and bones, not flesh and blood – blood is an earthly element.)

WHY MOST CHRISTIANS DON'T BELIEVE GOD HAS A BODY

The doctrine of a body-less God was developed when Hellenistic philosophy was inserted into Christian teachings several hundred years after Christ. This philosophy reasoned that anything physical or corporeal could not be divine, therefore God could not have a physical nature. In the third century the Christian theologian Origen wrote that:

"the Jews indeed, but <u>also some of our people</u>, supposed that God should be understood as a man, that is, adorned with human members and human appearance. <u>But the philosophers despise these stories</u> as fabulous and formed in the likeness of poetic fictions" [12]

The intellectual Greeks ridiculed the simple faith of the Christians in an anthropomorphic God, and ultimately the Christians "caved" and adopted a more "sophisticated" view of Diety to "fit in" to their society in the same way that many churches have today accepted the un-Biblical practices of ordaining women or sanctioning same-sex marriages.

Granted, there are a few verses in the Bible that seem at first glance to support the belief that God is "invisible" or "a spirit". The KJV states:

"no man has seen God at any time, the only begotten Son, which is in the bosom of the Father, he hath declared him."

—(John 1:18)

But John also wrote in the same volume:

"Not that any man hath seen the Father, <u>save he which is of God, he hath seen the Father.</u>"

—(John 6:46)

And the early Christian Father Irenaeus wrote in A.D. 180 (long before current Bible translations) that this scripture <u>should</u> be read:

"For no man," he says, *"hath seen God at any time, unless the only-begotten Son of God, which is in the bosom of the Father, He hath declared [Him]."* [13]

Who can we say from Scripture is "of God" and has seen God? Certainly Stephen, who saw Christ standing at the right hand of God when he was being stoned to death (Acts 7:56), or Jacob, when he had "seen God face to face" (Gen. 32:30), or Moses, and Aaron, Nadab, and Abihu, and seventy of the elders of Israel when *"they saw the God of Israel"* (Exodus 24:9-10) There are more, but you see my point, right?

To be fair, John also says that Jesus is *"the image of the invisible God"* (Col. 1:15). But what does "invisible" mean? What first comes to mind perhaps is the movie *"The Invisible Man"*, where special effects are used to create a see-through man. Is that how you envision God? But how about if we break down the word "invisible"? If we describe something as "not visible", is that a fair equivalent?

Yet something that is "not visible" to me or to you may be visible to someone who is "of God" or who is in a different place or situation. For example, if I'm in my hometown of Columbus, Georgia the city of Atlanta is "invisible" or "not visible" to me. But if I'm orbiting the earth in a space station and I have a strong telescope I can see them both. Or people in a dark place may be "not visible" to my eyes, but if I have some night-vision goggles I can see them clearly.

Lastly, John says: *God is a Spirit: and they that worship him must worship him in spirit and in truth.* (John 4:24) However <u>there is no article "a" in the Greek text</u>, and many translations including the NIV, NLT, ESV, NASB etc. do not use it. They say "God is spirit", or simply that God is a spiritual being. And indeed we must worship Him in a spiritual manner. But although our Lord Jesus Christ was fully man, <u>he was also fully God</u>. And although he was a spiritual being he also <u>had a physical body</u>.

In fact, Jesus took great pains to demonstrate his physical nature to his closest earthly associates when he appeared to the disciples in the Upper Room after his resurrection. Luke says they were "affrighted" because they thought they "had seen a spirit". Our Savior calmed their fears by saying to them: *"Behold my hands and my feet, that it is I myself: <u>handle me, and see; <i>for a spirit hath not flesh and bones, as ye see me have</i></u>"*

—(Luke 24:39).

On another occasion he ate fish and honeycomb in the presence of his disciples to demonstrate the physical nature of his resurrected body. (Luke 24:42) So I ask the questions: Was Jesus God? Was he <u>FULLY</u> God (especially in his glorified, resurrected condition)? Did he have a physical body? Of course he did! And did he not say "he that has seen me hath seen the Father" (John 14:9)? Since he was obviously not saying that he WAS the Father, then it is evident that he was saying that the Father was LIKE HIM. So ... does God the Father have a body?

What do you think?

OKAY THEN, WHAT DOES THE BIBLE SAY ABOUT THREE PERSONS CALLED GOD?

So let's forget all the creeds and "essence" and "nature" and the Greek philosophical stuff for a while and go back to the Bible and see what the Word of God tells us about the separate persons of the Father, Son, and Holy Ghost.

In the beginning was the Word, and the Word was with God, and the Word was God. The same was in the beginning with God. All things were made by him; and without him was not any thing made that was made.

—John 1:1-3

We know the Word is the pre-mortal Jesus, and he created the heavens and the earth under the direction of God the Father. These verses were once quoted on *"The Bible Answer Man"* program by the notorious anti-Mormon Walter Martin. He then elaborated, *"but the Word was <u>not</u> that <u>same</u> God that the Word was <u>with</u>"* (emphasis mine).

I think that's the only time I ever agreed with Walter.

LET'S LOOK AT WHAT THE BIBLE ACTUALLY SAYS

The best way to learn what the Bible really means is not to look at one or two "proof-texts" but to search the entire Word of God for ALL the references on a topic. The entire list is too long for this chapter but perhaps I'll put it in an appendix. Here are a few of the most popular verses:

See the table beginning on next page Bible verses describing "one God" Bible verses describing three separate Godhead members.

Bible verses emphasizing "One God"	Verses show 3 separate persons in Godhead
Deut 6:4 Hear, O Israel: The LORD our God is one LORD" (Known as the "schema")	**John 1:1** The Word was with God and the Word was God.
1 Corinthians 8:4 we know that an idol [is] nothing in the world, and that [there is] none other God but one.	**John 14:28** My father is greater than I.
Isaiah 45:18 I [am] the LORD; and [there is] none else.	**Matt 19:17** Why callest thou me good? there is none good but one, that is, God.
Isaiah 43:10 -11 – before me there was no God formed, neither shall there be after me. I, I am the Lord, and besides me there is no savior.	**John 5:19 - see also John 14:10.** The Son can do nothing of himself, but what he seeth the Father do.
Isaiah 44:6 - 8 Thus saith the LORD the King of Israel, and his redeemer the LORD of hosts; I am the first, and I am the last; and beside me there is no God. … Is there a God beside me? yea, there is no God; I know not any.	**Luke 22:42** Saying, Father, if thou be willing, remove this cup from me: nevertheless not my will, but thine, be done.
1 John 5:7 For there are three that bear record in heaven, the Father, the Word, and the Holy Ghost: and these three are one*. *** this text was inserted into the Bible in the 4th or 5th century - see note below**	**Matt: 3:16-17** And Jesus, when he was baptized, went up straightway out of the water: and, lo, the heavens were opened unto him, and he saw the Spirit of God descending like a dove, and lighting upon him: And lo a voice from heaven, saying, This is my beloved Son, in whom I am well pleased.
John 10:30 I and my Father are one.	**Matt. 17:1–6** While he yet spake, behold, a bright cloud overshadowed them: and behold a voice out of the cloud, which said, This is my beloved Son, in whom I am well pleased; hear ye him. **Acts 7:55-56** But he, being full of the Holy Ghost, looked up steadfastly into heaven, and saw the glory of God, and Jesus standing on the right hand of God, 56 And said, Behold, I see the heavens opened, and the Son of man standing on the right hand of God.

Hosea 13:4 Yet I [am] the LORD thy God from the land of Egypt, and thou shalt know no god but me: for [there is] no savior beside me.	**John 17:24** Father, I will that they also, whom thou hast given me, be with me where I am; that they may behold my glory, which thou hast given me: for thou lovedst me before the foundation of the world.
Galatians 3:20 - Now a mediator is not [a mediator] of one, but God is one.	**John 14:26** But the Comforter, which is the Holy Ghost, whom the Father will send in my name, he shall teach you all things
James 2:19 Thou believest that there is one God; thou doest well: the devils also believe, and tremble.	**John 3:16** For God so loved the world, that he gave his only begotten Son, that whosoever believeth in him should not perish, but have everlasting life.
Mark 12:32 And the scribe said unto him, Well, Master, thou hast said the truth: for there is one God; and there is none other but he:	**Matt. 12:31–32** And whosoever speaketh a word against the Son of man, it shall be forgiven him: but whosoever speaketh against the Holy Ghost, it shall not be forgiven him, neither in this world, neither in the world to come.
1 Tim 2:5 For there is one God, and one mediator between God and men, the man Christ Jesus	**1 Tim 2:5** For there is one God, and one mediator between God and men, the man Christ Jesus
Romans 3:30 Seeing it is one God, which shall justify the circumcision by faith, and uncircumcision through faith.	**Galatians 3: 28** There is neither Jew nor Greek, there is neither bond nor free, there is neither male nor female: for ye are all one in Christ Jesus. **Hebrews 1:3** Who being the brightness of [his] glory, and the express image of his person, and upholding all things by the word of his power, when he had by himself purged our sins, sat down on the right hand of the Majesty on high; **Matt 27:46** My God, my God, why hast thou forsaken me?

1 Cor 8:4 As concerning therefore the eating of those things that are offered in sacrifice unto idols, we know that an idol is nothing in the world, and that there is none other God but one.	**1 Cor. 8:6** But to us there is but one God, the Father, of whom are all things, and we in him; and one Lord Jesus Christ, by whom are all things, and we by him.
John 14:7-11 7 If ye had known me, ye should have known my Father also: and from henceforth ye know him, and have seen him. 8 Philip saith unto him, Lord, shew us the Father, and it sufficeth us. 9 Jesus saith unto him, Have I been so long time with you, and yet hast thou not known me, Philip? he that hath seen me hath seen the Father; and how sayest thou then, Shew us the Father?	**John 17:1-11** These words spake Jesus, and lifted up his eyes to heaven, and said, Father, the hour is come: glorify thy Son, that thy Son also may glorify thee: … 4 I have glorified thee on the earth: I have finished the work which thou gavest me to do. 5 And now, O Father, glorify thou me with thine own self with the glory which I had with thee before the world was. … 11 And now I am no more in the world, but these are in the world, and I come to thee. Holy Father, keep through thine own name those whom thou hast given me, that they may be one, as we are.
Colossians 2:9 For in him dwelleth all the fulness of the Godhead bodily.	**John 6:38** I came down from heaven, not to do mine own will, but the will of him that sent me.
John 14:10 Believest thou not that I am in the Father, and the Father in me? the words that I speak unto you I speak not of myself: but the Father that dwelleth in me, he doeth the works.	**Genesis 1:26** And God said, Let us make man in our image, after our likeness. **(The use of the plural pronouns "us" and "our" here make perfect sense when we realize that God the Father is talking to the Word, or Jesus/Jehovah.)**
Colossians 1:19 - For it pleased [the Father] that in him should all fullness dwell;	**Genesis 3:22** The LORD God said, 'Behold, the man has become like one of US, to know good and evil.
Zechariah 14:9 – And the LORD shall be king over all the earth: in that day shall there be one LORD, and his name one.	**Genesis 11:7** Come, let US go down and there confuse their language, that they may not understand one another's speech.

33

WAS THE BIBLE CHANGED TO SUPPORT TRINITARIAN DOCTRINE?

Okay, having seen above the comparison of Bible verses used to support and to refute the Trinitarian doctrine of the "orthodox" creeds, what do you think? Did I overlook any? Probably. There's one passage that I marked with an asterisk, and that's 1 John 5:7-8. In the baseball record books if you place an asterisk next to a statistic it means there is some question about it. So it is with this verse which says:

"For there are three that bear record [in heaven, the Father, the Word, and the Holy Ghost: and these three are one. And there are three that bear witness in earth], the Spirit, and the water, and the blood: and these three agree in one.

This verse contains some extra words (underlined in brackets above) known to Bible scholars as the "Johannine Comma" (also called the *Comma Johanneum*) that appear in some early printed editions of the Greek New Testament that were source material for the King James Version.

However these extra words are generally absent from the handwritten Greek manuscripts. In fact, they only appear in the text of four late medieval manuscripts. They seem to have originated as a marginal note added to certain Latin manuscripts during the middle ages that was eventually incorporated into the text of most of the later Vulgate manuscripts.

From the Vulgate, then, it seems that the Comma was translated into Greek and inserted into some printed editions of the Greek text, and in a handful of late Greek manuscripts. All scholars consider it to be spurious, and it is not included in modern critical editions of the Greek text, or in the English versions based upon them. The well-known Biblical scholar Norman Geisler wrote: This verse has virtually no support among the early Greek manuscripts... Its appearance in late Greek manuscripts is based on the fact that Erasmus was placed under ecclesiastical pressure to include it in his Greek NT of 1522, having omitted it in his two earlier editions of 1516 and 1519 because he could not find any Greek manuscripts which contained it.[14]

Theology professors Anthony and Richard Hanson explain the unwarranted addition to the text this way:

"It was added by some enterprising person or persons in the ancient Church who felt that the New Testament was sadly deficient in direct witness to the kind of doctrine of the Trinity

which he favoured <u>and who determined to remedy that defect</u>... <u>It is a waste of time to attempt to read Trinitarian doctrine directly off the pages of the New Testament</u>" [15]

WHERE AND WHY DOES THE OLD TESTAMENT SAY THERE IS ONLY ONE GOD?

The Old Testament has many references to one God, the YHWH (Jehovah) of the Israelites. The most often cited is the heart of Jewish worship, the recitation of the Schema: *"Hear, O Israel: The LORD our God is one LORD"* (Deut 6:4) In contrast to their pagan neighbors and enemies the Hebrews were distinguished by their monotheistic belief in Jehovah, the one God of Israel.

However, when we examine the word "echad," (translated "one" in the Schema), we discover an interesting meaning. This word, "echad," comes from a Hebrew root which does NOT always signify a <u>numerical</u> "one" but rather it sometimes means "to unify" or "to collect together," a "<u>united</u> one."

Like "one" bunch of grapes. (Strong's #259) We can get a better feel for its usage by examining a couple of additional verses that use the same Hebrew word. After the creation of man we find the establishment of the marriage relationship:

Therefore shall a man leave his father and his mother, and shall cleave unto his wife, and they shall be <u>ONE</u> (echad) flesh.
—Genesis 2:24, (Jewish Publication Society version, 1917)

Regarding the people of the earth after the flood we read:

And the LORD said: They are <u>ONE</u> (echad) people, and they have all one language.
—Genesis 11:6, (Jewish Publication Society version, 1917)

Christians recognize that the Jehovah of the Old Testament is Jesus Christ. In speaking of the Israelites wandering in the desert, Paul said *"that spiritual Rock that followed them: and that Rock was Christ."* (1 Cor. 10:4) In another place Paul differentiated between Jesus and God the Father: *"to us there is but <u>one God, the Father</u>, of whom are all things, and we in him; and <u>one Lord Jesus Christ</u>, by whom are all things, and we by him."* (1 Cor. 8:6)

So the New Testament gives us a much clearer picture of the separation between God the Father and God the Son.

DID THE JEWS ALWAYS BELIEVE IN JUST ONE GOD?

The excellent Methodist theologian Margaret Barker writes (emphasis mine):

The Deuteronomists were fervent monotheists, which has led us to believe that <u>all</u> the Old Testament describes a <u>strictly monotheistic religion</u>. They also said that God could not be seen, only heard. There were, however, ancient traditions which said <u>otherwise</u> in each case; there was, as we shall see, a <u>belief in a second divine being</u> who could have human form and <u>this became the basis of Christianity.</u>[16]

What has become clear to me time and time again is that even over so wide an area, the evidence points consistently in one direction and indicates that <u>pre-Christian Judaism was not monotheistic in the sense that we use the word.</u> The roots of Christian Trinitarian theology lie in pre-Christian Palestinian beliefs about the angels. There were many in first-century Palestine who still retained a world-view derived from <u>the more ancient religion of Israel</u> [that of the First Temple] in which <u>there was a High God and several Sons of God, one of whom was Yahweh, the Holy One of Israel.</u>

Yahweh, the Lord, could be manifested on earth in human form, as an angel or in the Davidic king. It was as a manifestation of Yahweh, the Son of God, that Jesus was acknowledged as Son of God, Messiah and Lord.[17]

Educated at Cambridge, Barker is a Methodist Bible scholar who has authored nine books and has published articles in a variety of academic journals in England and America. She is a recognized expert on temple symbolism and in 1998 served a term as the president-elect of the Society for Old Testament Study.

(www.trinity-bris.ac.uk/sots/pastconferences.html).

A number of her articles appear on Marquette University's web page at:

www.marquette.edu/maqom/

BUT WHAT OF ISAIAH 43:10-11? DOESN'T IT SAY THERE IS "ONE GOD" ONLY?

There are several ways to answer this question. It is a valid one, since the scripture seems to advocate a militant monotheism in these verses, where Gods says "no other God is formed beside me", and "I know none other". But let's look a bit closer at these verses …

- (1) Some scholars have reason to believe that several chapters of Isaiah that include these verses are not Isaiah's words at all, but were actually added to the manuscripts by Jewish scribes later. This would place their validity in question. (See unpublished paper by John Tevednes and Michael Griffith, *"The Problems of the Monotheistic Polemics in Isaiah 43".*)

- (2) Another approach to these verses might take into account the Fatherhood of God. If we were to substitute "Father" (the most-used term for God in the Bible) in these verses, they would say essentially that "I am your <u>Father</u> and you have no other <u>Father</u> besides me".

- I could say the same thing to my own children, and it would be a true statement. But at the same time it does not preclude the possibility of there being other fathers throughout the universe who have other children.

- (3) We know that the speaker in Isaiah 43:10 was Jehovah, the God of Israel. He was telling them the difference between him, the living God, and the false pagan idols of their neighbors that were **"<u>formed</u>"** from wood or iron. He says "there is no God formed beside me".

In other words, the real message here is that the inanimate objects <u>formed</u> by man are not really gods at all. But it does not preclude the possibility of <u>living</u> beings existing somewhere in Eternity who are also the same kind of being that God is. In fact...

- (4) When we consider who is actually talking here in Isaiah 43 (if indeed these verses are not spurious additions to Scripture), then we must put the remarks in their overall context. ("A text without a context is only a pretext".)

- A. The speaker is Jehovah, another name for the pre-mortal Jesus Christ; the "Rock" who followed Israel through the wilderness according to 1st Cor. 10:4.

- B. Jesus is indeed God the Son. And according to John 1:1 he "created the heavens and the earth".

But he did it under the direction of God the Father! When he spoke about his ascension after his resurrection, he said "I go unto my God and to your God".

- C. Now tell me... did Jesus know something at this later date that he didn't know when he spoke those words to Isaiah about "knowing no other God"? Of course not! What we have to do is look at Isaiah in its proper context, which is...

- (5) According to most serious Bible scholars, (including a direct quote I have from John Stewart, former Assistant Director of Walter Martin's Christian Research Institute) God has revealed Himself progressively to mankind over time, according to man's ability to understand Him. This means that —as Paul put it— He reveals the "milk" to those who are spiritually immature (as were the people of Israel in the days of Isaiah), and to others He reveals the "meat", as He did to the New Testament Saints, and to Joseph Smith and the Latter-day Saints.

- A. In Isaiah Jesus/Jehovah revealed the simple concept of one Living God contrasted with the pantheon of heathen "gods". Then later...

- B. In His mortal ministry, Jesus/Jehovah revealed that not only were He and His Father both called "God", but that there was also a third person, the Holy Spirit, who is also "God".

- C. This advanced concept of three persons —each of whom is God— is still misunderstood by the Jews today. They accuse Christians of "tri-theism" using the same Bible verses that anti-Mormon writers use to accuse the Latter-day Saints of "polytheism".

(We find that somewhat ironic! Doesn't that mean that the Christians are worshiping a "different God" from the God of the Jews? The Jews certainly think so!

- D. In continuing God's progressive revelation of Himself to mankind, He told Joseph Smith that there are not only were there three persons who are "Gods", but that godhood is the divine potential of every child of God. (Actually, this doctrine was also revealed to the New Testament church.) And although it was not part of the "milk" that was preserved in the 66 books of the current Protestant Bible, it was taught by almost all of the most orthodox early Church Fathers. (See articles on "Divinization" in Sunstone magazine, 1975 and 1984, and my chapter on Eternal Progression later on in this book.)

Yet the concept that there is ultimately only "one God" for us humans to worry about is maintained in the "positional" superiority of the Father in the Godhead. Or as Paul said, *"we worship the one God, the Father of our Lord Jesus Christ"*. This is also the theological position of the LDS Church.

ARE THE MEMBERS OF THE GODHEAD OF ONE "ESSENSE" OR "NATURE"?
The bishops and theologians in the Catholic Church councils of 325 AD and afterwards introduced confusion into the discussion of the godhead when they began to use non-Biblical terms like "essence" and "nature". But in a spirit of fairness I'll try to explain how to understand the godhead, even using these terms.

I've heard some pastors and Bible teachers try to explain their version of the "mystery of the Trinity" by saying the three members of the godhead are like ice, water, and water vapor. They are three versions of one substance.

I used to be a chemistry major at Georgia Tech, and I learned a little about chemicals and compounds. Each molecule of water is composed of two hydrogen atoms and one oxygen atom. That is its "essence" or "nature". As noted above, it can exist in different states of a solid, liquid or vapor according to its temperature. If I have three beakers of water sitting on a lab table they all share this same "essence" or "nature". But they are still three separate collections of water molecules. They are one compound, but three separate vessels or examples of that compound.

I can freeze one and heat another until it vaporizes and thus make them look different, but they are still separate. There is no co-mingling of the molecules necessary for them to each maintain their "one" identity as water. There are still three containers. Yet they are one "substance" — water. Likewise the three members of the godhead are three separate beings, each of whom has the same kind of molecules or qualities of divinity that makes each of them "God". Doesn't that make sense?

"THE TRINITY" WAS A NON-ISSUE IN THE NEW TESTAMENT CHURCH
It's important to realize that the New Testament Saints had no problem with their simple belief in the Father, the Son, and the Holy Ghost. Under the inspiration and guidance of the Apostles and those whom the Twelve had taught, there was an understanding of the Godhead that seems to have been lost to those Christians of later years. This understanding would not be found again on earth until the restoration of apostolic or "special" revelation, which we'll discuss later.

THE MYSTERY OF THE TRINITY SOLVED

The Latter-day Saint understanding of the "oneness" of the members of the Godhead is easily explained in the context of John chapter 17 where Jesus prayed to his Father that the twelve apostles and his other disciples be one even as he and the Father are one:

Holy Father, keep through thine own name those whom thou hast given me, that they may be one, as we are. ... Neither pray I for these alone, but for them also which shall believe on me through their word; That they all may be one; as thou, Father, art in me, and I in thee, that they also may be one in us: that the world may believe that thou hast sent me. And the glory which thou gavest me I have given them; that they may be one, even as we are one: I in them, and thou in me, that they may be made perfect in one;

—John 17:11-23

Based on Scripture, LDS President Gordon B. Hinckley stated the solution to the Trinitarian "mystery". I mentioned it before but it bears repeating here:

They are distinct beings, but they are one in purpose and effort. They are united as one in bringing to pass the grand, divine plan for the salvation and exaltation of the children of God.
—Gordon B. Hinckley, Ensign, March 1998

ONE IN PURPOSE

Although most non Latter-day Saint Christians still cling to the Trinitarian creedal statements that the three members of the godhead are one in "essence" or "nature", some of them seem to have reached an understanding through Bible study, reason and logic that the members of the godhead are "one" in purpose. This is similar to what Latter-day Saints have learned through modern prophetic revelation.

The following is from a discussion of John 10:30 which says: "I and my Father are one". (emphasis is mine) J. H. Bernard, in his commentary on John, explicitly takes this position:

A unity of fellowship, of will, and of purpose between the Father and the Son is a frequent theme in the Fourth Gospel (cf. 5:18,19; 14:9, 23 and 17:11, 22), and it is tersely and powerfully expressed here; but to press the words so as to make them indicate identity of OUSIA, is to introduce thoughts which were not present to the theologians of the first century. [18]

Similarly, R. V. G. Tasker, in his commentary on John, says that although the orthodox church fathers cited this verse in support of the doctrine that Christ was of one substance with the Father, *"the statement seems however mainly to imply that the Father and the Son are <u>united in will and purpose</u>"* [19]

Even John Calvin wrote:

<u>The ancients made a wrong use of this passage</u> (John 10:30) to prove that Christ is (homoousios) of the same essence with the Father. <u>For Christ does not argue about the unity of substance, but about the AGREEMENT which he has with the Father</u>, so that whatever is done by Christ will be confirmed by the power of his Father. [20]

SUMMARY

Critics of "Mormonism" continually say that the Latter-day Saint belief in three separate members of the Godhead is "another gospel", when in fact it is found explicitly taught in John's gospel, chapter 17. It is the mystical "triune" god that is the product of "another gospel" derived by the Hellenistic philosopher/ theologians over 300 years after the time of Christ.

So if anyone has a "different Jesus" from that of the Bible, it is those who cling to the man-made Trinitarian creeds, not the Latter-day Saints.

ENDNOTES FOR CHAPTER 2

1   Dr. Donald A. Carson is a professor of New Testament at the Trinity Evangelical Divinity School

2   Paul F. Achtemeier, ed. (1985), 1099; emphasis added.

3   Recorded by the author from broadcast on radio station KBRT in Los Angeles, CA

4   http://www.christianity.com/home/christian living features

5   http://carm.org/what-trinity

6   W. Le Saint, "Tertullian," The New Catholic Encyclopedia, Thompson Gale, 2003, Vol. 13, p. 837

7   R. L. Richard, "Trinity, Holy," in New Catholic Encyclopedia (New York: McGraw-Hill, 1967), 14:299.

8   Emil Brunner, The Christian Doctrine of God, Philadelphia: Westminster Press, 1949 pp. 205 & 236

9   George A. Lindbeck, Professor of Historical Theology, Yale University, The Nature of Doctrine, Philadelphia: Westminster Press, 1984, p. 92

10 http://www.livinghopelc.net/

11 (Against the Heresy of One Noetus, 1-4, 7-9)

12 Ronald E. Heine, Origin Homilies on Genesis Washington, DC: Catholic University of America, 1982, 89

13 Irenaeus, "Against Heresies," in Chapter 6 Ante-Nicene Fathers, edited by Philip Schaff (Christian Literature Publishing Co., 1886)1:427

14 Norman Geisler and Thomas Howe, 2008, pp. 540-541

15 Reasonable Belief: A Survey of the Christian Faith, (1980, p. 171)

16 Margaret Barker: The Gate of Heaven, p.7

17 Margaret Barker, The Great Angel: A Study of Israel's Second God (London: SPCK, 1992), p3

18 (A Critical and Exegetical Commentary on the Gospel According to St. John, International Critical Commentaries [Edinburgh: T & T Clark, 1928]).

19 (The Gospel According to St. John, Tyndale New Testament Commentaries [Grand Rapids: Eerdmans, 1960], 136). Other commentators make similar statements.

20 (Commentary on the Gospel According to John, trans. William Pringle (Grand Rapids: Eerdmans, 1949; orig. 1847], 416).

EVIDENCE 3

I AM SAVED BY GRACE

As a Latter-day Saint I believe I am redeemed by the blood of my savior Jesus Christ. I am saved by grace. I do NOT believe I can "earn" salvation by my good works, despite what some of the critics of my faith may claim. But neither do I believe I will be saved by faith or grace <u>alone</u>. I believe that my salvation is a free gift of grace from my savior Jesus Christ but it is a gift that comes with instructions, and those instructions must be followed if I am to benefit from the gift as Christ intended. I have to cooperate with Jesus and respond to his grace in the way he has taught us if I'm to be saved.

The Bible has some <u>apparently</u> conflicting statements on the subject of salvation, grace, faith, and works. And while The Church of Jesus Christ's means of resolving them may be different from that of Protestants, Catholics, or other Christians, I believe our teaching is a Biblical Christian belief. As the Bible says, "Come, let us reason together". (Isaiah 1:18)

INSIDE LATTER-DAY CHRISTIANITY

1. Okay, so how <u>is</u> it that we are saved? Is it by faith or works? There's not very much at stake: only our eternal salvation, right? And the answer is ……. (wait for it …) Yes.

    There are three of the Latter-day Saint Articles of Faith that speak of salvation:

2. We believe that men will be punished for their own sins, and not for Adam's transgression.

3. We believe that through the Atonement of Christ all mankind may be saved, by obedience to the laws and ordinances of the Gospel.

4. We believe that the first principles and ordinances of the Gospel are: first, Faith in the Lord Jesus Christ; second, Repentance; third, Baptism by immersion for the remission of sins; fourth, Laying on of hands for the gift of the Holy Ghost.

OUR COMMON GROUND

Again, despite what critics of "Mormonism" say, we believe that it is ONLY "through the atonement of Christ" (see #3 above) that we can be saved. In that regard we are in complete agreement with other Christians. Where we differ is in how we believe we must apply the sacrifice that Jesus made on our behalf. As LDS writer Jana Riess put it in a response to an article in *Christianity Today:* - *It is a gift, yes, but it's one we have to unwrap and put into play.*[1]

There is no way we mortals can live without sinning. And there is no way we can pay for our own sins, no matter how good we try to be or how many good works we do. As Nephi says in the Book of Mormon, *"after all we can do, it is by grace that we are saved."* (2nd Nephi 25:23) Okay, I turned the words around a bit in that verse, but it means the same thing and I like it better that way. Another way of putting it that may be easier for my Christian friends to understand is like this: "After we surrender our lives to Jesus, it is by grace that we are saved". Right? Really, that's "all we can do".

OUTSIDE LATTER-DAY CHRISTIANITY

Here are some comments from critics of "Mormonism" describing their (mis)understanding of our beliefs about grace, works, and salvation:

This Mormon concept of salvation being a result of works is vastly different from the commonly held Christian understanding of Salvation as an unmerited, unearned gift of God's grace.[2]

— Watchman Fellowship website

"Grace alone!" was the resounding cry of Martin Luther and the Protestant Reformation. Yet, this doctrine has been denounced by The Church of Jesus Christ of Latter-day Saints in the harshest of terms: Unfortunately, Mormons do not understand the biblical teaching of justification. Instead, they seek to be righteous by their own works and keeping the law.[3]

—Dave Johnson, Midwest Christian Outreach

When Latter-day Saints talk about salvation by grace, they're referring to what they themselves call "general salvation." By this, Mormons mean that everybody is going to be resurrected, after which they will be judged according to their works. In other words, everybody gets an entrance pass to God's courtroom, but once inside, they're on their own! This, of course, adds up to nothing more than salvation by works.[4]

–Hank Hanegraaff, Christian Research Institute

INSIDE CHRISTIANITY

So let's take a look at what true Christianity REALLY teaches about faith, works, and salvation.

THE THEOLOGY OF SOTERIOLOGY VS. THE APOSTLES OF GOD

A Lutheran friend of mine invited me to attend his Sunday school class where the topic was going to be Arminianism. I didn't want to seem ignorant, so I decided to do a bit of research on the topic. I've found a number of theological discussions on the internet about Arminianism, Pelagianism, semi-Pelagianism and lots of other "isms". Many of them were centered around the fine points of the roles that grace and works play in a person's salvation, or what they call "soteriology" (that was a new word for me).

I must admit that for me it seemed as though there was a great deal of "philosophies of men mingled with Scripture". There were many references to the writings of Arminius and his friends, of John Wesley, of John Calvin, and others who seem to have had a great deal of influence on the development of Christian theology. One of the most quoted was Augustine, the Bishop of Hippo about 400A.D, who was known as St. Augustine.

But I began to wonder why anyone should accept <u>their</u> interpretations of scripture any more than I should trust my <u>own</u>. These men were not prophets or apostles and received no special inspiration or special revelations from God that would make them authorities on the subjects they wrote about. If their writings are accepted by "orthodox" Christianity today, they can help to define <u>that</u> body of belief, but who is to say if their man-made conclusions were correct?

The Scriptures say in Amos 3:7 *"surely God will do nothing except he reveal it to his servants the prophets. "* These theologians upon whom so much Christian doctrine is based were not prophets.

According to his contemporary Jerome, Augustine *"established anew the ancient Faith. "*[5] By what authority? The New Testament says that Christ's Church will be built upon a foundation of apostles and prophets, not philosophers and theologians or bishops. Instead of "establishing anew the ancient faith", was not Augustine instead preaching a "different gospel"?

We are told in Ephesians 4:14 that the reason God gave us prophets and apostles is so that we would not be*"tossed to and fro with every wind of doctrine"*. The learned philosophers and theologians may babble all they want to about this or that particular verse, but to me their words are as the sounding brass and tinkling cymbal.

SALVATION BY FAITH ALONE?

When Martin Luther wrote *"Sola Fide"* in the margin of his bible he established a "declaration of independence" from what he perceived as the bonds of the sacraments and ordinances of the Roman Catholic church that he felt had shackled Christians for over a thousand years. Ever since that time around 1520 AD, a large segment of Christianity has had a sour taste in its mouth over the term "good works." In sermons, tapes and broadcasts of evangelism today we are constantly reminded that *"our righteousness is as filthy rags"* and that it is *"by grace that you are saved and not of works less any man should boast,"* etc.

The example is frequently given of the thief on the cross who repented shortly before his death and was allegedly "saved" without performing any good works. But what if the thief had not died, but had been taken off the cross still alive? What if he had recovered and continued in his old lifestyle of thievery and sin? When he ultimately died would he still have a place with Jesus in "paradise"? I think not.

Certainly good works in themselves do not save us and do not earn our entrance into the kingdom of God. There are many ethical and good people, perhaps those of the Jewish faith or Muslim faith or of no faith at all perform many good works, but unless they accept Christ as their Savior they will not enter into the kingdom of Heaven.

There's an old protestant song that I learned as a child (perhaps at the Baptist vacation Bible school?) that went something like this:

"Noah found grace in the eyes of the Lord,
Noah found grace in the eyes of the Lord.
Noah found grace in the eyes of the Lord
And he landed high and dry."

It was through the grace of God that Noah was told to build the ark to save his family from the coming flood. And it was through grace that he was instructed how to build it. It was the grace of God that brought the animals two by two to enter into the boat at the right time. But Noah still had to do the work that he was capable of and actually do the building of the ark. God did not magically build it for him. In order to be "saved", Noah had to cooperate with God.

Likewise, it was through the grace of God that the firstborn of the Children of Israel were saved from the angel of death at the first Passover in Egypt, but they had to do the "work" of putting lamb's blood on the frames of their doors or else the grace would be ineffective for them.

But has much of evangelical Christianity fallen into teaching "another gospel"? As one prominent bible teacher asks, has "cheap grace," or "easy believe-ism" become a popular doctrine taught by many pastors to those with "itching ears"? Let's look at *"The Rest of the Story"* as news commentator Paul Harvey used to say...

FAITH WITHOUT WORKS?

In James 2:20 we read that "faith without works is dead". James says *"show me your faith <u>without</u> your works and I'll show you my faith <u>by</u> my works."* Admittedly this verse is unpopular with many Christians today (and unknown to many). In fact, Martin Luther wanted to kick the epistle of James out of the canon of the New Testament primarily because of this verse. He called it the "Epistle of straw" and felt that it should be deleted from the Bible. That was a bit presumptuous and arrogant on Luther's part when you think about it.

Martin Luther himself is said to have coined this phrase and I've heard a number of evangelical pastors and teachers repeat it, that *"Faith alone saves, but the faith that saves is not alone"*. The contemporary Christain teacher R.C. Sproul says it this way:

"if good works do not follow from our profession of faith, it is a clear indication that we do not possess justifying faith. The Reformed formula is, "We are justified by faith alone but not by a faith that is alone."[6]

I suppose it could be viewed as either a rhetorical cop-out and verbal gymnastics, or a sincere attempt to explain that true faith in Christ is never really "alone". I like the latter better. And that's what we Latter-day Saints believe.

A CATHOLIC VIEW

In contrast to the protestant evangelical position on "faith alone", the Roman Catholic Church's beliefs in this matter seem much closer to our doctrine. From the Catholic Apologetics Network website we read (emphasis mine):

the Catholic Church does not teach "justification by faith alone" because <u>the Bible does not teach justification by faith alone!</u> The word "faith" appears in the New Testament 230 times, the word 'alone' 32 times. Paul uses "alone" more than any other New Testament author. <u>Yet Paul never puts "faith" and "alone" together.</u> One has to ask why is that? In only <u>one</u> instance in the Bible do these two words appear in the same verse. That verse ... is James 2:24 "You see that a man is justified by works and <u>not</u> by faith <u>alone</u>." How is it, then, that they can teach as true, <u>a doctrine that is explicitly denied by the plain reading of the text?</u>[7]

EVEN SOME EVANGELICALS UNDERSTAND – SORT OF

But even in the protestant evangelical branch of Christianity there are some pastors and teachers who seem to "get it" (from the Latter-day Saint perspective) about faith, grace, works, and salvation. When I lived in Southern California I used to listen to a well-known evangelical pastor on a radio program called "Grace to You". His name was John MacArthur, and although his views are not universally accepted among Christians, much of what he said made a lot of sense to me. I have his book called *The Gospel According to Jesus*. I think it might be useful to include a few quotes from that volume here to demonstrate that at least some Christians have an understanding of grace and works that is similar (but not identical) to what I've learned inside Latter-day Christianity: (underlining is mine)

<u>The Gospel in vogue today holds forth a false hope to sinners</u>. It promises them they can have eternal life, yet <u>continue to live in rebellion against God</u>. Indeed, it encourages people to <u>claim Jesus as Savior</u> yet defer until later the commitment to <u>obey him as Lord</u>.

—Page 15

... the Good News of Christ has given way to the bad news of an insidious <u>easy–believism</u> that makes no moral demands on the lives of sinners. <u>It is not the same message Jesus proclaimed</u>. ... The church's witness to the world has been sacrificed on the altar of <u>cheap grace</u>.

—Page 16

Works are not necessary to earn salvation. But true salvation wrought by God will not fail to produce the good works that are its fruit.

—Page 33

(Quoting Dr. H.A. Ironside) We have myriads of glib-tongued professors today who give no evidence of regeneration whatever. Prating of salvation by grace, they manifest no grace in their lives. <u>Loudly declaring they are justified by faith alone, they fail to remember that "faith without works is dead"</u>, and that justification by works before men is not to be ignored as though it were in contradiction to justification by faith before God.[8]

The language of the modern message sounds vaguely similar to (the hymn) "Just as I Am", but the difference in meaning is profound. <u>Sinners today hear not only that Christ will receive them as they are but also that he will let them stay that way!</u>

—Page 169

For those who insist on taking luggage, <u>the broad gate may be more appealing</u>. It is marked "Heaven". It may even be marked "Jesus", but it is not going to Heaven and it has nothing to do with Jesus. It is the gate of religion for the masses, a wide open gate through which anyone can pass without ridding himself of self-righteousness, pride, material possessions, or even sin. But <u>there is no salvation for those who choose this gate</u>.

—Page 183

The pattern of modern evangelism is to take people through a formula, get them to pray a prayer, sign a card, or whatever, then tell them they are saved and should never doubt it.

... <u>The teaching that Christians are freed from observing any moral law is rampant in today's evangelical community</u>. We are told that there is no reason to examine one's life

—Page 190

<u>Satan can do some amazing things, and he will do almost anything to deceive an individual into thinking he is saved</u>

—Page 191

Dr. MacArthur quotes from many Christian teachers in his Appendix (emphasis is mine):

Luther also wrote, "When we have thus taught faith in Christ, <u>then do we teach also good works</u>. These are good works, indeed, which flow out of this faith". ... He defended good *works arising from faith. ... Good works are according to him the end and aim of faith. ... "Where there are no good works, there is no Faith" Luther wrote, "if good works and love do not blossom forth it is not genuine faith, the Gospel has not yet gained a foothold, and Christ is not rightly known".*

—Page 224

From W. H. Griffith Thomas, founder of the Dallas Theological Seminary MacArthur quotes:

St. Paul uses Genesis 15 to prove the necessity of faith; St. James uses Genesis 22 to prove the necessity of the works. St. Paul teaches that works must spring from faith; St. James teaches that faith must be approved by works.[9]

—Page 234

ANTINOMIANISM

I find it ironic that even Martin Luther who is known for his "liberating" doctrine of "sola fide" found that many Christians of his day had gone too far with the idea that Christianity did not require any obedience to the commandments of Christ. He wrote a treatise *"Against Antinomianism"* where he coined that term which means: "The unbridled Christian belief against obeying any law." Many Christians today would be very surprised to read that Luther described the saving kind of faith as:

a living, creative, active and powerful thing, this faith. Faith cannot help doing good works constantly. It doesn't stop to ask if good works ought to be done, but before anyone asks, it already has done them and continues to do them without ceasing. Anyone who does not do good works in this manner is an unbeliever... Thus, it is just as impossible to separate faith and works as it is to separate heat and light from fire![10]

IS BELIEF ALONE ENOUGH FOR SALVATION?

There are several verses in the Bible that would seem to indicate that all a person has to do is believe that Jesus Christ is their Savior in order to be saved. For example Acts 16:31 says, *"Believe on the Lord Jesus Christ, and thou shalt be saved"*.

But other seemingly contradicting passages would seem to indicate that belief alone is not enough for salvation. Indeed in James 2:19 we read that, *"the devils also believe, and tremble"*. Are the devils then saved? I doubt it.

Since we all believe that the Bible doesn't <u>really</u> contradict itself, let's see if we can find a reasonable explanation for this <u>apparent</u> contradiction. If we look at the example above from Acts 16 in its <u>context</u>, we'll perhaps gain a better understanding of what is being said: Paul and Silas had been unlawfully imprisoned in Philippi. Then about midnight …

And suddenly there was a great earthquake, so that the foundations of the prison were shaken: and immediately all the doors were opened, and every one's bands were loosed. And the keeper of the prison awaking out of his sleep, and seeing the prison doors open, he drew out his sword, and would have killed himself, supposing that the prisoners had been fled. But Paul cried with a loud voice, saying, Do thyself no harm: for we are all here. Then he called for a light, and sprang in, and came trembling, and fell down before Paul and Silas, And brought them out, and said, <u>Sirs, what must I do to be saved</u>?

I guess it could be said that the jailor's question had two meanings or levels. On the one hand, his life was over if his prisoners escaped, and he was about to commit suicide. So he could have been asking Paul what must he do to save his mortal life. But the next verses indicate that more was at stake: *And they said, <u>Believe on the Lord Jesus Christ, and thou shalt be saved</u>, and thy house.*

Belief in Christ may or may not have prevented his physical execution (and that of his family?) if indeed his prisoners took advantage of the earthquake and ran away. But Paul and Silas had a greater purpose in mind:

And <u>they spake unto him the word of the Lord</u>, and to all that were in his house. And he took them the same hour of the night, and washed their stripes; <u>and was baptized</u>, he and all his, straightway.

— (Acts 16:26-33)

So we see that belief was only the first step. As Christ's servants "spoke unto him the word of the Lord" the jailor and his whole family were <u>baptized</u> "the same hour of the night". Thus Paul and Silas were fulfilling our Savior's Great Commission where he said "*he that believeth <u>and is baptized</u> shall be saved*". (Mark 16:16) This is just one of many examples in the New Testament illustrating <u>the proper order of response to the Good News</u> of the Gospel: <u>belief</u> is followed by <u>baptism</u>.

BELIEF VS FAITH

Those who say that "faith alone saves" may draw a distinction between belief and faith. I would tend to agree with that. I once heard a story that I think explains the difference between the two: As this story goes, there was a man who was among the first to walk across Niagara Falls on a tight rope. Others had done so using a balance pole, but this individual decided to cross the chasm on a tight rope pushing a wheelbarrow. As he addressed a large crowd of people before making his attempt, he asked if those present believed he could accomplish the task. "How many of you believe I will make it?", he asked. Most of the hands went up. He asked again, "how many of you <u>really</u> believe I can make it"? Again there were cheers of agreement. "Okay then", he said, "who wants to get in the wheelbarrow?" It was one thing to <u>believe</u>, but it took real <u>faith</u> to get in the wheelbarrow. Faith is a belief that motivates a person to <u>action</u>.

WHAT EXACTLY IS SALVATION?

The Bible uses the term "salvation" or "saved" in a number of verses that have different meanings. This can be confusing. For example, in Luke 18:42 Jesus heals a blind man and says *"receive thy sight. Thy faith hath <u>saved</u> thee."* Certainly his faith had saved him from a life of blindness, but was Jesus speaking in this case of the man's eternal spiritual salvation? Possibly, but the limited account in Luke doesn't make it clear.

In the very next chapter we read the account of Zacchaeus, a rich publican. Jesus went to his house and ate with him, and apparently this sinner repented of his evil ways.

"And Zacchaeus stood, and said unto the Lord; Behold, Lord, the half of my goods I give to the poor; and if I have taken any thing from any man by false accusation, I restore him fourfold. And Jesus said unto him, <u>This day is salvation come to this house</u>, forsomuch as he also is a son of Abraham. (v. 8-9)

I'm sure there are many evangelicals who would say that this man could not have been "saved" for his good works, so the "salvation" that was to come to his house "this day" must have meant something else than Saccaeus's eternal assurance of being with the Lord in heaven. On the other hand the change of heart that <u>motivated</u> those good works could be considered an indication that Zacchaeus was truly "born again".

So I ask again, what is salvation? Latter-day Saints believe that "salvation" means admittance into the Celestial Kingdom where both God the Father and Jesus dwell. This is what Paul called the "third heaven" or the kingdom like the "glory of the sun". (2 Cor. 12:2, 1Cor. 15:40-41) But the Bible also speaks of *"things that accompany salvation"* or <u>rewards</u>. More about this later.

IS CONFESSING WITH THE MOUTH ENOUGH FOR SALVATION?

Romans 10:9 is a popular verse among evangelical Christians. It says:

... if thou shalt <u>confess with thy mouth</u> the Lord Jesus, and shalt believe in thine heart that God hath raised him from the dead, <u>thou shalt be saved</u>.

As I read this and thought about it, it gave me an idea. I considered how effective it would be to confess with one's mouth that some drug or procedure is a cure for cancer, without taking the pill or undergoing the treatment required to cure the disease. So if you only *"confess with thy mouth the Lord Jesus"* without doing what Jesus says, what good is that? Think about it.

I think many Christians omit or forget the second part of that verse which places an emphasis on the need to believe in one's heart that God has raised Christ from the dead. And if we really "believe in our heart", is it a belief that motivates us to action? Which takes us back to the belief/faith issue.

Let's turn to Justin Martyr, one of the church fathers of the second century who wrote:

"And let those who are not found living as He taught, be understood to <u>be no Christians, even though they profess with the lip the precepts of Christ</u>; for <u>not those who make profession, but those who do the works, shall be saved</u>, according to His word:

"Not every one who <u>saith</u> to Me, Lord, Lord, shall enter into the kingdom of heaven, but he that <u>doeth</u> the will of My Father which is in heaven. For whosoever heareth Me, and doeth My sayings, heareth Him that sent Me.

And many will say unto Me, Lord, Lord, have we not eaten and drunk in Thy name, and done wonders? And then will I say unto them, Depart from Me, ye workers of iniquity. Then shall there be wailing and gnashing of teeth, when the righteous shall shine as the sun, and the wicked are sent into everlasting fire. For many shall come in My name, clothed outwardly in sheep's clothing, but inwardly being ravening wolves. By their works ye shall know them. And every tree that bringeth not forth good fruit, is hewn down and cast into the fire."

And as to those who are <u>not living pursuant to these His teachings</u>, and are <u>Christians only in name</u>, we demand that all such be <u>punished</u> by you.[11]

HOW MUST BELIEF OR FAITH OR GRACE BE APPLIED?

Having faith that Jesus died for our sins won't save us unless we <u>correctly apply</u> His atoning sacrifice.

For example, let's suppose that someone we'll call "John" has accidentally ingested a lethal dose of poison and only has a few minutes to live. Another person named "Jim" comes to John and says "I have a vial of liquid here that can save you from death." It's a true statement, and John believes Jim.

He says "okay, how do I use it?" If Jim tells John that he must rub it on his head to be saved from death but what John really needs to do is to swallow it, John will soon be dead if he follows Jim's instructions. Despite the fact that the antidote is real and Jim is sincere, he is tragically (and fatally for John) mis-informed.

It seems that this kind of mis-information was discovered by Paul when he visited Ephesus.

And it came to pass, that, while Apollos was at Corinth, Paul having passed through the upper coasts came to Ephesus: and finding certain disciples, He said unto them, Have ye received the Holy Ghost since ye believed? And they said unto him, We have not so much as heard whether there be any Holy Ghost. And he said unto them, <u>Unto what then were ye baptized?</u> And they said, Unto John's baptism. Then said Paul, John verily baptized with the baptism of repentance, saying unto the people, that they should believe on him which should come after him, that is, on Christ Jesus. <u>When they heard this, they were baptized in the name of the Lord Jesus. And when Paul had laid his hands upon them, the Holy Ghost came on them</u>; and they spake with tongues, and prophesied. And all the men were about twelve.
—(Acts 19:1)

It is apparent that some well-meaning teachers had taught the Good News of "Jesus and Him crucified" to these twelve men in Ephesus, but obviously those who taught them weren't authorized representatives of Christ. They did not know the fullness of the Gospel and had neither the knowledge nor the authority to preach and to bestow the gift of the Holy Ghost on believers through the laying on of hands. We'll get into the authority question later, but for now let's just say that those sincere believers who had taken it upon themselves to share the Gospel had not gotten the whole story of what was needed for salvation. They did not know fully how to APPLY the atoning sacrifice of Christ.

SO WHAT IS THE ANSWER? WHAT IS NECESSARY FOR SALVATION?

When a person first hears of what Jesus did for them and they believe it, the first question that naturally comes to mind is, "Okay, what do I do now?" As we discussed before, many sincere preachers and teachers will tell them that confessing their belief with their mouth is all they have to do to be saved. Others will pray with an individual who answers an altar call and then tell them that they are saved. But what is the New Testament answer to this question?

IF FAITH IS A BELIEF THAT LEADS TO ACTION, WHAT SHOULD THAT ACTION BE?

The Bible has a clear answer (at least it seems pretty clear to me). In the second chapter of Acts we read that Peter and the apostles were preaching to a crowd of at least 3,000 people on the day of Pentecost which was just fifty days after the crucifixion and resurrection of Christ. They said: *Therefore let all the house of Israel know assuredly, that God hath made that same Jesus, whom ye have crucified, both Lord and Christ. Now when they heard this, they were pricked in their heart, and said unto Peter and to the rest of the apostles, Men and brethren, what shall we do? Then Peter said unto them, Repent, and be baptized every one of you in the name of Jesus Christ for the remission of sins, and ye shall receive the gift of the Holy Ghost.*

—(Acts 2:37-38)

THE BIBLE'S REAL FOUR SPIRITUAL LAWS

A popular evangelical Protestant pamphlet talks about the "Four Spiritual Laws". This event in Acts 2:37-38 provides us a correct understanding of the Bible's real four spiritual laws - how a person is to respond to the "good news". That day of Pentecost sets a pattern that continues throughout the New Testament.

The people were "pricked in their hearts", meaning that the Holy Ghost had convicted them of the truth of the apostles' words. They were given through grace the gift of testimony and faith with no effort or "works" of their own. They received an instant confirmation in their hearts that Christ's special witnesses had spoken the truth.

They then exercised their (1) <u>faith</u> by asking "what shall we <u>do</u>?" Peter did <u>not</u> say as many Evangelical preachers do today: "You don't have to do anything. Jesus has already done it all for you." They were told to (2) <u>repent</u>, (3) be <u>baptized</u>, and (4) to <u>receive the Holy Ghost</u>. We've already seen from Acts 19 that this is done through the laying on of hands by one who has the authority to confer the gift of the Holy Ghost.

This Biblical example is how Christians must apply the atoning blood of Jesus Christ to their lives and to accept Him as their personal Savior. To teach any other response is to teach "another gospel", and we all know what the Bible says about that.

THE PATTERN OF SALVATION CONTINUES …
The Biblical response to the gift of salvation is illustrated several more times throughout the New Testament, showing a pattern that is different from what many preachers teach today.

In addition to the examples in Acts 2:37-38 and Ephesians 19, let's revisit Acts 16:30 and the jailer of Paul and Silas. As we discussed, after he was told "Believe on the Lord Jesus Christ, and thou shalt be saved', <u>he and his family were all baptized</u> "the same hour of the night".

Likewise when Cornelius, the first Gentile convert accepted Christ, what did he do? The Bible says that Peter "*commanded them to be baptized in the name of the Lord.*" (Acts 10:48) Are we starting to see a pattern here? This is what happens throughout the entire New Testament:

-faith – repentance – baptism – Holy Ghost.

Get it? Got it? Good.

Now let's go back and read again the 3rd and 4th LDS Articles of Faith.

3. We believe that through the Atonement of Christ all mankind may be saved, by obedience to the laws and ordinances of the Gospel.

4. We believe that the first principles and ordinances of the Gospel are: first, <u>Faith</u> in the Lord Jesus Christ; second, <u>Repentance</u>; third, <u>Baptism</u> by immersion for the remission of sins; fourth, Laying on of hands for the <u>gift</u> of the Holy Ghost.

These are the only "good works" necessary to enter the Celestial kingdom of God. Anything else has to do with rewards or the "things that accompany salvation". (Heb. 6:9)

IS WATER BAPTISM A "WORK"? IS IT REQUIRED FOR SALVATION?

The Latter-day Saints believe that baptism by immersion is more than just a good idea, or "an outward sign of an inward commitment". It is a necessary ordinance that is required for us to enter back into God's presence. I know that there are many Christians who disagree with us, but I think there are just as many or more on the other side who share this belief with us. The Roman Catholic Church teaches that baptism is one of the "sacraments" or ordinances required for salvation, and they are the largest Christian church in the world. Many Protestants also believe that water baptism is essential for salvation.

It might be said that baptism saves us in the same way that putting blood on the doorposts saved the children of Israel when God brought the plague of death upon the Egyptians. Sure, it was only a symbol and there was nothing inherent in the sheep's blood that saved them, but obeying that commandment was just as essential to their physical salvation as our obedience to the commandment to be baptized is to our spiritual life eternal.

BIBLE VERSES THAT SAY WATER BAPTISM IS ESSENTIAL FOR SALVATION

With all due respect to Christians who believe a verbal confession is all that's required to be saved, I think we've explained above why that teaching is not true nor is it Biblical. Let's see what the Bible says further about baptism:

Jesus answered, Verily, verily, I say unto thee, Except a man be born of water and of the Spirit, he cannot enter into the kingdom of God.

—John 3:5

Jesus says, "He that believeth and is baptized shall be saved; but he that believeth not (and therefore is not baptized) shall be damned."

—Mark 16:16

Then Peter said unto them, Repent, and be baptized every one of you in the name of Jesus Christ for the remission of sins, and ye shall receive the gift of the Holy Ghost.

—Acts 2:38

Robert Starling

Then they that gladly received his word were <u>baptized</u>: and the same day there were added unto them about three thousand souls.

—Acts 2:41

"....<u>whereunto even baptism doth also now save us,</u>

—1 Peter 3:21

Then cometh Jesus from Galilee to Jordan unto John, to be <u>baptized</u> of him. ... And Jesus answering said unto him, suffer it to be so now: for thus it becometh us <u>to fulfill all righteousness.</u> Then he suffered him. And <u>Jesus, when he was baptized,</u> went up straightway out of the water.

—Matt. 3:13-16 (also Mark 1:9 and Luke 3:21)

Go ye therefore, and teach all nations, <u>baptizing</u> them

—Matt 28:19

And all the people that heard him, and the publicans, justified God, being <u>baptized</u> with the baptism of John. But the Pharisees and lawyers <u>rejected the counsel of God</u> against themselves, being <u>not baptized</u> of him.

—Luke 7:29-30

And he (Peter) commanded them to be <u>baptized</u> in the name of the Lord.

—Acts 10:48

And now why tarriest thou? arise, and <u>be baptized</u> and wash away thy sins

—Acts 22:16

<u>Not by works of righteousness</u> which we have done, but according to his mercy <u>he saved us, by the washing of regeneration,</u> and renewing of the Holy Ghost;

—Titus 3:5

The contrast in this last verse also makes it very clear that baptism is NOT among the "works of righteousness" (the Law of Moses) that Paul says do <u>not</u> bring salvation. On the contrary, he says that it <u>IS</u> by "the washing of regeneration" (baptism) that God DOES "save us".

Okay, that's enough about baptism. Let's look at some other things ....

WHAT KIND OF "WORKS" DO LATTER-DAY SAINTS DO?

Many of the critics of "Mormonism" talk about the "works" that Latter-day Saints do, allegedly to "work our way to heaven". But what are they? Let's take a look at some of the kinds of "works" that members of The Church of Jesus Christ of Latter-day Saints might be "called" or asked to do (these are mostly things that I've done myself at one time or another):

1. offer prayers in our Sacrament Meetings or worship services, or in other meetings
2. give talks in some of those same meetings, or play a piano or lead the singing
3. visit other church members monthly as ministering brothers or sisters, to see how they are doing and to encourage them in their Christian walk
4. teach a class in Sunday School, Primary, Relief Society, Young Men/Women, or a priesthood quorum, or teach a Seminary class
5. serve as a class or quorum president or a counselor
6. sing in a choir or lead a choir
7. participate in a service project or help clean a chapel, mow grass or shovel snow
8. thin or pick peaches or some other plants on a welfare farm, or help with livestock on a ranch
9. help process foodstuffs at a church-operated cannery or other food preparation facility
10. help collect and sort donated clothing that will be given to the poor and needy
11. give ten percent of your income as tithing, and contribute other offerings as needed
12. serve as a Bishop, Stake President, Mission President or other administrative leader
13. give 18 months to two years of your life to serve as a full time missionary
14. serve part time as a local missionary or missionary leader
15. be a Scoutmaster or other Scout leader or Young Women leader
16. be a Relief Society or Primary president or president's counselor
17. perform or officiate in proxy baptisms and other ordinances in the temples
18. be a ward or stake clerk and keep church records
19. prepare, bless, and pass the Sacrament in church meetings
20. volunteer to help cleanup efforts in disaster areas

There are other things "Mormons" do that might be considered by some to be "works" that we simply consider obedience to God's commandments and receiving certain blessings from Him. Although we're imperfect and we don't always succeed, we strive diligently to:

21. demonstrate our faith in Christ and our repentance by being baptized by immersion and receiving the Gift of the Holy Ghost by the laying on of hands

22. keep the Sabbath day holy and obey all the Ten Commandments
23. abstain from sex before marriage and remain faithful in marriage
24. abstain from coffee, tea, tobacco, alcohol, illegal drugs, and other things harmful to the body
25. attend Sacrament meetings and other church meetings as needed
26. worthy males are ordained to various offices in the priesthood according to age and need
27. at an appropriate age, attend the temple and make additional covenants with God
28. return often to the temple to make those covenants by proxy for those who have died
29. wear temple garments (for those who have been to the temple) except when participating in sports, swimming, etc.
30. dress modestly and appropriately

While this may seem like a lot, many of these so-called "works" are things that many other Christians also do as a matter of course. And do you know what? Except for number 21 none of these has anything to do with being "saved" or "working our way to heaven". We do these things because:

  a. God has commanded it and we love Him and want to obey Him
  b. it makes our lives or the lives of others happier and more fulfilled
  c. it is our opportunity and privilege to use our God-given talents to build His kingdom

DO MORMONS HAVE TO BE "PERFECT" TO BE SAVED?

In Latter-day Saint meetings you'll sometimes hear about the need to strive for "perfection". This is not Joseph Smith's idea. It is a commandment from Jesus. It was our Savior who said *"Be ye therefore perfect, even as your Father which is in heaven is perfect."* (Matt. 5:48) We also read in LDS scriptures that *"the Lord cannot look upon sin with the least degree of allowance"* (Alma 45:16, D&C 1:31) But can we really be "perfect"? Does God really <u>expect</u> us to be "perfect"? Well, yes and no …

First of all, the word rendered as "perfect" in the KJV and other translations doesn't mean "without any error or blemish" as we consider the word in today's world. Unfortunately this mistranslation causes many folks a lot of anguish. The Greek text actually says that we should be "spiritually mature" or "complete". That makes a lot of difference, huh? (Can we all give a collective sigh of relief?) Secondly, there's nothing that says we have to become "complete" or without sin <u>all on our own</u>, or even that we have to do it all within the bounds of our mortal lives. Through <u>grace</u> and the proper application of the atonement of Christ we can be cleansed of all our sins and become "spotless" in God's sight. That's the "good news" of the Gospel! God doesn't expect me to become "perfect" in this life, but as long as I *"press toward the mark for the prize"* (Philippians 3:14), my confidence is in Christ that I will eventually attain that state in Eternity.

OUR GOOD WORKS ARE NOT AN ATTEMPT TO "EARN" OUR SALVATION OR TO "REPAY" OUR DEBT TO CHRIST

I've been fortunate for many years to have a neighbor next door who is also a good friend. His name is Larry and he's an expert at heating and air conditioning. In fact, he manages a company that is involved in that business. A few years ago it was a day of sweltering summer heat when the air-conditioning unit in my home broke down. Larry came over and took one look, and saw that we needed an entirely new heating and cooling unit. I was out of work and our family was in pretty dire financial straits at that time, and Larry's diagnosis was certainly something that I did not want to hear.

About that time a look came over his face as though he remembered something and he smiled. "Don't worry about it" and he said. "I have a customer who just upgraded to a larger unit for his home, and the unit that we removed would be perfect for your house. It is sitting on my warehouse floor right now. One of my installers owes me a favor, and I can have it installed and cooling your home by tomorrow." The heating and air conditioning unit for my home would have cost me several thousand dollars to purchase and install. With meager financial resources, there is no way I could have paid for it. It was a gift from my friend and neighbor.

Often now when it snows I will go over and shovel Larry's driveway and sidewalk. Sometimes when the garbage truck is coming, and his trash cans are not out on the street I'll go over and put them out for him. These are not things that I do to try to repay my friend. That is impossible. But I do them as a small token of my appreciation for his kindness and generosity.

Likewise, one day I was vacuuming carpets in the classrooms of my local LDS meetinghouse. As I was doing so, it occurred to me that many of my evangelical friends might think that I was trying to work my way to heaven. I quietly smiled to myself at their lack of understanding. I wasn't vacuuming for my salvation, nor was I trying to repay the great debt that I owe to my Savior. That is impossible. But the floors in the building where I worship Christ did need cleaning, and it was a privilege for me to be able to offer a small demonstration of my gratitude to Jesus for all he's done for me.

FAITH VS WORKS OR FAITH AND WORKS? WHAT DOES THE BIBLE SAY?

The apostle Peter warned us that in the specific area of salvation, it is dangerous to rely solely on the epistles of Paul because these writing were "difficult to understand" and if misunderstood could lead to destruction (2 Pet. 3:15-16). Many Christians do just that as they ignore any other Bible scriptures that encourage obedience and good works. But let's try an experiment. I've never seen anyone do this kind of comparison, so it should be interesting. Here are a few of the alleged "conflicting" statements about faith and works from the New Testament. But again, since we know the Bible doesn't contradict itself, there must be a way to reconcile "Column A" with "Column B" below: (see table next page)

COLUMN A	COLUMN B
Saved by Faith or Grace Alone? (Note: the phrase "works of the law" pertain specifically to keeping the Law of Moses)	**Saved/rewarded by our works or deeds?**
Ephesians 2:8-9 *For by grace are ye saved through faith; and that not of yourselves: it is the gift of God: **Not of works, lest any man should boast.*** (careful – don't look at verse 10 yet) OK –look to the right - -->	**James 2:24** *Ye see then how that by works a man is justified, and* <u>*not*</u> *by faith alone..* (oh look! – verse 10 is over here!) **Ephesians 2:10** *For we are his workmanship, **created in Christ Jesus unto good** works, which God hath before ordained **that we should walk in them.***
Romans 4:2 *For if Abraham were **justified by works**, he hath whereof to glory; but **not** before God.*	**James 2:21** ***Was not Abraham our father justified by works**, when he had offered Isaac his son upon the altar?*
Romans 3:27 *Where is boasting then? It is excluded. By what law? of **works**? Nay: but by the law of faith.*	**James 2:14** *What doth it profit, my brethren, though a man say he hath faith, and have not **works**? can faith save him?*
Isaiah 64:6 *But we are all as an unclean thing, and all our righteousnesses are as filthy rags* (note: the context of this verse is referring to the nation of Israel, not to individuals)	**James 2:17** *Even so faith, if it hath not **works**, is dead, being alone.*
Romans 4:6 *Even as David also describeth the blessedness of the man, unto whom God imputeth righteousness without **works**,*	**James 2:18** *Yea, a man may say, Thou hast faith, and I have **works**: shew me thy faith without thy **works**, and I will shew thee my faith by my **works**.*
Romans 11:6 *And if by grace, then is it no more of **works**: otherwise grace is no more grace. But if it be of **works**, then is it no more grace: otherwise work is no more work.*	**James 2:20** *But wilt thou know, O vain man, that faith without **works** is dead?*
Galatians 2:16 *Knowing that a man is not justified by the **works** of the law, but by the faith of Jesus Christ, even we have believed in Jesus Christ, that we might be justified by the faith of Christ, and not by the **works** of the law: for by the **works** of the law shall no flesh be justified.*	**Acts 26:20** *But shewed first unto them of Damascus, and at Jerusalem, and throughout all the coasts of Judaea, and then to the Gentiles, that they should repent and turn to God, and do **works** meet for repentance.*

Galatians 3:2 *This only would I learn of you, Received ye the Spirit by the* **works** *of the law, or by the hearing of faith?*	**Revelation 20:12** *And I saw the dead, small and great, stand before God; and the books were opened: and another book was opened, which is the book of life: and the dead were judged out of those things which were written in the books, according to their* **works**.
Galatians 3:5 *He therefore that ministereth to you the Spirit, and worketh miracles among you, doeth he it by the* **works** *of the law, or by the hearing of faith?*	**Revelation 20:13** *And the sea gave up the dead which were in it; and death and hell delivered up the dead which were in them: and* **they were judged every man according to their works**.
Galatians 3:10 *For as many as are of the* **works** *of the law are under the curse: for it is written, Cursed is every one that continueth not in all things which are written in the book of the law to do them.*	**2 Timothy 3:17** *That the man of God may be perfect, thoroughly furnished unto all good* **works**.
2 Timothy 1:9 *Who hath saved us, and called us with an holy calling, not according to our* **works**, *but according to his own purpose and grace, which was given us in Christ Jesus before the world began.*	**Philippians 2:12** *Wherefore, my beloved, as ye have always obeyed, not as in my presence only, but now much more in my absence,* **work out your own salvation with fear and trembling.**
Titus 3:5 *Not by* **works** *of righteousness which we have done, but according to his mercy he saved us, by the washing of regeneration, and renewing of the Holy Ghost;*	**1 Timothy 5:25** *Likewise also the good* **works** *of some are manifest beforehand; and they that are otherwise cannot be hid.*
Hebrews 9:14 *How much more shall the blood of Christ, who through the eternal Spirit offered himself without spot to God, purge your conscience from dead* **works** *to serve the living God?*	**1 Timothy 6:18** *That they do good, that they be rich in good* **works**, *ready to distribute, willing to communicate;*
Romans 9:11 *(For the children being not yet born, neither having done any good or evil, that the purpose of God according to election might stand, not of* **works**, *but of him that calleth;)*	**Titus 1:16** *They profess that they know God; but in* **works** *they deny him, being abominable, and* **disobedient**, *and unto every* **good work** *reprobate.*
Romans 9:32 *Wherefore? Because they sought it not by faith, but as it were by the* **works** *of the law. For they stumbled at that stumblingstone;*	**Titus 2:7** *In all things* **shewing thyself a pattern of good works**: *in doctrine shewing uncorruptness, gravity, sincerity,*

Titus 2:14 *Who gave himself for us, that he might redeem us from all iniquity, and purify unto himself a peculiar people, zealous of good* **works.**

Titus 3:8 *This is a faithful saying, and these things I will that thou affirm constantly,* **that they which have believed in God might be careful to maintain good works. These things are good and profitable unto men.**

Titus 3:14 *And let ours also learn to maintain good* **works** *for necessary uses, that they be not unfruitful.*

Hebrews 10:24 *And let us consider one another to provoke unto love and to good* **works:**

James 2:22 *Seest thou how faith wrought with his* **works,** *and by* **works** *was faith made perfect?*

James 2:25 *Likewise also was not Rahab the harlot justified by* **works,** *when she had received the messengers, and had sent them out another way?*

James 2:26 *For as the body without the spirit is dead, so faith without* **works** *is dead also.*

James 3:13 *Who is a wise man and endued with knowledge among you? let him shew out of a good conversation his* **works** *with meekness of wisdom.*

1 Peter 2:12 *Having your conversation honest among the Gentiles: that, whereas they speak against you as evildoers, they may by your good* **works,** *which they shall behold, glorify God in the day of visitation.*

Revelation 2:23 And I will kill her children with death; and all the churches shall know that I am he which searcheth the reins and hearts: and **I will give unto every one of you according to your works.**

	Revelation 2:26 *And he that over-cometh, and keepeth my **works** unto the end, to him will I give power over the nations:*
	Revelation 3:1 *And unto the angel of the church in Sardis write; These things saith he that hath the seven Spirits of God, and the seven stars; I know thy **works**, that thou hast a name that thou livest, and art dead.*
	Revelation 3:15 *I know thy **works**, that thou art neither cold nor hot: I would thou wert cold or hot.*
	Acts 9:36 *Now there was at Joppa a certain disciple named Tabitha, which by interpretation is called Dorcas: this woman was **full of good works** and alms deeds which she did.*
	1 Timothy 2:10 *But (which becometh women professing godliness) with good **works**.*
	1 Timothy 5:10 ***Well reported of for good works**; if she have brought up children, if she have lodged strangers, if she have washed the saints' feet, if she have relieved the afflicted, **if she have diligently followed every good work.***

Did I miss any? I'm sure I'll hear from you if I did.

JESUS AND GOOD WORKS

But, what did Christ himself say about doing "good works?"

Not in obedience to the old law of Moses (Paul made it clear that that was not a requirement for Christians), but in obedience to God's commandments given to the New Testament Church. What did our Lord say that he expected of his followers - those who would be his disciples and call themselves Christians?

The following passages may be unfamiliar, but look them up. They are in God's word just as much as those verses in Ephesians or Romans that we've already quoted that emphasize grace. And they're not just the words of the apostles, but of the Savior Himself.

Let your light so shine before men, that they may see your good <u>works</u>, and glorify your Father which is in heaven.

—Matthew 5:16

For the Son of man shall come in the glory of his Father with his angels; and then he shall reward every man according to his <u>works</u>.

—Matthew 16:27

Verily, verily, I say unto you, He that believeth on me, the <u>works</u> that I do shall he do also; and greater <u>works</u> than these shall he do; because I go unto my Father.

—John 14:12

... And ye shall be hated of all men for my name's sake: <u>but he that endureth to the end shall be saved.</u>

—Matthew 10:22, Matthew 24:13, Mark 13:13

IN CONCLUSION

This has been a pretty tiring chapter, huh? Maybe we should move on. But here's a thought before we leave it that I like from teacher Brad Wilcox:

"The question is not 'have you been <u>saved</u> by grace' but have you been <u>changed</u> by grace?'"

If your goal is just to slip into Heaven under the wire with the least effort possible, has the grace of Christ really changed your heart? Perhaps we all can benefit from these words often attributed to the founder of the Methodist church John Wesley:

"Do all the good you can. By all the means you can. In all the ways you can. In all the places you can. At all the times you can. To all the people you can. As long as ever you can."

I guess I can sum up my feelings on the whole subject of "soteriology" by just quoting the apostle James again. He's a pretty reputable source and he says it quite nicely: *Yea, a man may say, Thou hast faith, and I have works: shew me thy faith <u>without</u> thy works, and I will shew thee my faith <u>by</u> my works.* —James 2:18

END NOTES FOR CHAPTER 3

1   http://janariess.religionnews.com/2013/05/14/mormon-works-vs-evangelical-grace/#sthash.Zi9RZ7jb.dpuf

2   http://www.watchman.org/articles/mormonism/mormonism-explains-gods-grace-is-inadequate-for-salvation/

3   http://www.midwestoutreach.org/journals/mormon_view.html

4   http://www.equip.org/perspectives/do-mormons-accept-what-orthodox-christianity-considers-biblical-salvation/

5   *The American Heritage College Dictionary.* Boston, MA: Houghton Mifflin Company. 1997. p. 91. ISBN 0-395-66917-0.

6   *Essential Truths of the Christian Faith. p. 191*

7   http://www.canapologetics.net/sproul_4.html

8   A. Ironside, *Except Ye Repent*, Grand Rapids: Zondervan 1937, page 11

9   W. H. Griffith Thomas, *St. Paul's epistle to the Romans,* Grand Rapids: Eerdmans n.d. P. 371

10 "An Introduction to St. Paul's Letter to the Romans," Luther's German Bible of 1522

11 Justin Martyr *First Apology,*

Illustration by Allen Richardson

EVIDENCE 4

ONE TRUE CHURCH?

The evidence exists. I believe that The Church of Jesus Christ of latter-day Saints is the only church on earth today that contains the same form and teachings as the New Testament church that Jesus organized, and which has the sole authority to act for God here upon the earth.

We believe in the same organization that existed in the Primitive Church, namely, apostles, prophets, pastors, teachers, evangelists, and so forth.

—5th LDS Article of Faith

"For God is not the author of confusion, but of peace, as in all churches of the saints"

—1 Cor 14:33

"One Lord, one faith, one baptism."

—*Eph. 4:5*

"There are about <u>34,000</u> different Christian groups in the world since AD 30."
—*World Christian Encyclopedia – 2001*

I once asked my dear grandmother Clara Starling (we called her "Momo") how she ended up being a Methodist. She said "I was sitting in a Methodist Church when I came to know Jesus. What does it matter which building you sit in on Sunday, as long as you worship God?" I guess that's a fair question, and out of respect to Momo I'll try to give a fair answer.

Someone else very dear to me also asked me more recently if I believed I belong to the "one True Church." To be true to myself and to my faith I must confess that I do. I understand that many people (if not most) can't understand this position. It may seem to them very arrogant for a person or a church body to claim to have "the" truth or an authorization or approval from God that others don't have. It is not a "politically correct" way to believe. But then, neither was Jesus Christ himself politically correct. Particularly when He said things like: *"I am the way, the truth, and the life: no man cometh unto the Father but by me."*
—(John 14:8)

That didn't make him very popular with the Scribes and Pharisees of His day, and it doesn't make Latter-day Saints popular with other churches today.

THE HISTORY OF CHRISTIANITY IN A MINUTE (OR SO)

In a nutshell, here's what happened to Christianity: During his mortal ministry Jesus created an earthly organization that he called his church. After his death and resurrection and his departure from earth, his twelve apostles administered the workings of that church, which included the ordaining of others to various priesthood offices. (more about the priesthood in the next chapter) The apostles and prophets were the "foundation" of the church (Eph. 2:20). After all the apostles were killed, the "special revelation" that they received from God to guide the church was gone. Those left behind were on their own to continue the best they could by using their own interpretation of the apostles' writings.

The church began to split into many factions and the "falling away" (called apostasy) began (2Thess 2:3). Without the "special revelation" that the apostles had, the remaining bishops relied on their own understanding to try to hold the church together and maintain the correct doctrine. In 325 AD the Roman emperor Constantine called around 300 bishops together in a council to make some sense of the confusion caused by the many factions of

Christianity. Using debate and political wrangling they arrived at what they thought was a correct definition of the Trinity and some other items of business.

Not everyone really agreed, but they had to sign the documents or be banished. The one of the many factions that survived all this hoopla became the state religion of the Roman Empire and came to be known as the Roman Catholic Church. For centuries it was *de facto* the only recorded expression of Christianity on the planet except for the Eastern Orthodox Church, which maintained an uneasy alliance with the Roman church until the Great Schism of 1054 AD when they split altogether over doctrinal matters.

In the 1400's the Protestant Reformation began and many Christians "jumped ship" from the Roman church and started their own versions of Christianity. They have continued to split and divide for several hundred years until now there are over 3400 "flavors" of believers in Christ.

Paul told the Corinthians that already there were divisions among them even in his day
—(1 Cor. 11:18).

Did he say that was okay and that if they felt like it they could go down the road and start another church? NO. He said that he would come to them later and "set in order" the things that were wrong (11:34). Then all the apostles were killed there was no one left to "set in order" the church so the apostasy continued unabated. Later on I'll give you a step-by-step account of how that happened.

Latter-day Saints believe that almost all religions have some true parts of what we call the "fullness of the Gospel". Some of them take one small aspect of God's plan for mankind and build a whole religion around it. It's sorta like the story of the four blind men and the elephant. Do you remember that one? Each man felt with his hands a part of the elephant and assumed the whole animal was like a tree trunk (his leg), or a snake (his trunk), or a wall (his side), or a rope (his tail). Each one had a part of the truth but was ignorant of "the rest of the story". His error was in thinking that the part he knew about was all there was. Likewise today we find Christian denominations that build their whole faith structure around the seventh day observance, the indwelling of the Spirit, or unmerited grace, etc.

In 1830 God told a modern day prophet named Joseph Smith to restore the New Testament Christian church to the earth. It is called The Church of Jesus Christ of Latter-day Saints and it is one of the fastest-growing religions in the whole world. It is the literal fulfillment of Daniel's prophecy that in the last days the Kingdom of God would be like a stone cut out of the mountain without hands that would roll forth and fill the whole earth.

—(Daniel 2:31-45)

SO WHAT IS A CHURCH?

First of all, what is a "church"? The Greek word "**Ekklesia**" means "a called out assembly (of people)". To some folks a "church" is a building with a steeple on top and colored windows and Bibles inside. There's the Roman Catholic Church, which is the largest organized "assembly" of Christians on the planet. There are many different "denominations" of Christendom that are often called churches, and a growing number of non-denominational groups of believers that have organized themselves into groups called "churches". Then there's the un-organized mythical "body of Christ" that some refer to as "the church".

Sooo….. where do we go from here?

WHAT DOES THE NEW TESTAMENT SAY ABOUT THE CHURCH OF JESUS CHRIST?

It seems that to explore the topic reasonably and logically we need to ask several questions, and then search for their answers:

1. Did Jesus Christ establish an organized body of early "called out" believers that constituted an earthly Church?
2. What did he say about it?
3. What was it like? What were its identifying characteristics?
4. Did that organization continue on Earth after His death and resurrection?

    If so, how long? How long was it <u>supposed</u> to continue?

5. Was there a "falling away" prophesied? <u>From</u> the church? <u>Of</u> the church? Was a <u>restoration</u> also prophesied?
6. If the New Testament church did <u>not</u> continue to the present, what happened to it?
7. What Church organization on earth today (if any) most closely resembles the New Testament church?
8. How can I know what Church (if any) God wants me to join?
9. If Christ's earthly Church is on earth today, what can it offer that other bodies of believers cannot?

This is quite a job. I'll try to be up to this task, and with the Lord's help I can hopefully explain clearly my belief and understanding. You may not agree with me, but it will surely give you something to think about.

WHY ARE YOU A MEMBER OF YOUR CHURCH?

The great Christian thinker and author C.S. Lewis in his *Mere Christianity* supposed that when a person accepts Christ in a general sense he/she becomes a "mere" Christian, that is, not a part of any one sect or denomination or "church". At that point he likens them to someone who has entered a house and stands in a large hallway with many doors, each representing one of the "flavors" of Christianity. He writes:

And above all, you must be asking which door is the true one; not which pleases you best by its paint and paneling. In plain language, the question should never be: "Do I like that kind of service?" but "Are these doctrines true: Is there holiness here? Does my conscience move me towards this? Is my reluctance to knock at this door due to my pride, or my mere taste, or my personal dislike of this particular door-keeper?"[1]

Let's ask ourselves this. Why are people (why are you?) members of a particular church?

Here are a few reasons I've thought of (you may know of more):

1. Your parents were members there, or other family members (perhaps for generations).

(This is probably the biggest reason for most folks.)

2. It has a meeting place near your home. It's convenient.
3. Your friends are members there. It's a social thing.
4. There is a nice choir. You like the music.
5. You like the priest's or the pastor's preaching.
6. There a good youth program.
7. There's a lax dress code and you don't have to dress up (this is increasingly popular).
8. They serve free coffee before and after services.
9. You can find good business contacts there.
10. Teachings there are pretty much consistent with your own personal beliefs, wherever those beliefs come from or whatever they may be.

If your own reasons for belonging to your particular church fall into 1-9 above, then you may want to skip to the next chapter – unless you want to learn some really important stuff that might shake your world.

Here are a few other questions to consider;

Why is it important to find Christ's Church?

Can we agree that (unfortunately) there indeed are church organizations or groups of believers who are not Christ's church?

Can a person be saved just by joining any church, even Christ's church?

Can joining a church that is not Christ's Church prevent a person from being saved?

Can it prevent them from receiving the blessings from "things that accompany salvation"?

Is there a spectrum of belief? And how far along the spectrum must a church deviate before it is no longer Christ's church?

Then can we agree that almost any organized body of Christ's believers today seeks to imitate the New Testament church? The only question is, how successful are they?

WHY AM I A LATTER-DAY SAINT?

In my own life, at one time I would have admitted to #1 above. I was born and raised a Latter-day Saint. But I grew up in Georgia where most folks were either Baptists or Methodists, with a smattering of Presbyterians Lutherans, Catholics, Pentecostals, etc. They all got along fairly well, since none of them claimed to be the "only true Church". (Well I think the Catholics actually believed that, but they pretty much kept it to themselves.)

The claim to exclusivity has been one of the major reasons why "Mormons" have suffered opposition and persecution (up to and including beatings, burnings, rape and murder) from other so-called "Christians". Most of those things happened back in the 1800's and thankfully are in the past. However there are those today who still engage in character assassination and other slanders against those of my faith, often for the same reasons. If I'm to be true to Scripture I must "bring forth my strong reasons "to believe. (Isaiah 41:21) And like one of the great evangelical preachers said (I wish I could remember his name) "*I won't try to prove that my beliefs are true. I am just grateful for an opportunity to explain why I believe them".*

INSIDE LATTER-DAY CHRISTIANITY

Okay, so what does The Church of Jesus Christ of Latter-day Saints teach "inside" the walls of its chapels about the concept of being the "one true church"? Perhaps it is best to go back to the beginning …

I guess it's hard for secular-minded 21st-century Americans to believe, but in upstate New York in 1820 there was so much excitement about religion that it was later called the "burned-over district". A young boy named Joseph Smith who lived through the period described it this way:

> There was in the place where we lived an unusual excitement on the subject of religion. It commenced with the Methodists, but soon became general among all the sects in that region of country; indeed, the whole district of country seemed affected by it, and great multitudes united themselves to the different religious parties, which created no small stir and division amongst the people, some crying, "lo, here," and some "lo, there;" some were contending for the Methodist faith, some for the Presbyterian, and some for the Baptists. For, notwithstanding the great love which the converts for these different faiths expressed at the time of their conversion, and the great zeal manifested by the respective clergy, who were active in getting up and promoting this extraordinary scene of religious feeling, in order to have everybody converted, as they were pleased to call it, let them join what sect they pleased.
>
> Yet, when the converts began to file off, some to one party, and some to another, it was seen that the seemingly good feelings of both the priests and the converts were more pretended than real, for a scene of great confusion and bad feeling ensued; priest contending against priest, and convert against convert, so that all the good feelings, one for another, if they ever had any, were entirely lost in a strife of words, and a contest about opinions. … I often said to myself, What is to be done? Who of all these parties are right? Or, are they all wrong together? If any one of them be right which is it, and how shall I know it?
>
> While I was laboring under the extreme difficulties caused by the contests of these parties of religionists, I was one day reading the epistle of James, first chapter and fifth verse, which reads, **"*If any of you lack wisdom, let him ask of God, that giveth unto all men liberally and upbraideth not; and it shall be given him.*"**
>
> —Joseph Smith History Chapter 1 – Pearl of Great Price

75

Joseph took God's word literally and went to a nearby grove of trees to pray and ask which of the churches he should join. He said that he received a vision similar to that of Stephen in the New Testament (Acts 7:55-56), as God the Father and Jesus Christ appeared to him. And he got an answer to his question. Jesus did <u>not</u> say "join any of them, it doesn't really matter", or "just go to the one where you like the pastor's preaching the most". Joseph continued:

> I asked the personages who stood above me in the light, which of all the sects was right— and which I should join. <u>I was answered that I must join none of them, for they were all wrong</u>, and the personage who addressed me said that all their <u>creeds</u> were an abomination in His sight: that those professors were all corrupt; that *"they draw near to me with their lips, but their hearts are far from me"*
>
> — *(Isaiah 29:13);*

> *"they teach for doctrines the commandments of men: having a form of godliness, but they deny the power thereof."*
>
> — *(Mark 7:6-7)*

(Note: I've inserted the Bible references here to show that what seems to be a harsh description of those "professors" in the "wrong" sects did not originate with Joseph Smith but are actually quotes from Isaiah and Mark.)

In a later revelation from God after the church of Jesus Christ had been restored to the earth, the living Christ describes The Church of Jesus Christ of Latter-day Saints as:

"the only true and living church upon the face of the whole earth, with which I, the Lord, am well pleased"

—(Doctrine and Covenants 1:30)

DO LATTER-DAY SAINTS THINK MEMBERS OF ALL OTHER CHURCHES ARE GOING TO HELL?

The Church of Jesus Christ of Latter-day Saints does not believe nor teach that all other Christian churches are evil and that their members are going to hell. I was taught as a "Mormon" that there is a lot of truth in other churches and that there are many good and sincere people in them who love the Lord and try to live the teachings of Christ according to the light they've been given. Indeed my dear departed grandmother was one of them, as well as my uncle Rudolph who served his flocks faithfully for many years as a Methodist pastor.

Here are a few comments from "inside Mormonism", by leaders of the LDS Church speaking about those other churches:

Joseph Smith once observed:

> "If I esteem mankind to be in error, shall I bear them down? No. I will lift them up, and in their own way too, if I cannot persuade them my way is better; and I will not seek to compel any man to believe as I do, only by the force of reasoning, for truth will cut its own way. Do you believe in Jesus Christ and the gospel of salvation which he revealed? So do I. Christians should cease wrangling and contending with each other, and cultivate the principles of union and friendship in their midst."[2]

Gordon B. Hinckley, a more recent president of the LDS Church said:

> "We can respect other religions, and must do so. We must recognize the great good they accomplish. We must teach our children to be tolerant and friendly toward those not of our faith…We recognize the good in all churches, We recognize the value of religion generally. We say to everyone: live the teachings that you have received from your church. We invite you to come and learn from us, to see if we can add to those teachings and enhance your life and your understanding of things sacred and divine."[3]

One of the LDS apostles said this in a General Conference of the whole LDS Church:

> "These descriptions of a religious philosophy (the creeds) are surely undiplomatic, but I hasten to add that Latter-day Saints do not apply such criticism to the men and women who profess these beliefs. We believe that most religious leaders and followers are sincere believers who love God and understand and serve him to the best of their abilities. We are indebted to the men and women who kept the light of faith and learning alive through the centuries to the present day. We have only to contrast the lesser light that exists among peoples unfamiliar with the names of God and Jesus Christ to realize the great contribution made by Christian teachers through the ages. We honor them as servants of God."[4]

I will admit that I've also read statements from some LDS leaders that were less tolerant of other churches, but most of them were made in the 1800's when the Latter-day Saints were suffering a great deal of persecution from other so-called "Christians". It's easy to see how in that climate their rhetoric might have been a bit more volatile.

OUTSIDE LATTER-DAY CHRISTIANITY

Let's compare these bold statements from "inside" Latter-day Christianity with how the idea of having one true church of Jesus Christ is handled outside "Mormonism".

In October of 2011 Pastor Robert Jeffress of the First Baptist Church in Dallas, Texas touched off a firestorm of controversy with his statements on national news media that "Mormons" are a "cult" of people that are "not Christians". I wrote a letter to Pastor Jeffress (included herein as an appendix) explaining to him the error of his position from a Biblical and historical perspective, but somehow I don't believe he gave it much attention. Unfortunately there are quite a few people who are of the same persuasion as Pastor Jeffress. That's why I felt I needed to write this book. So what do some Protestant and Catholic leaders and teachers say about The Church of Jesus Christ of Latter-day Saints? The following is excerpted from the website of the Christian Broadcasting Network (CBN):

> Mormons are some of the most exemplary human beings, especially in regard to their behavior patterns and their adherence to the fundamental values of our society. But their religious beliefs are, to put is simply, wrong. They believe that an angel named Moroni left some gold tablets in upstate New York and that these tablets were discovered by a man named Joseph Smith. From these tablets, Joseph Smith "translated" the Book of Mormon, which is the foundation upon which Mormonism is built. Mormons also consider two other books, Doctrine and Covenants and The Pearl of Great Price, to be divinely inspired.

> Mormonism differs from biblical Christianity in several areas. Mormons do not believe, for example, that salvation comes through faith in Jesus Christ. Mormons must work their way to heaven.

> … In summary, the Mormon church is a prosperous, growing organization that has produced many people of exemplary character. But when it comes to spiritual matters, the Mormons are far from the truth. [5]

But this quote from an article in *Christianity Today* magazine has a different tone:

… in the big picture I'm not sad that they (the Billy Graham Evangelistic Association) are moving away from the word 'cult' for Mormonism. These days, the word is nothing more than a pejorative, and unhelpful in communicating the true gospel to Latter-Day Saints (LDS)." [6]

There's a fascinating reference to this topic by a Catholic official back in the 1920's when he spoke with an LDS apostle:

> Many years ago I had an interesting conversation with a man who was a member of the Roman Catholic church. He was a great scholar; he must have had a dozen languages at his tongue's end, and seemed to know all about history, science, law, philosophy, and all the rest of it. We were frank and friendly with each other, and one day he said to me:

"You 'Mormons' are all ignoramuses. You don't even know the strength of your own position. It is so strong that there is only one other position tenable in the whole Christian world, and that is the position of the Roman Catholic church. The issue is between 'Mormonism' and Catholicism. If you are right, we are wrong. If we are right, you are wrong, and that's all there is to it. These Protestant sects haven't a leg to stand on; for if we are right, we cut them off long ago, as apostates; and if we are wrong, they are wrong with us, for they were a part of us and came out of us. If we have the apostolic succession from St. Peter, as we claim, there was no need of Joseph Smith and

'Mormonism;' but if we have not that apostolic succession, then such a man as Joseph Smith was necessary, and 'Mormonism's position is the only consistent one. It is either the perpetuation of the Gospel from ancient times or the restoration of the Gospel in latter days."

"Doctor," said I, "that is a very clear and concise statement, and I agree with it in almost every particular. But don't deceive yourself with the notion that we 'Mormons' don't know the strength of our own position. We know it better than you do. We know it better than any other people can know it.

We haven't all been to college, we can't all speak the dead languages, and we may be ignoramuses as you say; but we know we are right, and we know you are wrong." I was just as frank with him as he had been with me.

—Elder Orson F. Whitney, *Conference Report,* April 1928, p. 60

HOW DO OTHER CHRISTIANS VIEW "THE CHURCH" AS THEY USE THE TERM?

Often I'll read articles or books where all of "traditional" or "orthodox" Christianity is generally referred to as "the church", as if there was some sort of universal or monolithic Christian body. And yet history shows that Christians have been not only disagreeing with each other but persecuting and killing each other for centuries over differences in beliefs.

Surely you've heard of the Spanish Inquisition? At a time when the Roman Catholic Church virtually ruled Europe with an iron fist, those who held different beliefs were declared "heretics". They were hunted down, tortured and murdered in the name of Christ. In 1655 tens of thousands of Protestant Waldenses in the mountain valleys of northern Italy were massacred and mutilated by Catholic soldiers.

Even after the Protestant Reformation in the 1500's, different "flavors" of Christians continued to fight and "convert" other Christians at the point of a sword. John Wycliff and others were hanged or burned at the stake for daring to translate the Bible into the common language of the people. Of particular horror is the persecution of the Anabaptists in supposedly civilized Europe. Thousands of these believers in Christ were murdered and treated worse than Hitler treated the Jews in WWII, simply because they practiced the baptism of adults rather than infants!

So is there a mythical entity called "the church" that encompasses believers of all "traditional"

Christian faiths? I'm sure many Christians would like to believe so, but I'm afraid it's just a myth. We're a long ways from the Biblical view of "one Lord, one faith, and one baptism". Let's go back in history and look at what "The Church" was like in New Testament times.

DID JESUS CHRIST ESTABLISH AN ORGANIZED BODY OF BELIEVERS THAT CONSTITUTED HIS EARTHLY CHURCH?

Apparently He thought so:

*Matthew 16:18 Upon this rock I will build my **church**.*

(We will examine later what the "rock" was)

Luke thought so:

*Acts 2:47 And the Lord added to the **church** daily such as should be saved.*

*Acts 5:11 And great fear came upon all the **church**,*

*Acts 11:26 they assembled themselves with the **church**, and taught much people*

*Acts 13:1 Now there were in the **church** that was at Antioch certain prophets and teachers;*

*Acts 14:23 And when they had ordained them elders in every **church***

Paul thought so:

*Corinthians 1:2 Unto the **church** of God which is at Corinth, to them that are sanctified in Christ Jesus, called to be saints*

*Corinthians 7:17 as the Lord hath called every one, so let him walk. And so ordain I in all **church**es.*

*Corinthians 11:16 But if any man seem to be contentious, we have no such custom, neither the **church**es of God*

WHAT WAS CHRIST'S CHURCH LIKE?

The New Testament church ("called out assembly") of Christ's followers was organized into local units in various cities.

*Acts 8:1 And Saul was consenting unto his death. And at that time there was a great persecution against the **church** which was at **Jerusalem***

Acts 9:31 Then had the churches rest throughout all Judaea and Galilee and Samaria

*Acts 13:1 Now there were in the **church** that was at **Antioch** certain prophets and teachers*

*Acts 15:41 And he went through **Syria and Cilicia**, confirming the **church**es.*

*Acts 18:22 And when he had landed at **Caesarea**, and gone up, and saluted the **church**, he went down to **Antioch***

*Acts 20:17 And from **Miletus** he sent to **Ephesus**, and called the elders of the **church**.*

*Romans 16:1 I commend unto you Phebe our sister, which is a servant of the **church** which is at **Cenchrea**:*

*Corinthians 16:19 The **church**es of **Asia** salute you.*

Local officers in these church branches were ordained by the apostles and by those whom they chose to be local stewards or overseers (Bishops).

*Corinthians 12:28 And God hath set some in the **church**, first **apostles**, secondarily **prophets**, thirdly **teachers**,*

*Acts 6:6 Whom they set before the **apostles**: and when they had prayed, **they laid their hands on them.***

*Acts 14:23 And when they had ordained them **elders** in every **church**,*

*Ephesians 4:11 And he gave some, **apostles**; and some**, prophets**; and some, **evangelists; and some, pastors and teachers;***

*Philippians 1:1 Paul and Timotheus, the servants of Jesus Christ, to all the saints in Christ Jesus which are at Philippi, with the **bishop**s and **deacon**s:*

*Titus 1:7 For a **bishop** must be blameless, as the steward of God; not selfwilled, not soon angry, not given to wine, no striker, not given to filthy lucre; The church branches were accountable to the twelve apostles who gave them guidance and instruction.*

*Acts 2:42 And they continued steadfastly in the **apostles**' doctrine and fellowship, and in breaking of bread, and in prayers.*

*Acts 14:27 And when they were come, and had **gathered** the **church** together*

*Acts 15:41 And he went through Syria and Cilicia, **confirming** the **church**es.*

*Acts 20:28 Take heed therefore unto yourselves, and to all the flock, over the which the Holy Ghost hath made you overseers, to feed the **church** of God,*

*Corinthians 7:17 But as God hath distributed to every man, as the Lord hath called every one, so let him walk. And so **ordain** I in all **church**es.*

*Corinthians 14:33 For God is not the author of confusion, but of peace, as in all **church**es of the saints.*

*Corinthians 16:1 Now concerning the collection for the saints, as **I have given order to the churches** of Galatia, even so do ye.*

*Corinthians 1:1 Paul, an **apostle** of Jesus Christ by the will of God, and Timothy our brother, unto **the church of God which is at Corinth**, with all the saints which are in all Achaia:*

*Ephesians 2:20 And are built upon the **foundation** of the **apostles** and prophets, Jesus Christ himself being the chief corner stone;*

*Peter 3:2 That ye may be mindful of the words which were spoken before by the holy prophets, and of **the commandment of us the apostles** of the Lord and Savior:*

So let's review:

1. The church that Jesus Christ himself organized was not a mythical union of all believers, but it was <u>an actual organization</u> built on a foundation of living apostles and prophets
—(Eph. 2:20).

2. It had <u>many local congregations</u> presided over by bishops and elders
— (Philippians 1:1, Titus 1:7).

3. It also had other <u>local offices such as deacons, teachers, etc.</u> (Ephesians 4:11) and a group of traveling ministers called "the seventy"
—(Luke 10:1, 17).

4. The apostles continually received revelations through the Holy Spirit for the guidance of the whole church.

5. They provided that <u>guidance to the local branches</u> of the <u>church</u> through letters, personal visits, and the work of other traveling leaders they called upon to help with the supervisory needs of the ministry.

6. The New Testament church had a canon of scripture (what we call the Old Testament), but as God's revelations were given to the apostles and prophets and written down in letters and Acts and the gospels, these were added to the canon as needed. <u>The canon of scripture was not closed,</u> but <u>all that was accepted as scripture was deemed useful for the church</u>.
— (2 Timothy 3:16)

DID JESUS PROMISE THAT HIS CHURCH WOULD NEVER BE TAKEN FROM THE EARTH?

Of course the LDS allegation that the New Testament church of Christ needed to be restored doesn't hold water if that church was never taken from the earth. This is the claim of the Roman Catholic Church. They claim an unbroken succession of Papal authority from God as witness that Catholicism has always been Christ's one "true" church. They believe that Peter was the first Bishop of Rome and that his successors have held the "keys of the kingdom" that Jesus conferred on him as head of his church. The Latter-day Saints along with the Protestants reject that claim on both Biblical and historical grounds. Let's take a look at it:

The key Bible verse (pun intended) on which the Roman Catholic Church makes its claims is Matt. 16: 16-19. Jesus has just asked the apostles who they thought he was. Peter says;

Thou art the Christ, the Son of the living God. And Jesus answered and said unto him, Blessed art thou, Simon Barjona: for flesh and blood hath not revealed it unto thee, but my Father which is in heaven. And I say also unto thee, That thou art Peter, and <u>upon this rock I will build my church</u>; and the gates of hell shall not prevail against it. <u>And I will give unto thee the keys of the kingdom of heaven</u>: and whatsoever thou shalt bind on earth shall be bound in heaven: and whatsoever thou shalt loose on earth shall be loosed in heaven.

— (Matt. 16: 16-19)

Catholics claim that Peter himself is the "rock" on which Jesus says he will build his church. But if it were to be built on any man it would be Christ himself, whom we're told in Ephesians 2 is the "chief corner stone" of the church.

A careful reading of the verses reveals that the context is Peter's confession that Jesus is the Son of God. And what was the source of his knowledge? God the Father had revealed it to Peter. It is that <u>revelation</u> of the testimony of Christ from God to man that is the "rock" upon the church would be built. It was that <u>revelation</u> through the Holy Spirit that "pricked the hearts" of over three thousand people on the day of Pentecost in Acts 2:37 and has pricked the heart of every true Christian convert for the last two thousand years.

Next, Jesus says that "the gates of hell shall not prevail against it". Most Christians think the "it" in this sentence refers to the <u>church</u>, but in reality it is <u>the "rock" of revelation</u>. The evidence of history proves that the "gates of hell" did indeed prevail against the church, whose corruption became so complete by the 2nd or 3rd centuries that God withdrew from it. In the 15th century the Reformers did the same. These verses do not guarantee that the earthly church would never fail. And the "gates of hell" have never prevailed against the "rock" of revelation. Each person can still receive the same witness of Christ as Lord that Peter received. It is revealed not by "flesh and blood" but by the whisperings of the Holy Ghost so their "hearts are pricked" and they come to know Jesus.

DOES THE BIBLE SAY THE CHURCH WILL "FALL AWAY" INTO APOSTASY?

The Bible not only says that the church Jesus organized CAN be taken from the earth, but it predicts that it indeed WILL happen.

Paul marveled at how quickly the Galatian Saints had "turned from the gospel"

—(Galatians 1:6-8).

Paul's second epistle to the church in Corinth mentions false apostles whom Paul describes as "ministers of Satan" (2 Corinthians 11:13-15). In his second epistle to Timothy, Paul says that *"all Asia is turned away"* (2 Timothy 1:15). In his letter to Gaius, John reports that in one unnamed branch of the church, the leader Diotrophes, will have nothing to do with John and his brethren. Not only does he refuse to accept John and his emissaries, but he opposes those who do want to accept them and "puts them out of the church" (3 John 1:9-10). In the book of Revelation, John writes inspired letters to seven of the churches in Asia, calling them to repentance for the most egregious of sins (Revelation 2–3).

So HOW and WHEN did the New Testament church "fall away"? I thought you'd never ask …

Here's a little timeline I put together:

"The Faith Once Delivered to the Saints": What Happened to It?

(A brief outline of the Apostasy and Restoration of the Church that Jesus Christ organized on the earth) References and citations to events presented here are included when possible and documentation is ongoing. Please do note that this is offered as a basis (or starting point) for further individual study or fellowship discussion. If you have any specific questions or comments re: conclusions reached or documentation for claims presented herein, I welcome your input.

1. Jesus Christ established an earthly organization (not just a mystical union of believers) which he called his Church, and which was also referred to as "the faith once delivered to the Saints".

—(Jude 1:3)

2. The Bible says that before the Second Coming of Christ, there would be an apostasy or falling away not only of individuals or groups from the true church of Jesus Christ, but that there would be an apostasy of the Church itself to the point where it would no longer be recognizable as His organization, and He would no longer recognize its authority to act for Him.

A. Isa. 24:5 "they have changed the ordinances, and broken the everlasting covenant..."
B. Amos 8:11 "a famine ... of hearing the words of the Lord: ... they shall wander from sea to sea ... and shall not find it"
C. Acts 20:29 "shall grievous wolves enter in among you, not sparing the flock"
D. Thes. 2:3 "(the Second Coming) shall not come, except there come a falling away first"
E. Tim. 3:5 "Having the form of Godliness, but denying the power thereof."
F. Rev. 2:2 "them which say they are apostles, and are not"

3. The Bible also states that before the Second Coming there would be a <u>restoration</u> of the Church that Jesus organized.
   Acts 3:21 "(the 2nd Coming will not occur until) the times of <u>restitution</u> (restoration) of all things"

   (see also the end of this paper)

4. History shows that the Great Apostasy <u>did indeed</u> take place:

Year (A.D.) --- Steps of the Apostasy
** Jerusalem (Headquarters of the New Testament church) is destroyed.

— Other cities such as Antioch, Alexandria, Ephesus, Corinth, and Rome began emerging as Christian centers.

** (approx) Death of the last of the original Twelve Apostles

(John was exiled to isle of Patmos, then disappeared from history after about 95 AD)

— With no more general Church authorities (Apostles and the Seventy), local authorities (Bishops) assumed leadership, but without jurisdiction to make decisions for the entire Church.

LOSS OF DIVINE AUTHORITY AND REVELATION FROM GOD TO THE CHURCH

A doctrine was developed by theologians regarding a "deposit of faith" consisting of the writings of the Apostles and earliest Church Fathers that could no longer be added to. Thus they claimed there was no more revelation needed from God.

** (approx) Irenaeus developed a theory that Bishops (at least those ordained directly by the Apostles) could justly claim to be equal in authority with the Apostles. He also theorized that churches with Apostolic foundation had "pre-eminent authority" over other churches.

** Tertullian (lawyer-turned-theologian) introduced the concept of the Godhead as a "corporation" (Latin personae), and coined the word "trinity". He also advocated a professional clergy.

— doctrine of baptism for the dead is lost.
— baptism of infants introduced.

** (approx) — use of crucifix & cross as a Christian symbol first began.

— artificial distinction created between laity and the "professional" clergy
— use of ceremonial robes for clergy

** —doctrine of man's pre-mortal existence was lost.

"Origin" (Bishop of Alexandria) was the last to teach it.

** Cyprian ("elected" Bishop of Carthage).

— expanded Irenaeus's theory to say that all Bishops were successors to the Apostolic authority.
— established doctrine that a council of Bishops could speak for the entire Church.

** Edict of Toleration (of Christians) issued by Galerius, thus ending Roman persecution.

313-324 ** Several Edicts by Constantine established Christianity as the favored State Religion of the Roman Empire. Constantine assumed the role of Pontifex Maximus or "chief priest" over the entire Roman Christian church.

** "Donatists" elect their own bishops in North Africa, and set up a separate Christian church which lasted until the Moslem conquest in the seventh century.

** Council of Arles was called by Constantine to settle the Donatist Schism. Precedent was set of the emperor (not Church authority) being called upon to settle Church matters.

** celibacy for the clergy was introduced, and monasticism.

** (approx) Arius (a young priest in Alexandria) taught that Jesus was not equally God with the Father, since he was "begotten" at some point in time and therefore was not co-eternal with the Father.

** Council of Nicea was called by the Roman emperor Constantine to settle the problem of the Arian "heresy". After two months of heated debate and deliberation by 274 bishops (mostly representing the Eastern church), a compromise concept called the Nicene Creed was formulated to "define" the Christian Godhead as the "Trinity".

Note: The council was not presided over by the Bishop of Rome (who was not even present), nor indeed any Bishop, but by the Emperor Constantine. It was he (an unbaptized pagan) whose power most directly influenced the formulation of the Creed and directed the outcome of the Council.

325+ ** The influence of Greek philosophy which had crept into Christian thinking continued to alter doctrines relating to the nature of God, and man's relationship to Diety.

(This was sometimes called Christian Neo-Platonism)

Some of the apostate doctrines that came out of this thinking were that:

— God was an ethereal, immaterial being who filled all space but who lived outside time and space. (Belief in an anthropomorphic God was prevalent until this time when it was lost.)
— Mortal, physical mankind could have no family relationship with such a God.
— Man is a mere created creature, like the animals.
— confession of sins to priests, and
— penance obligations assigned for sin
— Purgatory doctrine introduced (Augustine)

326+ ** Rise of "Caesaro-Papism", or support and dominance of the church by the Roman state.

** Augustine selected as a bishop. Trained as a lawyer and philosopher, he was known as the "Christian Plato". He greatly influenced Christian thought and introduced a number of apostate doctrines. Chief among these were:

— salvation by faith alone, without works
— original sin (defined as concupiscence or sexual lust)
— infant baptism
— predestination of salvation (which denies freedom or moral agency)

(Note: these doctrines were refined later by John Calvin and others.)

440-461 ** Title of "Pope" first used by Leo, Bishop of Rome (Note: "papa" or "pope" as well as "Vicar of Christ" were used by many bishops in different cities until the 6th century when it began to be reserved for the Bishop of Rome.

** Leo the Great begins building the Medieval Papacy into a political power.

(NOTE: None of the early Church Fathers who shaped the doctrine of the church were bishops of Rome.)

** Pope Gregory the Great established the Papal Kingdom (Vatican)

— paganism is mixed with Christianity in rituals, holidays, etc.

Example: December 25th, which was fixed as day to celebrate birth of Jesus, is actually the nativity date of the pagan god Mithras. (The actual date of Christ's birth was in the spring. This is the only time of year when shepherds spend the nights out in the field with their flocks because that is when the lambs are born.)

** Adoration of statues began (it was called the "Iconoclastic Movement")

— also veneration of relics

** Documents forged by some church leaders were alleged to be a handbook for church government put forth by "Pope" Sylvester in the 3rd century, supposedly giving support to the supremacy of the Bishop of Rome over other bishops. Called the "Forged Decretals", they were acknowledged as forgeries in 1440 by the Roman Catholic Church, but by then the Roman Papacy was well established. Thus the claim by some that the Roman Catholic Church was "built on lies and forgeries".

850-962 ** 112 years pass in which the Popes were chosen not by the Church, but by the Roman or German kings and emperors.

— doctrine established of a "treasury of merit", of excess good deeds by apostles and saints, etc. This merit could be dispensed to forgive or "absolve" the sins of <u>other</u> people, who could receive a "dispensation" under authority of the Pope. This led to the doctrine of "indulgences", wherein people could purchase forgiveness for sin from the church.

** Pope Benedict IX (12 years old when elected Pope) was such a farce that he was forced to resign the Papacy.

** The "Great Schism" occurs, when the Greek Orthodox and Roman Catholic branches of the Christian church excommunicated each other, formalizing a division that had actually been in existence for centuries.

** Pope Nicholas II institutes the College of Cardinals in an attempt to regain for the Church the control of the Papacy, and wrest it away from the political leaders of the state.

- 1216 ** Pope Innocent III acts as dictator, dominating the heads of state in England and Europe. (This was the reverse of "Caesaro-Papism" where the State ruled the Church.) In the papal bull "Deliberatio," Pope Innocent III said, "By me kings reign and princes decree justice."

12th Century — more apostate false doctrines were introduced:

— intercession of (& praying to) Mary and the saints
— use of Rosary
— use of crucifix
— incense burning
— ceremonial altars

** The doctrine of "Transubstantiation" was promulgated by Pope Innocent III as official dogma of the church. (it had been debated since the second century)

** Thomas Aquinas develops an explanation for the Transubstantiation doctrine.

** Conciliarism, and the 2nd Great Schism 3 Popes elected simultaneously in Rome & Pisa, Italy, & Avignon, France. They excommunicated each other, and confusion reigned for over 70 years (quite a break in the "unbroken succession"?) until 1449 when Pope Nicholas V of Rome outlived his competition.

(Where would the headquarters of the Church be if one of the others had lived longer?)

15th Century — "simony" introduced (purchase of priestly office with money)

— reading the Bible is forbidden to the laity, at times under penalty of death.

** The Council of Trent: met to <u>try</u> to reform the Catholic church's errors.

Later doctrines:

— Papal infallibility
— Papal decrees added to Bible and tradition as "basis of faith and doctrine"
— Perpetual virginity and assumption of Mary
— Prohibition against eating meat on Fridays

(first imposed, then rescinded in the 1960's, without any revelation from God for <u>either</u> doctrinal change)

THE PROTESTANT REFORMATION: SOME HITS AND SOME MISSES

** Peter Waldo of Lyons translated Bible into common tongue and distributed it. He founded the Waldensians, called the "first Protestants".

** John Wycliff translates the Bible into English (he is later burned at the stake) John Huss is executed for spreading Wycliff's work to Bohemia.

** Gerhard Groot started Bible studies in the Netherlands

** Martin Luther tacked 95 theses on Wittenburg church door, protesting sale of indulgences.

— Luther translated Bible into German.

— tried to reform Catholic church from within, at first.

He was a great reformer, but his <u>false</u> doctrines were:

— "sola fide", or salvation by faith alone (based on his interpretation of Rom. 1:17)
— he wanted to delete the book of James from the Canon because it disagreed with his "sola fide" doctrine.
— the "priesthood of believers", which stated that all believers had priesthood authority, but individuals didn't have enough to act for God. However when a congregation delegated all their individual "priesthood" to their pastor, he then had enough to perform ordinances, etc.

** King Henry VIII of England writes a rebuttal to Luther, thus earning himself the title (from the Pope) of "Defender of the Faith".

** A meeting between Luther and Swiss reformer Zwingli failed to reach unity.

Protestant faiths have diverged from one another ever since.

** The same Henry VIII defied Rome: he wanted to divorce his wife but the Pope said no.

** Henry declared himself head of the English Church, and separated it from Roman Catholicism into the Church of England (Episcopal Church)

** John Calvin developed doctrines from his study of the Bible that profoundly influenced the Presbyterian, Congregational and Baptist faiths, among others.

His "five points of Calvinism" (known by the acronym TULIP) are;

1. <u>T</u>otal depravity of man. (Man is incapable of good by himself.)

2. <u>U</u>nconditional Election (God chooses or "elects" those who will be saved.)

3. <u>L</u>imited Atonement (Christ died only for the Church, not for everyone.)

4. <u>I</u>rresistible Grace (Those predestined to salvation cannot resist God's "election".)

5. <u>P</u>erseverance of the Saints ("Once saved, always saved". You can't lose your salvation.)

TIME FOR THE RESTORATION

** Joseph Smith prays and asks "Which church to join?". In a daylight vision similar to that of Stephen in the New Testament he is visited by Jesus Christ who tells him to "join none of them", that they are all wrong. He is told that if he obeys God, he will be chosen to bring about the Restoration of New Testament Christianity in its pure form in these latter days.

After several years and a number of visits by heavenly messengers, he is ordained to the Apostolic Priesthood by the resurrected Peter, James, and John, and given authority to organize the Church of Jesus Christ once again on the earth.

The Bible's Restoration Prophecies are fulfilled:

A. Acts 3:21 "(the 2nd Coming will not occur until) the times of <u>restitution</u> of all things"
B. Daniel 2:44 "(<u>in the last days</u>) shall the God of heaven <u>set up a kingdom</u> which shall never be destroyed"
C. Rev. 14:6 "(in those days) I saw another angel flying in the midst of heaven, <u>having the everlasting gospel...</u>"
D. Isa. 29:14 "I will proceed to do a marvelous work and a wonder..."
E. Isa. 2:2 "the Lord's house shall be established in the tops of the mountains."

THE "FAITH ONCE DELIVERED TO THE SAINTS" IS RESTORED!

THE REFORMERS AND OTHERS RECOGNIZED THE REALITY OF THE APOSTASY AND THE NEED FOR A RESTORATION:

Are other Christians correct when they criticize Mormons for believing in a universal apostasy? Is it true that the New Testament church Christ established was preserved on the Earth?

Or did the "falling away" or apostasy of the church prophesied by Paul actually take place? (2nd Thessalonians 2:3)

These respected Christian leaders thought so:

But do I not preach a new doctrine? No. I simply say that <u>Christianity has ceased to exist</u> among those who should have preserved it—the bishops and scholars. —Martin Luther *Luther and His Times*, p. 509; — *Martin Luther*, p. 188

Robert Starling

Roger Williams, pastor of the oldest Baptist Church in America at Providence, Rhode Island, refused to continue as pastor on the grounds that,

"There is no regularly-constituted church on earth, nor any person authorized to administer any Church ordinance: nor can there be, until new apostles are sent by the great Head of the Church, for whose coming I am seeking."[7] Williams also said,

"The apostasy... hath so far corrupted all, that there can be no recovery out of that apostasy until Christ shall send forth new apostles to plant churches anew."[8]

Williams believed that divinely-given authority to men to act in the name of God (which we call the priesthood) had been lost from the earth. He looked forward to a time when Christ would send "*new apostles to recover and restore all the ordinances and churches of Christ out of the ruins of antichristian apostasy.*"[9]

In a work prepared by seventy-three noted theologians and Bible students, we read:

"...we must not expect to see the Church of Holy Scripture actually existing in its perfection on the earth. It is not to be found, thus perfect, either in the collected fragments of Christendom, or still less in any one of these fragments..."[10]

Dr. Harry Emerson Fosdick, prominent American Baptist clergyman and author, described the decadent condition of the Christian churches of the first half of the twentieth century in these words:

"A religious reformation is afoot, and at heart it is the endeavor to recover for our modern life the religion of Jesus as against the vast, intricate, largely inadequate and often positively false religion about Jesus. Christianity today has largely left the religion which he preached, taught and lived, and has substituted another kind of religion altogether. If Jesus should come back to now, hear the mythologies built up around him, see the creedalism, denominationalism, sacramentalism, carried on in his name, he would certainly say, 'If this is Christianity, I am not a Christian.'"[11]

John Wesley, the founder of Methodism, lamented that the Christians had apostatized from the gospel of Christ:

"It does not appear that these extraordinary gifts of the Holy Spirit were common in the church for more than two or three centuries. We seldom hear of them after that fatal period when the emperor Constantine called himself a Christian, ... From this time they almost totally ceased; very few instances of the kind were found. ... The Christians had no more of the Spirit of Christ than the other heathens. <u>The Son of Man, when he came to examine His Church, could hardly find faith upon the earth.</u> This was the real cause why the extraordinary gifts of the Holy Ghost were no longer to be found in the Christian Church because <u>the Christians were turned heathens again, and only had a dead form left.</u>"[12]

The Book of Homilies in the Church of England dates from about the middle of the sixteenth century. It officially affirms that the so-called Church and the whole religious world had been utterly apostate for eight centuries or more prior to the establishment of the Church of England.

"So that laity and clergy, learned and unlearned, all ages, sects, and degrees of men, women, and <u>children of whole Christendom</u> — an horrible and most dreadful thing to think — <u>have been at once drowned in abominable idolatry</u>; of all other vices most detested by God, and most damnable to man; and that by the space of eight hundred years and more."
—(Homily Against Peril of Idolatry)

In the words of one eminent historian,

<u>*"Christianity did not destroy paganism; it adopted it.*</u> *The Greek mind, dying, came to a transmigrated [new] life in the theology and liturgy of the Church."*
—*(Will Durant, The Story of Civilization, 3:595.)*

Historian Jesse Hurlbut says:

"For fifty years after St. Paul's life a curtain hangs over the church, through which we strive vainly to look; and when at last it rises, <u>about 120 A.D.</u> with the writings of the earliest church fathers, <u>we find a church in many aspects very different from that in the days of St. Peter and St. Paul</u>"[13]

Thomas Jefferson, though not a cleric in the usual sense, was a great student of Christianity. Even he acknowledged the loss of the original gospel and said that he looked forward to "the prospect of a restoration of primitive Christianity." In 1820 he wrote:

I hold the precepts of Jesus, as delivered by Himself, to be the most pure, benevolent, and sublime which have ever been preached to man. I adhere to the principles of the first age; and consider all subsequent innovations as corruptions of His religion, having no foundation in what came from Him. The metaphysical insanities of Athanasius, of Loyola, and of Calvin, are, to my understanding, mere relapses into polytheism, differing from paganism only by being more unintelligible.

... If the freedom of religion, guaranteed to us by law in theory, can ever rise in practice under the overbearing inquisition of public opinion, truth will prevail over fanaticism, and the genuine doctrines of Jesus, so long perverted by His pseudo-priests, will again be restored to their original purity. This reformation will advance with the other improvements of the human mind, but too late for me to witness it.

"Happy in the prospect of a restoration of primitive Christianity, I must leave to younger athletes to encounter and lop off the false branches which have been engrafted into it by the mythologists of the middle and modern ages."[14]

So we see that compared to the declarations of these many respected Christian pastors and teachers, Joseph Smith's statement about the existing churches that "they were all wrong" was quite mild by comparison!

SIGNS OR CHARACTERISTICS OF CHRIST'S NEW TESTAMENT CHURCH

The church of Jesus Christ as described in the New Testament had other characteristics as well. At this point I'd like to share a story about a group of students at Cal Tech who in 1941 searched through the New Testament to find the identifying characteristics of the church that Jesus organized. I first learned of this story by listening to audio tapes as a young missionary in 1966, and I later became acquainted with Floyd Weston, the person who recorded the account. Thus I was able to verify the truthfulness of the story for myself.

"FOUR OUT OF FIVE"
A Methodical Search for New Testament Christianity

By Robert Starling – based in a talk by Floyd Weston

The lecture hall was filled to overflowing with members of the faculty and student body of the California Institute of Technology. And why not? The speaker was none other than the eminent Albert Einstein, generally acknowledged to be perhaps the greatest scientific mind of the twentieth century.

Young Floyd Weston and his four student friends had wanted to hear the great man speak, but all they could do was sit outside in the hall and strain to listen, with an occasional peek through the crack in the big double doors.

For two and a half hours they sat enthralled as Einstein explained his theories and covered the giant chalkboard with formulas they couldn't hope to understand. But it was his closing remark that would shape the rest of their young lives. "Gentlemen, the deeper that I delve into the sciences of this universe, the more firmly do I believe that one God or Force or Influence has organized all of it for our discovery." With that remark, Einstein blew on his chalk and placed it in the tray of the chalkboard, and the five young students walked back to their dormitory in thoughtful silence.

One of them named John Vincent Dunbar had a pure photographic memory. He looked like a shorter version of Orson Welles, with a high forehead and deep set eyes. His academic brilliance had made him a sophomore at Cal Tech at the age of only seventeen. He would later become a leading scientist at the United States Air Force Technical Services, at Wright-Patterson AFB in Dayton, Ohio.

Like the others, John was shocked. They had all assumed that the great Albert Einstein was an atheist. When they reached his dorm room John reached into a desk drawer and slowly pulled out a Bible placed there by the Gideon Society. In this edition the words were printed in red wherever God the Father or Jesus was either speaking or was being directly quoted.

The five young men were from diverse religious backgrounds. John Dunbar was a Roman Catholic, and Floyd Weston had been raised as a Methodist. Donald Stonebreaker (who later became USAF Colonel was a Presbyterian. Williams was an Episcopalian, and "Junior" Glassie simply said, "there is no God". Glassie was embittered by an experience on a Missouri farm when his family had prayed for safety from an approaching tornado. The twister destroyed the farm and killed his uncle, and someone referred to it as an "act of God". He had decided at that moment that he wanted no part of a God who acted like that.

But on this day as they pondered Einstein's words, each of the five seemed to start over at "ground zero" on the question of faith in a Supreme Being. Dunbar turned in the Gideon Bible to a verse in Ephesians and read it to his friends. It said, "there shall be one Lord, and One Faith, and one Baptism". "If this is true" he said, "then why is there such a myriad of churches in the world today? I'm convinced that somewhere there should be this "one faith" that the Bible talks about. Somewhere there's the church that the Lord himself organized."

He left the room and returned about ten minutes later with a large chalkboard on wheels (the others never asked where he got it). He pushed it into the room, and his friends watched as he began to go through the Bible a page at a time, making notes on the board as he went. Over the next eight weeks the five would meet often in John's room to review his scribbled notes and discuss his progress from Genesis to Revelation. He was fortunate that his photographic memory allowed him to coast through his engineering classes with a minimal amount of study.

Using only the "red-letter" passages quoting the direct words of God, Dunbar carefully classified and copied down the references that he felt would allow anyone to objectively recognize and identify the Church that the Lord speaks of in the Scriptures. During this period of feverish activity John was obsessed with his task. His friends were welcome to come and visit his room, but they dared not accidentally brush up against the double-sided chalkboard and erase any of his notes!

At the end of two months, he called the group together and announced that his study was complete. He handed each student a three by five-inch card on which he had distilled his chalkboard notes into a typed list of seventeen specific characteristics or evidences of the original church organization that Jesus Christ had established during his ministry on Earth.

He said, "I'd like to suggest that we go out now and look for the church that is described in these evidences that I've extracted from the Scriptures". The proposal intrigued his friends. Although several of them were active in their own faiths, the search offered a challenging new adventure.

Dunbar's first requirement was that the Lord's church as described in the Bible would have no paid ministers. He quoted references that said that men should not preach for "filthy lucre" and that there should be "no hirelings in the flock", and so forth. This was somewhat disturbing to most of his friends, who knew that they belonged to churches with a professional clergy.

He also said that they would be looking for a church where the ministers had received authority from God to officiate in His name. He quoted Hebrews 5:4, "And no man taketh this honor unto himself, but he that is called of God as was Aaron." He explained that Aaron did not "volunteer" for the ministry, but that he has been called by the living prophet Moses (his brother) and ordained by Moses through the ordinance of the "laying on of hands".

The third characteristic they would be looking for was a church that practiced baptism by complete immersion in water. John cited several verses including the baptism of Jesus himself in the river Jordan, and John 3:5 which stated that no man can enter the Kingdom of Heaven without having been born of the water and of the Spirit.

He said that the church they were seeking must have an understanding of God and Jesus Christ as two separate persons, again citing the baptism of Jesus where the Lord was standing in the water, the Holy Spirit descended in the form of a dove, and the voice of God the Father spoke out of heaven. He rejected the notion that God was some sort of ventriloquist; therefore the Godhead must be comprised of three separate and distinct beings.

Having erased the chalkboard, Dunbar now used it to draw out an "organizational chart" of the New Testament church for his friends. He listed all the offices named in Scripture, and suggested that they search for a church with an organization as close to that of the Bible as possible.

The five students decided that they would use their Wednesday nights and their Sundays to search for the church described on their 3x5 cards. As Sherlock Holmes would have said, "the game is afoot"!

On the first Wednesday night they picked at random a small cobblestone Pentecostal-type church in Pasadena. The young minister had a drummer on the podium behind him, and the sermon was often punctuated by rim shots and drum rolls. Glassie turned to the others with a raised eyebrow and asked, "this is religion?"

The next Sunday they visited John Dunbar's Roman Catholic church and talked with Father "Whitey" Hill (formerly an All-American tackle at Notre Dame) at the Mission San Gabriel. In a long conversation, he discovered to his dismay that his church qualified on only one of the seventeen points on his card — they claimed to have divine authority. As they left, Father Hill said "Well John, don't worry about it son. If we're wrong there are five hundred million of us going down together."

Instead of comforting Dunbar this disturbed him. His photographic memory reminded him of the Bible verse, which said that "strait is the gate and narrow the way, and few there be that find it". He didn't think there would be any "security in numbers" where Heaven is concerned.

Floyd Weston made an appointment for the group to meet with Dr. Lee, the pastor of his Methodist church. A couple of Sundays later they were waiting in the church foyer when Dunbar noticed a financial statement on the bulletin board. "We might as well not waste our time here", he said. "It says here the pastor receives a salary".

And so it went for the next few weeks as they visited various churches, none of which met the criteria on their cards. Then suddenly the Japanese attacked Pearl Harbor, and the United States was at war.

Each of the five young students enlisted in the armed forces, and they went their separate ways. Floyd Weston soon found himself jogging down red clay roads in the Army Airborne training center at Fort Benning, Georgia. After completing the course himself, he began to teach other recruits how to jump out of perfectly good airplanes. One day an accident occurred, and a friend of Floyd's was killed when his parachute didn't open. It was while he was still pondering the larger questions of life and death that he met some recruits from Utah who seemed to have some of the answers he was seeking.

After some initial conversations he found that most of them were "Mormons" — members of The Church of Jesus Christ of Latter-day Saints. He had grown up with a number of Mormon kids in his high school in southern California, but wasn't familiar with what they believed. He got out his three-by-five card and asked one of the leaders of the Utah bunch about the 17 signs of Christ's church. To his amazement he found that the "Mormon" church met ALL of John Dunbar's criteria!

After some months of study (and more jumping out of airplanes!), the war ended and Floyd returned home to California. Soon after he was baptized in the Pacific Ocean and became a member of The Church of Jesus Christ of Latter-day Saints. Some time after that Floyd was attending a Stake Conference when he ran into John Dunbar at church. "What are you doing here?" he asked. Dunbar replied, "Well I belong here, what about you?" They fondly held an impromptu reunion right there in the foyer.

Later the two men looked up their other friends and found that Glassie —the atheist— had been a fighter pilot in North Africa where he'd been shot down and killed during the war. But their other two friends had survived. And amazingly enough, they too had both joined The Church of Jesus Christ of Latter-day Saints, primarily because of the 3x5 cards they each had carried which listed the seventeen signs of Christ's New Testament church. Four out of five had found the truth.

And the truth had set them free.

SOME MODERN-DAY EVIDENCES OF CHRIST'S TRUE CHURCH

In addition to the 17 signs discovered by Floyd Weston and his friends, my friend Kirk Magleby has added a few more evidences that The Church of Jesus Christ of Latter-day Saints is in reality the restored New Testament church of Jesus Christ. What do you think of these?

1. The name of the church. Yeah, it's pretty long, huh? That's why for many years lots of folks (including us) have preferred to used the shorter term "Mormon". But that's just a nickname. In reality, our church is one of the few churches on earth where every word in its name can be found in the Bible! (although rearranged a bit) But where in the Bible can you find the Southern Baptist Convention, the Roman Catholic Church, the Methodists, or the Presbyterians, etc.

2. <u>The method of succession to leadership of the church.</u> When the president of The Church of Jesus Christ of Latter-day Saints dies, there is no big convention called to elect a new leader. There is on lobbying or campaigning for votes or the summoning of a college of cardinals to send up white smoke when a new leader is elected. Instead, just as in the book of Acts, the remaining apostles hold a quiet and dignified meeting after fasting and prayer to select the new leader of the church, or new apostles to fill vacancies in the Quorum of the Twelve as directed by the Holy Spirit.

3. <u>The absence of corruption and accumulation of wealth by church leaders.</u> Most local pastors in most churches today are honest, hard-working servants who care for their flocks and are people of modest means. My uncle was a Methodist pastor who fit that description. But it seems that the larger the congregations or the greater the number of franchised churches in an organization, the higher the lifestyle of those at the top. It has become almost a common stereotype to see the senior pastors of giant megachurches or television ministries living in grandiose mansions and traveling in private jet aircraft.

It is not so with the Latter-day Saints. There are over sixteen million of us all over the world. We're the fourth largest church in America. Yet the First Presidency and other General Authorities hold the tithes and offerings of our members sacred. They each receive only a modest living stipend for their full-time service in the ministry. And local leaders serve part-time and receive no financial compensation at all. They are all volunteers. And you will not find any church-owned corporate jets at the Salt Lake City airport.

4. <u>The form of the church's organization.</u> The Church of Jesus Christ of Latter-day Saints is not a democracy or an affiliation of independent local churches who determine their own doctrines and elect their own leadership, etc. Like the congregations of the Church of Jesus Christ in New Testament times in Corinth, Ephesus, Thessalonia, Galatia, Rome, etc., the branches, wards and stakes of our church receive guidance and direction from the prophets, apostles, the seventy, and other "general authorities".

Like those who were "first called Christians" at Antioch, Latter-day Saint Bishops and Elders from Australia to Zimbabwe receive visits and directives from "church headquarters", which is not now in Jerusalem as in the days of Peter, but is now in Salt Lake City. Thus there is "one Lord, one faith, and one baptism" all over the world. You may discuss one Sunday School lesson in Atlanta, and the next week pick up with the next lesson in the series as you attend church in Saudi Arabia. (Yes, we have several branches and wards there!)

5. Another distinctive evidence of the Lord's church is <u>volunteerism</u>. I've visited a number of other churches where not only the pastors but the music leaders, youth and nursery leaders, etc. receive a salary. In a Latter-day Saint ward and stake, everyone is a volunteer, from the Stake President or Bishop down to the door greeter. Even outside the church, "Mormons" are known for their volunteerism in their communities. I'll explain more about this in chapter 12, but as a preview: A University of Pennsylvania Research study shows that on average Latter-day Saints volunteer <u>seven times</u> more than the average US citizen. The contributions of Latter-day Saints to worldwide disaster relief in recent years has become legendary, comparable to that of the Red Cross.

CONCLUSION

As we have seen, in1820 God told Joseph Smith that he would be an instrument to restore Christ's New Testament church to the earth.

In 1829 Joseph was ordained by heavenly messengers and given the priesthood authority and "keys of the kingdom" (like Peter received) needed to restore the church of Christ.

On April 6, 1830 The Church of Jesus Christ of Latter-day Saints was formerly organized. Like the "stone cut without hands", the kingdom of God that Daniel saw in vision has rolled forth and it is beginning to fill the whole earth. Today The Church of Jesus Christ of Latter-day Saints is found in over 175 countries with a worldwide membership of over 16 million (in 2019). It is the fourth largest church in America and it is growing at an accelerated rate.

As Floyd Weston and his four friends found for themselves during WWII, the LDS church matches the New Testament church of Christ in every aspect of its organization and doctrine.

The message of The Church of Jesus Christ of Latter-day Saints to the world is a message that John Wesley, Roger Williams and those other Christian leaders would have welcomed – that the times for the "restitution of all things" (Acts 3:21) has come, and that "primitive Christianity" has indeed been restored to the earth in these latter-days.

So … is there one "true church" representing Christ on the earth today? What do you think?

ENDNOTES FOR CHAPTER 4

1   C.S. Lewis, *Mere Christianity* (New York: Touchstone, 1996), pp. 11-12

2   Sermon delivered at the Nauvoo temple grounds on Sunday July 9, 1843 - Joseph Smith Diary

3   Gordon B. Hinckley, interview with Lawrence Spicer, London News Service, 28 Aug. 1995

4   Elder Dallin Oaks, Conference Reports, April 1995

5   http://www.cbn.com/spirituallife/cbnteachingsheets/faq_cult.aspx

6   Craig Hazen, professor of comparative religion and apologetics, Biola University http://www.christianitytoday.com/ct/2012/ october-web-only/should-billy-graham-have-removed-mormons-from-cult-list.html

7   (*Picturesque America, or the Land We Live In*, ed. William Cullen Bryant, New York: D. Appleton and Co., 1872, vol. 1, p. 502.)

8   (Underhill, Edward, "*Struggles and Triumphs of Religious Liberty*", cited in William F. Anderson, "*Apostasy or Succession, Which?* ", pp. 238-39)

9   (See John Catton, *A Reply to Mr. Williams ...*, ed. J. Lewis Diman, in *Complete Writings*, 2:14, 50, cited by Donald Skaggs, *Roger Williams' Dream for America*, Peter Lang Publ., NY, 1993, p. 43; as cited by R. I. Winwood, *Take Heed That Ye Be Not Deceived*, R.I. Winwood, SLC, UT, 1995, p. 12)

10   (Dr. William Smith, *Smith's Dictionary of the Bible*, Boston: Houghton, Mifflin and Company, 1896.)

11   *(Fosdick, Christianity and Progress, p. 196)*

12   *(Sermon 89 in The Works of John Wesley, Sermons 71-114, ed. A.C.* Outler, Nashville, Abingdon Press, 1986, 3:263-264, as cited by Winwood, pp. 12-13).

13   *The Story of the Christian Church, 1970, p. 33*

14   Letters to Dr. Benjamin Waterhouse and Reverend Jared Sparks, *The Writings of Thomas Jefferson* V15: Containing His Autobiography, Notes on Virginia, Parliamentary Manual, Official Papers, Messages and Addresses, And Other Writings And Private (Lipscomb and Bergh, Eds.; Kessinger Publishing, 2006), 15:288, 391

EVIDENCE 5

PRIESTHOOD AND AUTHORITY TO ACT FOR GOD

Here is another evidence in the case that The Church of Jesus Christ of Latter-day Saints has special authority to act for God, that other churches do not have.

I've often heard the phrase that someone has "chosen the ministry" to become a pastor or "chosen a vocation" as a priest or nun. But while it is admirable for people to want to dedicate their life to religious service, that alone does not give them the authority to act for God.

In like manner, a man can desire to be a policeman, but just putting on a uniform does not give him authority to act for the city government (even if he gets badge and a gun and a certificate from the Acme School of Law Enforcement). Unless he receives the proper authorization, his acts are not recognized by the organization he claims to represent.

One of our Articles of Faith in Mormonism says:

We believe that a man must be called of God, by prophecy, and by the laying on of hands by those who are in authority, to preach the Gospel and administer in the ordinances thereof.
—5ᵗʰ LDS Article of Faith

Jesus told his apostles when he gave them authority to act for him: *Ye have not chosen me, but I have chosen you, and ordained you,*

—John 15:16

He then sent them out into the world saying to them:

> *Go ye therefore, and teach all nations, baptizing them in the name of the Father, and of the Son, and of the Holy Ghost: Teaching them to observe all things whatsoever I have commanded you:*
>
> — *Matt. 28:19-20*

Latter-day Saints believe that after the death of the twelve apostles who were the "foundation" of the New Testament Christian church (Eph. 2:20) and those whom they had ordained to the priesthood, there were no more authorized representatives of God left on the earth, and the Church fell into apostasy and spiritual darkness. This led to that period history calls the "dark ages" that lasted over a thousand years. This is not to say that there were not some good people on the earth in those days who sought to worship God in the best way they knew how, but generally speaking the "lights had gone out" and the Church that Jesus has established on the earth was no longer here.

As I mentioned in the last chapter, this condition was recognized by Thomas Jefferson when he said:

> *"I hold the precepts of Jesus, as delivered by Himself, to be the most pure, benevolent, and sublime which have ever been preached to man. I adhere to the principles of the first age; and consider all subsequent innovations as corruptions of His religion, having no foundation in what came from Him."*

Jefferson also wrote in the same volume:

> *"Happy in the prospect of a restoration of primitive Christianity, I must leave to younger athletes to encounter and lop off the false branches which have been engrafted into it by the mythologists of the middle and modern ages."*[1]

The "restoration of primitive Christianity" that Jefferson anticipated came only four years after his death in 1826. I personally think that he was somewhere in heaven, smiling.

INSIDE LATTER-DAY CHRISTIANITY

On May 15, 1829 one of the most important events in the history of the world took place, and most people outside the LDS church are not even aware of it. Joseph Smith, with the assistance of Oliver Cowdery, was translating the Book of Mormon when he read about the performing of baptisms and wondered about the authority to do such.

He and Oliver retired to the wilderness and inquired of God about the authority to baptize. They were visited by John the Baptist, a resurrected person. He laid his hands on their heads and ordained them to the Aaronic Priesthood with the following words:

"Upon you my fellow servants, in the name of Messiah I confer the Priesthood of Aaron, which holds the keys of the ministering of angels, and of the gospel of repentance, and of baptism by immersion for the remission of sins; and this shall never be taken again from the earth, until the sons of Levi do offer again an offering unto the Lord in righteousness" [2]

He also told Joseph and Oliver that the priesthood they had received was the "lesser" of two priesthoods. It was the kind of authority given to Aaron and the "sons of Levi" or "Levites" to perform ordinances under the Law of Moses. It was called the "Aaronic" or "Levitical" priesthood.[3]

Some weeks afterwards they were visited by the resurrected Peter, James and John who likewise laid their hands upon them and ordained them to the higher priesthood after the order of Melchizedek.

— (Heb. 7:11)

Peter gave to Joseph Smith the same "keys to the kingdom" that he had received from Jesus – the power to bind or loose on earth that which would be bound or loosed in heaven. Thus the authority for men to act for God was restored once more to the earth after being missing for over 1500 years. It has been described "inside Mormonism" as follows:

"The Priesthood is an everlasting principle, and existed with God from eternity, and will to eternity, without beginning of days or end of years. The keys have to be brought from heaven whenever the Gospel is sent."[4]

—Joseph Smith

It is veritably <u>the power of the Almighty given to man to act in His name</u> and in His stead. It is a delegation of divine authority, different from all other powers and authorities on the face of the earth. Small wonder <u>that it was restored to man by resurrected beings who held it anciently</u>, that there might be no question concerning its authority and validity. <u>Without it there could be a church in name only, lacking authority to administer in the things of</u>

God. With it, nothing is impossible in carrying forward the work of the kingdom of God. It is divine in its nature. It is both temporal and eternal in its authority.[5]

—Gordon B. Hinckley, May 15, 1988

In The Church of Jesus Christ of Latter-day Saints every worthy male is ordained to first the Aaronic and then the Melchizedek priesthood. This follows the New Testament practice of the earliest Christians as illustrated by Peter's statement to them that:

"ye are a chosen generation, a royal priesthood, an holy nation, a peculiar people"

—1 Peter 2:9

There was then (and is now) no separate class of "clergy" among members of the church of Jesus Christ. That distinction was an apostate practice that began after the death of the original apostles when the "falling away" began.

WHY DO WE NEED AUTHORITY FROM GOD?

In his Great Commission to the New Testament apostles our Savior said: Go ye into all the world, and preach the gospel to every creature. He that believeth and is baptized shall be saved; but he that believeth not shall be damned.

—Mark 16: 15-16

On this occasion Jesus gave his disciples two directives: to teach and to baptize. First let's talk about the teaching or preaching. There are two kinds. There is the sharing of one's personal testimony and understanding of the Scriptures, which requires no special authority or commission. Any believer in Christ can -and indeed should- use every opportunity available to share his or her testimony and beliefs with others.

Then there is another kind of teaching. The Bible speaks of those who were ordained by Jesus to "speak with authority" (Titus 2:15). When they did so under the inspiration of the Holy Spirit their words (whether written or spoken) were not just their own interpretation of Scripture or their own opinion. They were giving forth the mind and will and word of God. In theological circles this kind of inspiration enjoyed by the apostles is called "special revelation".

Those who are ordained ("set apart" in the Greek) were also authorized to perform the second part of the Great Commission – to baptize those who responded to the preaching of the Gospel. In addition their ordination authorized them to administer other ordinances of

Christ's church such as the sacrament instituted by Jesus at the Last Supper and others that we'll discuss later.

The authority to act for God as His representative on earth is not something that can be assumed by an individual, no matter how strongly he or she feels a "call" or a "vocation" to do so. The Bible is very clear on this:

And no man taketh this honour unto himself, but he that is called of God, as was Aaron.
—*Hebrews 5:4*

How was Aaron called? Aaron did not decide to take the priesthood upon himself, but he was called by Moses, who was instructed by the Lord and who had authority over him.

And thou shalt <u>put upon Aaron the holy garments, and anoint him</u>, and sanctify him; that he may minister unto me in the priest's office. And thou shalt bring his sons, and clothe them with coats: <u>And thou shalt anoint them</u>, as thou didst anoint their father, <u>that they may minister unto me in the priest's office: for their anointing shall surely be an everlasting priesthood</u> throughout their generations. Thus did Moses: according to all that <u>the LORD commanded him</u>, so did he.
—*(Exodus 40:13-16)*

Later Moses was also commanded to also ordain Joshua by the laying on of hands:

And the LORD said unto Moses, Take thee Joshua the son of Nun, a man in whom is the spirit, and <u>lay thine hand upon him</u>; And set him before Eleazar the priest, and before all the congregation; and <u>give him a charge</u> in their sight. <u>And thou shalt put some of thine honour upon him</u>, that all the congregation of the children of Israel may be obedient.
—*(Numbers 27:18-20)*

This priesthood authority is sacred and cannot be bought.

And when Simon saw that <u>through laying on of the apostles' hands the Holy Ghost was given</u>, he offered them money, Saying<u>, Give me also this power</u>, that on whomsoever I lay hands, he may receive the Holy Ghost. But Peter said unto him, Thy money perish with thee, because <u>thou hast thought that the gift of God may be purchased with money.</u>
—*(Acts 8:18-20)*

WHAT IS THE PRIESTHOOD?

The priesthood is the authority to act for God. And God is pretty particular about who receives this authority and what they do with it. The Old Testament prophets were given priesthood authority beginning with Adam. I don't think anyone will argue that Noah, Enoch and others were called and set apart by God for their ministries. We know that Abraham was a prophet and he gave tithes to Melchisedec, so both of them must have been God's authorized servants. In fact, in the 5th chapter of Hebrews the office of High Priest is called "after the order of Melchisedec".

When Moses delivered the tribes of Israel out of bondage in Egypt and brought them to the foot of Mount Sinai to meet their God, they refused that honor (Exodus 20:18-19). When he came down the mountain after talking with God and found the Israelites conducting an orgy in their worship of a golden calf, Moses was angry and he threw down on the ground and broke the first set of stone tablets (Ex. 32:19). These were the tablets on which God has written His commandments with his own finger.

Moses himself then made a new set of tablets (Ex. 34:4), then went back up on Mount Sinai and received a "lesser" law for the people to live and a lesser priesthood to administer that law. Note that under this "lesser law" the priesthood was only given to the "sons of Levi", or members of only one of the twelve tribes of Israel. This "lesser" priesthood (also called "the order of Aaron" or the Aaronic Priesthood) was differentiated in the New Testament from the "order of Melchisedec" or the Melchisedec priesthood.

And verily they that are of the sons of Levi, who receive the office of the priesthood, have a commandment to take tithes of the people according to the law, that is, of their brethren, though they come out of the loins of Abraham: If therefore perfection were by the Levitical priesthood, (for under it the people received the law,) what further need was there that another priest should rise after the order of Melchisedec, and not be called after the order of Aaron? For the priesthood being changed, there is made of necessity a change also of the law.

—Hebrews 7:5, 11-12

The writer of Hebrews says that under the new covenant of Christ the old Levitical or Aaronic priesthood had to be "changed" along with the changes that fulfilled the Law of Moses. When Jesus ordained Peter and his other apostles and they in turn ordained others, they were given the authority of the Melchisedec or "greater" priesthood, so that when they performed church ordinances such as the laying on of hands to bestow the gift of the Holy Ghost, whatever they "sealed on earth" would be "sealed in heaven".

—(Matt. 16:19)

JESUS GAVE PRIESTHOOD AUTHORITY TO HIS DISCIPLES

The Bible is pretty clear that Jesus received power and authority from God the Father, and he then conferred priesthood authority on his disciples:

For as the Father hath life in himself; so hath he given to the Son to have life in himself; And hath given him authority to execute judgment also, because he is the Son of man.

—*John 5:26-27*

THEN he called his twelve disciples together, and gave them power and authority over all devils, and to cure diseases. And he sent them to preach the kingdom of God, and to heal the sick.

—*Luke 9:1-2*

And he ordained twelve, that they should be with him, and that he might send them forth to preach.

—*Mark 3:14*

Beginning from the baptism of John, unto that same day that he was taken up from us, must one be ordained to be a witness with us of his resurrection.

—*Acts 1:22*

And when he had called unto him his twelve disciples, he gave them power against unclean spirits, to cast them out, and to heal all manner of sickness and all manner of disease.

—*Matthew 10:1*

Whereunto I am ordained a preacher, and an apostle, (I speak the truth in Christ, and lie not;) a teacher of the Gentiles in faith and verity.

—*1 Timothy 2:7*

The apostles ordained others and gave them a portion of this authority: For this cause left I thee in Crete, that thou shouldest set in order the things that are wanting, and ordain elders in every city, as I had appointed thee...

—*Titus 1:5*

And when they had <u>ordained them elders in every church</u>, and had prayed with fasting, they commended them to the Lord, on whom they believed.

—*Acts 14:23*

This authority was passed directly from God the Father, to Jesus Christ, to the Apostles, to the Elders, and to others. It was a priesthood which any worthy man could have, if he lived worthy of it. It was also necessary for the establishment of the Church. Christ left this priesthood authority on the earth when He ascended into heaven, so that the Church could still function.

For the Son of man is as a man taking a far journey, who left his house, <u>and gave authority to his servants</u>, and to every man his work.

—*Mark 13:34*

So now that we've seen how the priesthood is used and conferred in Christ's church, what is the teaching and practice on priesthood in other churches today?

OUTSIDE LATTER-DAY CHRISTIANITY

A good friend of mine named Jerry (now deceased) was a deacon in a prominent Baptist church in my hometown in Georgia. Jerry was a great guy and I had the utmost respect for him. I've discussed with him his experiences as a member of the selection committee for a new pastor at his church where he interviewed candidates, etc. I believe he also participated in the passing of the bread and wine used in communion, the collection of offerings, etc. I also have a cousin Mark who recently was made a deacon in another Baptist church in Georgia. He explained to me how the pastor had ordained him.

I need to ask my uncle Rudolph (Mark's father, who is a retired Methodist minister) if the process is similar in the Methodist church. And to make sure I've done my homework I'll need to learn how it's done by Presbyterians, Lutherans, Catholics, etc. I have some friends who are members of those faiths, so I should be able to find out. Perhaps I'll put that in my next book. But whether the ordination is done by a pastor or a seminary faculty or the College of Cardinals, it is irrelevant if that person or group did not have the authority from God to bestow His priesthood.

You see, this question of priesthood authority is an important one. In fact, it's one of the major differences between Latter-day Saints and other Christians. In contrast with the

"Mormon" doctrine of the priesthood we have two different views in the Catholic and Protestant traditions. Let's examine them separately.

THE CATHOLIC VIEW OF THE PRIESTHOOD

The Catholics believe their authority to act for God comes from Christ through the apostle Peter in an unbroken line succession from one Pope to another down through the centuries. The Latter-day Saints also believe their priesthood authority comes from Christ through Peter, but by a different historical process involving resurrected beings as I've explained.

As far as I can tell, most non-Catholic Christians claim to have received from their study of the Bible a "priesthood of all believers" that was first taught by Martin Luther as we'll discuss later.

My good Catholic friends include some who are learned apologists for their faith. As I just mentioned, they say that the Roman Catholic Church derives its priesthood authority from an unbroken line of succession of Popes beginning with the apostle Peter, whom they claim was the first bishop of Rome.

They say that succeeding bishops of Rome received his same apostolic authority and passed it on through the centuries to the present day. And they say that because Rome was the largest Christian church it was only logical that the Bishop of Rome should have more authority than other bishops and thus become the leader of the entire church.

My Evangelical Protestant friends will join me in challenging that claim. This is one of many areas where Latter-day Saints and Evangelicals are in agreement (Surprise! We're in agreement with many teachings of Catholics, too.) Let's examine the errors of the Catholic view on priesthood in detail:

WAS PETER GIVEN AUTHORITY TO LEAD CHRIST'S EARTHLY CHURCH?

It's true that Jesus gave to Peter the keys to priesthood authority in his church and chose him as its earthly head. The Bible is pretty plain in this regard. It was first to Peter that Christ said:

And I will give unto thee the keys of the kingdom of heaven: and whatsoever thou shalt bind on earth shall be bound in heaven: and whatsoever thou shalt loose on earth shall be loosed in heaven.

—Matthew 16:19

113

Matthew called Peter "the first" among the apostles, although he was not the first chronologically to be called. (Matthew 10:2) It was to Peter that Jesus said several times, *"feed my sheep".* (John 21:15) Paul acknowledged that Peter, along with James and John *"seemed to be pillars,"* of the infant New Testament church. (Galatians 2:9) It was Peter who received the revelation from God and told the other apostles how repentance and salvation had been granted to the Gentiles. (Acts 11:1-18, 15:7) After His resurrection, Jesus visited Peter before any of the other apostles. (1 Corinthians 15:5) Okay then, if Peter was the head of the Biblical church of Christ, does that make the Catholics right? Not so fast ….

BISHOPS ARE NOT THE SAME AS APOSTLES

In his letters to both the Corinthians and the Ephesians the apostle Paul lists several offices in the priesthood, as did Luke in the book of Acts. As we noted in the previous chapter there were pastors, teachers, evangelists, deacons, the seventy, elders and bishops, all built on the "foundation" of living apostles and prophets. It is very clear that bishops are not the same as apostles. They were local church officers who were ordained by and presided over by the apostles. Thus Peter would never have acted as the bishop of Rome. He and his fellow apostles provided guidance and direction for all the bishops of the entire church.

WHAT ARE PRIESTHOOD "KEYS"?

The "keys" that Jesus gave to Peter pertained not only to his calling to preside over the other twelve apostles but also over the church as a whole. The holder of priesthood keys has authority to act independently over his stewardship and to ordain others to the priesthood without permission and approval from those under whom he serves. For example a bishop had the keys to preside over his own congregation and to ordain deacons, elders, teachers, etc. But he had no keys of authority over other congregations and he could not ordain other bishops. Those church-wide keys belonged exclusively to the apostles.

Only Peter held all the keys for the church as a whole, although those presiding keys were also vested in the twelve acting as a quorum. Thus when Judas killed himself the remaining eleven apostles were able to act together to ordain Matthias as his replacement. —(Acts 1:23-26) When the apostles were all scattered and killed and could not re-constitute the quorum of twelve there was no authority remaining to ordain new apostles. When existing bishops undertook to ordain new bishops themselves, those ordinations were not according to the order of the church that Jesus had given, and they were not recognized by God. They could ordain new elders, deacons, etc. but <u>eventually all those who held any priesthood keys died out</u> and the power to act for God was lost from the earth.

CATHOLIC POPES ARE ORDAINED BY CARDINALS, NOT APOSTLES

As I understand it, Roman Catholic popes today are elected and ordained by a "college" of Cardinals. First of all the office of Cardinal is not found in the Bible. Secondly the cardinals are definitely not apostles, hence they cannot ordain bishops. But even if they could, what does history tell us about the so-called "unbroken" line of Papal succession?

AN UNBROKEN LINE OF POPES?

I'm aware that the Roman Catholic church has a list of an alleged unbroken line of the bishops of Rome that are called "Popes" from which they supposedly derive their "apostolic" authority. But as we've seen above, the offices of bishop and apostle are totally different and cannot be confused. And even if their claims to original authority were true, there are some problems with their "unbroken" line of succession.

Of course only one broken link in a chain is enough to sever the connection, but let's consider the following:

In 1378 the Roman Catholic Church experienced the 2nd Great Schism, also called the Western Schism. At that time three different Popes were elected simultaneously in Rome & Pisa, Italy, & Avignon, France. They excommunicated each other, and confusion reigned for over 70 years (quite a break in the "unbroken succession"?) until 1449 when Pope Nicholas V of Rome outlived his competition. (Where would the headquarters of the Church be if one of the **others** had lived longer?) I could give other evidence of breaks in the "unbroken succession", but as I said, only one break in the chain is enough to sever the connection. Even if the Pope at one time had apostolic authority (which he did not), it has not been passed down to the present.

"DOES PRIESTHOOD AUTHORITY COME FROM THE BIBLE"?

Knowing or studying the Bible does not give a person the authority to act for God any more than knowing or studying a law book or the Constitution gives him or her the authority to act for the law. Can you imagine what would happen if anyone who felt "called" to be a policeman, a district attorney, or a judge were to assume the duties of that office merely because they had studied the civil code or some other law book? What if someone decided that they wanted to be an FBI agent, so they went out and got themselves a badge and a gun and a black suit and tie? He or she might get a friend to administer the oath of office to them, but where would their authority come from? Certainly not from the law book, even though it may have all the valid laws enumerated in it and they had studied to know all the correct procedures to be followed.

THE "PRIESTHOOD OF ALL BELIEVERS"

Most Evangelical Protestants think they get the power to act for God from the "priesthood of all believers". But where does that idea come from? What does it mean?

While Martin Luther did not use the exact phrase "priesthood of all believers", he describes a general priesthood in Christendom in his 1520 essay *To the Christian Nobility of the German Nation* in order to dismiss the medieval view that Christians in the present life were to be divided into two classes: "spiritual" and "secular". In his opposition to the priesthood hierarchy of the Catholic Church he <u>invented</u> the doctrine that all baptized Christians are "priests" and "spiritual" in the sight of God;

That the pope or bishop anoints, makes tonsures, ordains, consecrates, or dresses differently from the laity, may make a hypocrite or an idolatrous oil-painted icon, but it in no way makes a Christian or spiritual human being. In fact, <u>we are all consecrated priests through Baptism</u>, as St. Peter in 1 Peter 2:9 says, "You are a royal priesthood and a priestly kingdom," and Revelation 5:10, "Through your blood you have made us into priests and kings."[6]

Two months later Luther would write in his *On the Babylonian Captivity of the Church* (1520): *How then if they are forced to admit that <u>we are all equally priests, as many of us as are baptized</u>, and by this way we truly are; while to them is committed only the Ministry (ministerium Predigtamt) and consented to by us (nostro consensu)? If they recognize this they would know that they have no right to exercise power over us (ius imperii, in what has not been committed to them) except insofar as we may have granted it to them, for thus it says in 1 Peter 2. "You are a chosen race, a royal priesthood, a priestly kingdom." In this way we are all priests, as many of us as are Christians. <u>There are indeed priests whom we call ministers</u>. They are <u>chosen from among us</u>, and who do everything in our name. <u>That is a priesthood</u> which is nothing else than the Ministry. Thus 1 Corinthians 4:1: "No one should regard us as anything else than ministers of Christ and dispensers of the mysteries of God."*[7]

Please note the context of Luther's remarks here. He is declaring independence from the Pope, the bishops and priests of the Roman Catholic Church by saying that *"they have no right to exercise power over us".* He <u>assumes</u> that 1 Peter 2 gives every baptized believer the power of God's priesthood.

But that is a mistaken and an un-Biblical assumption. In Peter's day in the New Testament church every worthy male was ordained to the priesthood, so his remark about "a royal priesthood" makes sense in that context. But it does not grant to the un-ordained the power to act for God. Those whom Luther calls "ministers" he says, *are chosen from among us, and who do everything in our name".* Certainly one whom a congregation chooses to be their minister can act in <u>their</u> name, but not in the name of God unless he has been ordained by one who has the "keys" of authority to make the ordination.

WHAT IF SOMEONE ASSUMES PRIESTHOOD AUTHORITY?

So… What if a person sincerely believes he has priesthood authority and attempts to use it to perform ordinances, etc.? Will God recognize them? Perhaps a couple of examples from the Bible will give us some insight:

1. In Acts 19 we read of twelve people in Ephesus who had been baptized by someone with authority from God. Or so they thought …

And it came to pass, that, while Apollos was at Corinth, Paul having passed through the upper coasts came to Ephesus: and finding certain disciples, He said unto them, Have ye received the Holy Ghost since ye believed? And they said unto him, We have not so much as heard whether there be any Holy Ghost. And he said unto them, <u>Unto what then were ye baptized? And they said, Unto John's baptism.</u> Then said Paul, John verily baptized with the baptism of repentance, saying unto the people, that they should believe on him which should come after him, that is, on Christ Jesus. When they heard this, <u>they were baptized in the name of the Lord Jesus.</u> And when Paul had laid his hands upon them, the Holy Ghost came on them; and they spake with tongues, and prophesied. And all the men were about twelve.

— Acts 19:1-7

So we have a case here where sincere believers <u>thought</u> they had been baptized by someone with proper priesthood authority "unto John's baptism". Paul recognized that John's baptisms were valid for repentance prior to the organizing of the church of Jesus Christ, but because these disciples had not been taught about receiving the Holy Ghost, he realized that whoever performed their baptisms did not have proper authority to do so. <u>He corrected the error by re-baptizing them</u>, and then performed the ordinance that always accompanies baptism in

Christ's church – he laid his hands upon them that they might receive the gift of the Holy Ghost.

(Likewise, if you were to find that the person who performed your marriage ceremony was not authorized to do so, you'd want to be re-married by someone with the proper authority wouldn't you?) There are a couple of other examples in the Bible of people attempting to assume for themselves the power of God's priesthood, with disastrous results:

2. Aaron's sons offered unauthorized sacrifices:

And Nadab and Abihu, the sons of Aaron, took either of them his censer, and put fire therein, and put incense thereon, and offered strange fire before the LORD, which **he commanded them not.** *And there went out fire from the LORD, and devoured them, and they died before the LORD.*

—Leviticus 10:1-2

3. And what happened when the sons of Sceva tried to cast out evil spirits without authority?

Then certain of the vagabond Jews, exorcists, took upon them to call over them which had evil spirits the name of the Lord Jesus, saying, We adjure you by Jesus whom Paul preacheth. And there were seven sons of one Sceva, a Jew, and chief of the priests, which did so. And the evil spirit answered and said, Jesus I know, and Paul I know; but who are ye? And the man in whom the evil spirit was leaped on them, and overcame them, and prevailed against them, so that they fled out of that house naked and wounded.

—Acts 19:13-16

WHO IS ELIGIBLE TO HOLD PRIESTHOOD OFFICES?

One of the criticisms often leveled at my church is that our Deacons are ordained at the age of twelve, as I was. Critics say that the Bible requires that a Deacon in Christ's church be "a husband of one wife" and therefore the LDS practice of ordaining young unmarried boys to the priesthood is unbiblical and therefore un-Christian. A similar verse is used to declare that when the "Mormons" were practicing polygamy in the 1800's and ordained Bishops who had multiple wives, they were acting contrary to the Bible. We'll deal with the polygamy question later, but for now let's stay with the question of priesthood authority for deacons and other offices in the church.

So, is it Biblical for LDS boys to be ordained Deacons without being married to "one wife"? Perhaps a closer look at the Bible verse in question is warranted. The Bible (at least the KJV) does indeed say that one of the qualities looked for in deacons in the church organized by Christ and directed by His apostles is that they *"be the husbands of one wife, ruling their children and their own houses well."*

—(1 Timothy 3:12)

If a man is already a husband and father, certainly he should be acting well in that role before being ordained to the church office of a deacon. Adult male converts to the LDS church who are husbands and fathers are ordained Deacons or Priests in the Aaronic Priesthood before later becoming Elders. But is it a requirement for ordination that he be a father? Or a husband for that matter?

The translation of the Greek word "andres" ("husband" in this verse) is dependent on the context. In the KJV it is translated "man" or "male" 156 times, and translated "husband" only 50 times. It should be noted that under Jewish law a boy became a "man" in the eyes of his community when he performed his Bar Mitzvah at about the age of 13. This may be something akin to the experience of the boy Jesus when he taught in the temple at Jerusalem at age 12.

The phrase translated in the KJV as "husband of one wife" means literally in the Greek that a Deacon be the kind of man who would be faithful to his wife or a "one woman man", whether he is actually married or not. So Mormon Deacons don't HAVE to be married, they just have to be "morally straight" (and since most of them are Boy Scouts they promise to do that in the Scout Oath every week at their troop meetings). But I digress. Let's get back to the authority thing.

WOMEN NOT ORDAINED TO THE PRIESTHOOD
In recent years some churches have begun ordaining women to their priesthood offices. This is a practice that is clearly prohibited in the Bible as well as in LDS scriptures. It is true that even in the LDS church some women have asked to be ordained, but that is not in God's plan. Nevertheless in our ward and stakes and even at a worldwide level, women hold administrative callings that require far more responsibility than that exercised by women serving in most other churches. But they are not ordained to the priesthood.

HISTORICAL LIMITATIONS ON THE PRIESTHOOD

Some people have criticized our church because men of African descent were not ordained to the priesthood until a revelation was given to the prophet of the church in 1978 permitting the practice. That restriction was never based on skin color, but on lineage. There has been some confusion over the reasons for this historical limitation, and in 2013 the church leaders released a statement clarifying the issue.

However it must be remembered that restrictions on priesthood ordination based on lineage has precedence in the Bible. Among the twelve tribes of Israel only those of the tribe of Levi were given priesthood responsibilities. And until Peter received a direct vision from God, the Gentiles were prohibited not only the priesthood but even membership in the church. I wrote a complete essay on this topic in 1976 that I'll put in the back of this book as an appendix.

PRIESTHOOD AUTHORITY VERSUS POWER OF THE PRIESTHOOD

It is important to remember that while a man may be ordained to the priesthood, the exercise of the authority of God with true priesthood power can only be operated on the principles of righteousness. We are told that:

"the rights of the priesthood are inseparably connected with the powers of heaven, and that the powers of heaven cannot be controlled nor handled only upon the principles of righteousness. That they may be conferred upon us, it is true; but when we undertake to cover our sins, or to gratify our pride, our vain ambition, or to exercise control or dominion or compulsion upon the souls of the children of men, in any degree of unrighteousness, behold, the heavens withdraw themselves; the Spirit of the Lord is grieved; and when it is withdrawn, Amen to the priesthood or the authority of that man. Behold, here he is aware, he is left unto himself, to kick against the pricks, to persecute the saints, and to fight against God.

—D&C 121: 34-38

CONCLUSION

And so we see that even if a church gets all the doctrines and teachings right, without the priesthood it cannot provide the necessary ordinances for salvation and exaltation. Ephesians tells us that the church and kingdom of Christ is based on "a foundation of apostles" who hold the priesthood of God.

Without living apostles and prophets who hold priesthood keys there can be no valid ordinations.

The "good news" that the Latter-day Saints have to share with the world is that now those keys have been restored to the earth.

ENDNOTES TO CHAPTER FIVE

1   *Letter to Dr. Benjamin Waterhouse, in The Writings of Thomas Jefferson V15: Containing His Autobiography, Notes on Virginia, Parliamentary Manual, Official Papers, Messages and Addresses, and Other Writings and Private Letters (Lipscomb and Bergh, Eds., Kessinger Publishing, 2006), 15:288, 391*

2   Doctrine and Covenants, Section 13

3   Leviticus 8:1-12, Numbers 3:5-7

4   *Teachings of Presidents of the Church: Joseph Smith [2007], 104.*

5   "Priesthood Restoration," *Ensign,* Oct. 1988, 71

6   *The Protestant Heritage*, Encyclopedia Britannica, 2007

7   *Weimar Ausgabe*, vol. 6, p. 407, lines 19–25 as quoted in Timothy Wengert, "The Priesthood of All Believers and Other Pious Myths," page 12

Illustration by Allen Richardson

EVIDENCE 6

GOD'S WORD

I believe the Bible to be God's word in its original form when first written. But I don't believe that it's all of God's word to His children. Nor do I believe that any one translation available today is totally free from error. As I read the Chicago Statement on Biblical Inerrancy that is accepted by most Christians, I pretty much agree with most of it. (see below) In other words, I do believe the Bible to be the word of God. You're not going to find me or any other faithful Latter-day Saint attacking the Bible. I love the Bible and I study it deeply and often. I receive great comfort and knowledge from it. But I recognize both what it <u>IS</u> and what it <u>ISN'T</u>, from history and from the Bible itself. It is not God's <u>only</u> word, and not God's <u>uncorrupted</u> word. We're lucky that most of it is pretty reliable as scripture, but we have to be realistic and recognize its limitations as well.

INSIDE LATTER-DAY CHRISTIANITY

As a member of the Church of Jesus Christ of Latter/daySaints, I have read and studied the King James Version of the Bible all my life. From the time I was a young child attending Primary and Sunday School classes in our little Latter-day Saint congregation in Georgia, I learned about Adam and Eve, Noah, Abraham, Moses, Samuel, Samson, David and Goliath, and most importantly about Jesus. I was taught about our Savior's birth in Bethlehem, his ministry throughout the Holy Land, his crucifixion at Calvary, and his glorious resurrection. I learned about Peter and Paul, and all the way to the Revelation of John. But as Paul wrote to Timothy,

"All scripture is given by inspiration of God, and is profitable for doctrine, for reproof, for correction, for instruction in righteousness: That the man of God may be perfect, thoroughly furnished unto all good works."

— (2 Tim. 3:16-17)

And I don't believe that the 66 books of the Protestant canon represent ALL of the scripture that God has given to man.

Our eighth Article of Faith states:

"We believe the Bible to be the Word of God, as far as it is translated correctly. We also believe the Book of Mormon to be the Word of God."

I'll talk more about *The Book of Mormon: Another Testament of Jesus Christ* in the next chapter. For now we'll concentrate on the Bible. In addition to the Bible and the Book of Mormon, we have two other books that are also part of our "Standard Works", or those writings we accept as part of our "canon", and consider equal with the Bible as Scripture. These are called the *Doctrine and Covenants*, and the *Pearl of Great Price*.

How do we get "scripture" or the word of God? Peter wrote:

For the prophecy (scripture) came not in old time by the will of man: but holy men of God spake as they were moved by the Holy Ghost.

— (2 Peter 1:21)

This thought is amplified in our Doctrine and Covenants:

And whatsoever they (God's prophets and apostles) shall speak when moved upon by the Holy Ghost shall be scripture, shall be the will of the Lord, shall be the mind of the Lord, shall be the word of the Lord, shall be the voice of the Lord, and the power of God unto salvation.

— (D & C 68:4)

So in other words, Latter-day Saints agree with the apostle Paul that ALL scripture is profitable, etc, not just the 66 books that Martin Luther decided should be in the Protestant canon. (see below for details) Of course you have to realize that for the New Testament saints, "all scripture" as we think of it was limited to the books of what we now call the Old Testament. (these were the "holy scriptures" that Timothy had known as "a child" - 2 Tim 3:15) But new "scripture" was being spoken and written daily by the apostles. Paul knew this when he wrote to the Corinthians:

"the things that I write unto you are the commandments of the Lord"

—1 Cor. 14:37

Towards the end of his life Joseph Smith was working on a new version of the Bible based on the KJV and revelations he received from God. However he was not able to finish it before he was murdered. Those revisions that he did make were published as the "Joseph Smith Translation" and are often used by Latter-day Saints to clarify certain passages and mis-translations of the Bible.

OUTSIDE LATTER-DAY CHRISTIANITY - CLAIMS THAT MORMONS DO NOT USE THE BIBLE

It's unfortunate that many people are so uninformed about the beliefs and practices of "Mormonism" that they actually believe the misrepresentations of some of our critics who say that we don't use the Bible or that we try to undercut the Bible or to destroy confidence in the Bible. One of these critics writes: (underlining added)

"Janet went on to say that it was a glaring revelation to her as a Mormon, before she was converted to Christ, that she was in the same camp with atheists and all other cults, <u>who did not believe in the sufficiency or accuracy of the Bible"</u>.

—Floyd McElveen, God's Word, Final, Infallible, And Forever, p. 171

But what is the truth? You might be surprised!

WHAT LATTER-DAY CHRISTIANS BELIEVE ABOUT THE BIBLE

Latter-day Saints use the Bible as much as any other Christian faith (or more!). It is one of our four "standard works" and is usually mentioned first in the list of our "canon", followed by the *Book of Mormon*, the *Doctrine and Covenants* and the *Pearl of Great Price*. The church officially uses the King James Version of the Bible and we have published our own edition for many years, with appropriate study guides and footnotes, etc. related to topics of interest to Latter-day Saints.

In September 2010 the Pew Research center released a study showing that Latter-day Saints have a better knowledge of the Bible than any other group of people, including a score ten percent higher than Evangelicals![1]

In 1979 a new English edition of the Bible was printed by our Church with expanded references and a new topical reference guide. On October 15, 1982, the Layman's National Bible Committee presented an award to The Church of Jesus Christ of Latter-day Saints for outstanding service to the Bible cause through the publication of its new edition. A Spanish LDS Bible was published in 2009 that was based mainly on the 1909 edition of the Reina-Valera version.

Here is what the leaders of The Church of Jesus Christ of Latter-day Saints have had to say in support of the Bible as God's word:

"I believe the Bible as it read when it came from the pen of the original writers"[2]

—Joseph Smith

"Take up the Bible, compare the religion of the Latter-day Saints with it and see if it will stand the test,"[3]

—Brigham Young

In the Church's worldwide General Conference in April 2007, one of the Apostles, M. Russell Ballard said:

"It is a miracle that we have the Bible's powerful doctrine, principles, poetry, and stories. But most of all, it is a wonderful miracle that we have the account of the life, ministry, and words of Jesus, which was protected through the Dark Ages and through the conflicts of countless generations so that we may have it today."

He noted that in a recent conference our LDS leaders had quoted from the Bible nearly 200 times. Former Church President Thomas S. Monson said:

"The entire message of the New Testament breathes a spirit of awakening to the human soul."[4]

THE BIBLE IN MORMON STUDY CURRICULUM

The importance of the Bible to Latter-day Saints can be highlighted by the fact that it is studied on equal basis with other scriptures in an eight-year program of adult Sunday School classes. An entire year is devoted to the Old Testament and another year to the New Testament in the eight-year rotation of lessons. A similar period of study of the Bible is given to our high school-aged students in the Church Seminary program.

BIBLE VIDEOS PRODUCED BY LDS CHURCH

In recent years our Church has spent a great deal of funds and effort to create a number of high-quality and historically accurate Bible videos that it has made available to everyone freely on the internet. The quality and value of these videos have been recognized with numerous awards. Links to these videos can be found here:

http://www.lds.org/bible-videos/?lang=eng

The Church also produced several award-winning TV specials celebrating the 400th anniversary of the first printing of the King James Version. These can be seen online here: http://www.youtube.com/watch?v=7JjwhVAPXtc&feature=player_embedded

FREE BIBLES OFFERED TO THE PUBLIC FROM OUR WEBSITES

The LDS Church has also printed and given away hundreds of thousands of free copies of the KJV through its website: www.mormon.org/free-bible

So … do Latter-day Saints respect, read, and study the Bible? What do you think now?

INSIDE CHRISTIANITY
CHRISTIAN ATTITUDES VARY TOWARD THE BIBLE

There's a great deal of variation among various Christian denominations regarding their outlook toward the Bible, ranging from those who will accept only the King James version as "God inspired" to those who have a position similar to Latter-day Saints, to the liberal extreme of those who do not accept the Bible to be literally God's word but only a collection of inspirational writings. It's always puzzled me why many Christians should make it a "litmus test" of one's Christianity to accept the 66 books of the Protestant Bible as a closed canon. According to them, our Heavenly Father slammed shut the windows of heaven with the last writings of the Apostles and their contemporaries and said, "Sorry my children, that's all of my Word you're gonna get. There won't be any more till my Son comes again in glory". But personally I don't buy that.

CATHOLIC BIBLES HAVE ADDITIONAL BOOKS

First of all let's take a look at the Catholic view of scripture, since it's much closer to Latter-day Saint teachings than the Protestant or Evangelical view (and since Catholics make up the largest single body of Christians on the planet).

Like the Latter-day Saints, the Roman Catholic Church places additional scriptures on a par with the 66 books of the Protestant canon. The Roman Catholic Bible currently has seven more books than the current Protestant versions (this is down from 14 additional books in earlier versions). These are called the "Deuterocanonical" ("secondary canon") books or simply the "Aprocypha". (Apocrypha means "hidden things" in Greek.) These books are: Tobit, Judith, 1 and 2 Maccabees, Wisdom of Solomon, Ecclesiasticus (or Sirach), and Baruch. Catholic Bibles also include an additional six chapters in Esther and three chapters in Daniel.

These books were included in many of the early Protestant translations of the Bible as well, including editions of the King James Version from 1611 up until 1885. They were interspersed among other books of the old and new testaments. Martin Luther's first German translation (1534) and the English Cloverdale Bible (1535) segregated the books of the Apocrypha into a separate section. When Martin Luther dropped them entirely from his later editions, subsequent Protestant Bibles followed this practice. But the Roman Catholic Council of Trent, on the other hand, declared in 1546 that the Deuterocanonical books were indeed divine, and many Catholic Bibles still include the Apocrypha today.

We'll talk more later about who "chose and closed" the canon and why. You can read more here: http://wiki.answers.com/Q/Why_does_the_Protestant_Bible_have_66_books_while_the_Catholic_Bible_has_73_books#ixzz1xdk6HhJL

CATHOLICS BELIEVE CHURCH TRADITION IS EQUAL TO SCRIPTURE

Roman Catholic "orthodoxy" also teaches that traditions of their church carry a weight equal to the Bible in determining the beliefs and practices of Catholics:

"Therefore both sacred Tradition and Scripture are to be accepted and venerated with the same devotion and reverence".[5]

Their position (which in my opinion has some validity) is that the church Jesus organized was in existence over a hundred years before the canon of the New Testament was established, therefore Christians were being taught about Christ and being saved long before there was a Bible as we know it.

The first Christians "occupied themselves continually with the apostles' teachings" (Acts 2;42) long before there was a Bible. <u>The fullness of Christian teaching was found, right from the first, in the Church</u> as the living embodiment of Christ, <u>not in a book</u>. The teaching Church, with its oral traditions, was authoritative.
— *Karl Keating,* Catholicism and Fundamentalism, *p. 138*

The Roman Catholic Church defines their Tradition (with a capital "T") as follows:

Tradition means <u>the teachings and teaching authority of Jesus and, derivatively, the apostles</u>.

These have been handed down and entrusted to the Church (which means to its official teachers, the bishops in union with the Pope). It is necessary that Christians believe in and follow this Tradition as well as the Bible.
—Karl Keating, *Catholicism and Fundamentalism*, p. 137

This is in complete <u>opposition</u> to the Protestant belief in the doctrine of *sola scriptura* that was developed by Martin Luther as part of the Reformation of Christianity.

WHAT IS "SOLA SCRIPTURA"?

Sola scriptura (Latin ablative, "by scripture alone") is the doctrine that the Bible contains all knowledge necessary for salvation and holiness. Or as some say, it is "sufficient".

According to Catholic sources, the very earliest mention of the doctrine of *Sola Scriptura* was by Martin Luther as he was questioned in the Synod of Augsburg (Germany) in October 1518. In his appeal to the Council, Luther placed the Bible and his interpretation of it, above the Pope. Even so he admitted the authority of the Synod and of the Bible were equivalent, only in the hope that the Synod would give him a favorable decision. In the Leipzig Disputation in July 1519, Luther went a step further and declared that Scripture ranked above the church councils, and that Ecumenical Councils had already erred in matters of faith. As a result he was branded a heretic.

There seems to be a contradiction here, as Luther was a Catholic Augustinian Monk, and therefore was well aware it was Catholic Church Councils that finalized the canons of both the Old and the New Testaments. Now at Leipzig, he declared that the product of the Councils ranked above the Councils themselves.

Luther was warned by the Church in June 1520, in the Papal Bull *Exsurge Domine*. According to Catholics the Church did everything it could to reconcile with him but he refused, thus setting the stage for his self ex-communication. He was formally ex-communicated on January 3, 1521 through the Papal Bull *Decet Romanum Pontificem*.

Other Reformers have followed Luther in setting the authority of the written words of the Bible above the authority of the church that determined its content. As John Wesley stated in the 18th century (referring to Roman Catholicism):

"In all cases, the Church is to be judged by the Scripture, not the Scripture by the Church."[6]

Modern Catholic writers have argued that without the authority of the Church to interpret what is meant by verses in scripture, the Bible alone is subject to private interpretation and therefore is NOT "sufficient" to provide an infallible guide to correct doctrine and practice:

> Scripture alone, as the tragic history of Protestantism has shown, becomes the private play toy of any self-styled "exegete" who wishes to interpret God's Word to suit his own views. The history of Protestantism, laboring under "sola scriptura", is an unending kaleidoscope of fragmentation and splintering. It cannot provide any sort of doctrinal certitude for the Christian, because it is built on the shifting sand of mere human opinion - what the individual pastor thinks Scripture means.
>
> Even Martin Luther saw the inescapable principle of fragmentation and disunity that lies at the heart of ***sola scriptura***. In a letter to Urlich Zwingli, he complained bitterly about the doctrinal anarchy that was even then rampant among Protestants: "If the world lasts, it will be necessary, on account of the differing interpretations of Scripture which now exist, that to preserve the unity of faith, we should receive the [Catholic] councils and decrees and fly to them for refuge."[7]

Oddly enough, the concerns about "private interpretation" of the Bible mentioned by this Catholic author are echoed in the words of one of the most respected Protestant preachers in America:

"I think we have misinterpreted the Scriptures many times and we've tried to make the Scriptures say things that they weren't meant to say." [8]

—Billy Graham

THE TRANSLATORS OF THE KING JAMES VERSION
ADMITED THAT IT WAS NOT PERFECT

In the original 1611 edition of the King James Version there was a lengthy preface (not included in most modern editions) called "The Translators to the Reader". The 54 translators explained that the KJV was not translated from Greek and Hebrew texts for the most part, but that they relied heavily on previous existing translations, primarily the Geneva Bible and the Bishops Bible. The translators wrote that: "perfection is never attainable by man, but the word of God may be recognized in the very meanest translation of the Bible." They also explained that their numerous changes made from those previous translations do not imply faults in the book, but that "the whole history of Bible translation in any language … is a history of repeated revision and correction." [9]

The respected Bible scholar F.F. Bruce writes in the preface to his book History of the English Bible:

"Traduttore traditore" says an Italian proverb: "The translator is a traitor". An exaggeration certainly; yet an honest translator is bound to confess that something is lost, something is changed, in the course of translation. … but what of those translations where the translators deliberately introduce their own peculiar ideas of religious belief and practice? Must they not be condemned? Indeed they must … Let us remember too that it is usually our unconscious prejudices and preferences that do the most damage.[10]

Between the 1611 and the 1769 editions of the KJV there were over 100,000 changes made.

HOW REFORMED CHRISTIANS VIEW THE "SUFFICIENCY" OF THE BIBLE

The impact of the "sola scriptura" doctrine advanced by Luther and followed by other Reformers can be seen in some of their statements of belief and practice:

"The whole counsel of God, concerning all things necessary for his own glory, man's salvation, faith, and life, is either expressly set down in Scripture, or by good and necessary consequence may be deduced from Scripture: unto which nothing at any time is to be added, whether by new revelations of the Spirit, or traditions of men...
—Westminster Confession of Faith (6) (emphasis added)

Now this "Westminster Confession of Faith" is taken as "gospel" (pun intended) by many faiths as a binding statement of what Christians believe. Yet it rejects the possibility of God giving any more of His Word to man, even by "new revelations of the Spirit". Sounds a bit cocky to me!

Where do they get the authority to limit the workings of the Holy Spirit? Here'what some of the major churches say about it:

METHODIST
The Bible is sacred canon for Christian people, formally acknowledged as such by historic ecumenical councils of the Church. Our doctrinal standards identify as canonical thirty-nine books of the Old Testament and the twenty-seven books of the New Testament. Our standards affirm the Bible as the source of all that is "necessary" and "sufficient" unto salvation (Articles of Religion) and "is to be received through the Holy Spirit as the true rule and guide for faith and practice" (Confession of Faith). ... While we acknowledge the primacy of Scripture in theological reflection, our attempts to grasp its meaning always involve tradition, experience, and reason.[9]

SOUTHERN BAPTIST
The Holy Bible was written by men divinely inspired and is God's revelation of Himself to man. It is a perfect treasure of divine instruction. It has God for its author, salvation for its end, and truth, without any mixture of error, for its matter. Therefore, all Scripture is totally true and trustworthy.

—The Baptist Faith and Message

http://www.sbc.net/bfm/bfm2000.asp

EVANGELICAL LUTHERAN CHURCH IN AMERICA
The canonical Scriptures of the Old and New Testaments are the written Word of God. Inspired by God's Spirit speaking through their authors, they record and announce God's revelation centering in Jesus Christ. Through them God's Spirit speaks to us to create and sustain Christian faith and fellowship for service in the world.

This church accepts the canonical Scriptures of the Old and New Testaments as the inspired Word of God and the authoritative source and norm of its proclamation, faith, and life.

—ELCA Confession of Faith - Constitution of the
Evangelical Lutheran Church in America.

EDGEWOOD BAPTIST

Out of respect to my friend Jerry who was a Deacon at Edgewood Baptist Church in my hometown in Georgia, I'm going to include the statement of belief about the Bible from his church; *We understand this to mean that the whole Bible is inspired in that holy men of God "were moved by the Holy Spirit," (II Peter 1:21) to write the very words of Scripture. We believe that this divine inspiration extends equally and fully to all parts of Scripture* as it appeared **in the original manuscripts**. *We believe* that the whole Bible **in the original** is therefore without error.

— Statement of Beliefs http://edgewoodbaptistchurch.us/jesus

(Actually, this is exactly the Latter-day Saint belief as well, as stated in the 8th LDS Article of Faith. Unfortunately "the whole Bible **in the original**" does not exist.)

HOW WE GOT THE BIBLE - WHY 66 BOOKS?

For many Protestants … (for convenience here I'll use the term "Protestant" to refer to all non-Catholic Christians, although I realize there are some Baptists and others who do not feel that term accurately describes them. Please forgive my laziness but for now let's go with it, okay?)

All right, let's start again: For many English-speaking Protestants the King James Version (KJV) is the most familiar translation of the Bible or the "gold standard", although some use newer versions or even paraphrased editions that make no claim to be "translations" in the traditional sense. Other popular Bibles are the New International Version (NIV), the New American Standard Bible (NASB) the English Standard Version (ESV), the New Living Translation (NLT), etc. The list goes on and on.

The American Bible Society says that there are almost a thousand different translations and paraphrases of the Bible in use today, and that's just in the English language![10] But they all contain the same 66 books (except the Catholic Bibles, as I've already explained). Why?

The first century Christians did not have a "bible" as we know it. They had collections of writings of various apostles and church leaders that would be read and taught in their church meetings. But each local church had its own favorites, and they were not universally the same.

The first known list of books approved for worship (at least approved by that unknown author) is called the "Muratorian Fragment". It was found in the eighth century in the

Ambrosian Library in Milan Italy, copied from a Greek text that apparently dates to about 170 AD. The list was made in response to another group of Christians called "Marcionites" who were using a different set of writings in their worship, to which the Muratorian author objected.

The Muratorian Fragment includes most of the books of the current canon, but it omits Hebrews, 1 and 2 Peter and James, and adds the *Apocalypse of Peter* and the *Shepherd of Hermas*.

The first list of books approved for use in all the Catholic churches was decided by the Council of Florence in 1451. It was similar to the canonical list used today, but not quite identical. It included the Deuterocanonical books of the Apocrypha. The first collection that mirrors our modern Protestant Bible was Luther's German Bible of 1534. On April 24, 1870 the first Vatican council approved the addition of some verses to Mark, Luke and John in Catholic bibles that are not present in early manuscripts but are contained in the Latin Vulgate edition.

WHAT BIBLE MANUSCRIPTS EXIST, AND HOW ACCURATE ARE THEY?

There are over 2500 fragments of manuscripts containing various verses from our modern Bible, with one or two dating to as early as 2nd century. But many of these fragments only contain a verse or two. There are only three main manuscripts of the complete text. They are:

1. **Codex Sinaiticus** (from the 5th century AD or possibly the 4th, found by Konstantin von Tischendorf in a monastery on Mt. Sinai in 1844, now in the British Museum. Its canon contains the *Shepherd of Hermas* and *The Epistle of Barnabas)*

2. **Codex Vaticanus** (4th century, Vatican Library, Rome)

3. **Codex Alexandrinus** (5th or 6th century, British Museum) (Two of these three manuscripts contain books that are not part of the 66 listed in today's canon.) So the earliest manuscript copies that we have date to no earlier than the 4th century. That's up to 300 years removed from the original texts! Is it not conceivable that in 300 years of copying manuscripts there were some errors introduced by the foibles of human scribes and translators? Fredrick C. Grant of Union Theological Seminary thinks so. He writes:

> "of the New Testament writings the period of greatest change and alteration was the 2nd century, but from this century we have only one tiny scrap of papyrus – the Rylands

fragment of John. From the 3rd century we have only the Chester Beatty fragments. ... From the 5th and 6th centuries we have an increasing quantity of manuscripts ... but the greater number of manuscripts does not compensate for the lack of manuscripts from the earliest and most ancient period."

"of the abundant variations and disagreements between manuscripts (John Mill in 1707 estimated them at 30,000) the vast majority are merely errors due to mistaken copying. ... More serious are the **intentional changes** introduced by scribes and before them the owners of the manuscripts who wished to improve or correct their text ... Finally the work of **revisers** who **worked in the interest of some dogmatic view** or other also must be taken into account."

"Contrary to the popular notion that anyone who can read English can interpret the Bible, it is clear that sound judgment in exegesis requires long training and much experience."[11]

Margaret Barker is a respected Methodist Bible scholar. Educated at Cambridge, Barker has authored nine books and has published articles in a variety of academic journals in England and America. She is a recognized expert on temple symbolism and in 1998 served a term as the president-elect of the Society for Old Testament Study.

www.trinity-bris.ac.uk/sots/pastconferences.html

A number of her articles appear at Marquette University's page at

www.marquette.edu/maqom/

Here is what Margaret Barker writes about the reliability or "inerrancy" of the New Testament texts:

Recent work on the transmission of the New Testament has shown convincingly that what is currently regarded as "orthodoxy" was constructed and imposed on the text of the New Testament by later scribes, "clarifying" difficult points and resolving theological problems... It may be that those traditions which have been so confidently marginalized as alien to Christianity on the basis of the present New Testament text, were those very traditions which later authorities and their scribes set out to remove.[12]

Robert Starling

EVEN THE KEY MANUSCRIPTS SHOW SIGNS OF EARLY TAMPERING

Noel B. Reynolds is a professor at Brigham Young University and he has been a visiting professor at Harvard Law School, Edinburgh University and Hebrew University of Jerusalem. He recounted a surprising experience regarding Bible "inerrancy":

> A few years ago I had a personal experience .... I was a guest of the director of the Vatican Library in Rome, and he brought out their fourth century copy of the complete Bible for me to see — Codex Vaticanus B. The first page we looked at had numerous erasures, additions, and changes written right on the page in different inks and different hands!

> I asked, pointing to some of these, "What is that?" The reply: "Oh, that's where they made corrections." Over the last two decades, many New Testament scholars have argued convincingly that the final texts of the gospels and the epistles that were eventually canonized, took shape during a long period in which they were modified as necessary to support the emerging theological orthodoxy among the leaders of the Christian churches. Their principal evidence comes from scriptural quotations in second century documents which are different and which would not have supported the theological orthodoxy that emerged later.[13]

MOST CHRISTIANS UNDERSTAND LIMITATIONS ON THE BIBLE - IS ALL OF THE BIBLE "TRANSLATED CORRECTLY"?

So we see that except for a few die-hard fanatics, most Christians, even among the Protestants and Evangelicals, accept that there have been errors in the transmission and the translation of the Bible from one language to another. In fact, most will take the position identical to that of the Latter-day Saints — they would be indeed "verbally inspired" or God's infallible word IF we had the original autographs written by the original authors. The "Chicago Statement on Biblical Inerrancy" correctly notes:

> Since God has nowhere promised an inerrant transmission of Scripture, it is necessary to affirm that only the autographic text of the original documents was inspired and to maintain the need of textual criticism as a means of detecting any slips that may have crept into the text in the course of its transmission. The verdict of this science, however, is that the Hebrew and Greek text appears to be amazingly well preserved, so that we are amply justified in affirming...a singular providence of God in this matter and in declaring that the authority of Scripture is in no way jeopardized by the fact that the copies we possess are not entirely error-free...Similarly, no translation is or can be perfect, and all translations are an additional step away from the autographa.[14]

So let's see … many pastors and teachers say that Latter-day Saints are not "Christians" because we accept the Bible as the word of God only "as far as it is translated correctly", and yet most of them believe the same thing. How logical is that?

WHAT ABOUT ADDING TO THE BIBLE?

Another reason many folks want to keep the Mormons out of their Christian "club" is that we believe God has given us other scripture outside of those famous 66 books that were first published in that format by Luther in 1534 and in the English Cloverdale Bible the following year. (What about all the Christians before that time?) I've already shown that if you follow that logic you'd also have to deny Catholics that "Christian" status as well, thus eliminating the largest Christian faith group on earth.

The single Bible verse these folks rely on to say there can be no additional scripture is Revelations 2:18:

"For I testify unto every man that heareth the words of the prophecy of this book, If any man shall add unto these things God shall add unto him the plagues that are written in this book."

Because the Book of the Revelation of St. John is the last book in most modern Bibles, then many suppose it means that there can be no more of God's word added to the Bible. The problem is, there are several things wrong with their position and their interpretation:

1. At the time John wrote this verse there was no "Bible" per se. The 66 books had not been decided on nor collected into one volume. Therefore his curse of "plagues" can only apply to "any man" adding to "this book", which is his Revelation only. If one were to use the misguided logic of the critics of Mormonism regarding this verse, then they would have to throw out all of the Bible following Deuteronomy which says:

Ye shall not add unto the word which I command you, neither shall ye diminish ought from it, that ye may keep the commandments of the Lord your God which I command you. (4:2)

And What thing soever I command you, observe to do it: thou shalt not add thereto, nor diminish from it. (12:32)

2. John did not say that God himself could not add to His word at some later time, only that "any man" could not add unauthorized text to his Revelation. In fact, John wrote his

own Gospel AFTER he wrote the Revelation, and several other New Testament books were written after that time.

THE JOHANNINE COMMA – ADDED TO THE BIBLE

It's somewhat hypocritical to claim that Latter-day Saints can't be Christians because they've added to Scripture when the King James Version itself contains additions added by Christian theologians.

Perhaps the most glaring example is the so-called "Johannine Coma" in 1 John 5:7-8.

For there are three that bear record in heaven, the Father, the Word, and the Holy Ghost: and these three are one. And there are three that bear witness in earth, the Spirit, and the water, and the blood: and these three agree in one.

These emphasized words above are generally absent from the Greek manuscripts. In fact, they only appear in the text of four late medieval manuscripts. They seem to have originated as a marginal note added to certain Latin manuscripts during the Middle Ages, which was eventually incorporated into the text of most of the later Vulgate manuscripts. … From the Vulgate, then, it seems that the Comma was translated into Greek and inserted into some printed editions of the Greek text, and in a handful of late Greek manuscripts.

All serious scholars consider it to be spurious, and it is not included in modern critical editions of the Greek text, or in the English versions based upon them. It was mistakenly added to the KJV.

—See Bruce Metzger, The Text of the New Testament, pp. 101 f.

IS THE CURRENT PROTESTANT CANON ALL OF GOD'S WORD?
WHAT ABOUT THE MISSING BOOKS FROM THE BIBLE?

When the early Christians started gathering together the Apostles' writings and formulating the canon of scripture, were there books that had been lost? Would some of those writings have blessed our knowledge of Jesus and his teachings?

John wrote: (emphasis mine)

"Many other signs also Jesus worked in the sight of His disciples, WHICH ARE NOT WRITTEN IN THIS BOOK. But these are written that you may believe that Jesus is the Christ, the Son of GOD, and that believing you may have life in His Name."

—John 20:30-31

and also:

"There are, however, many other things that Jesus did; but if every one of these should be written, NOT EVEN THE WORLD ITSELF, I THINK, COULD HOLD THE BOOKS THAT WOULD HAVE TO BE WRITTEN."

—John 21:25

Obviously Holy Scripture itself has said very clearly, that everything is NOT in the Bible. Yet who can deny that our lives would not be blessed by having more? For example, Paul writes in 1st Corinthians 5:9 that he had written a <u>previous</u> letter to those Saints. What happened to that letter, and wouldn't it be wonderful to have that counsel and those teachings as well as the two letters that are in the canon? I wonder, if that letter were to be discovered today as the Dead Sea Scrolls were discovered in 1947, would we accept it into the New Testament? Why not?

My friends John Tvetdnes and Matt Roper have listed several other books that are mentioned in Scripture but are missing from the Bible as we now have it:

BOOKS MENTIONED IN THE BIBLE THAT ARE NOT IN THE CURRENT CANON
the Book of the Covenant (Exodus 24:7; cf. Exodus 32:15 19, 32 33),
the Book of the Wars of the Lord (Numbers 21:14),
the Book of Jasher (Joshua 10:13; 2 Samuel 1:18),
the Manner of the Kingdom, written by Samuel (1 Samuel 10:25),
the Book of the Acts of Solomon (1 Kings 11:41; cf. 1 Kings 4:32 33?),
the Book of Samuel the Seer (1 Chronicles 29:29),
the Book of Gad the Seer (1 Chronicles 29:29),
the Book of Nathan the Prophet (1 Chronicles 29:29; 2 Chronicles 9:29),
the Prophecy of Ahijah (2 Chronicles 9:29),
the Visions of Iddo the Seer (2 Chronicles 9:29; 12:15; 13:22),
the Book of Shemaiah the Prophet (2 Chronicles 12:15),
the Acts of Abijah . . . in the Story of the Prophet Iddo (2 Chronicles 13:22),

the Book of Jehu (2 Chronicles 20:34),

the Acts of Uzziah written by Isaiah the Prophet (2 Chronicles 26:22),

the Sayings/Words of the Seers (2 Chronicles 33:18 19).

If these books were to be discovered, would they be added to the Christian canon or rejected?

IN "TRADITIONAL" OR "ORTHODOX" CHRISTIANITY, READING THE BIBLE WAS BANNED FOR CENTURIES – WHY?

Can you imagine a church in which you could be killed for reading or even owning a Bible? One might believe such a case if you were living in a Communist or some other totalitarian dictatorship, but for many centuries, that was the position of "traditional" or "orthodox" Christianity. In Medieval Europe few people excepting the clerics and nobles could read anyway, but having or reading the Bible was punishable by death unless you were a church official. The reformers believed it was because the Catholic Church wanted to keep people ignorant of what the Gospel really taught, so they would not see how far the clerics had drifted from Biblical principles. Perhaps they were correct. Valiant men like John Wycliffe, and William Tyndale were burned at the stake for the "crime" of translating the Bible into English for the common man to read. Tyndale said to one cleric:

"I defy the Pope and all his laws. If God spares my life, before many years pass I will make it possible for the boy who drives the plough to know more of the Scriptures than you do." [15]

Through the grace of God we now have easy access to the Bible in many languages.

WHAT DO THE BIBLE AND THE BOOK OF MORMON SAY ABOUT EACH OTHER?

The Bible actually mentions the Book of Mormon and its people, though not by name.

Genesis 49 speaks of a branch of the tribe of Joseph that would "go over a wall", or in other words to a far place.

"Joseph is a fruitful bough, even a fruitful bough by a well; whose branches run over the wall:"

—Genesis 49:22

In Ezekiel 37 we read about the coming forth of the Book of Mormon and how it will be used alongside the Bible as a second witness of Christ:

The word of the Lord came again unto me, saying, Moreover, thou son of man, <u>take thee one stick, and write upon it, For Judah,</u> and for the children of Israel his companions: then <u>take another stick, and write upon it, For Joseph</u> the stick of Ephraim, and for all the house of Israel his companions: And join them one to another into one stick; and <u>they shall become one in thine hand.</u>

—*Ezekiel 37:15-17*

The Bible is the "stick of Judah" and the Book of Mormon is the "stick of Joseph".

In like manner Jesus also spoke of the people he was going to visit after his resurrection – a visit that was recorded in the Book of Mormon. He said:

<u>And other sheep I have, which are not of this fold: them also I must bring, and they shall hear my voice;</u> and there shall be one fold, and one shepherd.

—*John 10:16*

Some believe Jesus was speaking of the Gentiles as his "other sheep". But when he visited the "branch" of the tribe of Joseph that was living in the Americas, he said:

And verily I say unto you, that ye are they of whom I said: <u>Other sheep I have which are not of this fold</u>; them also I must bring, <u>and they shall hear my voice</u>; and there shall be one fold, and one shepherd.

And they understood me not, for <u>they supposed it had been the Gentiles</u>; for they understood not that <u>the Gentiles should be converted through their preaching</u>.

And they understood me not that I said they shall hear my voice; and they understood me not that <u>the Gentiles should not at any time hear my voice</u> - that I should not manifest myself unto them save it were by the Holy Ghost.

—*3 Nephi 15:21-23*

The prophet Nephi foresaw that many would reject additional scripture when the Book of Mormon came forth in 1830. He wrote accurately many centuries ago:

... and my words (in the Book of Mormon) shall hiss forth unto the ends of the earth, for a standard unto my people, which are of the house of Israel;

141

And because my words shall hiss forth—many of the Gentiles shall say: A Bible! A Bible! We have got a Bible, and there cannot be any more Bible.

But thus saith the Lord God: O fools, they shall have a Bible; and it shall proceed forth from the Jews, mine ancient covenant people. And what thank they the Jews for the Bible which they receive from them?

— 2 Nephi 29:2-4

WHY DOES A CLOSED CANON PERSIST?

Does the principle of continued revelation from God embarrass those who don't receive it themselves? To whom should new revelation come? Is it binding on other Christians? Are these questions too sticky for both Catholics and Protestants who don't want to have to deal with them? Is it easier to just say dogmatically that the Heavens are closed?

Our 9th Article of Faith is a more open and reasonable approach:

"We believe all that God has revealed, all that He does now reveal, and we believe that He will yet reveal many great and important things pertaining to the Kingdom of Heaven."

But we'll get into that more in another chapter. For now, have I convinced you that Latter-day Saints believe in the Bible? I hope so, because it is true.

ENDNOTES TO CHAPTER 6

1   *Who Knows What About Religion* September 28, 2010, The Pew Forum on Religion and Public Life http://www.pewforum.org/U-S-Religious-Knowledge-Survey-Who-Knows-What-About-Religion.aspx#Bible

2   *Teachings of the Prophet Joseph Smith, sel. Joseph Fielding Smith* [1976], 327

3   Brigham Young, May 18, 1873, *Journal of Discourses*, vol. 16, p. 46

4   "The Spirit Giveth Life," *Ensign*, June 1997, 2

5   *Vatican II, Dei Verbum, 9*

6   *The Works of the Rev. John Wesley, vol. XV, p. 180, London (1812)*

7   *Patrick Madrid, Sola scriptura: A Blueprint for Anarchy, Mar-Apr.* 1996 issue of "Catholic Dossier"

8   David Frost, "Doubts and Certainties: David Frost Interview (BBC-2, 1964)," in *Billy Graham: Personal Thoughts of a Public Man – 30 Years of Conversations with David Frost* (ColoradoSprings: Chariot Victor, 1997), 73-74.

9   F.F. Bruce, History of the Bible in English, The Lutterworth Press, Cambridge, England, 1961, p. 101

10   ibid, p. ix

11   *From The Book of Discipline of The United Methodist Church - 2008. Copyright 2008 by The United Methodist Publishing House. (emphasis added)*

12   http://news.americanbible.org/article/number-of-english-translations-of-the-bible

13   Fredrick C. Grant, Union Theological Seminary, *Bible 12: The Text of the New Testament, p. 699*

14   Barker, "The Secret Tradition," *Journal of Higher Criticism* 2/1 (1995): 50. She is citing Bart D. *Ehrman, The Orthodox Corruption of Scripture: The Effect of Early Christological Controversies on the Text of the New Testament (New York: Oxford University Press,1993).*

15   Noel B. Reynolds – BYU-Idaho Devotional June 15, 2004

16   Chicago Statement on Biblical Inerrancy, 1978, ICBI, *Exposition* 17 As quoted in the *Foxe's Book of Martyrs* by John Foxe

EVIDENCE 7

THE BOOK OF MORMON

I told the brethren that the Book of Mormon was ... the keystone of our religion. — Joseph Smith

I believe there is sufficient evidence (and more!) to consider *The Book of Mormon* to be the word of God. I believe that it is an authentic record of ancient peoples who were led by the hand of God to journey from the Old World to the western hemisphere and establish great civilizations in the Americas.

I know, I know, there are lots of folks who say *The Book of Mormon* is a wild folk tale written by Joseph Smith. Why would a reasonably intelligent person such as myself (ahem!) give any credence to what some critics have called "youthful gibberish"?

Well if you'll have a bit of patience with me, I'll show you my "strong reasons" why I believe. And if you knew even half of what I know, perhaps you might believe, too.

You see, in the many years since I first felt the witness of the Holy Spirit telling me in my heart and soul that *The Book of Mormon* was true I've been blessed to study and learn about a wide variety of external evidences supporting the historical validity of that book. I've served on the board of directors of two different organizations dedicated to the scholarly study of ancient America (one "Mormon" and one non-Mormon). I've been honored to associate with and come to know on a first-name basis dozens of top scholars and researchers in the field, both Latter-day Saints and non-LDS. In 2005 I spent some time in Guatemala studying ancient ruins and learning how they related to the historical claims of *The Book of Mormon.* It's been a fascinating ride!

My visit to Tikal, Guatemala 2005

But enough about me. Let's talk about the book itself.

WHERE DID THE BOOK OF MORMON COME FROM?

You see, here's the deal. The book exists. It has over 250,000 words, 531 pages (in the English version), 239 chapters, and claims to have over 21 authors, all prophets of God who lived in ancient America from 2200 BC to 400 AD. Its existence has got to be explained somehow. You can't just ignore it and hope it will go away. Any thoughtful and reasonable person has to decide either to (a) accept the story that comes with it as to its origin, or (b) to come up with a more plausible explanation of how it came to be. So what are the possibilities? Either:

1. It is what Joseph Smith claimed it to be: a record written by ancient prophets in America that he translated from metal plates "by the gift and power of God".
    or

2. Joseph Smith wrote it out of his fertile imagination, possibly plagiarizing parts of it from the Bible, from Ethan Smith's *"View of the Hebrews"*, or Solomon Spaulding's *"Manuscript Lost"*.
    or

3. Someone else wrote it and for some reason allowed Joseph Smith to take the credit for it. Some have accused his friend Sidney Rigdon of being the real author. (Although he did not meet Joseph until AFTER the publication of the book!)
    or

4. Joseph wrote it under the influence of some Satanic spirit that dictated it to him.
    or

5. It dropped out of the sky from a UFO (in the handwriting of Joseph Smith's scribes) and Joseph did a Spock-type "mind meld" to convince everyone around him to go along with his deception. (Okay, I'm having some fun what this last alternative, but …)

Actually he would have had to fool a lot of folks that were close to him. This would include his wife Emma and several other people who acted as scribes while he dictated the translation.

INSIDE LATTER-DAY CHRISTIANITY

Okay, where do Latter-day Saints say the book came from?

The Book of Mormon was written on various thin metal plates by numerous prophet-scribes in ancient America over a period of time from approximately 2200 BC to 400 AD. Toward the end of that period a prophet named Mormon consolidated the records into an abridgement that he wrote on a new set of golden-colored metal plates. His son Moroni added a few of his own words before burying the plates in a stone box in what is now upstate New York, to be preserved for future generations. In September of 1823 this same Moroni appeared to Joseph Smith as a resurrected person or "angel" and led him to the location of the records on a hillside near his home in Palmyra, New York.

After a period of time Joseph was allowed to take the plates from their hiding place and translate a portion of them into English. The translation took less than 90 working days, often interrupted by persecutions from people hostile to Joseph. Part of the translation was accomplished using a device that had been buried with the plates called in the Bible the Urim and Thumim (Ex. 28:30; Levi 8:8.). This device consisted of a breastplate and a pair of lenses similar to modern eyeglasses. But it operated by spiritual principles, not on a mechanical basis. Another part of the record was translated using a "seer stone", which operated on the same spiritual principles. It seems to be related to the "white stone" with writing on it mentioned in Rev. 2:17 that will be given to each person who "overcomes" the world. After the translation the angel took the plates from Joseph, and their location at present is unknown.

In 1830 *The Book of Mormon* was first published by the Grandin Press in Palmyra, New York. Since that time it has been printed in many editions worldwide in more than 107 languages. *The Book of Mormon* is in the top five of the most-printed books in the world, with over 150 million copies in distribution. In 1982 its title was amended to read "*The Book of Mormon: Another Testament of Jesus Christ*". It is the foundational religious text of the fourth largest Christian church in America.

All this sounds kinda weird, right? I realize that the story of the origin of The Book of Mormon seems a bit "far out" to someone who is not familiar with it. The appearance of angels, records written on metal plates buried in stone boxes, translation of languages using ancient spectacles —it all seems preposterous to the modern mindset. But I bear you my humble witness and testimony that all of it is absolutely true, and I'm joined by over 16 million others, many of whom are among the most enlightened and intelligent folks on the planet.

I'll bet you're asking yourself, "how can that be"? Well, in this chapter I will "bring forth my strong reasons" (Isa. 41:21) for this "hope that is in me" (1 Pet. 3:15), and by the end of it I'll show how <u>you</u> can also know if it is true or not. Does that sound fair?

The acceptance of The Book of Mormon as ancient scripture and the word of God is a fundamental part of Mormonism. You can't really be a faithful Latter-day Saint and not believe that, although there are some folks who are born in the faith and have their doubts just like people in any religion have doubts.

Our eighth Article of Faith states:

"We believe the Bible to be the Word of God, as far as it is translated correctly. We also believe the Book of Mormon to be the Word of God." Latter-day Saints believe that The Book of Mormon: Another Testament of Jesus Christ is <u>scripture</u> just like the Holy Bible and the other two volumes of what we call our "standard works", The Doctrine and Covenants and The Pearl of Great Price.

And as Paul wrote to Timothy, *"<u>All</u> scripture is given by inspiration of God, and is profitable for doctrine, for reproof, for correction, for instruction in righteousness: That the man of God may be perfect, thoroughly furnished unto all good works."* (2 Tim. 3:16-17) We believe that includes *The Book of Mormon.*

That does not mean Latter-day Saints believe *The Book of Mormon* is perfect or without any error (just as our modern Bible is not without any error), although some critics of our faith try to hold it to that standard. And in the non-English versions we would have to apply the same caveat to it as we do to the Bible. It is considered the word of God "as far as it is translated correctly". Even in the various English editions there have been numerous corrections of spelling, grammar, typesetting errors, etc. It is similar to the Bible in that regard. Do you remember what I said in the last chapter? Between the 1611 first edition of the King James Version and 1769, there were over 100,000 changes in that translation of the Bible.

But it <u>is</u> "profitable for doctrine" and the other good uses that Paul attributes to "all scripture" in the verse above. Joseph Smith described it thusly:

*I told the brethren that the Book of Mormon was the <u>most correct</u> of any book on earth, **<u>and the keystone of our religion,</u>** and a man would get nearer to God by abiding by its precepts, than by any other book.*

—History of the Church, November 28, 1841.

He wasn't describing it as "most correct" in a literary or grammatical sense, but rather that its doctrine and teachings were correct, and that it contains God's word in the most pristine or unfiltered state of any other book. Brigham Young elaborated on the process of receiving God's word in this way:

When God speaks to the people, he does it in a manner to suit their circumstances and capacities.... Should the Lord Almighty send an angel to re-write the Bible, it would in many places be very different from what it now is. And I will even venture to say that if the Book of Mormon were now to be re-written, in many instances it would materially differ from the present translation. According as people are willing to receive the things of God, so the heavens send forth their blessings.[1]

I love *The Book of Mormon*. It has given me comfort and a great knowledge of God and his plan for me, and it has helped me to understand many of the "plain and precious truths" that were taken out of the Bible over the centuries. It fills in many of the gaps in the writings of Paul that Peter said were "hard to be understood". (2 Pet. 3:16) It also explains many of the mysteries of the history of ancient America that have baffled historians, archaeologists and anthropologists for centuries.

HOW CAN ONE KNOW IF *The Book of Mormon* IS REALLY TRUE?

There are many external evidences to the historicity of *The Book of Mormon* which I'll get to later on, but the most fundamental method of knowing the truth about it comes in part from the Bible, and partly from the book itself.

for the Spirit searcheth all things, yea, the deep things of God. For what man knoweth the things of a man, save the spirit of man which is in him? <u>*even so the things of God knoweth no man, but the Spirit of God.*</u> *... that we might know the things that are freely given to us of God, ... not in the words which man's wisdom teacheth, but* <u>*which the Holy Ghost teacheth;*</u> *comparing spiritual things with spiritual.*

—1 Corinthians 2:10-12

The Holy Ghost has taught me that the Book of Mormon is the historical document that it claims to be, and that it is God's word and "another testament of Jesus Christ". The apostle James wrote that if we lack wisdom about something we should ask God, who gives answers "liberally" if we will only ask in faith.

"If any of you lack wisdom, <u>let him ask of God</u>, that giveth to all men liberally, and upbraideth not; <u>and it shall be given him</u>. But let him ask in faith, nothing wavering".

—James 1:5-6

Similarly, in Moroni's closing words he said:

"And when ye shall receive these things, I would exhort you that ye would ask God, the Eternal Father, in the name of Christ, if these things are not true; and if ye shall ask with a sincere heart, with real intent, having faith in Christ, he will manifest the truth of it unto you, by the power of the Holy Ghost."

—Moroni 10:4-5

What better evidence can you have than the witness of the Holy Spirit himself to let you know that *The Book of Mormon* is true? But I realize that for skeptics that's a pretty large leap of faith, so later on I'll give you some evidence that can help you shrink down the length of that jump, okay?

OUTSIDE LATTER-DAY CHRISTIANITY

The *Book of Mormon* has many critics outside The Church of Jesus Christ of Latter-day Saints.

Unfortunately most of them have never read the book themselves, although some have. In the spirit of full disclosure, here are some of their opinions:

Mark Twain wrote this in *"Roughing It – A Personal Narrative"* as he tried to figure out the Mormons during his two-day visit to Great Salt Lake City on his way to silver mines of Nevada: *All men have heard of the Mormon Bible, but few, except the elect have seen it or at least taken the trouble to read it. I brought away a copy from Salt Lake. The book is a curiosity to me. It is such a pretentious affair and yet so slow, so sleepy, such an insipid mess of inspiration. <u>It is chloroform in print.</u> ... "And it came to pass," was his (Joseph Smith's) pet (phrase). If he had left that out, his bible would have been only a pamphlet.*

More recent critics have also shared their thoughts on the book:

It is difficult to believe that, after having seen the evidence, any honest person could accept the Book of Mormon as being inspired by God. There are simply too many things wrong with it. The evidence of mistakes, error, and fraud is so obvious that it stands as a barrier to any acceptance of this book.[2]

Not only does the Book of Mormon plagiarize heavily from the King James Bible, but it betrays a great lack of information and background on the subject of world history and the history of the Jewish people. ... Joseph Smith was a poor student of history and of Hebrew customs.[3]

Your recent inquiry concerning the Smithsonian Institution's alleged use of the Book of Mormon as a scientific guide has been received in the Office of Communications. The Book of Mormon is a religious document and not a scientific guide, The Smithsonian Institution has never used it in archeological research and any information that you have received to the contrary is incorrect.[4]

WAS MARK TWAIN RIGHT ABOUT THE BOOK OF MORMON?

As I quoted above, Mark Twain wrote that the Book of Mormon to him was so dull that it was "chloroform in print". But some modern readers and scholars respectfully disagree with Twain about his "chloroform" statement, giving *The Book of Mormon* more credence as a literary document. Daniel Walker, who won a Pulitzer Prize in History, wrote:

> **True or not, the Book of Mormon is a powerful epic written on a grand scale** with a host of characters, a narrative of human struggle and conflict, of divine intervention, heroic good and atrocious evil, of prophecy, morality and law. **Its narrative structure is complex...** the dominant themes are Biblical, prophetic, and patriarchal, not democratic or optimistic. It tells a tragic story of a people who, though possessed of the true faith, fail in the end. Yet it does not convey a message of despair, God's will cannot ultimately be frustrated. **The Book of Mormon should rank among the great achievements of American literature,** but **it has never been accorded the status it deserves**, since Mormons deny Joseph Smith's authorship, and non-Mormons, dismissing the work as a fraud, have been more likely to ridicule than read it.[5]

COULD JOSEPH SMITH HAVE WRITTEN *THE BOOK OF MORMON?*

Even if Joseph Smith had been the world's greatest author and scholar on geography and ancient American history and archaeology etc. he could not have written *The Book of Mormon* based on his own knowledge, as I'll explain later. But in fact he was an unlearned young frontier farmer with only about a third grade education. His own wife Emma said:

Robert Starling

"Joseph Smith could neither write nor dictate a coherent and well-worded letter; let alone dictating a book like the Book of Mormon."[6]

COULD SIDNEY RIGDON OR ANYONE ELSE HAVE WRITTEN IT?

Although Sidney Rigdon, Oliver Cowdery and a few of Joseph Smith's other close associates had more education and writing ability than Joseph did, could they (and would they?) have written it either singly or together and then given the credit to Joseph?

Most of them left the church and became disaffected with Joseph at some point and would have had good reason to "blow the whistle" on him if that were the case. But such a thing never happened. Sidney Rigdon never even met Joseph Smith until after *The Book of Mormon* was published. Oliver Cowdery wrote:

"I wrote, with my own pen, the entire Book of Mormon (save a few pages), as it fell from the lips of the Prophet Joseph Smith, as he translated it by the gift and power of God... Sidney Rigdon did not write it. Mr. Spaulding did not write it. I wrote it myself, as it fell from the lips of the Prophet."[7]

DID JOSEPH PLAGIARIZE THE WORKS OF OTHER AUTHORS?

A number of critics of *The Book of Mormon* have claimed that Joseph Smith wrote it by plagiarizing either Solomon Spaulding's unpublished manuscript about ancient America or Ethan Smith's *View of the Hebrews*, or *The Great War*, all of which had some superficial similarities to the story of Lehi and his family's voyage to America from Jerusalem.

For several decades the Spaulding manuscript was lost and unavailable for comparison. Unfortunately for the critics, it was discovered in Hawaii in 1884. It only takes a cursory examination of either of these candidate texts and a comparison with *The Book of Mormon* to quickly see that these theories as to the origin of *The Book of Mormon* are groundless, to say the least. If you really want to check out the plagiarism option in detail check here:

http://www.fairlds.org/authors/misc/ask-the-apologist-solomon-spaulding-and-the-book-of-mormon

Here are some other resources on this topic:

Spencer J. Palmer and William L. Knecht, "View of the Hebrews: Substitute for Inspiration?" *BYU Studies* 5 (Winter 1964), pp. 105-13;

Hugh Nibley, "The Comparative Method," *Improvement Era*, Oct. 1959, pp. 744-59 and Nov. 1959, pp. 848, 854, 856;

Hugh Nibley, *No Ma'am That's Not History* (Salt Lake City: Bookcraft, 1946); and Bruce Blumell, *Ensign*, Sept. 1976, pp. 84-87, (each available as reprints).

See also Ariel L. Crowley, "Analysis of Ethan Smith's 'View of the Hebrews': A Comparison with the Book of Mormon," in *About the Book of Mormon* (Salt Lake City: Deseret News Press, 1961); William Riley, "A Comparison of Passages from Isaiah and Other Old Testament Prophets in Ethan Smith's *View of the Hebrews* and the Book of Mormon," - Master's thesis, Brigham Young University, 1971.

As you can see, Latter-day Saint scholars have not ignored claims of the critics but instead have thoroughly researched and refuted them.

DID JOSEPH SMITH PLAGIARIZE THE BIBLE?

There are those who say that much of *The Book of Mormon* simply copies the King James Version of the Bible. It's true that the 2nd Book of Nephi quotes long passages from Isaiah. Nephi loved Isaiah and quoted extensively from that prophet's writings. Joseph Smith was familiar with the KJV and when Nephi's quotes were essentially the same as the words of Isaiah the KJV he translated using the text he was familiar with. However it is important to note that variants in *The Book of Mormon* version often agree with the scholarship of more recent –and more accurate- Isaiah translations.

The same thing occurs in 3rd Nephi verses that describe the words of Christ to his disciples in the Americas. Jesus intentionally repeated the Sermon on the Mount to his "other sheep" that lived in the New World, so in Joseph Smith's translation of the record he used the familiar wording of the KJV. If he were the charlatan that critics try to make him out to be, and if he was as devious as many claim him to be, don't you think he would have tried to disguise his "plagiarism" more than he did? I would have, wouldn't you?

CAN ANY OF TODAY'S BRIGHTEST MINDS DUPLICATE THE FEAT OF WRITING *THE BOOK OF MORMON*?

Dr. Hugh Nibley was widely acknowledged by Latter-day Saints and non-Mormons alike as one of the brightest minds of our day. Nibley began his studies at University of California, Los Angeles, graduating *summa cum laude*, and earned a doctorate as a University Fellow at the University of California, Berkeley in 1938. Before his death in 2005 he was a professor of

Ancient Scriptures at Brigham Young University for almost fifty years. Nibley could read, write or speak 16 languages, and he published articles in numerous peer-reviewed journals and authored several scholarly books.

At BYU Dr. Nibley would regularly challenge his university students, as described by Alan Miner:

> Since Joseph Smith was younger than most of you and not nearly so experienced or well educated at the time he copyrighted the Book of Mormon, it should not be too much to ask you to hand in by the end of the semester (which will give you more time than he had) a paper of, say, five to six hundred pages in length. Call it a sacred book if you will, and give it the form of a history. Tell of a community of wandering Jews in ancient times; have all sorts of characters in your story, and involve them in all sorts of public and private vicissitudes [daily activities]; give them names — hundreds of them — pretending that they are real Hebrew and Egyptian names of circa 600 B.C.; be lavish with cultural and technical details — manners and customs, arts and industries, political and religious institutions, rites, and traditions, include long and complicated military and economic histories; have your narrative cover a thousand years.
>
> Keep a number of interrelated local histories going at once; feel free to introduce religious controversy and philosophical discussion, but always in a plausible setting; observe the appropriate literary conventions and explain the derivation and transmission of your varied historical materials.
>
> Above all, do not ever contradict yourself! For now we come to the really hard part of this little assignment. You and I know that you are making this all up — we have our little joke — but just the same you are going to be required to have your paper published when you finish it, not as fiction or romance, but as a true history! After you have handed it in you may make no changes in it. ...
>
> What is more, you are to invite any and all scholars to read and criticize your work freely, explaining to them that it is a sacred book on a par with the Bible. If they seem over-skeptical, you might tell them that you translated the book from original records by the aid of the Urim and Thummim — they will love that! Further to allay their misgivings, you might tell them that the original manuscript was on golden plates, and that you got the plates from an angel. Now go to work and good luck![8]

Then Alan Miner added his own additional challenge to Dr. Nibley's:

> To this I would like to add an additional challenge, though it shouldn't be hard, living as we do in the computer world of the Internet:

Because your story is supposed to be a religious record, include in your paper over 500 different descriptive titles for deity, all within a proper religious context that will not only explain these titles in relation to what we have in the Bible, but give added meaning and understanding. Because this is supposedly an ancient Hebrew record, <u>give numerous and multiple examples of ancient parallelistic Hebrew literary forms. Have whole pages, even chapters and larger sections written in parallelistic patterns.</u> Weave in an underlying theme of covenants with the Lord, both culturally and scripturally. In fact, it would be a good idea to make every part of your narrative not only covenant-related, but Christ-related as well.

For one final challenge - <u>you must dictate your story to a scribe without the aid of a written script.</u> While you may be allowed to tell your scribe to adjust the spelling of proper names, you must leave your script as you dictate it, and <u>never ask your scribe to tell you where you left off after lunch or the end of a day.</u> On his own, your scribe can adjust capitalization, punctuation, the spelling of traditional words, and some simple grammar, but that is all. Dictate parts of your story in non-chronological order, <u>and be sure to credit these parts of your story to different writers, varying your manner of using words so that a distinct separation of language style can be detected.</u>[9]

So what do you think? Could you do it? Think of the smartest person you know. Could he or she do it? I had the highest SAT scores in my high school and I attended five years of college on academic scholarships. I can't even come close to doing it. *The Book of Mormon* meets every one of these challenges, and more.

And ...

During the actual 75 days or so that Joseph Smith spent in translation he did not have the luxury of a calm writing environment. His world was in constant mental and emotional turmoil because of the persecutions that were being heaped upon him.

So as Dr. Nibley told his college students, "Good Luck!"

IS THERE ANY SCIENTIFIC, HISTORICAL OR ARCHAEOLOGICAL EVIDENCE TO SUPPORT THE CLAIMS OF THE BOOK OF MORMON?

Before we can answer this question, we have to determine just what ARE the historical and cultural claims of *The Book of Mormon*. In a nutshell they are:

1. There were three migrations of peoples from the Middle East to the Americas by boat, at approximately 2200 BC, 600 BC, and 585 BC.

2. The first migration was led by two brothers. One was named Jared, so *The Book of Mormon* called his group "Jaredites". They lived at the time of the Tower of Babel in ancient Sumaria (present-day Iraq) when the Bible says God confounded the languages of people who were trying to build a tower to heaven.

3. The Jaredites brought to the New World various animals, seeds, honeybees, etc. in their eight "barges" – boats built similar to the ark of Noah. These boats had no windows and were sealed "tight like a dish" so that they could travel through heavy seas and survive being completely submerged at times. They had ports that could be opened for fresh air when necessary.

4. The Jaredites traveled to the Americas around 2200 BC and established a colony and a civilization that lasted about 1600 years before they destroyed themselves in a civil war.

5. The second migration consisted primarily of two families who fled Jerusalem about 600 BC shortly before it was destroyed by the Babylonians. A prophet named Lehi led them through the desert south and east through the Arabian "empty quarter" until they came to a secluded oasis on the coast of the Indian Ocean that they called "Bountiful". There God instructed them how to build a ship and they sailed to the Americas.

   They too established a colony, but soon after their arrival Lehi's third son Nephi and his followers separated themselves from the two oldest brothers Laman and Lemuel. The two groups became known as "Lamanites" and "Nephites" respectively.

6. The Nephites built great cities, highways, etc. and established a more advanced civilization, while the darker-skinned Lamanites remained in a less civilized state. The Nephites and Lamanites were not the only inhabitants of the New World. In fact the boundaries of their entire history of over a thousand years for the most part was contained in a geographical area only a few hundred miles in diameter.

7. After his crucifixion and resurrection in the Holy Land, Jesus appeared to this remnant of Israelites living in the Americas. He had a brief ministry there and then he left, promising to return at a later date.

8. About 400 AD the Lamanites destroyed the Nephites in a war of virtual extinction. Remnants of the Lamanites can be found among many of the native peoples throughout the Americas.

If The Book of Mormon is what it says it is, then any valid historical, linguistic, archaeological or other scientific discoveries about ancient America will not contradict the eight claims I've staked out above. At the time *The Book of Mormon* was published in 1830 its claims about the cultures and peoples of ancient America were considered to be something akin to science fiction. In fact some of those claims above were totally in <u>opposition</u> to the knowledge base of 1830 when the book was published. But as that knowledge base has changed and been enlarged over the last 180-plus years, many of the historical and cultural claims of *The Book of Mormon* have been <u>vindicated</u>, not contradicted. I'll show you a few...

DID ANCIENT PEOPLES WRITE ON METAL PLATES?

Did Joseph Smith translate an ancient record written on metal plates? This was something that was entirely unknown in 1830 and Joseph Smith was often ridiculed for claiming to translate from such plates. But in the 180-plus years since the publication of *The Book of Mormon*, numerous examples of writing on metal plates have been discovered in both the Old World and the New. Here are a few:

• In 1938 archaeologists from the University of Chicago discovered at Persepolis (Iran) <u>silver and gold tablets </u>inside a stone box laid in the foundation of the palace. The tablets bore inscriptions from Darius I of Persia. They are dated to 522 BC and they describe the boundaries of his kingdom in three languages. The surviving plates are in the National Archaeological Museum in Tehran, Iran.

• In July1964 <u>gold plates</u> written in Etruscan and Phoenician were found in the ancient port of Pyrgi at the Etruscan city of Caere. They are dated to around 500 BC. (Journal of Near Eastern Studies, Vol. 51, No. 2, Apr., 1992)

• Mariano Eduardo de Rivero, director of Lima's National Museum, and his associate, Juan Diego de Tschudi, asserted that there were two kinds of ancient **Peruvian** writing:

"The one and surely the most ancient consisted of certain hieroglyphic characters; the other of knots made with strings of various colors. The hieroglyphs, very different from the Mexican ones, were sculpted in stone or <u>engraved in metal</u>."[10]

• According to one nineteenth-century Mesoamerican historian in Oaxaca, the ancestors of the Mixtecs kept hieroglyphic records on <u>thin gold plates</u>.

(Jose Antonio Gay, *Historia de Oaxaca,* vol.1 Mexico, 1881, pp.4, 62)

- A Creek Indian group in Alabama called the "Tukabatchi had certain metal records that they had preserved from time immemorial as recorded in the *Handbook of Indians North of Mexico Part 2*. According to well-known Indian historian James Adair in his *History of the Indians* p. 178 (1775) there were <u>plates of both copper and brass</u>.[11]

- Traveller Bird wrote a history of his blood ancestor known as Sequoyah, the alleged inventor of the Cherokee syllabary or"alphabet". But he revealed the <u>actual</u> source of the Cherokee writing system as follows:

Before the white man came, there had been received into the population of [the Cherokee] a small group of immigrant Indians from the Southwest. ... Less than twenty-five survivors remained of this tribe. ... The ragged people brought with them little more than the clothes on their backs, but even in this moment of deep hurt and humiliation they brought, of themselves as a people, one great gift — <u>the thin gold plates of their written language.</u>

... So the teaching began in October 1795. In each village chiefs council, the people gathered and were informed about the ninety- two symbols that represented parts of syllables in their language, <u>and were shown the ancient thin gold plates upon which the symbols were engraved by their forefathers</u> — the Taliwa.[12]

As I said, NONE of this was widely known in 1830 when *The Book of Mormon* was published.

Joseph Smith's "fairy tale" about an ancient record written on metal plates was a pretty lucky guess, huh? Want more? See this article by John Tvedtnes on storing metal plates in stone boxes: <u>http://maxwellinstitute.byu.edu/publications/books/?bookid=9&chapid=75</u>

DID ANYONE BESIDES JOSEPH SMITH SEE THE GOLDEN PLATES?

Critics of *The Book of Mormon* claim that there never were any golden plates at all for Joseph Smith to translate. Joseph said the angel Moroni took the plates from him after the translation work was done. (Considering how many documented attempts were made to steal the "non-existent" plates from him while they were in his possession, that was probably a good idea.) But in the opening pages of every copy of the book we find the testimonies of eleven other people who say that they saw and handled the plates. Three of them also testify that the angel Moroni appeared to them in a daylight visit and testified to the truthfulness of Joseph's translation. How many witnesses are needed in a modern courtroom to establish the facts of a case? Certainly eleven would be enough, right? And these eleven witnesses were not deadbeats but upstanding citizens of their communities.

VALIDITY OF THE WITNESSES

"But …" you say, "maybe Joseph bribed these witnesses or tricked them somehow into making their statements. Perhaps they were friends of his who just let him use their names to perpetuate his hoax". Well, that theory might hold some water except …

What would be their motivation? Joseph had no money to pay them, and friendship or even family relationship only goes so far. (Would you do such a thing for your sibling or your child?) The eleven witnesses suffered tremendous persecution throughout their lifetimes for their testimonies regarding *The Book of Mormon*. At some point <u>every one of them became disaffected with Joseph</u> and turned against him, <u>but not one of them ever denied their testimony</u> as written in the *The Book of Mormon*.

In fact one of them named David Whitmer went to extreme measures to make sure his position was understood. Whitmer was excommunicated from the LDS church and did not go west with the Mormons, but in 1881 his testimony of *The Book of* Mormon was challenged, so he took out ads in the newspapers of the area and published a "Proclamation" that said:

"I wish now, standing as it were, in the very sunset of life, and in the fear of God, once for all to make this public statement: That <u>I have never at any time denied that testimony or any part thereof,</u> which has so long since been published with that Book, as one of the three witnesses. Those who know me best, well know that I have always adhered to that testimony. And that no man may be misled or doubt my present views in regard to the same, <u>I do again affirm the truth of all of my statements, as then made and published.</u> He that hath an ear to hear, let him hear; it was no delusion!"[13]

THE MIRACLE OF TRANSLATION

As I've said before, Joseph Smith translated *The Book of Mormon* "by the gift and power of God", and not by means of any earthly scholarship. He used the Urim and Thummim and a seer stone, both of which were called "interpreters". In each case the English translation of the ancient words written on the plates in Reformed Egyptian were revealed to him by divine means, just as the high priests of ancient Israel were commanded to use the physical objects of the Urim and Thummim to seek the mind and will of God.

—(Leviticus 8:8, Exodus 28:30, Ezra 2:63, Numbers 27:21)

Some critics have gotten a big laugh from the idea of Joseph Smith looking into a hat to read the words of translation as they appeared on the seer stone. And yet someday in the future I would imagine they themselves will hope to be reading from a stone of their own as described by John in the book of Revelations:

To him that overcometh will I give to eat of the hidden manna, and will <u>give him a white stone, and in the stone a new name written</u>, which no man knoweth saving he that receiveth it.

—Rev. 2:17

In approximately 63 working days he dictated the text to several different scribes, most notably Oliver Cowdery, averaging about 8 pages per day and sometimes as many as 15 pages per day. According to the documented accounts of eyewitnesses, Joseph never used any notes or reference materials in the translation process. When he returned to the translation each day or after a break, he never asked for any text to be read back to him, and his first draft was the final draft that was sent to the printer.

This book that you are reading has taken me more than thirty years to write, with the aid of many reference books and the internet. I've gone through several drafts and revised the text many times. I could not have completed it without the aid of a computer and word processing software. No one who has not written a book can understand what a miracle it is to complete a work of this magnitude, even with a good education and all the modern tools available.

I have a friend in Texas named Bill Boushka who is a doctor – a radiologist. He also has a degree in engineering. One day Bill called me and explained that he had been pondering the miracle of Joseph Smith's translation of The Book of Mormon. He said "As a doctor, I write reports every day on the status of my patients. I dictate for a living, yet there is no way that I could have accomplished what Joseph Smith did. It was truly a miracle."

OTHER EVIDENCES

Let's explore some other claims of *The Book of Mormon*. What about those migrations of people coming from the Middle East to the Americas before Columbus? How outlandish, right? Doesn't everyone know that the inhabitants of the western hemisphere were Mongolians who came across the Bering Strait after the Ice Age, and that except for a few wandering

Vikings in Nova Scotia nobody else sailed to the New World before Christopher Columbus? I mean, that's what we're all taught in school, and what modern DNA evidence proves, right?

Hold on a minute .....

NO OUTSIDERS BEFORE COLUMBUS?

For the last 40 years or so I've been compiling research for a 6-hour documentary I hope to produce (someday when I can get the funding) called "The Columbus Conspiracy" (AKA "They All Discovered America). I've learned a few things along the way that I'm happy to share with you about pre-Columbian visits to the Americas from peoples of many lands and cultures. Obviously I can't pack six hours worth of evidence into a couple of pages or less, but let's just look at some of the highlights and approximate dates:

- 7500 BC – date of remains of Kennewick (Washington) man found on banks of Columbia River in 1996, with Caucasian features and bone structure.

- 3600 BC – date of Jamon pottery from Japan found in Ecuador in 1964

- 3500 BC – date of a Sumerian tablet found Near La Grange, Georgia in Mrs. Joseph Hearn's garden about 1933 (Sumeria is where the Tower of Babel was built) Some artifacts and ancient legends in Peru also point to one or more ancient Sumerian voyages to that land.

- 2800 BC – date of a Minoan inscription found on a stone near Columbus, Georgia by Manfred Metcalf about 1966 (Minoans lived on the Mediterranean isle of Crete)

- 499 AD Chinese explorer Hui Shen sailed across the Pacific to Mexico and other places in the Americas then returned home to write his memoirs.

- 565 AD – Brendan "The Navigator" (known as "Saint Brendan" in the Roman Catholic church) sailed from Galway, Ireland to America in a 38-ft. ox-hide *currach* or giant kayak with sails, and returned to Ireland to write about his voyage. Some historians believe that Columbus followed Brendan's directions to America.

- 670 AD (or 1170 AD?) – According to legend the Welsh Prince Madoc sailed from Wales to a bay near Mobile, Alabama, liked what he saw and returned home to get his friends and more ships. He sailed away from Wales once more and was never heard of again. Later, indians of the Mandan tribe in the Upper Mississippi valley were observed speaking archaic Welsh in tribal ceremonies. Ancient Welsh-style fortifications were found in north Alabama and Kentucky.

These are only a few of the fascinating evidences I've found in over 40 years of research on the topic. For more you'll have to watch my documentary on PBS or the Discovery Channel (when I get it produced).

"But", you say, "you haven't mentioned any <u>Jewish or Hebrew</u> visitors to the Americas like those mentioned in *The Book of Mormon*".

… I thought you'd never ask …

IS THERE ANY EVIDENCE OF HEBREWS IN ANCIENT AMERICA?

What about the story of Lehi and his family (and others) coming from Jerusalem to America about 600 BC? If that's true there should be SOME kind of evidence of pre-Columbian Hebrew culture in the New World, right?

Well, it would depend on how much of an impact the immigrants made on the existing folks who were here when they arrived. And they weren't the only Israelites who came to this Promised Land over the centuries. In fact, in the 18th and 19th centuries there were <u>many</u> well-educated people who thought that perhaps ALL of the native peoples of the Americas were descendants of the Lost Tribes of Israel. Why would they think that?

My first exposure to the idea (outside my Mormon upbringing) came when I was a child and I visited the "Indian" portion of our local city museum in Columbus, Georgia. The curator was Dr. Joseph Mahan (a non-Mormon), who would also sometimes lecture my school classes on historical matters. Later we became great friends, as I may have already mentioned.

Dr. Mahan was probably the world's greatest authority on the Yuchi tribe that was indigenous to our area (except for the Yuchi themselves, and he knew perhaps even more than most of them). He once took a six-month sabbatical to travel to Pakistan in search of details on the Yuchi legends that told of a migration over the seas from a distant land.

"Joe" (as I called him) had created an exhibit in the museum with a large mural on one wall depicting the Yuchi harvest festival called <u>the Green Corn Ceremony</u>. On the opposite wall was a glass case with a large Bible opened up to the 23rd chapter of Leviticus wherein is described the Jewish Feast of the Tabernacles. Dr. Mahan found many striking similarities between the two customs.

LORD KINGSBOROUGH

The Irish Viscount of Kingsborough Edward King, a member of the British Parliament, was passionate about his belief that the indigenous peoples of the Americas were descended from the Lost Tribes of Israel. He spent his entire fortune publishing facsimiles of Mesoamerican codices. His 1831 publication of volume one of *Antiquities of Mexico* landed him in debtors prison where he later died. Volumes 2 and 3 were published posthumously.

(Note that this was after the 1830 publication of The Book of Mormon.)

Kingsborough expressed the opinion that *"the colony which arrived in early ages in America from the East, were Jews from Alexandria; (Vol. 1 p. 51)*

JAMES ADAIR

Explorer James Adair was –according to his own words- "chiefly engaged in an Indian life ever since the year 1735". In 1775 he published a classic account of his experiences of 40 years trading among the American indians while he ... *lived with them as a friend and brother. My intentions were pure when I wrote, truth hath been my standard, and I have no sinister or mercenary views in publishing.*

Adair also wrote:

Observations, and arguments, in proof of the American Indians being descended from the Jews.

... From the most exact observations I could make in the long time I traded among the Indian Americans, I was forced to believe them lineally descended from the Israelites, ... This descent, I shall endeavour to prove from their religious rites, civil and martial customs, their marriages, funeral ceremonies, manners, language, traditions, and a variety of particulars...[14]

Note: one of the discoveries that led Adair to his conclusions was the fact that many native American tribes worshipped as their principal deity the god ***"Yo-He-Wah"***. Doesn't that sound like "Je–hovah"? It sure does to me.

Robert Starling

PHYLACTERIES

At a symposium in Westville, GA in 1973 (which I attended), Dr. Lynn Holmes of West Georgia College reported two recorded instances where phylacteries (rawhide boxes tied around the arm) were found among the Native Americans. Inside the boxes were pieces of parchment with sections of scripture from the writings of Moses. One of these small rawhide boxes, with the parchment inside written in Hebrew, was found in 1815 in Pittsfield, Massachusetts. The other phylactery contained parchment of Hebrew extracts from Exodus and Deuteronomy. These were found in Fort Leavenworth, Kansas in 1854.

THE NEWARK OHIO HOLY STONES

In 1860 Methodist preacher David Wyrick discovered several Hebrew artifacts in a mound near Newark, Ohio that date to the pre-Columbian era. These included a stone bowl, a triangular shaped stone, and a small stone box with an inscribed tablet inside. The tablet featured a picture of a man believed to be Moses. Around the edges and back of the tables are inscribed the Ten Commandments in an ancient form of Hebrew.

Here is a photo I took of these artifacts when they were taken to Georgia for a symposium in 1973.

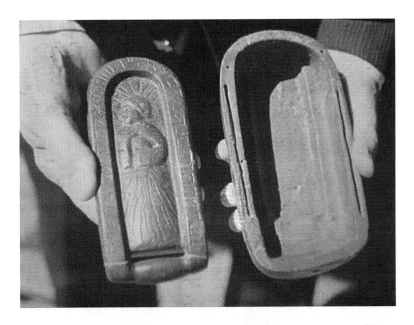

You can find much more info on the Newark Holy Stones here: http://www.econ.ohio-state.edu/jhm/arch/wyrick/transcrpt.pdf

NEW MEXICO'S "MYSTERY MOUNTAIN" AND DECALOGUE STONE

A few miles south of Albuquerque, New Mexico near a town called Las Lunas is a place known locally as Mystery Mountain. On top of the mountain there are ruins of a pre-Columbian fortress of some sort, and about halfway up the slopes is a large slab of rock with a Hebrew Inscription of the Ten Commandments (or "Decalogue"). No one knows the date of its origin, but it was there when the first white settlers arrived. I visited the Mystery Mountain site in October 2010. More info on the Decalogue Stone is here:

http://www.econ.ohio-state.edu/jhm/arch/loslunas.html

Me with the Decalogue Stone at Las Lunas, NM

Robert Starling

ISRAELITES IN TENNESSEE?

Perhaps one of the most persuasive pieces of evidence of Hebrews or Israelites in ancient America is the Bat Creek Stone, an artifact discovered in an official Smithsonian archaeological dig in 1885 in Bat Creek, Tennessee. This candy bar-sized stone was found in an unusual indian mound underneath the head of a skeleton that was quite different from other such burials.

The Bat Creek stone contained some strange letters inscribed on it which were thought for many decades to be Cherokee script. This did not attract much notice, so the stone was stashed away in the bowels of the Smithsonian archives for many years like the Lost Ark in the Indiana Jones movie.

But fortunately in the 1960's it was rediscovered and the writing on it was found to be an ancient form of Hebrew! It says "for the land of Judah" and it dates to around 135 A.D. It may or may not have anything to do with the people of the Book of Mormon, but it dates to the correct time period and it is definitely of Israelite origin. Like many ancient artifacts this one has been called a hoax by some detractors, but no one has come up with a reasonable method or motive for creating a hoax there.

A BOOK OF MORMON STORY RECORDED IN STONE?

In 1941 Smithsonian archaeologist Matthew Stirling recorded the discovery of a large complex of sculptured stone pillars or "stelae" at a place near the southern border of Mexico called Itzapa. One of them that he designated "Stela 5" bears a pictorial record of a scene that is remarkably similar to several Middle Eastern depictions of the Tree of Life.

Some Latter-day Saint scholars have identified artistic elements on the stone that seem to link it to Lehi's vision of the Tree of Life found in the first book of Nephi in *The Book of Mormon*. One researcher found what he believed to be 55 specific correlations between Nephi's account and the artifact. But there still remains a lot of controversy about the stone.

I first learned about Stela 5 or the "Lehi Stone" when I was a missionary in Pima, Arizona in 1967. A local family named Kimball had obtained a replica of the stone made from a rubber cast. This photo is of me kneeling beside that replica. One day I hope to go to Mexico to see the original!

Yep, that's me in 1967 in Arizona!
Here's a link to more info on Stela 5 Itzapa:
http://maxwellinstitute.byu.edu/publications/jbms/?vol=8&num=1&id=180

EVIDENCE IN ARABIA FOR THE BOOK OF MORMON

According to *The Book of Mormon*, the prophet Lehi and his family left Jerusalem in 600 BC and traveled through the Arabian desert for several years before arriving at a costal oasis where they built a ship and sailed to a "promised land" in the Americas.

169

In 1830 when *The Book of Mormon* was published very little was known about Arabia. The first western explorers did not publish anything about that desolate corner of the world until well after 1830, so Joseph Smith could not have had any knowledge of the area to write about it accurately. And yet … modern adventurers have made some astounding discoveries after spending years looking through the desert sands of the "Empty Quarter" for connections to *The Book of Mormon*. Here's a little of what they found:

1. About three day's journey south of the northern-most part of the Red Sea (by camel and on foot) lies a secluded valley with high rock walls. The Wadi Tayyib Al-Ism corresponds perfectly to the valley of Lemuel as described in 1 Nephi 2:6, 8:1. http://maxwellinstitute.byu.edu/publications/jbms/?vol=8&num=1&id=185&print

2. Even more astounding, running through the center of that valley is a small trickle of a stream (called a "river" in the desert) that flows all year round, just as Nephi recorded:

And it came to pass that when he had traveled three days in the wilderness, he pitched his tent in a valley by the side of a river of water. … And it came to pass that he called the name of the river, Laman, and it emptied into the Red Sea; and the valley was in the borders near the mouth thereof.

—(1 Nephi 2:6-10)

3. After running in a south-southeast direction for many miles the Arabian "Frankincense Trail" (probably followed by Lehi but totally unknown to Joseph Smith) takes an abrupt turn to the east at a place that is today called Nahem or NHM, just as recorded by Nephi (1 Nephi 17:1)). Additionally, "Nahem" is translated as a "place of mourning". Nephi says that one of their party –a man named Ishmael- died and was buried there. Nehem in the Jawf Valley in Yemen is the location of one of the largest burial sites in Arabia.

Altar in southern Arabia with the inscription "NHM"
Image courtesy of Warren P. Aston

4. Nephi writes that after journeying east through the desert as directed by God, they found a narrow valley that led down to an oasis on the seashore they called Bountiful. There they found water, abundant food, and trees to build their ship. They also found iron ore to smelt into metal for shipbuilding tools.

—(1 Nephi 17:5-10)

That all sounds pretty convenient, huh? What a storyteller that Joseph Smith was! All those geographical details in the Book of Mormon about Arabia, a place he had never seen and knew nothing about. And yet guess what?

Over a hundred years later Mormon researchers discovered just such an oasis near a place called Salalah on the southern coast of Oman, east of Nahom right where Nephi said it was!

Oasis at Khar Karfot, believed to be Nephi's "Bountiful"
Image courtesy of Warren P. Aston

And you know that <u>boat</u> Nephi said they built to sail to America? Well, it happens that the nearby city of Salalah is a seaport with a tradition of shipbuilding going back to the time of Lehi, about 600 BC. In 2009 a replica of the same type of ship was built from ancient drawings and sailed from Salalah to re-enact a Phoenician voyage around the horn of Africa.

So…… Where did this ignorant farm boy from upstate New York find out in 1830 so much accurate information about unknown Arabia to write in his book? I happen to believe it came from the hand of Nephi as written on those golden plates. If you can come up with a better answer please let me know will you? Please?

LINGUISTIC EVIDENCES
Speaking of an "unlearned" Joseph Smith … The 23-year old young man with only a third grade education… Let's talk about writing skills.

The Book of Mormon is claimed to have been written by more than 21 different authors over a period of more than a thousand years. Then around 400 AD their writings were abridged by the prophet Mormon who also added his own commentaries. Not only should it not contain any jargon or figures of speech common to 1830 (a modern example might be something like "show me the money" or "where's the beef?"), but the writing styles of each individual author should be evident in the chapters attributed to them. And none of them should be similar to Joseph Smith's own writing style as revealed in his personal papers and other writings. Such a literary feat would be a tall order for the brightest PhD in English at Harvard, right? Yep, that's what I think too. And yet …

WORDPRINT ANALYSIS, or STYLOMETRY
Several different computer-aided studies in a field called "wordprint analysis" or "stylometry" have been applied to *The Book of Mormon* with amazing results. An initial study done in 1979 using 1,000-word samples showed that neither Joseph Smith, Sidney Ridgon, Oliver Cowdery nor Solomon Spaulding could have written The Book of Mormon, and that in fact each of the texts of the 21 Book of Mormon authors differed from each other (as they should).

Another study done at the University of California at Berkley in the 1990's used a 5,000-word sample from each alleged author to compare non-contextual word patterns. This peer-reviewed study found that there is a <u>one in 15</u> <u>trillion chance</u> that the books of Nephi and Alma were written by Joseph Smith or any other single author.

<u>http://en.fairmormon.org/Book_of_Mormon/Wordprint_studies</u>

CHAISMUS
Okay, let's suppose Joseph Smith was such a genius that he was able to fake 21 different writing styles (although no modern author has been able to do so), how much do you think he might have known about ancient Hebrew poetry forms? Even ones that were almost totally unknown by anyone in the world in 1830?

In the mid 1960's a Latter-day Saint missionary named John W. Welch discovered in the text of *The Book of Mormon* many instances of a little-known Hebrew poetic structure called "chiasmus". Chiasmus was used often in the Bible but became a lost art that was virtually unknown in 1830 when *The Book of Mormon* was published.

It is a parallelistic literary structure where a group of lines of text are written in a certain order, then slightly re-phrased and re-written in a reverse order. A short simple chiasmus looks something like this:

A
  B
    C
  B
A

The Book of Mormon contains hundreds of chiasms, many of them very long and very complex. The entire 36th chapter of Alma is a complete chiasm. How could Joseph Smith (or anyone of his time) have constructed such elaborate literary parallels in a technique that was known only to a few scholars in the entire world? Of course for Nephi and his successor prophets who were "skilled in the learning of the Jews" it was a simple matter …

"AND IT CAME TO PASS"

Do you remember a few pages back what Mark Twain said about the phrase *"and it came to pass"* that is repeated so often in *The Book of Mormon*? Twain said that if it were taken out of the book we would only be left with a thin pamphlet. Many other critics have also made fun of that phrase, saying that Joseph Smith probably used it to "pad" the book and make it longer. But the phrase is a common Hebrew construction that is not unique to *The Book of Mormon.* It occurs 526 times in the Old Testament and 87 times in the New Testament. And it does appear a lot in *The Book of Mormon* – over 1500 times when you count different variations.

But guess what? It is also a common phrase in the Maya language, where it is reduced to a single word that sounds something like "utchi". At the ruins of Palenque and other places there is found a common glyph that represents the phrase. So a Mayan glyph that can be translated "and it came to pass" is almost as ubiquitous in ancient American writing as it is in *The Book of Mormon?* It looks like Joseph Smith somehow made another "lucky" guess, huh?

DID CHRIST VISIT ANCIENT AMERICA AS THE BOOK OF MORMON CLAIMS?

Okay, let's get down to the real nitty-gritty. The central claim of *The Book of Mormon* is that Jesus Christ visited a remnant of Israelites living in the Americas shortly after he was resurrected. In fact, the full name of the volume is *The Book of Mormon: Another Testament of Jesus Christ*. If this is true, then it provides positive <u>proof</u> of his resurrection (and thus of his divinity) that should be welcome news to any Christian.

We have the testimony of two textual witnesses to Jesus as the Lord and Savior of mankind (the *Bible* and *The Book of Mormon*) that was prophesied in the Old Testament by the prophet Ezekiel:

"Moreover thou son of man, <u>take thee one stick and write upon it for Judah</u> and for the children of Israel his companions; then <u>take another stick, and write upon it. For Joseph</u>, the stick of Ephraim, and for all the house of Israel his companions: And join them one to another into one stick: and <u>they shall become one in thine hand</u>.

—Ezekiel 37: 16-17

Jesus himself told the people in Jerusalem that he would visit his "other sheep" and that they would "hear his voice".

"And other sheep I have which are not of this fold: them also I must bring, and they shall hear my voice; and there shall be one fold, and one shepherd."

—John 10:16

Many have supposed that he was referring to the Gentiles in this verse, but there are a couple of problems with that interpretation:

1. Jesus never personally taught any Gentiles (although his disciples did later). They never "heard his voice". That was not his mission. He said:

2. *"I am not sent but unto the lost sheep of the House of Israel"*

—(Matt. 15:24)

THE BOOK OF MORMON ACCOUNT OF CHRIST'S VISIT TO THE AMERICAS

The New Testament account of the crucifixion of Christ says that at his death there were "great earthquakes" and "darkness" in Jerusalem that lasted for about three hours.

—(Luke 23:44-45)

The Book of Mormon account in 3rd Nephi of that same event records that the upheavals and commotion of the elements were even more severe and lengthy on the American continent.

Cities were burned and sunken in the seas, mountains fell down and valleys were thrust up and the whole face of the landscape was changed. A mist of darkness covered the land for three days. Many thousands (possibly tens or hundreds of thousands) of people died in the destruction that took place.

Then the people began to hear a still, small voice that gradually became louder, and they saw a light in the sky. Soon they discerned the figure of a man descending from the heavens until finally he stood among them and said:

And verily I say unto you, that ye are they of whom I said: Other sheep I have which are not of this fold; them also I must bring, and they shall hear my voice; and there shall be one fold, and one shepherd.

And they understood me not, for they supposed it had been the Gentiles; for they understood not that the Gentiles should be converted through their preaching. And they understood me not that I said they shall hear my voice; and they understood me not that I should not manifest myself unto them save it were by the Holy Ghost.

—3rd Nephi 15:21-23

The visit of the resurrected Jesus Christ is the most important event that ever occurred in the western hemisphere, and as we'll see later it did not go unnoticed or unrecorded in the history of the indigenous peoples there. Jesus spent many days among the people and taught them many things. He chose twelve disciples as special witnesses of his mission and his divinity just as he had done in the land of Israel. He repeated to them the Sermon on the Mount almost verbatim, and he performed many miracles among them. He organized his earthly church among the people just has he had done in the Old World. Then he left, saying that he was going to visit still more of his "other sheep" but that someday he would return. He ascended into heaven as he came.

—(3rd Nephi 18:39)

The account in *The Book of Mormon* of Christ's ministry in the Americas stands as a second witness with the Bible as to his divine role as the Only Begotten Son of God and as the savior and redeemer of mankind. It is indeed *Another Testament of Jesus Christ*.

So.... If *The Book of Mormon* is a true historical record, shouldn't there be some evidence of Christ's visit in other historical sources? Well, let's see ….

THE WHITE AND BEARDED GOD OF ANCIENT AMERICA

Historians almost universally agree that the most important of all the deities worshipped by the inhabitants of the Americas before the Spaniards brought Catholic Christianity to the New World was a white and bearded god who appeared about 33 A.D. (how curious!) He was called Quetzalcoatl by some but he had other names among different peoples. He was known as Kulkulcan, Itsamna, Viracocha and other titles from one end of the continent to another. But the description of him is the same: He was a kind and gentle man with white skin and a beard. He wore long flowing robes. He commanded them to cease their practices of human sacrifice. He healed the sick and raised the dead. He taught them better ways of raising crops. Some legends say that he told people had he had been crucified in a far-off land, and that he had risen from the grave on the third day.

The deity Quetzalcoatl was so loved and respected that some native rulers later adopted his name. (Just as later Roman rulers adopted the name Caesar.) One particular leader named Quetzalcoatl who lived about 1100 AD is often mixed up with the original person of that name. This has caused confusion among some historians.

After a period of time this white and bearded god left each of the groups that he visited, but he promised to return at a later time. When the Spaniard Cortez came to Mexico he easily conquered the mighty Aztec nation partly because their emperor Montezuma believed he was the returning god Quetzalcoatl.

I first learned about the legends of the white and bearded god when I read a book called *He Walked The Americas* by a non-Mormon author named L. Taylor Hansen. She became fascinated with the many oral histories about this pervasive legendary personality and tracked down and recorded the accounts from many cultures and tribes throughout the Americas. She wrote:

He told them he was born across the ocean where all men had beards. Even in the legends, he told them of his <u>virgin birth</u> and about the <u>bright star that shone over his city of his birth.</u> The heavens opened up and <u>winged beings sang chants</u> of exquisite beauty.When the University of Oklahoma was digging the Spiro Mound, they found much pottery showing winged beings singing, and also the hand with the cross through the palm. To them, <u>He was known as Chee-Zoos,</u> the Dawn God, and they whisper of Him about the campfires when no white man can listen.[15]

Certain aspects were common to almost all the descriptions of this multi-named person:

- He was a white man with a beard
- He said He came from across the sea
- He would choose twelve "disciples" wherever he went
- He spoke of His Father's Kingdom
- He wore a bright white garment with golden sandals
- He made references to the future
- He had control over the wind and all elements
- He had the ability to heal wounds
- He taught love and peace
- He taught that good deeds were important
- He referred them to the Dawn Star

Although Ms. Hansen was not a member of The Church of Jesus Christ of Latter-day Saints when she wrote the book in 1963, according to a blog entry (reportedly by her niece) she became a Latter-day Saint seven years before her death in 1976.

Many other historians have recorded info about the white and bearded god. My friend Kirk Magleby served as an LDS missionary in Peru, and while there he collected accounts written by Spanish Conquistadors who had lived and served in that area. In 1984 he wrote an article citing four of them in particular. He summarized:

> Synthesizing elements from all four Peruvian versions of the white god tradition into one composite description, an interesting portrait of the god Viracocha emerges. He was a creator god who came to visit the men he had created, to instruct and organize them. With white skin and a medium to large build, he wore a white tunic girded at the waist that hung down to his feet. Past his youth, he was slender and had white hair. When he walked, he carried a staff and a book in his hands, and sometimes he was seen with a crown on his head. He demonstrated supreme authority, yet spoke with love and humility, calling everyone his sons and daughters.

> Appearing long before the time of the Inca empire, the coming of this Viracocha constituted the single most important tradition of the Andean Indians. For many days prior to his coming, the sun was darkened and the people suffered tremendous privations from lack of sunlight. Only after intense praying and supplication was the light restored, after which Viracocha appeared. Everywhere he went in the mountains of Peru, he performed miracles. He lowered the hills and raised up the level places to become mountains. He drew water from rocks, gave life to animals and men, and walked on water.

He healed the sick with only a touch of his hand, and spoke all the diverse languages of the region with equal fluency.

He gave commandments to men that they love their neighbor and have charity, and he chastised the people for their wrongdoings. He gave them a copy of his discourse, written on a stick, then reviewed it with them for emphasis. Speaking to a large congregation, he told them of events to come, warning them that some would come in his name, falsely claiming to be the Viracocha. Then he promised to send them true messengers and servants in future ages to teach and support them. Having no earthly possessions, Viracocha went off into the ocean after concluding his visit, and the people never heard from him again.[16]

For me personally, *The Book of Mormon* is indeed *"Another Testament of Jesus Christ"*. In 1979 I wrote the script for a feature documentary film called *"In Search of Historic Jesus"* that was produced by Schick Sunn Classic Pictures. It was released in theaters in 1980 and after a successful theatrical run was shown on TV all over the world including the NBC television network in the U.S. My original idea for the movie was: "What if a person did not accept the Bible as a historical document? What other sources are there to determine if Jesus Christ ever lived on earth as a real person?

Among the other historical sources I included the account in *The Book of Mormon* of his visit to ancient America. I had shortly beforehand read a book called *"The Passover Plot"* that attempted to explain away the resurrection and divinity of Jesus by attacking and tearing down the Biblical account. For me, *The Book of Mormon* provided an independent witness to support the Bible and testify to the world of the resurrection and divinity of my Lord and Savior.

I've shared with you some of my "reasons to believe", and I hope it has been illuminating for you. Far from being a "fanciful fiction", The Book of Mormon is a real history of real people, a branch of the House of Israel who came to the Americas in ancient times. Most importantly it truly is *"Another Testament of Jesus Christ"*. It is the "stick of Joseph" that has now joined the "stick of Judah" (the Bible) as an irrefutable witness that Jesus Christ is indeed our Lord and Savior, the Only Begotten Son of God who visited his "other sheep" in the New World.

Not all the physical evidence has yet come forth, but there is more support every day for this sacred volume of scripture. DNA evidence of Middle Eastern blood types that was lacking in 2003 was discovered in 2006. The remains of horses dating to Book of Mormon times have recently been excavated in Mexico and other sites in Mesoamerica. Impatient critics decry the book saying, "where are the coins or cities mentioned in the book"? There are already many more important evidences than that, but remember the geographical location of the city of Troy was considered a myth until Henry Schlieman found it in 1888 and announced it to the world.

Can the city of Zarahemla be next?

ENDNOTES FOR CHAPTER 7

1   *Journal of Discourses* 9:311. [13 July 1862]

2   Jon Gary Williams, The Book Of Mormon: A Book Of Mistakes, Error, And Fraud, p.17, Apologetics Press, Inc., Montgomery, AL

3   *Walter Martin, Kingdom of the Cults - http://www.waltermartin.com/mormon.html*

4   *Smithsonian Institution form letter 4/1/1998 PIMS/ANT01/4-1-98*
    (note: an earlier Smithsonian statement published in 1996 was much more critical of The Book of Mormon, but after LDS Scholars pointed out the errors in that statement it was replaced with the above response. Nevertheless, many anti-Mormon critics continue to quote the outdated Smithsonian document.)

5   *What Hath God Wrought?—The Transformation of America, 1815- 1848", P. 314 (Quoted by LDS researcher George Potter)*

6   Interview by Parley P. Pratt, Jr. recorded by Nels Madsen, 27 November 1931, LDS Archives; cited by *Mormon Enigma*, 2nd ed., 297–298.

7   Reuben Miller Journal, 21 October 1848, LDS Church Archives, Salt Lake City, Utah, cited in *Deseret News*, 13 April 1859

8   *The Prophetic Book of Mormon, F.A.R.M.S., 221-222*

9   ibid

10 *(Antiquidades Peruanas, Vienna: Imprenta Imperial de la Corte y del Estado, 1851, vol. 5, p. 101.)*

11 (Smithsonian Institution Bureau of American Ethnology, *Bulletin 30*, p.833, Wash. 1910)

12 *Tell Them They Lie: The Sequoyah Myth* by Traveller Bird. Los Angeles CA: Westernlore Publishers, 1971. pp. 31,83.

13 *[Richmond] Conservator - March 24, 1881*

14 James Adair (c.1709-1783) *History of the Indians*, London: Edward & Charles Dilly, 1775) pp. 14-15

15 L. Taylor Hansen, *He Walked the Americas*, Adventures Unlimited Press (February 12, 2014)

16 https://www.lds.org/new-era/1978/12/four-peruvian-versions-of-the-   white-god-legend?lang=eng&query=magleby

EVIDENCE 8

PROPHETS AND REVELATION

There is evidence that God speaks to man on earth today just as he did in Biblical times. He is "the same yesterday, today, and forever. (Heb. 13:8) However just as he gave man a "new covenant". (Heb. 12:24) when Jesus came to earth (as uncircumcised Gentiles were admitted into the church), he sometimes changes the way he works with mankind. That's why there is a need for modern prophets and modern revelation. I believe man not only <u>can</u> see God but that he <u>has</u> seen God in these latter days. God has called modern prophets to be his mouthpiece on earth today just as in Biblical times, beginning with the Prophet Joseph Smith in 1820.

This belief in continuing revelation is explained in one of our Latter-day Saint **Articles of Faith**:

"We believe all that God has revealed, all that He does now reveal, and we believe that He will yet reveal many great and important things pertaining to the Kingdom of God."

—*LDS 9th Article of Faith*

It is based on Bible teachings expressed in both the Old and New Testaments:

"Surely the Lord GOD will do nothing, but he revealeth his secret unto his servants the prophets."

—*Amos 3:7*

"Upon this rock (of Revelation) I will build my church..."

—Matthew 16:18

<u>*And he gave some, apostles; and some, prophets*</u>*; and some, evangelists; and some, pastors and teachers; For the perfecting of the saints, for the work of the ministry, for the edifying of the body of Christ: Till we all come in the unity of the faith, and of the knowledge of the Son of God, unto a perfect man, unto the measure of the stature of the fullness of Christ*<u>*: That we henceforth be no more children, tossed to and fro, and carried about with every wind of doctrine*</u>*, by the sleight of men, and cunning craftiness, whereby they lie in wait to deceive;*

—Ephesians 4:11-14

Peter adds:

"For the prophecy came not in old time by the will of man: but <u>*holy men of God spake*</u> *as they were moved by the Holy Ghost."*

—2 Peter 1:21

And as expressed plainly in the LDS Church:

"Joseph Smith, the Prophet and Seer of the Lord, has done more, <u>*save Jesus only,*</u> *for the salvation of men in this world, than any other man that ever lived in it".*

—John Taylor

"Praise to <u>*the man who communed with Jehovah*</u>*, Jesus anointed that prophet and seer."*

—LDS Hymn # 27

I believe that Jesus truly "anointed that prophet and seer". Joseph Smith was called by God just as Moses and other ancient prophets were, to be his mouthpiece and to reveal his will to men. Joseph Smith was called by God just as Peter was, to direct the work of Christ's Church upon the earth.

Brigham Young and Joseph's other successors down to the present day have continued in that same calling. One might call Joseph Smith "Mormonism's first Christian". At least I do.

I believe that God did not shut the door on heavenly revelation when the 66 books of the Protestant Bible were canonized by un-inspired church councils. Although the earth went through a long period prophesied by the prophet Isaiah when "a darkness shall cover the earth" (Isaiah 60:2) and when men would "run to and fro to seek the Word of God and shall not find it" (Amos 8:11), there was also a "restitution of all things" in these latter days, including the gift of prophecy. (Acts 3:21)

INSIDE LATTER-DAY CHRISTIANITY

The Church of Jesus Christ of Latter-day Saints is led by a Prophet and President who is assisted by two counselors. They are called the First Presidency of the church. The general leadership of the church also includes The Quorum of the Twelve Apostles. Each year in a General Conference of church members worldwide we have the opportunity to raise our hands in a sustaining vote of these men as "prophets, seers, and revelators".

Another group of men called the Seventy work under the direction of the First Presidency and the Quorum of the Twelve to administer the guidance and direction of the church. These men are called "General authorities". Their calling is to give all of their daily efforts to building the Kingdom of God, and they may be asked to go anywhere on earth to perform their service to the Lord. Their ministry is different from the part-time work of unpaid local volunteer church leaders, and they receive a small stipend for the support of their families.

OUTSIDE LATTER-DAY CHRISTIANITY

To my knowledge there is no major Christian religion today that claims to have a prophet at its head in the same sense as in the New Testament church. The Roman Catholic Pope may come the closest to that claim in that his teachings are believed by Catholics to be "infallible" or speaking for God when he speaks "ex cathedra" (in his official position as the Pope). But I don't think he claims to be a prophet.

Most Christian teachers accept the concept of "general revelation", meaning that God is revealed in the glory of his handiwork, but they deny the continuance of "special revelation" (the kind that prophets experienced in the Bible) beyond the close of the New Testament. Some churches expressly <u>deny</u> the possibility of God speaking to mankind today as in Bible times.

The Westminster Confession of Faith (1646 A.D.) says:

"The whole counsel of God, concerning all things necessary for his own glory, man's salvation, faith, and life, is either expressly set down in Scripture, or by good and necessary consequence may be deduced from Scripture: unto which <u>nothing at any time is to be added, whether by new revelations of the Spirit,</u> or traditions of men"

It also says:

"those former ways of God's revealing his will unto his people being now ceased."[1]

HAS GOD STOPPED USING PROPHETS TO TALK TO MANKIND?

Why do many ministers and teachers in the world today so vehemently deny that God uses prophets today in the same way He did in Biblical times? Is it because they just don't know of any? One of the verses they use to support this position is this one:

God, who at sundry times and in divers manners spake in time past unto the fathers by the prophets, Hath in these last days spoken unto us by his Son, whom he hath appointed heir of all things, by whom also he made the worlds;

—Hebrews 1:1-2

They say that because Jesus came to earth and God has "*spoken to us by his Son*", there is no more need for prophets. But Paul wrote in his epistle to the Ephesians (long after Jesus had been resurrected and left the earth) that Christ gave us "apostles and prophets" along with pastors and teachers.

And for what purpose would we need these offices in the Church?

"For the perfecting of the saints, for the work of the ministry, for the edifying of the body of Christ"

And for how long would we need them?

"Till we all come in the unity of the faith"'

And why did our Lord give these to his Church?

(continuing) "That we henceforth be no more children, tossed to and fro, and carried about with every wind of doctrine, by the sleight of men, and cunning craftiness, whereby they lie in wait to deceive"

—Ephesians 4:11-14

I believe that God loves his children who live upon the earth in the 21st century just as much as those who lived during the time that the New Testament books were being written. There are those who quote those first two verses in Hebrews and interpret them to indicate that all revelation was completed in Jesus Christ. But if that were true, then all of the revelation of God's Word in the rest of the New Testament after the Gospels would be invalid.

Paul speaks of <u>new</u> knowledge from God coming <u>AFTER</u> the mortal ministry of Christ

*"Which in other ages was not made known unto the sons of men, **<u>as it is now revealed unto his holy apostles and prophets by the Spirit</u>**;*

— Eph. 3:5

Paul also wrote that the apostles and prophets are the "foundation" of Christ's church. (Eph. 2:20) So if the New Testament church of Jesus Christ is to be found on the earth today, one of its characteristics is that it will still have a "foundation" of living apostles and prophets. Doesn't that make sense? It sure does to me.

I realize that many people interpret the Bible to say that the "foundation" is the <u>writings</u> of the original twelve apostles and prophets, but in my view they are "straining at a gnat" to reach that interpretation and "wresting the scriptures" to meet their own preconceived views.

We find in the first chapter of Luke's message to Theophilus that we call the Acts of the Apostles, that after Jesus was *"taken up ... he through the Holy Ghost had given commandments unto the apostles whom he had chosen"*. In verses 23-25 we see that when one of the original twelve apostles died (Judas), the first order of business was to select a new apostle to *"take part of this ministry and apostleship"*, … *And they gave forth their lots; and the lot fell upon Matthias; and he was numbered with the eleven apostles."* And thus the Bible is clear that the intent and practice of the New Testament church was to maintain a quorum of twelve <u>living</u> apostles.

(A side note: I believe there is some confusion because the scripture says they "gave forth their <u>lots</u>" to select Matthias as an apostle. Some folks may think this was something like rolling dice because our modern usage of the term "casting lots" implies gambling or and element of chance. But the Greek word used in this verse refers to an "assignment" such as one's "lot" in life. Thus the will of the Holy Spirit was confirmed as the assembled disciples cast their sustaining votes to give Matthias his ministry assignment or "allotment" to become one of the twelve apostles. This is the same procedure used today to select a new apostle in The Church of Jesus Christ of Latter-day Saints.)

Robert Starling

JOSEPH SMITH, A PROPHET OF GOD

Just as God called a young boy named Samuel to be his mouthpiece and to receive revelations in the Old Testament days, he called another young boy named Joseph in our own time to receive revelations from God to man. Just as Samuel said, "here I am Lord", so did Joseph Smith accept the difficult burden of speaking the word of God to mankind. Joseph was warned that he would be persecuted. He was told that his name would be had for both good and evil upon the earth.

John Taylor, the third president and prophet of The Church of Jesus Christ of Latter-day Saints wrote:

> "Joseph Smith, the Prophet and Seer of the Lord, has done more, save Jesus only, for the salvation of men in this world, than any other man that ever lived in it. In the short space of twenty years, he has brought forth the Book of Mormon, which he translated by the gift and power of God, and has been the means of publishing it on two continents; has sent the fullness of the everlasting gospel, which it contained, to the four quarters of the earth; has brought forth the revelations and commandments which compose this book of Doctrine and Covenants, and many other wise documents and instructions for the benefit of the children of men; gathered many thousands of the Latter-day Saints, founded a great city, and left a fame and name that cannot be slain. He lived great, and he died great in the eyes of God and his people; and like most of the Lord's anointed in ancient times, has sealed his mission and his works with his own blood; and so has his brother Hyrum. In life they were not divided, and in death they were not separated!"
>
> —Doctrine and Covenants 135:3

THE MANTLE OF THE PROPHET IS PASSED ON

After the martyrdom of Joseph Smith the mantle of the prophet was passed to Brigham Young just as the mantle of leadership of the children of Israel was passed from Moses to Joshua. And just as God demonstrated his acceptance of Joshua by giving him the power to divide the River Jordan so that the children of Israel might cross into the Promised Land, on August 8, 1844 a miracle occurred to demonstrate God's acceptance of Brigham Young as the prophetic successor to Joseph Smith.

A MIRACULOUS MANIFESTATION

In a conference of the Church called to decide its new leadership, Brigham Young took the podium and began to speak. Immediately those present witnessed a transformation. Brigham took on the voice and the face of Joseph Smith, as testified by those present. Hundreds of people saw and heard not Brigham Young, but Joseph.

In succeeding years as Brigham Young and his successors finished their earthly ministries, God revealed to the Quorum of the 12 apostles whom each successor was to be. This was done in the same manner as we've seen described in the New Testament wherein the successor to Judas was revealed to the remaining apostles.

HOW DOES GOD REVEAL HIMSELF?

Revelation can come in many forms. The most common form is the "still small voice" that speaks to our hearts and minds when we seek God's will in our individual lives. When Moses was on Sinai, God's revelation took the form of stone tablets in which God wrote his will and his commandments with his own finger in stone. When the prophet Balaam tried to travel in the wrong direction, revelation from God took the form of human speech coming forth from his donkey. When Stephen was being stoned to death, revelation took the form of a vision of God the father, and God the son standing on his right hand. Similarly when Saul/Paul was on the road to Damascus, revelation took the form of his vision of a glorified Savior and the voice of God speaking from the heavens.

When Peter needed direction from God as to whether Gentiles could become members of Christ's Church, revelation took the form of a dream in which he saw a sheet let down at four corners containing animals that were considered unclean according to the previous revelation of Jewish law.

IS MODERN-DAY REVELATION NECESSARY?

There are those who say that what we read in the Bible is all we need of God's Word. One might as well say that the meal I eat today is all the food I will ever need. The revelation of God's will to mankind is the "rock" upon which Jesus said that he would build his church. (Matt. 16:17-18) The popular Christian singer Sandi Patti emphasizes this principle in her song "Upon This Rock", which is one of my favorites:

Upon this rock, I'll build my kingdom
And on this rock, forever and ever it will stand.
Upon the rock of revelation, I'll build a strong and mighty nation
And it shall stand the storms of time, Upon this rock[2]

The need for continuing revelation became evident very early in the New Testament church after the ascension of Jesus into heaven. As noted above, God revealed to the eleven remaining apostles who should take the place of Judas. Not too much later the question of whether Gentiles should be allowed membership in the church was answered through the revelation of Peter's vision or dream. The question of whether non-Jewish converts to Christianity need to be circumcised was a BIG question in the New Testament church that also had to be decided by revelation.

After the death of the original apostles (who were also prophets) the remaining bishops and other church officers tried to substitute the deliberations and decisions of various ecumenical councils for revelation from God. But without true prophets to guide the church, the edicts from one council were soon replaced by even more questions, requiring more councils and so forth. Indeed the Christians were "tossed to and forth, by every wind of doctrine". Often the decision of a council was based more on politics than on sound doctrine and scripture. In today's complex world there are many situations that require revelation from God to direct his church on earth. Same-sex marriage comes to mind. That's certainly one that's not spoken of in the Bible! And even though homosexuality is condemned in the Bible as a sin, the acceptance of it as "normal" in many Christian churches today shows how critical it is to know God's will in all matters.

CAN GOD CHANGE HIS MIND?

The whole purpose of continuing revelation is so that God can reveal his will when there is a need to give new information to mankind, or for a change in the way God wants things done among his people. That is why Peter received the vision of the unclean animals to tell him that Gentiles were permitted to join the New Testament church. That is why Joseph Smith received a commandment that the Mormons should practice plural marriage, and in 1890 Wilford Woodruff received another revelation giving the Church permission to end the practice. That is why Spencer W. Kimball in 1978 received a revelation granting permission for all worthy males in the LDS church to receive the priesthood.

Early in his presidency it was revealed to Gordon B. Hinckley that the LDS church should expand the building of temples around the world. When I was a young missionary serving in the 1960's there were only 13 temples in the entire world. As of 2019 there are almost 200 temples either completed or under construction. As in Biblical times, our Father in Heaven has prepared the way for the growth of his kingdom upon the earth in these latter days through continual revelation to his servants.

God never intended that his people should only have the guidance of scriptures that were given to them 2000 years ago. In the Bible Amos wrote, *"God will do nothing except he revealeth his secrets unto his servants the prophets"* (Amos 3:7). There was no expiration date put on that scripture or on that promise. So we see that there is a need for continuing revelation today.

DO WARNINGS OF FALSE PROPHETS MEAN THERE ARE NO TRUE ONES?

In the minds of many people in our modern-day world, the word "prophet" is almost always preceded by the word "false". I wonder why that is? Perhaps it is because they've never heard of a true prophet except in the Bible. It is correct to say that the Bible warns us of false prophets. Here are a few examples:

Beloved, do not believe every spirit, but test the spirits to see whether they are from God, for many false prophets have gone out into the world.

—1 John 4:1

But false prophets also arose among the people, just as there will be false teachers among you, who will secretly bring in destructive heresies, even denying the Master who bought them, bringing upon themselves swift destruction.

—2 Peter 2:1

"Beware of false prophets, who come to you in sheep's clothing but inwardly are ravenous wolves.

—Matthew 7:15

For false Christs and false prophets will arise and perform great signs and wonders, so as to lead astray, if possible, even the elect.

—Matthew 24:24

'I know your works, your toil and your patient endurance, and how you cannot bear with those who are evil, but have tested those who call themselves apostles and are not, and found them to be false.

—Revelation 2:2

Okay, I could go on and on with more verses, but you get the picture, right? However if there were to be no <u>true</u> prophets then all these warnings against <u>false</u> prophets would be unnecessary, right? The Word would simply say there will be no more prophets. But instead Scripture says we must TEST the prophets.

HOW DO WE TEST A PROPHET?

Certainly our Father in Heaven does not want his children to live in confusion about prophets or anything else:

For God is not a God of confusion but of peace. As in all the churches of the saints,

—1 Corinthians 14:33

So he has given us guidance in how to test to see if prophets are true: Beloved, do not believe every spirit, but <u>test</u> the spirits to see whether they are from God, for many false prophets have gone out into the world.

—1 John 4:1-6

"I know your works, your toil and your patient endurance, and how you cannot bear with those who are evil, but have <u>tested</u> those who call themselves apostles and are not, and found them to be false."

—Revelation 2:2

IS A PROPHET ONLY A FORETELLER? HOW ABOUT A FORTH-TELLER?

There are some folks out there who only talk of one test of a prophet. Has he made any predictions of the future, and have they come true? Is he an accurate foreteller? And yet Moses was one of the greatest prophets of all time and he is known primarily as "the lawgiver". Although he did foretell the plagues that would befall Egypt, his major contribution was to bring forth to the children of Israel the Ten Commandments and the laws of God by which they should be governed. He was a "forth-teller" and a leader of God's people. Just like the prophet Joseph Smith and his latter-day successors.

In addition to bringing forth *The Book of Mormon* and other additional scriptures to guide our lives, Joseph Smith was instrumental in restoring the New Testament church of Jesus Christ and many teachings and principles that traditional Christianity had lost over the ages. He founded what has become the fourth largest church in America and one of the fastest-growing faith groups on earth. His teachings about the gospel of Jesus Christ have blessed the lives of over fifteen million current members of the LDS church worldwide. The Bible says "by their fruits ye shall know them", and in a later chapter I will share in greater detail the good "fruits" of Latter-day Christianity.

Yet some of the critics of Joseph occasionally trot out a list of alleged "failed prophesies" that they have circulated in hopes to prove him a liar. They quote a verse in Deuteronomy

(18:20-22) that says if a man's prophecies don't come true then he is a false prophet. I only bring it up here so you'll know that I'm aware of that criticism. But I'm also aware (as Joseph's detractors are apparently not) of a thorough study that completely refutes their list. I won't go into it in this volume but if you want to read it you can find it here:

http://en.fairmormon.org/Joseph_Smith/Alleged_false_prophecies#Fulfilled_prophecies

PROFILE OF A (TRUE) PROPHET

When I was a missionary in California and Arizona in the 1960's I often listened to an audio recording of a talk given by LDS leader Hugh B. Brown called "Profile of a Prophet". In it he described a meeting he held in 1939 with a member of the House of Commons who was a former justice in the Supreme Court of England. The gentleman said to him: "I cannot understand how a barrister (lawyer) and solicitor from Canada, a man trained in logic and evidence, could accept such absurd statements. What you tell me about Joseph Smith seems fantastic, but I think you should take three days at least to prepare a brief and permit me to examine it and question you on it." Instead Elder Brown suggested they begin immediately. He laid out for this friend what he called a "profile of a prophet" showing that Joseph Smith fulfilled every Biblical requirement for a true prophet of God.

His complete discussion of the matter can be found here:

http://speeches.byu.edu/?act=viewitem&id=114

In summary, first he asked these questions of his friend, to which he received all affirmative answers:

"I assume you believe in the Bible—the Old and New Testaments?"
"Do you believe in prayer?"
"You say that my belief that God spoke to a man in this age is fantastic and absurd?"
"Do you believe that God ever did speak to anyone?"
"Do you believe that contact between God and man ceased when Jesus appeared on the earth?"
"Do you believe that Jesus was the Son of God?"
"Do you believe a tentmaker by the name of Saul of Tarsus—when on his way to Damascus talked with Jesus?"
"So was it standard procedure in Bible times for God to talk to man?"
"Yet you believe it stopped shortly after the first century of the Christian era?"

Finally, he got some "no" answers when he asked:

"Can you give me a reason for your belief that God stopped talking to man?"

"Is it that He cannot, that He has lost the power to do so?"

"Is it that He doesn't love us anymore and He is no longer interested in the affairs of men?"

"Is it that we don't need Him?"

Elder Brown said they then agreed that the following characteristics would create a "profile" of a man who claims to be a prophet.

1. He will boldly claim that God had spoken to him.

2. Any man so claiming would be a dignified man with a dignified message—no table jumping, no whisperings from the dead, no clairvoyance, but an intelligent statement of truth.

3. Any man claiming to be a prophet of God would declare his message without any fear and without making any weak concessions to public opinion.

4. If he were speaking for God he could not make concessions, although what he taught would be new and contrary to the accepted teachings of the day.

5. Such a man would speak in the name of the Lord, saying, "Thus said the Lord," as did Moses, Joshua, and others.

6. Such a man would predict future events in the name of the Lord, and they would come to pass, as did those predicted by Isaiah and Ezekiel.

7. He would have not only an important message for his time but often a message for all future time, such as Daniel, Jeremiah, and others had.

8. He would have courage and faith enough to endure persecution and to give his life, if need be, for the cause he espoused, such as Peter, James, Paul, and others did.

9. Such a man would denounce wickedness fearlessly. He would generally be rejected or persecuted by the people of his time, but later generations and descendants of his persecutors would build monuments in his honor.

10. He would be able to do superhuman things—things that no man could do without God's help.

11. His teachings would be in strict conformity with scripture, and his words and his writings would become scripture. *"For the prophecy came not in old time by the will of man: but holy men of God spake as they were moved by the Holy Ghost"* (2 Peter 1:21).

Elder Brown testified to his friend, and I testify to you, that Joseph Smith fulfills every one of these Biblical requirements for a true prophet. One of the "superhuman things" that Joseph did was the translation of *The Book of Mormon* – something that no man could have done without God's help. And as I've shown in a previous chapter, the coming forth of *The Book of Mormon* as a true record of God's people in ancient America is an undeniable evidence of Joseph Smith's prophetic calling.

DOES A PROPHET ALWAYS SPEAK AS A PROPHET?

Some people misunderstand the calling of a prophet. They expect that every word that comes out of his mouth should be the inerrant word of God. Yet even in the Bible Paul was careful to declare that some of his counsel (particularly regarding marriage) was being given "by permission and not of commandment " (1 Cor. 7:6, 12). In other words, it was his personal opinion.

In the Catholic church there is an understanding that the Pope is only infallibly speaking doctrine for the whole church when he speaks *"ex cathedra"*, or in his official Papal communications. Likewise, Joseph Smith and his successors have said that "a prophet is a prophet only when he speaks as a prophet". As a man he also has personal opinions but they are not prophetic. In other words if the president and prophet of the LDS church walks out the front door of his house and says "It looks like it's going to rain", is he then a false prophet if the sun shines? Hardly.

Both Joseph Smith and Brigham Young have been reported to have given their opinions about people living on the sun, or about men being on the moon. In the first place the validity of these reports is very suspect because they were third-hand accounts written down decades after they were supposedly uttered. But even if they did say those things it would have been personal opinions and not "false prophesies".

In considering the role of a prophet it's important to realize that in The Church of Jesus Christ of Latter-day Saints there is an established procedure for recognizing any new prophetic revelation as being the word and will of the Lord and binding on the whole church. A perfect example would be the revelation on ordaining all worthy males to the priesthood that was given in 1978. President Spencer W. Kimball had been praying mightily about the welfare of many LDS members of black African descent who were beginning to come into the Church in great numbers in Africa and Latin America, but who could not hold the priesthood under then-current Church policy.

After he received the revelation in answer to prayer, he presented it to the rest of the First Presidency and the Quorum of the Twelve Apostles. They in turn gave it prayerful consideration and gave it their unanimous support. The revelation was then presented to the entire membership of the church for their common consent and vote before it was published as doctrine and added to the Doctrine and Covenants as new scripture.

WHY DO WE NEED NEW REVELATION?
So then let me try to answer this question: "If Jesus Christ was and is the only way, why on earth did Joseph Smith need to receive a new revelation?" Actually, if mankind would have understood perfectly and followed perfectly the "way" that Jesus outlined for us, there would be no need for the "new revelation" of the Gospel plan that our Heavenly Father gave to the prophet Joseph. But that did not happen.

When he went into that grove of trees to pray in 1820, Joseph only wanted to know which of the existing Christian churches he should join. If the true Church of Jesus Christ had been preserved on earth since New Testament times, the Savior would have simply directed him to join that church.

Believe me, his life would have been much simpler and easier, and he would have lived much longer instead of being murdered in the prime of his life. But as you know, even those closest to Jesus in his mortal ministry misunderstood a great deal of what he tried to teach them. And as the fledgling New Testament church began to grow, it was almost ripped apart with dissention by those who misunderstood how we are to "come unto Christ".

It took a "new revelation" to the apostle/prophet Peter to straighten things out so that Jewish Christians would accept Gentiles into the Church. So there is nothing new or unique about having "new revelation" in the Church of Jesus Christ. If you want to "stick to the facts", the fact is that continuing revelation is an identifying hallmark of the New Testament church that is conspicuously missing in the Protestant and Catholic versions of Christianity that we find today.

Paul said that the "falling away" of the church from the original truth Christ taught had already begun in his own time, and he prophesied that it would continue. But Peter said that there would be a restitution (or restoration) of the Gospel plan before the Second Coming of Christ. Obviously there is no need to "restore" something that was never gone!

Jesus Christ certainly is the only way to heaven. It is definitely not by Joseph Smith or by works. But the true knowledge of how mankind can "come unto the Father" through the grace of Jesus Christ had been lost through apostasy by the third century AD. Therefore it was necessary that our Father give a "new revelation" of that truth to someone here on earth. It just happened to be a man named Joseph Smith.

Paul told the Ephesians that in addition to the Chief Cornerstone of Jesus Christ, the Church is built on a foundation of living apostles and prophets. The continuing revelation that they receive to guide the Church is necessary so that we "be not tossed to and from with every wind of doctrine". He said they would be needed "until we all come to a unity of the faith", which we certainly haven't done yet.

Joseph Smith serves the same function in "Mormonism" as Peter or Paul. No more, no less. But since even Peter said that much of Paul's writings were "hard to be understood", I'm grateful that God gave us a prophet in our own time to provide us a more complete understanding of the truth of Christ's Gospel.

SHOULD WE BLINDLY FOLLOW A PROPHET?

In the Latter-day Saint Primary classes our little children are taught a song that says:

Follow the prophet, follow the prophet,
Follow the prophet; don't go astray.
Follow the prophet, follow the prophet,
Follow the prophet he knows the way.

— Primary Songbook pages 110-111

But does that mean that Latter-day Saints are like "sheep" as some critics claim, who follow their prophets blindly? Well, Jesus himself described those who follow him as sheep, so that part is not as awful as it might seem. But what did Brigham Young himself say about following the prophets?

"I am more afraid that this people have so much confidence in their leaders that they will not <u>inquire for themselves of God whether they are led by him</u>. I am fearful they settle down in a state of blind self-security, trusting their eternal destiny in the hands of their leaders with a reckless confidence that in itself would thwart the purposes of God in their salvation, and weaken that influence they could give to their leaders, <u>did they know for themselves, by the revelations of Jesus, that they are led in the right way</u>"

—(Discourses of Brigham Young, *135*)

IS A TRUE PROPHET A PERFECT MAN?

There was only one perfect man who ever walked the earth, and that was Jesus Christ. God has always called prophets who were imperfect men. Adam partook of the forbidden fruit. Noah got drunk. Jonah got mad when God did not destroy Nineva. Moses was denied entry to the Promised Land because he did not give Jehovah the glory when he struck a rock and provided water for the children of Israel in the desert. Peter denied Christ three times. Paul contended with Peter and the other apostles. Joseph Smith was stopped by the Lord from translating *The Book of Mormon* for a time because of his transgressions. Brigham Young and his successors have all had their human weaknesses. But in none of these cases did the mistakes of these men mean that they were false prophets. At times they suffered the chastisement of the Lord but they continued to be true prophets.

WAS JOSEPH SMITH A POWER HUNGRY WOMANIZER AND A PEDOPHILE?

While Joseph Smith was not a perfect man as we've discussed, neither was he the power-hungry and over-sexed scoundrel that many of his critics accuse him of being.

Like the Biblical prophet David who was "beloved of the Lord", Joseph was a young man when he was called by God to an extraordinary life's mission. When he went into the woods to pray at age 14, he only wanted to know which church he should join. If he wanted a life of power and ease, he certainly failed miserably at that objective. Even when he became the leader of a new church with tens of thousands of followers, he and his wife Emma continued to serve others. Their home was always open to those needing shelter and care, and they often gave up their own beds and slept on the floor to provide shelter for the needy.

While it is true that he became the mayor of Nauvoo, the largest city in Illinois at the time, and he was a candidate for President of the United States and the military leader of the Nauvoo Legion, those roles were thrust upon him as civic duties required to maintain the order and growth of the church as God commanded him to do.

And what about his plural wives, some of whom were teenagers? The whole discussion of polygamy has been much misunderstood, from the 1830's when the principle of celestial marriage was revealed by God until he no longer required it of the Church and the practice was abolished in 1890. A great deal of valuable research and information on this topic can be found on an excellent website: https://josephsmithspolygamy.org/

But let me try to summarize in the limited space here some of the most important points to know and understand:

1. While studying the Old Testament, Joseph inquired of the Lord about the prophets Abraham, Isaac, Jacob and others who had multiple wives, apparently with God's approval. (Example: The twelve tribes of Israel came from the four wives of Jacob.)

2. God asked Joseph "Do you really want to know?, because if I reveal this principle to you, you'll have to live it." I'm pretty sure brother Joseph wished for the rest of his life that he had replied, "Never mind, I don't need to know."

3. After receiving the commandment to take a plural wife, it took Joseph a long time to reluctantly obey after a great deal of insistence from God, including a visit from an angel with a drawn sword who threatened his life if he did not proceed.

4. Many of Joseph's "sealings" to women (including all of those to women already married to other men) were for "eternity only" and were not in effect during their mortal lives. These sealings were not consummated as earthly marriages.

5. In the 1800's it was not uncommon for girls to marry as young as 16. Joseph was sealed to two young women under 15, but there is no evidence that those sealings were ever consummated as earthly marriages.

    (Note: my own mother and father were married during WWII when she was 17.)

6. While it is not known how many of Joseph's plural marriages were consummated sexually or how often relations occurred, DNA evidence shows that he had NO blood descendants from these sealings. Yet he produced several children with his first wife Emma.

So, was Joseph Smith a power hungry womanizer and a pedophile? Apparently not.

CONCLUSION

In a world filled with human foibles and uncertainty, I am eternally grateful that God our Father has seen fit to call modern prophets to lead and guide us as he did in ancient times. To me it is a testament of his great love for us his children. Now we just need to have the faith to follow the prophets, for therein is truth and safety, and ultimately eternal life.

END NOTES FOR CHAPTER 8

1 Westminster Confession of Faith, Chapter 1, VI, http://www.reformed.org/documents/index.html?mainframe=http://www.reformed.org/documents/westminster_conf_of_faith.html
2 Sandi Patti, "More Than Wonderful" album, 1991, Columbia Records/ Sony

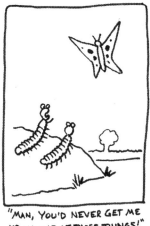

"MAN, YOU'D NEVER GET ME UP IN ONE OF THOSE THINGS!"

Illustration by Allen Richardson

EVIDENCE 9

ETERNAL PROGRESSION

Did you hear the story about the two caterpillars?
One looks up and sees a butterfly and says to the other,
"Boy, you'll never get me up in one of those things!"
Jesus "shall change our vile body, that it may be fashioned like unto His glorious body"
—Philippians 3:21

The sign in the window of the "Ex-Mormons For Jesus" Visitors center loudly proclaimed, "LDS Robert Starling Admits Men Can Become Gods!" Well the good news is, I not only "admit" it, but I joyfully <u>proclaim</u> it to the ends of the earth. I exhort all mankind to diligently seek it, as I echo the word of Paul in saying:

"<u>let this mind be in you</u> as it was in Christ Jesus, who, being in the form of God, thought it not robbery to be equal with God."

—(Philippians 2:5-6)

I am a child of God, and that I'm hoping to grow up to be like my Heavenly Father. I believe that as a child of the King I'm also heir to a throne, and that as a child of God I have within me the capacity to become as He is. So … do Mormons believe they can become gods? Yep, and so did the first-century Christians! If you don't believe it, just keep reading. I'll present the evidence.

WHAT IS MAN THAT THOU SHOULD BE MINDFUL OF HIM?

This doctrine of "Eternal Progression" or recognition of mankind's divine potential is one of the most misunderstood teachings of The Church of Jesus Christ of Latter-day Saints. In fact, notwithstanding the above quoted words of Paul, it is considered by many good Christians to be the ultimate heresy.

This attitude is no doubt rooted in many things. One of these is the notion fostered by St. Augustine, and later by Calvin and other Reformation thinkers that man is some lowly creature who is the handiwork of a Creator God in the same category as a painting or a piece of sculpture, or in a more modern context perhaps like Ghepetto's puppet Pinoccio, or a Frankenstein creature or an artifically intelligent computer robot. But Pinoccio wanted to be a "real boy" – a true son to Ghepetto. The glorious news of the Restoration of New Testament Christianity is that we are "real boys" to God. As Paul said, we are his "offspring".

Martin Luther was one of the first in the Reformation who "admitted" that the Christian church of his time had "fallen away" and had lost many of the simple truths of the "faith once delivered to the saints". An important part of that which was lost was a knowledge of the nature of God and man's relationship to Him. Shortly after the Apostolic era the Hellenizing of the Christian God began, ending with a depersonalized Essence of Being which bore no recognizable relationship to the God of Abraham, Isaac, and Jacob! No wonder then that the doctrine that we are indeed the "offspring" of God should be lost, hidden, or mythologized into obscurity.

In order to really see what our Father wants for his children, we have to take off the lens of the Reformation thinkers through which much of the modern Christian world views its theology and get back to the words of scripture itself and see what was taught and believed in the early Christian church.

So hang on, dear reader – this chapter may be a bumpy ride!

Warning – you're gonna have to open up your mind a bit and consider some things that may sound a bit strange and even blasphemous at first. But if you'll stay with me, I'll show you that everything I have to say is based on Biblical principles. It's kinda like when Paul wrote to the Corinthians and told them they were not ready to be taught the deeper doctrines of God:

And I, brethren, could not speak unto you as unto spiritual, but as unto carnal, even as unto babes in Christ. I have fed you with milk, and not with meat: for hitherto ye were not able to bear it, neither yet now are ye able. For ye are yet carnal:

— 1 Cor. 3:1-3

And the writer to the Hebrews said likewise:

For when for the time ye ought to be teachers, ye have need that one teach you again which be the first principles of the oracles of God; and are become such as have need of milk, and not of strong meat. For every one that useth milk is unskilful in the word of righteousness: for he is a babe. But strong meat belongeth to them that are of full age, even those who by reason of use have their senses exercised to discern both good and evil.

— Hebrews 5: 12- 14

What we're gonna talk about in this chapter is getting into the "meat" of the Gospel of Jesus Christ. If you've only heard the "milk" before, I hope that you'll be "able to bear it". Ordinarily the kinds of things we'll be discussing here are reserved for "them that are of full age" in their Christian walk and study. However because critics of my faith have raised these issues in public forums I feel I need to share them with you here, even though I'm taking a chance in doing so "out of order".

One of the early Church Fathers was Clement, a first century bishop of Rome. He is said to have been instructed personally by the Apostle Peter. He wrote:

The teachings of all doctrine has a certain order. There are certain things that must be delivered first, others in second place and others in third place and so on. If they be delivered in their order they become plain, but if they be brought forward out of order they will seem to be spoken against reason.

– Clementine Recognitions III

You see, it's hard to explain theological calculus or even trigonometry and algebra to folks who haven't yet studied the spiritual arithmetic or geometry. This is not meant to demean the intelligence of my dear readers, but you can't know what you haven't been taught, and I'm pretty sure your pastor or priest hasn't shared these spiritual "advanced mathematics" with you.

Heck, even most Latter-day Saints are not aware of the background behind most of this stuff even though they believe the basics of it.

INSIDE LATTER-DAY CHRISTIANITY

The doctrine of "eternal progression" as it is known in Latter-day Christianity is found in part in the 132nd section of the Doctrine and Covenants. It describes the condition in heaven (not here on earth) of men and women who are faithful to Christ in obeying his commandments and who enter into special covenants with him and subsequently remain faithful to those promises:

Then shall they be gods, because they have no end; therefore shall they be from everlasting to everlasting, because they continue; then shall they be above all, because all things are subject unto them. Then shall they be gods, because they have all power, and the angels are subject unto them.

– D&C 132:20

In contrast, those who do <u>not</u> make and keep those covenants with God but do accept Christ as their savior and otherwise live his commandments are described thusly:

For these angels did not abide my law; therefore, they cannot be enlarged, but remain separately and singly, without exaltation, in their saved condition, to all eternity; and from henceforth are not gods, but are angels of God forever and ever.

– D&C 132:17

So if you only want to be <u>saved</u> and not <u>exalted,</u> you can stop reading now. But you may want to take a little peek behind the veil to see what the Bible calls "the things that accompany salvation".

Perhaps the most extensive explanation of this doctrine is found in a sermon given by Joseph Smith in 1844 shortly before his death. The occasion was the funeral of a man named King Follett, and it is known as the King Follett Discourse. He said:

Here, then, is eternal life — to know the only wise and true God. And <u>you have got to learn how to be gods yourselves</u> — to be kings and priests to God, the same as all Gods have done — by going from a small degree to another, from grace to grace, from exaltation to exaltation, until you are able to sit in glory as do those who sit enthroned in everlasting power.[1]

(Note that this pertains to both men and women. The "exaltation" that elevates mankind to godhood through the grace of Christ does not happen to single individuals, but to couples sealed in the New and Everlasting Covenant of eternal marriage. But if you're single now don't worry. Our Father has prepared a way for all his children to partake of these blessings, in the next life if not in this one.) The LDS prophet Lorenzo Snow in 1840 expressed this doctrine that we call "eternal progression" in a short couplet that kinda sums it up nicely.

"As man is, God once was. As God is, man may become."

Here then, is the "meat" of the Gospel of Jesus Christ: To understand that <u>salvation is only the beginning</u> of what God wants for his children. To know that the ultimate goal of our Heavenly Father is <u>to make us like himself</u>. This is the second "good news" that Latter-day Christianity brings to the world. (The first is that Christ died for our sins and was resurrected on the third day so that we can be saved.) But as Clement said, if this news is brought forth "out of order" (that is, without a solid foundation of knowledge) then it will seem to the uninformed Christian "milk drinkers" to be "against reason". For this reason the doctrine of eternal progression to become like God has drawn lots of fire from outside The Church of Jesus Christ of Latter-day Saints.

OUTSIDE LATTER-DAY CHRISTIANITY

Criticism of this doctrine ranges from good-natured kidding to outright hostility. One of the most-quoted lines from song "I Believe" in the popular Broadway musical "The Book of Mormon" says:

I believe that God has a plan for all of us. I believe that plan involves me getting my own planet.

A critic Bill McKeever writes:

Isaiah 43:10 makes it clear that no man, Mormon included, will ever attain Godhood for it says, "I am He; before Me there was no God formed, neither shall there be after Me." ...

Regardless of what Joseph Smith and other Mormon leaders have said about men passing on to Godhood, the fact remains that the God of the Bible, who is all knowing, says He knows of no other Gods

—(Isaiah 44:8). ...

The possibility of man becoming divine is a man-made promise that the true God will not honor. It was His plan that we become His children by faith in Jesus Christ, to live with Him throughout eternity as His people (not fellow Gods).

—http://www.mrm.org/lorenzo-snow-couplet

But McKeever and other critics of this teaching just don't understand it. And as one of the early church fathers said:

"men are apt to deride what they do not understand. The ignorant, still ... condemn what they ought most to venerate." – St. Cyril of Alexandria - seventh book against Julian:

And so I will say to McKeever and others of his persuasion as the writer to the Hebrews said: (and I know I'm repeating myself here, but perhaps it bears repetition)

For <u>when for the time ye ought to be teachers, ye have need that one teach you again</u> which be the first principles of the oracles of God; <u>and are become such as have need of milk, and not of strong meat.</u>

– Hebrews 5: 12- 14

INSIDE MERE CHRISTIANITY
GODHOOD: SOMETHING TO ASPIRE TO? OR BLASPHEMY TO CONSIDER?

(Are ya'll ready for this? Hang on, this is gonna blow your mind!) The doctrine that men can become gods is something found in the Bible and almost everywhere among the earliest Christians if you only know where to look for it.

All Christians believe that we have a Father in Heaven. Jesus taught us to pray "Our Father, which art in heaven …" In Hebrews the Bible says that he is the father of our spirits. (Heb. 12:9) In Isaiah we read that Lucifer who was called "son of the morning" rebelled against God and was cast out of heaven for seeking to exalt his throne above that of our Heavenly Father. (Isa. 14:13) When Lucifer met Adam and Eve in the Garden of Eden, he told them that if they partook of the forbidden fruit that they would be as gods, knowing good and evil. (Gen. 3:5) Many people have said that was the big lie that the "serpent" told. Although he told many lies, was that particular statement a lie? We find a few verses later that when God came into the garden, he turned and said to Jesus Christ, his son, who helped in the creation: *"look, man has become as one of us, knowing good and evil"*.

—(Gen. 3:22)

So that particular statement that Adam and Eve "would be as gods, knowing good and evil" was not a lie. By coming to "know good and evil" Adam and Eve gained at least that one quality of godhood.

Indeed we are children of God, and not in just a mythical or metaphysical sense, but literally of the same heavenly species. He is "the father of our spirits," (Heb. 12:9) and as Paul said "we are the offspring of God" (Acts 17:29) Jesus himself said that our ultimate goal is to be *"perfect* (in the Greek "spiritually mature" or "complete"), *even as your Father in Heaven is perfect."* (Matt 5:48) Man was separated from God by transgression with the fall of Adam. Then Christ came "to reconcile us with the Father" so that the separation might be only temporary.

Thus, we know that when the glorified, resurrected and exalted Jesus returned to the being whom he called "my father and your father, my god and your god" (John 20:17) he was leading the way for us to do the same. Even though we now *"see through a glass darkly",* (1 Cor 13:12) We know that *"when we see him we shall be like him,"* (1 John 3:2) because Paul said that we should *"let this mind be in us as it was in Christ Jesus, who being in the form of God thought it not robbery to be equal with God."*

—(Philippians 2:6)

The mistaken doctrine of the depravity of man as some sort of worm rather than as a child of God flourished in the medieval church and was "canonized" in the Reformation by Calvin and others. But this was an apostate doctrine. It was not the view of our relationship to himself that God wishes us to have. Indeed the Psalmist said *"what is man that thou art mindful of him. Thou has created him a little lower than the angels"* (Psalms 8:5). In fact, the word there used for "angels" in the King James version is actually ***Elohim*** which in other Bible verses is translated "gods". So the correct reading should be: *"what is man that thou art mindful of him? Thou has created him a little lower than the Gods."*

So what IS man? Is he simply a creation of God like a woodcarver creates a puppet? Is man a "Pinocchio", or is he a "real boy"? - is he the "offspring" of God as Paul tells us? Is God the

Father of our spirits in the same way that our earthly fathers and mothers are the "creators" of our bodies? And as our father, <u>what does he want for his children?</u> What has he <u>promised</u> us through his Only Begotten Son?

There are lots of religion teachers out there that would have you settle for less than your full inheritance. Let's look at it this way: Suppose your father was a king (or at least very rich) and he prepared for you an elaborate seven-course meal. Then someone came along and diverted your invitation, and convinced you that all you should expect from your parent was soup and an appetizer. Would that person be your friend? On one of the LDS blogs we read this:

"A mortal father would want his children to inherit his kingdom/business/etc. So why would an immortal, exalted father be any different? How could a "loving Father" want to withhold His divine inheritance from His children?

It is my firm belief that he simply WOULDN'T and DOESN'T. Sure, [anti-Mormons] like to misconstrue it and call it blasphemy, but seriously, WHY are we here if not to gain exaltation? Does God just think it's funny to send His children to earth to starve, fight in wars, and struggle all the days of their lives only to have them return home to live....exactly as they lived before with NO progression or true reward? That doesn't sound like any father I know.

... I want to be like my Father. Not kind of like Him, and not ALMOST like Him, but EXACTLY like Him. Put simply: <u>I want to inherit a portion of His company... not just to work as a cashier in one of His chain stores.</u> And I believe this is what He wants as well. For ALL of His children."

– From "The Lola Letters" – commenter on

http://askmormongirl.wordpress.com/2012/01/02/do-mormons-believe-people-can-become-gods/

SOME MODERN CHRISTIANS "GET IT" ABOUT MEN BECOMING GODS

One of the great thinkers in modern Christianity is C. S. Lewis. Not only did he write great Christian-themed novels like *The Chronicles of Narnia*, but he authored many theological classics that are treasured by Christians worldwide. In some of them he wrote:

It is a serious thing to live in a society of possible gods and goddesses, to remember that the dullest and most uninteresting person you talk to may one day be a creature which, if you saw it now, you would be strongly tempted to worship....

– C. S. Lewis, The Weight of Glory, p. 9

God said to this hairless monkey, "get on with it, become a god."

—C. S. Lewis, A Grief Observed, p. 72

(God) said that we were "gods" and He is going to make good His words. If we let Him, for we can prevent Him if we choose. He will make the feeblest and filthiest of us into a god or goddess, dazzling, radiant, immortal creature, pulsating all through with such energy and joy and wisdom and love as we cannot now imagine, a bright stainless mirror which reflects back to God perfectly (though, of course, on a smaller scale) His own boundless power and delight and goodness. The process will be long and in parts very painful; but that is what we are in for.

—C. S. Lewis, Mere Christianity 174-5

Morality is indispensable: but the Divine Life, which gives itself to us and which calls us to be gods, intends for us something in which morality will be swallowed up. We are to be remade... we shall find underneath it all a thing we have never yet imagined: a real man, an ageless god, a son of God, strong, radiant, wise, beautiful, and drenched in joy.

– C. S. Lewis, The Grand Miracle, p. 85.

BUT IF THE BIBLE TALKS OF ONLY "ONE GOD" — CAN WE STILL BECOME GODS?

I quoted earlier from an anti-Mormon writer verses in Isaiah 43 and 44 that are used frequently by many critics of this LDS doctrine of eternal progression in attempts to refute it. But "a text without a context is a pretext for a prooftext" (am I repeating myself here?), and we need to look at what the entire Bible says about this, rather than selecting only one or two verses.

There are many ways to answer this question. It is a valid one, since the scripture seems to advocate a militant monotheism in these verses, in which Gods says "no other God is formed beside me", and "I know none other". How then can we reconcile them with the Mormon doctrine of becoming gods?

(1) A reasonable approach to these verses might take into account the Fatherhood of God. If we were to substitute "Father" (the most-used term for God in the Bible) in these verses, they would say essentially that "I am your <u>Father</u> and you have no other <u>Father</u> besides me". I could say the same thing to my own children and it would be a true statement. But it does not negate the fact that there are other fathers who have other children.

(2) We know that the speaker in Isaiah 43:10 was Jehovah, the God of Israel. He was telling the Israelites the difference between him, the living God, and the false pagan idols of their neighbors that were "formed" from wood or iron. He says "*there is no God formed beside me*".

In other words, the real message here is that the inanimate objects "formed" by man are not really gods at all. But it does <u>not</u> preclude the possibility of there being living beings somewhere in Eternity who are also the same kind of being that God is. In fact...

(3) When we consider who is actually talking here in Isaiah 43, we must put the remarks in their overall context.

- A. The speaker in Isaiah is Jehovah (YWYH), another name for the pre- mortal Jesus Christ; the "Rock" who followed Israel through the wilderness according to 1st Cor. 10:4.
- B. Jesus is indeed God the Son. And according to John1:1 he "created the heavens and the earth". But he did it under the direction of God the Father. When he spoke about his ascension after his resurrection, he said "*I go unto my God and to your God*". (John 20:17)
- C. Now tell me... did Jesus know something at this <u>later</u> date that he <u>didn't</u> know when he spoke those words to Isaiah about "knowing no other God"? Of course not! He knew about his father when he spoke to Isaiah just as he did when he spoke the words recorded in John's gospel. What we have to do is look at Isaiah in its proper context, which is...

(4) According to most serious Bible scholars, (including a direct quote I have from John Stewart, former Assistant Director of Walter Martin's Christian Research Institute) God has <u>revealed Himself progressively</u> to mankind, according to man's ability to understand Him. This means that —as Paul put it— He reveals the "milk" to those who are spiritually immature

(as the people of Israel were in the days of Isaiah), and to others He reveals the "meat", as He did to the New Testament Saints, and to Joseph Smith and the Latter-day Saints.

Let's look at the progression:

A. In Isaiah Jesus/Jehovah revealed the simple concept of one Living God as contrasted with the pantheon of heathen "gods" formed of iron and wood.
B. In His mortal ministry, Jesus/Jehovah revealed that not only were He and His Father both called "God", but that there was also a third person, the Holy Spirit, who is also "God".

This advanced concept of three persons —each of whom is God— is still misunderstood by the Jews today. They accuse Christians of <u>tri-theism</u> using the same Bible verses that anti- Mormon writers use to accuse the Latter-day Saints of "polytheism". (We find that somewhat ironic! Doesn't that mean that the Christians are worshiping a "different God" than the God of the Jews? The Jews certainly think so!)

C. In these latter days God the Father and Jesus revealed to Joseph Smith an even <u>more</u> advanced concept. It was a doctrine that had been lost from traditional Christianity – that God wants his children to grow and progress until they can become like him.

Where is the proof you say? Okay, let's look at what some other Bible verses say about this topic:

THE BIBLE SAYS THAT MEN WERE CREATED TO BECOME LIKE GOD

* *Let **us** make man in **our** image, after our likeness ... male **and female** created he the*
  —(Gen. 1:27-28)

* *man is **become as one of us**, knowing good and evil ...*
  —(Gen. 3:22)

* *thou hast made him **a little lower than the gods***
  —(KJVsays angels but the Greek is gods), (Ps. 8:5)

* ***Ye are gods**; and all of you are children of the most High,*
  —(Ps. 82:6)

209

Robert Starling

- *Jesus answered them, Is it not written in your law, I said, **Ye are gods**? If he called them gods, unto whom the word of God came, and the scripture cannot be broken;*
  —*(John 10:34-35)*

- *Be ye therefore perfect (Gr. "Spiritually mature or complete"), **even as your Father** in heaven is perfect*
  —*(Matt. 5:48)*

- *we are **the offspring of God**,*
  —*(Acts 17:29)*

- *The Spirit itself beareth witness with our spirit that **we are the children of God**: And if children, then heirs; **heirs of God**, and **joint-heirs with Christ**; if so be that we suffer with him, that **we may be also glorified** together.*
  —*(Rom. 8:17)*

- *Wherefore thou art no more a servant, but a son; and if a son, then **an heir of God through Christ**.*
  —*(Gal. 4:7)*

- *be in subjection unto **the Father of spirits**, and live,*
  —*(Heb. 12:9)*

- *Beloved, **now are we the sons of God**, and it doth not yet appear what we shall be: but we know that, **when he shall appear, we shall be like him**; for we shall see him as he is*
  —*(1 John. 3:2)*

- *to him that overcometh I will grant to **sit with me in my throne**, even as I also overcame, and am set down with my Father in His throne."*
  —*(Rev. 3:21)*

- *Whereby are given unto us exceeding great and precious promises: that by these ye might be **partakers of the divine nature** ...*
  —*(2 Pet. 1:4)*

- *He that overcometh **shall inherit all things**; and I will be his God, and he shall be my son.*
  —*(Rev. 21:7)*

"ORTHODOX" EARLY CHRISTIAN FATHERS TAUGHT THAT MEN CAN BECOME GODS

Now lest you think that the Latter-day Saints have mis-interpreted some of the above scriptures and we've gotten the wrong idea about "becoming god" or this "partaking of the divine nature" thing, lets look at what some of the earliest Christian pillars of orthodoxy had to say on the matter: (And let's keep in mind the big difference here between Satan's plan to become equal with God <u>on his own</u>, and God's plan that we can become like Him <u>through the work of our savior Jesus Christ.</u> As Paul said, that plan is not robbery.)

- "And how shall <u>man pass into God</u>, If God (Christ) had not been caused 'to pass into man?"
    —Ireneaus, (*Against the Heretics III.* 18.7, IV.20.5-6). (IV.33.4)

- "We were not made gods at our beginning, but <u>first we were made men, then, in the end, gods.</u>
    —*Irenaeus, Against Heresies, 4:37*

- "How then will any <u>be a god</u>, if he has not first been made a man? ... For one's duty is first to observe the discipline of man and thereafter to <u>share in the glory of God</u>."
    —Irenaeus, *Against Heresies,* 4:39

- "the Logos [Word] of God had become man so that you might learn from a man <u>how a man may become God.</u>"
    —Clement of Alexandria, *Exhortation to the Greeks* 1.8.4

- "the soul [which is kept pure], receiving the Lord's power, <u>studies to become a god</u>"
    —Clement of Alexandria, *Stromata* VI. 14

- "Many become gods by participation in God; we should flee with all our power from being men and <u>make haste to become gods.</u>"
    — Origin (*On the Gospel of John* 11.3,19, cf. 20.29)

- "He (Christ) was made man <u>that we might be made God</u>"
    — Athanasius, *On the Incarnation of the Word* 65. Cf., *Oration Against the Arians* 1.11.38-39, ll, 19.47, and throughout his writings.)

- "<u>I may become God</u> to the same extent as He became man."

  — Gregory of Nazianus, *Orations* 29:19

- It is demonstrated that <u>all men are deemed worthy of becoming "gods,"</u> and of having power to become sons of the Highest."

  —Justin Martyr, *Dialogue With Trypho,* 124

- For <u>we shall be even gods,</u> if we shall deserve to be among those of whom He declared, "I have said, Ye are gods,' and, 'God standeth in the congregation of the gods.' But this comes of His own grace, not from any property in us, <u>because it is He alone who can make gods."</u>

  —Tertullian, *Against Hermogenes* 5

- "<u>To make gods those who were men</u>, He (Christ) was made man who is God."

  —St. Agustine, *("Augustine's Conception of Deification," "Journal of Theological Studies",* Gerald Bonner NS, Vol. 37, pt.2, P. 376)

- The Only Begotten Son of God, wanting to make us <u>sharers in his divinity,</u> assumed our nature so that he, made man, might <u>make men gods</u>.

  —Thomas Aquinas, (paragraph 460 of the *Roman Catholic Catechism*)

Do you want more? Here's more:

- "But if thou art desirous of also <u>becoming a god,</u> obey Him that has created thee, and resist not …"

  — *Hippolytus,* Refutation of all Heresies *10:29*

- "We declare that the Logos of God became man for the purpose of our salvation, <u>so that we might receive the likeness of the Heavenly One and be made God</u> after the likeness of the true Son of God according to nature and the Son of man according to the flesh, our Lord Jesus Christ."

  — Appolinaris of Laodicea

- let us become the image of the one whole God, bearing nothing earthly in ourselves, so that we may <u>consort with God and become gods, receiving from God our existence as gods</u>

  — St. Maximus the Confessor

- Souls wherein the Spirit dwells, illuminated by the Spirit, themselves become spiritual, and send forth their grace to others. Hence comes... abiding in God, then <u>being made like to God,</u> and, highest of all, <u>then being made God</u>

  —St. Basil the Great, (*On the Spirit.*)

- every believer must, through participation in Christ, <u>be born a Christ</u>" ... "He was made man <u>that we might be made Gods</u>".

  — Methodius (cited, Inge, "*Christian Mysteries* p. 357)

- the chaste man will become "<u>identical in all respects with God.</u>"

  —Lactantius (about 325 AD)

- in the "future life" we will be among gods ... those who have become perfect ... and become pure in heart ... <u>They are called by the appellation of gods, being destined to sit on thrones with the other gods</u> that have been first put in their places by the Savior."[1]

  — Clement of Alexandria (d. A.D. 215)

- "other beings besides the true God, <u>who have become gods</u> by having a share of God."

  —Origen of Alexandria (d. A.D. 251)

- "God made man for that purpose, that from men <u>they may become gods</u>. ... They who cease to be mere men, abandon the ways of vice, and are become perfect, are <u>gods and sons of the Most High.</u>

  —St. Jerome (d. A.D. 419)

So — are we talking about just a "weird" Mormon doctrine? Heck no! The Bible teaches it, and the greatest leaders of the early Christian church taught it. This sublime doctrine of man's eternal potential to "partake of the divine nature" is ubiquitous in the early church. <u>How then, did it become lost?</u> (At least it was lost in the western branch of Christendom. It is still taught to some extent in the eastern Orthodox churches.)

One of the most powerful influences on Christian theology was <u>Agustine</u>, the bishop of Hippo (450 AD). Although he taught this doctrine of "divinization" or "theosis" in his early writings, he seems to have changed his mind somewhere along the line and he denies it in his later teachings. In my personal opinion, Agustine is responsible for much of the "falling away" of the church from Christ's original doctrines, and we'll get into some of that in other chapters.

But some modern Christian thinkers and writers have not been fooled. They "get it". Let's see what they say ….

A CATHOLIC MONK WHO UNDERSTANDS DIVINIZATION

Jordan Vajda is a Roman Catholic Dominican monk. His master's thesis completed at the Graduate Theological Union at the University of California, Berkeley in 1998 is called *"Partakers of the Divine Nature"*. In it he compared the Latter-day Saint doctrine of eternal progression with the teachings of the early Church fathers.

Although he does not fully agree with all the ramifications of Latter-day Saint doctrine (or else he would have become a Latter-day Saint!), from his studies he draws the following conclusion: *The three persons who are <u>God by nature</u>—the Father, the Son, and the Holy Spirit— make created persons who are human by nature to be <u>"gods by grace"</u> through participation in their divinizing energies. <u>Divinized human persons</u>, without ceasing to be human, <u>become what they were not— gods.</u> The revelation of Christ and the dispensation inaugurated by him, according to the Greek Fathers of the Church, makes clear and accomplishes <u>what in God's plan is the purpose of human existence—to become a god</u>.*[3]

THE BOTTOM LINE?

If the Latter-day Saint doctrine of eternal progression is not a Christian teaching, then you will have deny the label of "Christian" to the inspired authors of the Bible, most of the early Church Fathers, and C.S. Lewis, among others. It is a sublime doctrine that was lost to Christendom in the Dark Ages. Thankfully it has been restored to the earth in these latter days so that we can learn how to become the "partakers of the divine nature" that our Heavenly Father intends us to be.

In the 1980's anti-Mormon Ed Decker made a lot of money by producing and distributing his film *"The Godmakers"*. He ridiculed this doctrine of eternal progression. He and his friends even sued me personally <u>twice</u> for millions of dollars (unsuccessfully, thank the Lord) because I pointed out the errors in his movie to others (see appendix 4). Like other anti-Mormons he can be described as St. Cyril of Alexandria said centuries ago:

"men are apt to <u>deride</u> what they do not understand. The ignorant, still … <u>condemn</u> what they ought most to venerate."

— *Cyril, Bishop of Alexandria (d. 444 AD), 7th Book Against Julian*

This ancient lost teaching of mankind's eternal potential is one of the most illuminating and inspired doctrines restored to the earth through Latter-day Christianity. "Mormons" are not "Godmakers". It is our Heavenly Father himself and his son Jesus Christ who are the "Godmakers". And it is their whole purpose to make us "partakers of the divine nature". God said *"this is my work and my glory, to bring to pass the immortality and eternal life of man"*
—(Moses 1:39 in *The Pearl of Great Price*)

Dear reader you can deny this if you wish, but if you do so it puts you in opposition to the Bible, to the Early Church Fathers, and to some of the brightest Christian scholars of our day. Right now you and I are like caterpillars. We creep along the earth slowly and laboriously and hardly ever look up to the sky. As Paul said we "see through a glass darkly" (1 Cor. 13:12). And someday we will sleep in the tomb like the caterpillar does in his cocoon.

But like the caterpillar we will awaken from our sleep and emerge as something vastly different from what we are now. If we do not rebel against our Father and "prevent" him (as C.S. Lewis cautioned) from granting us the blessings he stands waiting to give us, we shall not only "see him as he is" but "we shall be like him". (1 John 3:2) We will not only sing praises and worship God, but we will also be invited to sit on a throne with our Savior (Rev. 3:21) How glorious is that?! How wonderful!

I pray that you will not be like the other caterpillar who looked up at the butterfly and said, "You're never gonna get me up in one of those things".

ENDNOTES TO CHAPTER 9

1   Ensign, April 1971, King Follett Sermon, https://www.lds.org/ensign/1971/04/the-king-follett-sermon?lang=eng

2   (Clemens von Alexandrien, Werke, ed. 0. Stahlin, in the series Die Griechischen Christlichen Schriftsteller der ersten Jahrhunderte (1905-1936)

3   *Jordan Vajda, 'Partakers of the Divine Nature': A Comparative Analysis of Patristic and Mormon Doctrines of Divinization (master's thesis, Graduate Theological Union, 1998)*

EVIDENCE 10

TEMPLES OF THE MOST HIGH GOD

I believe in lost doctrines of Christianity that are now found only in Latter-day Saint temples.

One of the most distinctive features of the worship and practice of the Latter-day Saints is a series of ordinances performed in special buildings called temples. The temples are different from everyday meetinghouse or chapels. There are (as of 2019) only about 163 operating LDS temples in the world, while there are over 17,000 regular chapels or meetinghouses in over 190 countries.

While critics of the Church sometimes ridicule these temple ordinances and call them "weird", I will show that temple worship was not only a part of the religion of God's people, the ancient Israelites, but that it was also practiced by early Christians in New Testament times. Unfortunately the whole concept of temple worship was lost in later centuries because of the "falling away" of Christianity that we discussed earlier.

INSIDE LATTER-DAY CHRISTIANITY

The LDS beliefs about temple worship are simple and direct. The website temples.lds.org contains a page called "Why Latter-day Saints Build Temples" that starts like this:

From the days of the Old Testament, the Lord has commanded His people to build temples, -sacred structures where He could teach, guide, and bless them. For example, the Lord told the Israelites to build a portable tabernacle that would be their temple while they traveled in the wilderness (see Exodus 26-27; 40:35).

Additional Old Testament references to temples are found in 2 Chronicles 5:1-14; 7:1-2 (Temple of Solomon) and Ezra 3:1-13; 6:3 (Temple of Zerubbabel).

A TEMPLE ONLY IN JERUSALEM?

Some critics of my faith claim that God only commanded one temple to be built on earth for his children because the Bible only mentions the temple in Jerusalem, the capital of the Jewish nation. However recent archaeological and historical research has discovered evidence of more than fifteen other temples among the Israelites. For just one example see the March/April 1987 *Biblical Archaeology Review.* (See also the article here:

http://en.fairmormon.org/Book_of_Mormon/Anachronisms/Temple_in_New_World

When I was a child growing up in Georgia there were only thirteen temples in the entire world.

Latter-day Saints who did not live in areas with large Mormon populations had to travel great distances to participate in temple ordinances. My parents drove over two thousand miles from Georgia to Utah when I was a baby so that we could be sealed together as an eternal family. (more about that later).

The Bible tells us how Joseph and Mary and many of their neighbors and kin traveled to their temple in Jerusalem when Jesus was twelve years old. I can relate to their "temple excursion", a practice that Latter-day Saint families and wards in many areas of the world still engage in today. (they often charter tour buses for this purpose, which are much more comfortable than the caravans and wagon trains used by worshipers in earlier centuries, or even the 1943 Ford used by my mom and dad!).

Fortunately now there are many more temples all over the world so that they are closer to the homes of members of the Church wherever they may live. A complete list of LDS temples from Aba, Nigeria to Winter Quarters, Nebraska (none in Zanzibar – yet!) can be found at: https://www.lds.org/church/temples/find-a-temple?lang=eng

WHAT GOES ON IN THE TEMPLES?

While the ordinances themselves are not revealed outside the temple, there is much that we can discuss about what goes on inside those buildings. One of the temple ordinances - baptism for the dead- is mentioned in 1 Cor. 15:29. Other ordinances involve ceremonial washings and anointings, the receiving of a "new name", the use of certain handclasps, the donning of special articles of clothing, etc. My friend Dr. John A. Tvetdnes has written one of many excellent research articles that discuss some of the elements of temple worship. He provides evidence that they were part of the beliefs and practices of Jews and early Christians. His article in its entirety can be found here:

http://www.fairlds.org/fair-conferences/1999-fair-conference/1999-early-christian-and-jewish-rituals-related-to-temple-practices

OUTSIDE LATTER-DAY CHRISTIANITY

But uninformed (or just plain hostile?) critics of Mormonism use temple ordinances as an easy target for their polemics against the Saints because most people know little about the subject.

Since they are "exotic" or "different" from the practices of other Christians they are singled out for controversy. One anti-Mormon critic writes:

The Mormon walks out of these rituals bound to darkness by bloody oaths and occult incantations; sealed to the very principalities and powers we are told to be at war against ...

He stands encased in a secret set of magic underwear operating as an occult talisman.

—Ed Decker "Temple of the Godmakers"

SECRET OR SACRED?

The Church of Jesus Christ of Latter-day Saints has received criticism because we consider the covenants we make with God in our temples too sacred to discuss outside the Lord's house. We refer to these things as "sacred, not secret". I understand how it might be hard to see the difference from an outsider's viewpoint. But I think of it as a matter of intent. Is the intention to cover up something that is evil and dark (with secrets), or is it to preserve the sanctity of something that is beautiful and righteous (and sacred)? Jesus instructed his disciples not to share sacred things with those who would not understand or who would ridicule them:

Give not that which is holy unto the dogs, neither cast ye your pearls before swine, lest they trample them under their feet,

—Luke 6:37-42

Robert Starling

For nine years I was employed by an aerospace company that built the B-2 "Stealth" bomber, the most advanced aircraft of our time. In the name of national security I held a Top Secret security clearance with the Department of Defense and I signed documents promising never to reveal some of the things that I saw and learned about our nation's defensive technologies. One might ask whether my silence on those matters was "secret" or "secure". I prefer the latter, although I can see where others might not perceive that fine distinction.

BLOOD OATHS?

What is a "blood oath"? It sounds terrible, doesn't it? I suppose for someone wanting to paint a lurid picture of "Mormonism" it's a juicy couple of buzz words they like to use for shock value. But if one's motives are to inflame rather than to inform, any kind of distortion of the truth will suffice. For example; the enemies of early Christians claimed that those Saints were practicing "ritual cannibalism" every week at the Sacrament of the Lord's Supper because they would eat and drink bread and wine that represented the flesh and blood of Jesus Christ. I suppose if someone wanted to distort the truth badly enough they could say that I take a "blood oath" every Sunday at church. When I partake of the little cup of water it is blessed …

"to the souls of all those who drink of it, that they may do it in remembrance of the blood of thy Son, which was shed for them"

—(D&C 20:79)

In the Sacrament prayers I promise to take the name of Christ upon me, to remember him, and to keep his commandments. If that is a "blood oath", then so be it. I'm guilty as charged.

NO SECRET DOCTRINES IN CHRISTIANITY?

Critics of the Church of Jesus Christ of Latter-day Saints often say that in true Christianity there are no secret doctrines. They say that the Bible has plainly and simply set forth all that there is to do with the Christian religion, and nothing should be hidden from anyone. They cite certain verses to bolster this position:

Nothing is covered up that will not be revealed, or hidden that will not be known.

—Luke 12:2 also Matt. 10:26-28

For nothing is hidden that will not be made manifest, nor is anything secret that will not be known and come to light.

—Luke 8:17

(note that the context of these verses is the sins that people are hiding, NOT the teachings of the church)

Some leaders among these critics have gone so far to say that "Mormonism" is another form of gnosticism and that the very existence of secret doctrines not available to the public or to the neophyte church member brands the faith as a "non-Christian cult."

But the Bible does not always speak of secret things in a negative light:

"The secret things belong to the Lord our God,

—Deuteronomy 29:29

It is the glory of God to conceal things,

—Proverbs 25:2

So that your giving may be in secret. And your Father who sees in secret will reward you.

— Matthew 6:4

Argue your case with your neighbor himself, and do not reveal another's secret,

—Proverbs 25:9

In fact there were many instances in which Jesus taught things to his disciples that were too sacred to be shared with a disbelieving and disrespectful public:

And he said unto them, Unto you it is given to know the mystery of the kingdom of God: but unto them that are without, all these things are done in parables:

—Mark 4:11

Howbeit <u>we speak wisdom among them that are perfect</u> (Greek = "spiritually mature"): yet not the wisdom of this world, nor of the princes of this world, that come to naught: But <u>we speak the wisdom of God in a mystery, even the hidden wisdom, which God ordained before the world unto our glory</u>

—1 Corinthians 2:6-7

Let a man so account of us, as of the ministers of Christ, and <u>stewards of the mysteries of God</u>.

—1 Cor. 41

221

And he charged them that they should tell no man: but the more he charged them, so much the more a great deal they published it;

—Mark 6:37

And Jesus said to him, See you tell no man; but go your way, show yourself to the priest, and offer the gift that Moses commanded, for a testimony to them.

—Matt. 8:4

John the Revelator was told to write parts of his vision of the Apocalypse, but not other parts: I was about to write: and I heard a voice from heaven saying unto me, Seal up those things which the seven thunders uttered, and write them not.

—Rev. 10:4

Paul said that he received a vision from God in which he

"heard unspeakable words, which it is not lawful for a man to utter."

—2 Cor. 12:4

While Jesus taught parts of his message to anyone who would listen, he reserved some of his teachings only for the twelve apostles and others who were more spiritually mature. Paul and the writer of Hebrews also taught that there was a difference between the "milk" and the "meat" of the Gospel, and that there were those who were not yet ready to receive the "meat".

I have fed you with milk, and not with meat: for hitherto ye were not able to bear it, neither yet now are ye able. For ye are yet carnal:

—1 Cor. 3:1-3

For every one that useth milk is unskilful in the word of righteousness: for he is a babe. But strong meat belongeth to them that are of full age,

—Hebrews 5: 12- 14

Likewise Clement, an early Christian bishop of Alexandria who was taught personally by the apostles, wrote that there was an "order" to teaching the doctrines of Christ. Some of the more advanced teachings were to be reserved for those who had already received a firm foundation in the faith:

The teachings of <u>all doctrine has a certain order</u>. There are certain things that must be delivered <u>first</u>, others in second place and others in third place and so on. If they be delivered in their order they become plain, <u>but if they be brought forward out of order they will seem to be spoken against reason.</u>

— *Clementine Recognitions III*

The bottom line here is that none of the advanced or "secret" teachings of Christianity (or of Latter-day Christianity) are reserved for any "elite" few. <u>Anyone</u> who is willing to commit their life to Christ and obey his commandments is invited to partake of the higher ordinances of the gospel that are available in the temple to all who are prepared to receive them.

ANCIENT ORIGINS OF TEMPLE WORSHIP

Did Joseph Smith just dream up all this temple stuff, or is there more to it than that? Is it part of "another gospel" or was it practiced and taught by Christians in the New Testament era?

Here the story gets interesting. In the first hundred years or so after Christ, there were several competing versions or "flavors" of Christianity in existence, just as there are thousands of different Christian churches on earth today. They all claimed to believe in Christ but they differed in doctrine and in their interpretation of the writings of the apostles (sound familiar?). They called each other Gnostics or heretics. Eventually one "flavor" became large enough or politically-connected enough that it was able to get rid of the other "heretics", often by killing them and burning their books. This dominant strain or "flavor" of Christianity was largely represented by the Roman church, although in the Great Schism of 1054 A.D. the Eastern Orthodox Christians broke off and became their own "flavor".

In 1945 – about the same time as the discovery of the Dead Sea Scrolls- another similar cache of ancient records was discovered at the site called Nag Hammadi in Egypt. But whereas the DSS were primarily Jewish writings, the Nag Hammadi codices (books) were written by some of the earliest Christians in the 2nd and 3rd centuries. These writings contain many references to advanced Christian teachings that sound an awful lot like the Latter-day Saint temple ceremonies. That kinda rules out the theory that Joseph Smith made it all up out of his fertile imagination, right? It does for me.

ARE LATTER-DAY SAINT TEMPLE CEREMONIES DERIVED FROM MASONIC RITUALS?

While some of the Masonic orders may have more recent origins, the roots of Freemasonry go back to the builders of the Temple of Solomon in Jerusalem. The masons who built the temple were also knowledgeable about the ceremonies performed therein. It therefore stands to reason that there would be at least some similarities between the Masonic rites and the ancient temple ceremonies. I realize that there may be some folks who have issues with some of the practices of modern Masons (and perhaps rightfully so), but that's another subject. The same folks may also have issues with the practices of individual Baptists, Methodists, Catholics, Pentecostals, and even Latter-day Saints. (and perhaps rightfully so)

But the Latter-day Saint temple ceremonies are not derived from Masonic rituals. They came from the same source as the rituals practiced in the Temple of Solomon and in early Christian temples in Nag Hammadi and elsewhere. They are a restoration of the "meat" of the gospel of Jesus Christ that was revealed to Adam, Noah, Enoch, Abraham and other prophets, and was practiced by Christians in the New Testament era.

In the 1800's there was sometimes tremendous persecution of the "Mormons" involving murder, rape, burning of homes and farms, etc. At one time Joseph Smith and some of the other Latter-day Saint leaders joined Masonic lodges hoping that the pledges of mutual protection in that fraternal order might provide their people some safety. Unfortunately in most cases it did not work.

If indeed the Latter-day Saint temple ordinances are a restoration of ancient Christian practices (as the Nag Hammadi records indicate), and if Christian temple worship is rooted in antiquity going back to the days of Solomon's Temple and beyond, then once more it stands to reason that there should be at least some similarities between those ancient rites and Latter-day Christianity.

BAPTISMS FOR THE DEAD

Another distinctive practice of the Church of Jesus Christ of Latter-day Saints is the baptizing of church members on behalf of the dead. Latter-day Saints believe that baptism is an ordinance necessary for salvation, and that by performing the ordinance vicariously or via proxy for those that have passed on that they allow those departed souls an opportunity to receive the blessings of baptism in the hereafter. This practice was followed by the Corinthian saints as evidenced by Paul's reference to it in 1 Corinthians 15:29

Else what shall they do which are baptized for the dead, if the dead rise not at all? why are they then baptized for the dead?

Most scholars agree that Paul here referred to a well-known practice among the Corinthian saints of its members being baptized vicariously for the dead. He used it to illustrate that they had forgotten the reason they were performing the ordinance as some of them were losing faith in the doctrine of the resurrection. He explained to them that the whole point of performing these ordinances was that there would be a resurrection. Although this practice is not heard of in the Christian church after 250 A.D. it was well known before that time as will be evidenced later. Thus, far from being an "occultic practice" as claimed by critics of the Latter-day Saints, it is in fact proof that "Mormonism" is indeed a restoration of New Testament and First Century Christianity.

THE TEMPLE ENDOWMENT

Perhaps the least understood of all Latter-day Saint temple ordinances among non-Mormons is the temple endowment ceremony. Participation in this ordinance usually takes about two hours to complete. During the endowment ceremony, temple patrons are instructed in God's plan for mankind from the beginning of creation as they follow a symbolic Adam and Eve through the Garden of Eden experience, temptation by Lucifer, the fall of Adam, and the instructions as to the saving nature of the atonement of Jesus Christ whereby they may receive forgiveness of their sins.

At certain points in the ceremony they make special promises to God to be obedient to his commandments and to make sacrifices of their time and talents and even earthly possessions where necessary to build of the kingdom of God upon the earth. In return for entering into these covenants with their Heavenly Father, they are promised special blessings that come from obedience to God's commandments. These blessings have nothing to do with one's salvation. Rather they are spoken of Biblically as "rewards." They are some of the "rewards" that the writer of Hebrews spoke of as "the things that accompany salvation." (Hebrews 6:9) The making of these covenants is accompanied by the receiving of certain "signs and tokens" which are sacred and are not discussed outside the temple.

Brigham Young expressed the nature of the "signs and tokens" and their purposes in the following manner:

"Your endowment is, to receive all those ordinances in the house of the Lord, which are necessary for you, after you have departed this life, to enable you to walk back to the presence of the Father, passing the angels who stand as sentinels, being enabled to give them the key words, the signs and tokens, pertaining to the holy Priesthood, and gain your eternal exaltation in spite of earth and hell." [1]

At one point in the endowment ceremony, temple worshippers receive a "new name" similar to that mentioned in the book of Revelation.

"Him that overcometh ... I will write upon him my <u>new name</u>.

—*Rev. 3:12*

While the temple endowment ceremony practiced by early Christians has largely been lost to the rest of Christendom, those Latter-day Saints who have received their endowments will recognize many similarities to the ceremonies used to initiate new members into one of the monastic orders of the Greek Orthodox Church:

Stage 1: The initiate is given "a **new name**" and is invested with **a tunic and a headdress**.
Stage 2: The service is symbolic of three things: (#1) a second baptism or washing, (#2) the return of the prodigal son, and (#3) marriage. **The initiate goes to the Royal Doors and altar** [i.e., the iconostasis/**veil**] where the abbot (**who represents the father** from the prodigal son parable) meets him. There is an exchange of questions and answers between them which begins with the abbot **inquiring why the initiate has come there** and the initiate responds by announcing his intent. The questions and answers that follow incorporate the taking of **"formal vows" of obedience, chastity**.
The abbot reminds the initiate that "invisible angels are present recording [his] vow." The initiate is then invested with ecclesiastical clothing, a girdle, and a headdress. At the end of the ceremony the initiate and the initiator embrace.
Stage 3: The initiate is invested with the full religious dress which includes "an elaborately embroidered **apron**." This apron includes a symbol of Adam and also the acronymn for Paradise. The **clothing** given to the initiate in this stage of his progression is **never to be taken off**—day or night, "even in death." Monks at this stage of initiation vow to "renounce the world and the things of the world" [2]

TEMPLE MARRIAGES FOR ETERNITY

Some Latter-day Saint couples are married in regular chapels in a traditional "till death do you part" wedding. However worthy Latter-day Saints are encouraged to be married in the temples "for time and all eternity" in a special ceremony which creates a family unit that can last beyond the grave. (Note: Although most Protestants and Catholics have an innate or intuitive belief that husbands and wives and families will be together in the hereafter, their theology does not teach this and their wedding contract by definition ends with "till death do you part.")

Latter-day Saints believe that when Jesus gave to Peter (the head of the apostolic church) the "keys of the kingdom" and gave him the power such that whatsoever he "bound on earth" would be "bound in heaven" that he was committing to him the same divine authority to create eternal families that has been restored to the earth in these latter days and as presently found in those who officiate in Latter-day Saint temples. This concept of eternal marriage and eternal family is not new with "Mormonism" but was found in the early Christian church as we shall see later.

When an LDS temple marriage or sealing is performed, both the bride and groom are dressed in white clothing. They kneel on opposite sides of a low altar and clasp hands. A limited number of family and close friends are seated on opposite sides of the special "sealing room" that has mirrors on both walls. As the couple look at each other and repeat their vows they can see their images reflected back and forth into infinity, symbolizing the eternal nature of their commitment to each other. It is a very simple and dignified ceremony. I still remember fondly that day in the Salt Lake Temple when I knelt across the altar from my sweet bride and we were sealed together as man and wife for "time and all eternity".

TEMPLE GARMENTS

Much has been said and written in recent years about the so-called "magic underwear" that LDS members wear after they have received their endowments in the temple. It is unfortunate that many people who would never be so disrespectful as to make fun of a nun's habit or a Catholic or Lutheran pastor's robes or vestments or collar or a Jew's skull cap or yarmulke, yet they find it "okay" to mock the sacred clothing of the Latter-day Saints.

The Latter-day Saint temple garments are worn as a reminder of the covenants we have made to God in the temple. They are also given as an encouragement to dress modestly so as not to flaunt the sacred undergarments. They are representative of the garments of skins made by God himself and given to Adam and Eve in the Garden of Eden.

"Unto Adam also and to his wife did the Lord God make coats of skins, and clothed them"
—(Genesis 3:21).

Such clothing, fashioned by the very hands of God would surely be of a sacred nature. The Bible also makes mention of the sacred "garment of salvation" (Psalms 132:16; Isaiah 61:10; Revelation 3:4-5; 6:11). Other references to sacred clothing are found in many places in the Bible:

And I will clothe him with thy robe, and strengthen him with thy girdle, and I will commit thy government into his hand: and he shall be a father to the inhabitants of Jerusalem, and to the house of Judah. And the key of the house of David will I lay upon his shoulder; so he shall open, and none shall shut; and he shall shut, and none shall open. And I will fasten him as a nail in a sure place; and he shall be for a glorious throne to his father's house.
—Isaiah 22:21-23

I will greatly rejoice in the Lord, my soul shall be joyful in my God; for he hath clothed me with the garments of salvation, he hath covered me with the robe of righteousness, as a bridegroom decketh himself with ornaments, and as a bride adorneth herself with her jewels.
—Isaiah 61:10

Perhaps the reference to the Latter-day Saint undergarments as "magic" refers to the fact that one of the promises given to those who make these covenants in the temple is that the garment will be a protection to them. It is easy for unbelievers to mock and scoff at things they do not understand, and certainly Jesus himself suffered plenty of that even in the face of the many miracles he performed. But there are hundreds if not thousands of documented cases where the temple garment has protected its wearers from both physical and spiritual harm.

For example: My own father Austin Starling was once welding some metal in our basement when the torch slipped and the flame touched his leg. His outer clothing was burned away but his temple garment underneath was not even singed, and his leg was not burned. A similar event happened to my wife Sharon with an accident involving fireworks.

A more dramatic example is the account of Rachelle Wallace who was in a blazing airplane crash. She was burned over almost every square inch of her body EXCEPT the parts that were covered by her temple garments. Sister Wallace later entered a burning building to save a neighbor and was subsequently named California's Woman of the Year. I personally met her and heard her story first hand at a meeting in Los Angeles. Details of the account are in her book *The Burning Within* published in 1994 by Gold Leaf Press.

I suppose any miracle of God is considered "magic" by those who do not understand spiritual gifts. More about the LDS temple garments can be found on the Church's official web site: http://www.mormonnewsroom.org/article/temple-garments

(It includes a video that shows what they look like.)

WHAT DOES A MORMON DO TO ENTER THE TEMPLE?

Participation in temple ordinances is limited to those Latter-day Saints who are living their lives in obedience with the commandments of God, so as to be "worthy" to enter into the temple. Worthiness is determined in an interview held every two years with their Bishop and Stake President to determine if they are living in accordance with the principles of the gospel of Jesus Christ. New members of the church must usually wait one year after baptism before they can participate in temple worship. Upon successful completion of the interview the member is issued a temple "recommend" or certificate which is presented at the entrance to any temple for admission.

The questions asked in a temple recommend interview are simple and direct. There is nothing mysterious or secret or hidden about them. They are:

1. Do you have faith in and a testimony of God the Eternal Father, His Son Christ, and the Holy Ghost?

2. Do you have a testimony of the Atonement of Christ and of His role as Savior and Redeemer?

3. Do you have a testimony of the restoration of the gospel in these the latter days?

4. Do you sustain the President of the Church of Jesus Christ of Latter-day Saints as the Prophet, Seer, and Revelator and as the only person on the earth who possesses and is authorized to exercise all priesthood keys? Do you sustain members of the First

Presidency and the Quorum of the Twelve Apostles as prophets, seers, and revelators? Do you sustain the other General Authorities and local authorities of the Church?

5. Do you live the law of chastity?

6. Is there anything in your conduct relating to members of your family that is not in harmony with the teachings of the Church?

7. Do you support, affiliate with, or agree with any group or individual whose teachings or practices are contrary to or oppose those accepted by the Church of Jesus Christ of Latter-day Saints? (referring to anti-Mormon groups who actively oppose the LDS Church)

8. Do you strive to keep the covenants you have made, to attend your sacrament and other meetings, and to keep your life in harmony with the laws and commandments of the gospel?

9. Are you honest in your dealings with your fellowmen?

10. Are you a full-tithe payer?

11. Do your keep the Word of Wisdom?

12. Do you have financial or other obligations to a former spouse or children? If yes, are you current in meeting those obligations?

13. If you have previously received your temple endowment: Do you keep the covenants that you made in the temple? Do you wear the garment both night and day as instructed in the endowment and in accordance with the covenant you made in the temple?

14. Have there been any sins or misdeeds in your life that should have been resolved with priesthood authorities but have not been?

15. Do you consider yourself worthy to enter the Lord's house and participate in temple ordinances?

So you see, there's nothing secret or sinister about what you have to do in order to enter the temple.

TEMPLE WORSHIP IS THE ULTIMATE CHRISTIANITY

In conclusion let me say that the "meat" of the gospel of Jesus Christ that we receive in the temple is a wonderful gift from God. I call it "graduate level Christianity". The baptisms for the dead that make salvation available to those who have died without knowledge of Christ makes perfect sense to me.

And the promise of a celestial marriage to those who are sealed in the temple "for time and all eternity" is far superior to a union that is only "till death do us part".

The Bible says that after the resurrection of Christ, he visited with his apostles, *being seen of them forty days, and speaking of the things pertaining to the kingdom of God* (Acts 1:3) What did he teach them for forty days? The Bible is silent, and perhaps for good reason. Perhaps that is when he instructed them in temple worship. At any rate, I'm just glad that he restored it to us in these latter days.

END NOTES FOR CHAPTER 10

1   *Discourses of Brigham Young,* sel. John A. Widtsoe [Salt Lake City: Deseret Book Co., 1941], p. 416
2   Graham Speake, *Mount Athos: Renewal in Paradise* [New Haven, CT: Yale U. Press, 2002], 209– 15, cited in

EVIDENCE 11

MIRACLES AND SPIRITUAL GIFTS

I have a strong belief in the Biblical gifts of the spirit, and in modern miracles. I have personally experienced many of these gifts and I've known others who have had some marvelous experiences.

The Bible speaks of spiritual gifts that are given to the followers of Christ, according to their needs and their worthiness. Jesus said:

And these signs will accompany those who believe: in my name they will cast out demons; they will speak in new tongues; they will pick up serpents, and if they drink any deadly thing, it will not hurt them; they will lay their hands on the sick, and they will recover."

—Mark 16:17-18

And Paul wrote to the Corinthians:

For to one is given by the Spirit the word of wisdom; to another the word of knowledge by the same Spirit; To another faith by the same Spirit; to another the gifts of healing by the same Spirit; To another the working of miracles; to another prophecy; to another discerning of spirits; to another divers kinds of tongues; to another the interpretation of tongues:

—1Cor. 12:8-10

The presence of these gifts is one of the characteristics of the Church of Jesus Christ. The absence of these gifts is a characteristic of a church that does NOT belong to Jesus.

Robert Starling

INSIDE LATTER-DAY CHRISTIANITY

Our seventh Article of Faith states:

We believe in the gift of tongues, prophecy, revelation, visions, healing, interpretation of tongues, and so forth.

—*LDS Articles of Faith*

Of course as the Bible says, not every man or woman has every gift: Are all apostles? are all prophets? are all teachers? are all workers of miracles? Have all the gifts of healing? do all speak with tongues? do all interpret?

—*1 Cor. 12:29-30*

But within the whole church all the gifts are present, just as in the New Testament church.

OUTSIDE LATTER-DAY CHRISTIANITY

There are many among various Christian churches who believe that the age of miracles is past, and that there is no place or need today for spiritual gifts. These folks are often called "cessationists" because they believe miracles and spiritual gifts have "ceased". There are quite a number of debates on this topic that have been going on for centuries and continue even today.

In October 2013 at Grace Community Church in Sun Valley, California an Evangelical Bible teacher named Tim Pennington gave a seminar talk called "The Case for Cessationism". In his presentation he said:

So what do we mean by cessationism? We mean that the Spirit no longer sovereignly gives individual believers the miraculous spiritual gifts that are listed in the Scripture and that were present in the first century church. It is neither the Spirit's plan, nor His normal pattern to distribute miraculous spiritual gifts to Christians and churches today as He did in the times of the Apostles. Those gifts ceased as normative with the apostles.[1]

On the other hand, among those who believe that the Holy Spirit is still working and that spiritual gifts are for today's Christians is Mark Rutland, who wrote this on the Charisma News website about those who deny that such gifts exist today:

Denouncing all who dare to believe in the validity of biblical gifts in this and every age is a cave-dweller's point of view: Because I have never seen a train, there are no trains. It also smacks of an incredible conceit. "If God were going to manifest His gifts anywhere in any time among any group, it would surely be now among me and my friends." Hmmmm.[2]

The great reformer and founder of the Methodist church John Wesley acknowledged that a loss of spiritual gifts was a sign that the apostacy or "falling away" of New Testament Christianity was complete in his day:

It does not appear that these extraordinary gifts of the Holy Spirit were common in the church for more than two or three centuries. We seldom hear of them after that fatal period when the emperor Constantine called himself a Christian. ... The Christians had no more of the Spirit of Christ than the other heathens. ... This was the real cause why the extraordinary gifts of the Holy Ghost were no longer to be found in the Christian Church because the Christians were turned heathens again, and only had a dead form left.

—Wesley's Works, vol. 7, 89:26, 27

SPIRITUAL GIFTS AND MIRACLES IN THE RESTORATION

Latter-day Saints agree that the Holy Spirit withdrew from most of mankind after that "fatal period" identified by John Wesley. I'm sure there were occasions when individual believers in Christ prayed for and received miracles, but I'm equally sure that the "traditional" or "orthodox" church organization "had only a dead form left" and was devoid of spiritual guidance.

The "good news" that Latter-day Saints bring to other Christians today is that those New Testament spiritual gifts have been restored and are once again found on the earth. In the first recorded miracle of the Restoration, Joseph Smith cast a devil out of Newel Knight: He sent for the prophet, who, when he came found Newel in a sad condition and suffering greatly. His visage and limbs were distorted and twisted in every shape imaginable. At last he was caught up off the floor and tossed about most fearfully.

The neighbors hearing of his condition came running in. After he had suffered for a time the prophet succeeded in getting him by the hand, when Newel immediately spoke to him, saying he knew he was possessed of the devil, and that the prophet had power to cast him out. "If you know I can, it shall be, done," replied the prophet; and then almost unconsciously he rebuked Satan and commanded him to depart from the man. Immediately Newel's contortions stopped, and he spoke out and said he saw the devil leave him and vanish from sight[3].

HEALING MIRACLES

Almost everyone in The Church of Jesus Christ of Latter-day Saints can share an experience (or several!) recounting a time when they've personally seen the power of God evident in physical healing. The Saints believe literally in the Biblical instruction to "call for the elders of the Church" when someone is sick or injured.

Is any sick among you? let him call for the elders of the church; and let them pray over him, anointing him with oil in the name of the Lord:

—James 5:14

In The Church of Jesus Christ of Latter-day Saints the anointing of the sick is a simple and dignified procedure. One priesthood holder anoints the head of the sick or injured person with a single drop of olive oil that has previously been blessed or "consecrated" in a separate ordinance or ritual. He places his hands on the person's head. Then calling the person by name he gives a prayer of anointing in the name of Jesus Christ and by the power of the priesthood. The other elder then joins in a separate prayer where they both place their hands on the person's head and he "seals" the anointing and gives whatever blessing he is impressed by the power of the Holy Spirit to give at that time.

Any two holders of the Melchizedek Priesthood may participate in the administering to the sick, and in an emergency both the anointing and the sealing blessings can be given by one elder.

A personal example: When my wife Sharon and I were first married she was subject to occasional migraine headaches that were quite painful. One night she awoke at about two in the morning crying in pain. She asked me to give her a blessing, which I did immediately. In an instant the pain went away and we both were able to get back quickly to a peaceful sleep. Not all healings by the Spirit are that immediate or dramatic, but we were very grateful for God's grace and power on that night.

OTHER EXAMPLES OF HEALING MIRACLES

From the very beginnings of The Church of Jesus Christ of Latter-day Saints there are accounts of healings:

"Ezra Booth, of Mantua, a Methodist preacher of much more than ordinary culture, and with strong natural abilities, in company with his wife, Mr. and Mrs. Johnson, and some other citizens of this place, visited Smith at his house in Kirtland, in 1831. Mrs. Johnson had

been afflicted for some time with a lame arm, and was not at the time of the visit able to lift her hand to her head. The party visited Smith, partly out of curiosity, and partly to see for themselves what there might be in the new doctrine.

During the interview the conversation turned upon the subject of supernatural gifts; such as were conferred in the days of the apostles. Some one said: 'Here is Mrs. Johnson with a lame arm; has God given any power to men on the earth to cure her?' A few moments later, when the conversation had turned in another direction, Smith rose, and walking across the room, taking Mrs. Johnson by the hand, said in the most solemn and impressive manner: "Woman, in the name of Jesus Christ, I command thee to be whole; and immediately left the room. The company were awestricken at the infinite presumption of the man, and the calm assurance with which he spoke. The sudden mental and moral shock—I know not how better to explain the well attested fact—electrified the rheumatic arm—Mrs. Johnson at once lifted it with ease, and on her return home the next day she was able to do her washing without difficulty or pain."[4]

Nauvoo, IL 22 July 1839

Brother Joseph walked up to Brother Fordham and took him by the right hand; in his left hand he held his hat. He saw that Brother Fordham's eyes were glazed, and that he was speechless and unconscious. After taking hold of his hand, the Prophet looked down into the dying man's face and said, "Brother Fordham, do you not know me?" At first he made no reply; but we could all see the effect of the Spirit of God resting upon him.

Joseph again said, "Elijah, do you not know me?" With a low whisper, Brother Fordham answered, "Yes." The Prophet then said, "Have you not faith to be healed?" The answer, which was a little plainer than before, was, "I am afraid it is too late. If you had come sooner, I think I might have been." He had the appearance of a man waking from sleep. It was the sleep of death. Joseph then said, "Do you believe that Jesus is the Christ?" "I do, Brother Joseph," was the response. Then the Prophet of God spoke with a loud voice, as in the majesty of the Godhead, "Elijah, I command you, in the name of Jesus of Nazareth, to arise and be made whole!"

The words of the Prophet were not like the words of man, but like the voice of God. It seemed to me that the house shook from its foundation. Elijah Fordham leaped from his bed like a man raised from the dead. A healthy color came to his face, and life was manifested in every act. His feet were done up in Indian-meal poultices. He kicked them off his feet, scattered the contents, then called for his clothes and put them on. He asked for a bowl of bread and milk and ate it. Then he put on his hat and followed us into the street to visit others who were sick.

As soon as we left Brother Fordham's house, we went into the house of Joseph B. Noble, who was very low and dangerously sick. When we entered the house, Brother Joseph took him by the hand, and commanded him, in the name of Jesus Christ, to arise and be made whole. He did arise and was immediately healed[5]

Matthew Cowley was a Latter-day Saint Apostle who served as a missionary in Polynesia. In a famous talk he gave on "Miracles" at Brigham Young University in 1953 he described several miraculous experiences. On one occasion he was asked to perform the ordinance of blessing a baby (similar to a christening) by a family in New Zealand:

> I said, 'All right, what's the name?' So he told me the name, and I was just going to start when he said, 'By the way, **give him his vision when you give him a name. He was born blind.** '

> It shocked me, but then I said to myself, why not? Christ said to his disciples when he left them, 'Greater things than I have done shall you do.' (See John 14:12) I had faith in that father's faith. After I gave that child its name, **I finally got around to giving it its vision**. That boy is about twelve years old now.

> The last time I was back there I was afraid to inquire about him. I was sure he had gone blind again. That's the way my faith works sometimes. So I asked the branch president about him. And he said, **'Brother Cowley, the worst thing you ever did was to bless that child to receive his vision. He's the meanest kid in the neighborhood; always getting into mischief.'** Boy, I was thrilled about that kid getting into mischief!

In the same speech he also spoke about another miracle that was even more dramatic - raising the dead.

> I was called to a home in a little village in New Zealand one day. There **the Relief Society sisters were preparing the body of one of our saints.** They had placed his body in front of the big house, as they call it, the house where the people come to wail and weep and mourn over the dead, when in rushed the dead man's brother. He said, 'Administer to him.' And the young natives said, 'Why, you shouldn't do that; **he's dead'**. The younger native got down on his knees and he anointed this man. Then **this great old sage got down and blessed him and commanded him to rise**. You should have seen the Relief Society sisters scatter! **He sat up and said, 'Send for the elders; I don't feel very well.'** … We told him

he had just been administered to, and he said, 'Oh, that was it.' He said, 'I was dead. I could feel life coming back into me just like a blanket unrolling.' He outlived the brother that came in and told us to administer to him.[6]

Although many miracles occurring in The Church of Jesus Christ of Latter-day Saints come through the use of the priesthood, the Bible says "the prayers of a righteous man availeth much", and Latter-day Saint do not have a monopoly on miracles. Here is a non-Mormon example of a modern-day miracle:

> In an airport one day I picked up a copy of the Dallas Morning News. My eyes were drawn to a columnist's report of a letter detailing a remarkable miracle. The writer's five-year-old granddaughter, Heather, suddenly became feverish and lethargic. She breathed with difficulty, and her lips turned blue. By the time she arrived at the hospital, her kidneys and lungs had shut down, her fever was 107 degrees, and her body was bright red and covered with purple lesions. The doctors said she was dying of toxic shock syndrome, cause unknown. As word spread to family and friends, God-fearing people from Florida to California began praying for little Heather. At the grandfather's request, a special prayer service was held in their Church of Christ congregation in Waco, Texas.
>
> Miraculously, Heather suddenly came back from the brink of death and was released from the hospital in a little over a week. The columnist concluded that Heather "is living proof that God does answer prayers and work miracles." [7]

WHAT ABOUT THE GIFT OF TONGUES?

Our Pentecostal Christian friends put great emphasis on the gift of tongues in their worship. Many of them go so far as to say that if a person doesn't "speak in the Spirit" he or she is not really "saved". Some mainline Christians kinda look down on them because of that (and perhaps some Mormons, too), but Latter-day Saints do believe in the gift of tongues along with other miracles. I like to divide the topic into two areas I call "known tongues" and "unknown tongues".

KNOWN TONGUES

We read in the New Testament that fifty days after the crucifixion of Jesus an amazing miracle happened as the believers in Christ met together:

And when the day of Pentecost was fully come, they were all with one accord in one place. And suddenly there came a sound from heaven as of a rushing mighty wind, and it filled all the house where they were sitting. And there appeared unto them cloven tongues like as of *fire, and it sat upon each of them. And <u>they were all filled with the Holy Ghost, and began to speak with other tongues,</u> as the Spirit gave them utterance.*

And there were dwelling at Jerusalem Jews, devout men, out of every nation under heaven. Now when this was noised abroad, the multitude came together, and were confounded, because that <u>every man heard them speak in his own language.</u> And they were all amazed and marvelled, saying one to another, Behold, are not all these which speak Galilaeans? And how hear we every man in our own tongue, wherein we were born? Parthians, and Medes, and Elamites, and the dwellers in Mesopotamia, and in Judaea, and Cappadocia, in Pontus, and Asia, Phrygia, and Pamphylia, in Egypt, and in the parts of Libya about Cyrene, and strangers of Rome, Jews and proselytes, Cretes and Arabians, <u>we do hear them speak in our tongues the wonderful works of God.</u> And they were all amazed, and were in doubt, saying one to another, What meaneth this?

—Acts 2: 1-13

We don't know what language was being spoken by the Galilean believers, but it is apparent that observers from many different lands were able to understand them, each in his or her own language.

This phenomenon of speaking or understanding a "known tongue" (but unknown to the speaker or listeners) has been experienced a number of times in Latter-day Christianity. For example: In the South Pacific in 1913, John Alexander Nelson Jr. spoke Samoan but not Tongan. When he arrived for an assignment in Tonga, he found that he had been scheduled to speak to a congregation of 300 Wesleyan Methodists. He began in faith by speaking a few sentences of greeting he knew in the Tongan language, and then suddenly found himself continuing to speak in Tongan. He spoke without hesitation for nearly an hour "as fluently as any native."[8]

INTERPRETATION OF TONGUES

David O. McKay, who was the President of the Church when I was growing up wrote:

> "One of the most important events on my world tour of the missions of the Church was the gift of interpretation of the English tongue to the Saints of New Zealand, at a session of their conference, held on the 23rd day of April, 1921, at Puke Tapu Branch, Waikato District, Huntly, New Zealand.

> "When I looked over that vast assemblage and contemplated the great expectations that filled the hearts of all who had met together, I realized how inadequately I might satisfy

240

the ardent desires of their souls, and I yearned, most earnestly, for the gift of tongues that I might be able to speak to them in their native language. "Until that moment I had not given much serious thought to the gift of tongues, but on that occasion, I wished with all my heart, that I might be worthy of that divine power.

... "When I arose to give my address, I said to Brother Stuart Meha, our interpreter, that I would speak without his translating, sentence by sentence, what I said, and then to the audience I continued:

"'I wish, oh, how I wish I had the power to speak to you in your own tongue, that I might tell you what is in my heart; but since I have not the gift, I pray, and I ask you to pray, that you might have the spirit of interpretation, of discernment, that you may understand at least the spirit while I am speaking, and then you will get the words and the thought when Brother Meha interprets.'

"My sermon lasted forty minutes, and I have never addressed a more attentive, a more respectful audience. My listeners were in perfect rapport—this I knew when I saw tears in their eyes. Some of them at least, perhaps most of them, who did not understand English, had the gift of interpretation.[9]

SPEAKING IN KNOWN TONGUES IN MODERN TIMES

While serving on the Japanese island of Kyushu, Elder Yoshihiko Kikuchi had an experience that proved to be pivotal in his life. Elder Gordon B. Hinckley, then a member of the Council of the Twelve, visited Japan and spoke at a missionary zone conference. Yoshihiko was the only Japanese elder present.

"We had a testimony meeting, and I was the last one to bear my testimony," Elder Kikuchi relates. "I stood and began to speak in Japanese. Suddenly, a very warm spirit came over me and, without knowing what I was saying, I started speaking in English. I didn't know what I said. But I remember the beautiful feeling I felt." After he went back to his seat, Elder Hinckley stood and pronounced a special blessing on Elder Kikuchi.

—Ensign, Dec. 1984

UNKNOWN TONGUES

The speaking in "unknown" tongues (technically called "glossolalia") is a gift of the Spirit that is claimed to be practiced frequently by many Pentecostal Christians. It is quite rare among the Latter-day Saints but there have been some recorded instances of it. I was curious about it so a number of years ago I did some research and wrote a paper about it and presented it to a Sunstone conference of LDS people. Rather than go into it here in detail I think I'll just put it at the end of this book in an appendix. Suffice it to say, the Latter-day Saints DO believe in "speaking in tongues" – a legitimate Bible gift of the Spirit given to "them that believe".

OTHER DRAMATIC MIRACLES

Author Eric B. Shumway describes many other miracles experienced in the Pacific islands among the people there of great faith. For example, in the midst of the furious hurricane that devastated Vava'u in 1961, a Tongan father reasoned that he had priesthood power to heal a body and saw no reason why he could not also "heal" the raging storm. Brother Shumway writes, "His dramatic blessing at the peak of the hurricane saved his home and the people who took refuge there." [10]

In another experience, heavy ocean waves were crashing onto a beach at a time when the missionaries had scheduled some baptisms. An elder "stepped out and blessed the ocean, commanding it to be still so these sacred ordinances could be accomplished." Almost instantly the ocean calmed down and five people were baptized. Then as the party started up the path from the ocean, "the waves came crashing in again over the very spot where the sacred ordinances were held".[11]

I myself experienced the power of God's love in a miraculous way when I lived in Los Angeles in the 1980's. I have only shared this experience before with a few family members and close friends because it is very sacred to me, but I'm impressed to share it here.

It was Christmas time and my family had already flown to be with my parents in Georgia for the holidays. I had stayed behind to finish up some work on a movie project. On the morning that my flight was to leave I was dismayed to hear on the radio that the Los Angeles airport was covered in fog and that no flights were landing or departing. Fearing that I might be separated from my family for the holidays, I knelt down in our apartment and prayed earnestly that our Heavenly Father would part the clouds so I could leave. I said, "Father I know this is a small matter in the eternal scheme of things, but for my sake and that of many others traveling to be with their families for Christmas, could you bless us with just a small miracle?"

It was then that I received a distinct impression in my mind that said: "I've given to you the same priesthood power that Moses used to part the Red Sea. If you have sufficient faith, you have permission to use that power yourself." Boy was I ever surprised! But then I realized that it was true. With a hopeful heart and with faith that God really can perform miracles, I raised my right arm to the square and reached out my left hand towards LAX and in the name of Christ I commanded the clouds to depart. Within an hour the planes were landing and departing, and I was able to be with my dear ones that year to celebrate the birth of our Savior. Some might say it was a just a coincidence, but I personally believe it was the power of God. In fact I know it was.

THE MIRACLE OF THE GULLS

One of the most famous miracles among the Latter-day Saints took place shortly after their arrival in the Salt Lake Valley in July of 1847. Their newly planted crops had barely started to sprout when clouds of grasshoppers or locusts descended from the skies and began to gobble up the plants they needed to survive the winter. After trying in vain to beat them back with their own strength, the pioneers knelt and prayed in their fields and asked God for help. Immediately flocks of seagulls appeared and began eating the insects. Some observed the birds vomiting up the pests and then returning to eat more. The crops were saved, and today the seagull is protected as the state bird of Utah. The "miracle of the gulls" was depicted in the climactic final scenes of the movie "Brigham Young" produced by Twentieth Century Fox in 1941. You should watch it!

CONCLUSION

I could go on and on. There have literally been dozens of books written recounting hundreds and thousands of miracles – testaments to the power of God in these latter days. Suffice it to say that the Latter-day Saints -like the New Testament saints- believe in the same Biblical spiritual gifts and in the power of God to work miracles in the world today.

ENDNOTES TO CHAPTER 11

1 http://www.gty.org/resources/sermons/TM13-7/a-case-for-cessation ism-tom-pennington

2 http://www.charismanews.com/opinion/41499-john-macarthur-cessation-theology-and-trainspotting-for-cave-dwellers

3 *Brigham H. Roberts, "The Testimony of Miracles," in New Witnesses for God, 3 Vols., (Salt Lake City: Deseret News, 1909[1895, 1903]), 1:254–255*

4 *Brigham H. Roberts, "The Testimony of Miracles," in New Witnesses for God, 3 Vols., (Salt Lake City: Deseret News, 1909[1895, 1903]), 1:255–256.*

5 Joseph Smith, *History of The Church of Jesus Christ of Latter-day Saints*, 7 volumes, edited by Brigham H. Roberts, (Salt Lake City: Deseret Book, 1957), 4:3, footnote; see also Wilford Woodruff, *Leaves from My Journal*, 75–79 and *History of Wilford Woodruff*, p. 326

6 *"Miracles", Brigham Young University Speeches of the Year (5 Apr. 1966, rebroadcast from a speech delivered 18 Feb. 1953)*

7 *Sometimes, 'Miracles' Are Just That,* Dallas Morning News, 30 Jan. 2000, p. 31A.

8 *Teachings of Gordon B. Hinckley (1997), 343.*

9 David O. Mackay, *Cherished Experiences*, 73–74

10 Eric B. Shumway, trans. and ed., *Tongan Saints: Legacy of Faith* (1991), 45.

11 Op cit, p 84

EVIDENCE 12

BY THEIR FRUITS YE SHALL KNOW THEM

I confess. I believe in doing good works. Not for my salvation, but because, well, it's a good thing to do. Good works are the "fruits" of my religion. Our Savior had some things to say about fruits and the trees that bear them in Matthew chapter 7:

Even so every good tree bringeth forth good fruit; but a corrupt tree bringeth forth evil fruit. A good tree cannot bring forth evil fruit, <u>neither can a corrupt tree bring forth good fruit</u>. Every tree that bringeth not forth good fruit is hewn down, and cast into the fire. Wherefore <u>by their fruits ye shall know them</u>[1]

Obviously we live in a fallen world and we're all sinners, and only once in a while do we rise to our full potential or become our best selves. And even a good tree will have some rotten apples at times. But generally our Lord's observation is a true one. So we must ask: What are the "fruits" of Latter-day Christianity? Our 13th LDS Article of Faith says:

We believe in being honest, true, chaste, benevolent, virtuous, and in doing good to all men; indeed, we may say that we follow the admonition of Paul—We believe all things, we hope all things, we have endured many things, and hope to be able to endure all things. If there is anything virtuous, lovely, or of good report or praiseworthy, we seek after these things.

In John 1:46 when Philip told Nathaniel that Jesus of Nazareth was the long-awaited Messiah, Nathaniel asked, "can any good thing come out of Nazareth?" Philip responded, "come and see".

There are many skeptics in the world today who ask, "can any good thing come out of Mormonism". I will give the same answer as Philip: "come and see".

IS "MORMONISM" A CULT?

I guess this is as good a place as any to address one of the biggest misconceptions that many folks have about Latter-day Christianity – that we are supposedly a "cult". I can see how critics of my faith like to use that pejorative term, because it's an easy way to say "bad" or "weird", and that's how they want others to see us. But let's look at some of the characteristics often used to describe a "cult", and see if our church fits. If it doesn't walk like a duck or quack like a duck, hopefully reasonable people will not call it a duck, right? Here are a few:

At Miriam-Webster.com (or in an old-fangled dictionary) the definition starts like this:

"a small religious group that is not part of a larger and more accepted religion and that has beliefs regarded by many people as extreme or dangerous"

"Small"?

There are over 16 million members of The Church of Jesus Christ of Latter-day Saints worldwide. It is the fourth largest church in the United States – larger than many so-called "mainline" churches. I don't call that small.

"not part of a larger and more accepted religion"

If you haven't understood by now after reading the preceding 11 chapters that Latter-day Christianity is a restoration of original New Testament Christianity (that is certainly accepted by millions of people around the world), then like Cool Hand Luke, we're really having a "failure to communicate".

"has beliefs regarded by many people as extreme or dangerous"?

"Mormonism" may have a few beliefs that some folks consider peculiar (see the next chapter), but has anything I've described about my faith so far seemed "extreme" or "dangerous"? I don't really think so. But I've heard of some Pentecostals who handle live rattlesnakes in their services, and I regard THAT as "extreme and dangerous".

There is however one dictionary definition of a "cult" that fits the earliest Christians and I suppose I have to confess that I share it: *"formal religious veneration"* and *"great devotion to a person".* I have great devotion and love for my Lord and Savior Jesus Christ, and if that makes me part of the "cult" of Christianity, then so be it.

INSIDE LATTER-DAY CHRISTIANITY

Some of the basic "fruits" of Latter-day Christianity include the following:

1. We have a better understanding of who God and Jesus are, and the relationship of the three members of the Godhead to each other.

2. We have additional scripture to provide a "second witness" of Jesus Christ, and better understanding of his life and mission on earth.

3. We have living prophets and continuing revelation from God.

4. We have an accurate understanding of man's relationship to our Father in Heaven and why we are here on earth, where we came from, and where we're going.

Of course I know that there are critics of my faith who challenge whether these are actually good fruits or not. They claim that "Mormonism" produces "evil" fruits, and have sought to destroy it. For example:

OUTSIDE LATTER-DAY CHRISTIANITY

In addition to (and perhaps because of) being a "peculiar" people, the Latter-day Saints have often been a **persecuted** people. For example:

* The Latter-day Saints were driven out of New York, Pennsylvania, Ohio, Missouri, and Illinois by angry mobs. Has any other church in America been driven so far and for so long?

* In 1838 the Governor of Missouri Lilburn Boggs issued an unconstitutional "extermination order" that made it legal for anyone to kill "Mormons" who would not leave that state.

(that order was not officially rescinded until 1976)

* Few members of any other church in America have had to flee as a body from their homes and their country to find safety thousands of miles away. The Latter-day Saints finally found a desert valley home that nobody else wanted in present-day Utah, which at that time was outside the United States.

* Some scholars have estimated that at least 7,000 Latter-day Saints lost their lives along the wagon trail between Nauvoo, Illinois and Salt Lake City between 1846 and 1869.

* No U.S. President has called for war upon any other church, nor ordered the U.S. Army to march on the city of its headquarters as did U.S. President James Buchanan in the "Utah War" of 1857. Over one-third of the existing Union army was sent to quell an alleged "Mormon Rebellion" in the Territory of Deseret. (fortunately the situation was resolved without bloodshed)

* No members of any other church in America have had legislation passed against them in Congress as The Church of Jesus Christ of Latter-day Saints Church suffered with the 1887 Edmunds-Tucker Act. That unconstitutional law took almost all the Church's property, disenfranchised the members, put the leaders in prison (at least those who hadn't gone into hiding), took away their civil rights of voting and even citizenship. In effect, it took away all their First Amendment rights.

* Around the turn of the century in 1900, Elder B.H. Roberts was elected to the U.S. House of Representatives but was denied the right to take his seat in Congress. Has any member of any other church been denied a Congressional seat for religious reasons?

* No other church has been part of the platforms of so many political parties, as The Church of Jesus Christ of Latter-day Saints. In the 1850's the new Republican Party was established to eliminate the "twin pillars of barbarism" which it defined as slavery and polygamy.

* No national political party has ever been set up to specifically oppose any church, except the American Party, which was organized in 1906 specifically to oppose "Mormonism".

One would hope that religious persecution would be an evil that was left in the past, but even in the present we find:

A New York Times online op-ed piece published in January 2012 presented some opposing views. In a section called "Room for Debate", screenwriter Ian Williams wrote: *With no marriages outside the church, zero tolerance of homosexuality and very little coffee, the L.D.S. worldview would positively smother most Americans. It might be smothering most Mormons; Utah's antidepressant use makes it one of the most-medicated states in the country.*

In the same article Sally Denton said:

*Mormonism is a valid issue of concern not as a religious test for office, but for its most distinctive characteristic — <u>male authoritarianism</u>. The controversial and secretive religion is **a** <u>multibillion-dollar business empire</u> ruled by a stern patriarchal gerontocracy.*

Jane Barnes who co-wrote the 2007 PBS TV series "*The Mormons.*" contributed:

When it comes to the social agenda, <u>the Mormon Church does not respect separation of church and state.</u> It has used its mobilizing genius to pursue political goals, and individual Mormons have obeyed like sheep.

INSIDE CHRISTIANITY

Well I guess I could spend your time refuting some of those outrageous criticisms, but perhaps the more "Christian" thing to do would be to give you some irrefutable facts and figures and let you decide for yourself whether the "fruits" of Mormonism are corrupt or good. First we'll examine the "institutional" fruits of The Church of Jesus Christ of Latter-day Saints itself, and then the "individual" fruits in the lives of members of the church.

INSTITUTIONAL FRUITS -- MODEL COMMUNITIES

The Church of Jesus Christ of Latter-day Saints first became a sizeable organization in Kirtland, Ohio where in 1836 the "Saints" erected a beautiful temple and created a society of their own. Thousands of converts came from America and from Europe, and they built farms and shops and prospered under the leadership of the prophet Joseph Smith.

Later they moved their community to the banks of the Mississippi River in Illinois where they drained a swamp and built the town of Nauvoo. This beautiful city became a showplace of industry and order with clean streets and neat homes and shops, markedly different from other sprawling frontier towns.

At one time Nauvoo was larger than Chicago and it was crowned by another beautiful temple.

Religious persecution caused the Mormons to flee from their beautiful city in the winter of 1847 and they endured a merciless forced march to a new home in the Rocky Mountains, far beyond the reach of those who would do them harm. Tens of thousands of men, women and children were led by Brigham Young to a desert valley on the shores of the Great Salt

Lake that was then outside the boundaries of the United States. In a land that nobody else wanted, they introduced irrigation and made the desert "blossom as the rose".

The beautiful metropolis of Salt Lake City today is a testament to the industriousness of the Saints and the foresight of their leader Brigham Young. But it was just the beginning. They built orderly communities of law-abiding citizens and colonized much of western America. In addition to their towns in Utah and Arizona, the Latter-day Saints founded the cities of San Francisco and San Bernardino, CA, Las Vegas, NV and Colonia Juarez in Mexico.

EDUCATIONAL INSTITUTIONS

The Latter-day Saints started the first public university west of the Mississippi (The University of Utah) in Salt Lake City, and later built others in Provo (Brigham Young University) and Logan (Utah State University). Education was (and still is) a hallmark of Mormon communities.

BYU is the largest private university in America and is known as the "Harvard of the West". It is renowned for its scholarship and the success of its graduates, as well as the beauty of its campus and the clean-cut image of its students. The University of Utah is distinguished in the fields of medicine and computer science and was one of the first five universities that originally collaborated to build the internet. Utah State has one of the nation's oldest undergraduate research programs, second only to MIT.

The Church of Jesus Christ of Latter-day Saints also founded the Church Business College in Salt Lake City, the Church College of Hawaii (now BYU Hawaii), and Ricks College (now BYU Idaho) in Rexburg, Idaho. Several other secondary schools have been established in Mexico and elsewhere.

HOSPITALS AND MEDICAL RESEARCH

Both LDS Hospital and Primary Children's Hospital in Salt Lake City were established by the Latter-day Saints. Though later divested by the Church, they still serve the community. Medical research at the University of Utah led to the development of the world's first artificial heart and ground-breaking heart transplant techniques.

A WORLD-RENOWNED CHOIR

The Mormon Tabernacle Choir (now called the Choir at Temple Square) is acknowledged as one of the greatest choral organizations in the world and was named "America's Choir" by President Ronald Reagan. It has thrilled audiences all over the world, and their weekly program "Music and the Spoken Word" from Temple Square in Salt Lake City is the longest-running national radio program in history.

HUMANITARIAN AID PROGRAMS

The Welfare Programs of The Church of Jesus Christ of Latter-day Saints constantly inspire amazement among relief workers and government leaders from all over the world. The Church has numerous ranches, orchards and farms to grow food that is processed in its own canneries and provided free of charge to the needy all over the world, both Latter-day Saints and non-Mormons alike.

A network of thrift stores similar to Goodwill Industries (called Deseret Industries) provides employment opportunities and low-cost clothing and other goods that are sold to the public. A worldwide distribution system of warehouses and retail-like outlets called Bishop's Storehouses give essential food to those in need, along with free clothing and other goods from the Deseret Industries stores.

When natural disasters strike, The Church of Jesus Christ of Latter-day Saints has become one of the premiere first-responders to render humanitarian aid anywhere on earth. The Church maintains a number of strategically pre-positioned tractor-trailer trucks in various locations all over the U.S. and in some other parts of the world loaded with disaster supplies to be dispatched at a moment's notice.

Latter-day Saint volunteers are also mobilized to help in disaster situations. Dressed in yellow T-shirts or vests with the "Mormon Helping Hands" logo, they give up their weekends and vacation days to journey to stricken areas and provide assistance when needed.

In April of 2011 I had the privilege of participating personally in one of these disaster relief volunteer groups. A series of devastating tornados created a mile-wide swath of destruction through the southeastern United States, killing 243 people in Alabama. I joined over a hundred and twenty volunteers from the Columbus, Georgia Stake (a group of about eight congregations or "wards") who drove to Birmingham, Alabama to help in cleanup efforts after the storm. With our work gloves and chain saws in hand, we traveled more than a hundred miles at our own expense, rising at 4AM on a Saturday morning.

We camped out on the lawn of a Latter-day Saint meetinghouse (chapel) that served as a command center where we joined hundreds of other Latter-day Saint volunteers from throughout the South. With the efficiency of a well-oiled machine we were given work orders to cut and remove fallen trees from the homes of tornado victims in a devastated community southwest of Birmingham. Most of them (if not all) were the homes of people not of our faith.

It was nice to see that other churches were also involved in the relief efforts. One of the local Baptist congregations came around the storm-damaged neighborhoods in a pickup truck handing out water and sandwiches to the Latter-day Saints and other relief volunteers. I really enjoyed seeing the cooperative spirit of followers of Christ supporting and helping each other.

We worked all day Saturday, got a bit of rest, and then started again on Sunday after a brief worship service. Since the "ox" was definitely "in the mire", one of the men said it was a unique opportunity for him to use his chainsaw on a Sunday without breaking the Sabbath! At the end of the day we were a very tired group of people, but as we drove back to Columbus we had the satisfaction of knowing that we had been of service to our fellow man. The expressions of gratitude we received from the families we had helped certainly warmed our hearts.

My experience in Alabama has been duplicated all over the world by Latter-day Saints serving others from Alaska to Argentina, from Madagascar to Morocco, and from Paris to Pretoria. Over 6,000 volunteers went to help those devastated by the super-storm Sandy that hit the northeastern U.S. in 2012. Sometimes those being helped don't even know where the assistance is coming from. After one major hurricane hit Florida several years ago, local leaders said there were two main groups that came to the aid of citizens in the area. They were "the Mormons" and "The Church of Jesus Christ of Latter-day Saints".

According to the LDS online publication Meridian Magazine, Christian principles of compassion and caring for others have always been fundamental teachings of the Church. An organized humanitarian service was formed in 1985 when Church leaders asked Latter-day Saints in the United States and Canada to participate in two special fast days to raise money for famine relief in Ethiopia, Chad and other sub-Saharan nations. By going without two meals on the designated days and contributing at least the value of the meals missed, Latter-day Saints donated in excess of $11 million, all of which went directly into relief efforts with the Church bearing all administrative expenses.

(Note: this was the largest contribution by any group or government to provide relief from that terrible 1985 famine.)

Since 1985, The Church of Jesus Christ of Latter-day Saints has mounted more than 144 major disaster relief projects worldwide. Overall humanitarian assistance rendered since

1985 totals over $89 million in cash donations and more than $456 million in material assistance. All activities are supported largely by Church member donations of funds and volunteer labor.

FRUITS OF LATTER-DAY SAINT PEOPLE AS A GROUP
In addition to the institutional fruits of the official church organization, what about the fruits of Latter-day Christianity in the lives of church members? The Bible says that God's people should be "in the world but not of the world". In other words they should be different. In 1 Peter 2:9 the New Testament saints were told *"ye are a chosen generation, a royal priesthood, an holy nation, a peculiar* people".

Sometimes Latter-day Saints jokingly refer to certain members of their ward as a bit more "peculiar" than others, using the modern definition of the word as "odd". (I've been called that myself a few times.) But more accurate Bible translations render the KJV "peculiar" as "God's own possession", or "treasured".

So how are Latter-day Saints different from other people? In a nutshell, Latter-day Christianity produces members who are for the most part (with occasional exceptions):

- a happy people
- an educated people
- a worshipful people
- a healthy people
- a giving people
- a serving people
- a fasting people
- a law-abiding people
- a people who value marriage and family
- a Sabbath-observing people
- a prosperous people
- a missionary people
- a talented people
- a cultured people
- a worldwide people
- an industrious people

Even the most ardent critics of "Mormonism" (well, at least most of them) readily admit to these positive qualities of the Latter-day Saint people.

There are a few qualities of Latter-day Saints that I pulled out of that list for special mention. Latter-day Saints are also known as:

- a <u>healthy</u> people: According to a 1995 report by the American Cancer Society active Mormons die from cancer at about <u>one-third the national average</u> rate.

A 1989 UCLA study confirms that the healthiest active Latter-day Saints have <u>a life expectancy that is eight to 11 years longer</u> than the general population in the United States.

<u>http://articles.latimes.com/1997-04-26/local/me-52680_1_mormon-doctrine</u>

- a **happy** people: While some may think Latter-day Saints are a strict, somber group of folks, quite the opposite is true. One of my favorite verses in *The Book of Mormon* says that "men are that they might have joy". In 2012, CNN reporter Richard Guest visited the campus of my alma mater Brigham Young University to see what the Latter-day Saint students there were like. He said they were: *"Neat. Tidy. Oh, and everyone smiles. The woman at the ice cream shop smiled. The guides showing me round the university smiled."* He was impressed with the happy students he found there.

- a **patriotic** people: There are unusually high percentages of Latter-day Saint people serving in the Armed Forces, and in government service in the FBI, CIA, NSA, etc. where love of country is valued and respected. Latter-day Saints who have excelled in the military include my own cousin's husband General David Haight who in 2012 served as the Commandant of the U.S. Army's Infantry School at Ft. Benning, GA.

- a **trustworthy** people: This quality of Latter-day Saints is recognized by many of those above-mentioned government agencies, who do a lot of recruiting at Brigham Young University. Many private corporations recruit Latter-day Saint employees for the same reason. The billionaire Howard Hughes was known to have hired Latter-day Saints almost exclusively for his inner circle of employees.

A personal note: In November of 1982 I was employed by the NBC television network to work at their studios in Burbank, California. As a new hire I had the "privilege" of working during the Christmas holidays while others were on vacation. One of the NBC vice presidents invited me to stay in his mansion in the Hollywood Hills and look after it while he was gone to England for the holidays.

I was surprised, and I told him "but you don't even know me. I've only worked for you for a few weeks. You're going to just give me the keys to your house?" He looked at me quizzically and said "well, you're a Mormon aren't you? " I have never felt more proud to be a Latter-day Saint than at that moment.

And speaking of "trustworthy" – that's the first word of the Scout Law. As an avid Boy Scout and a long time Scout leader, I have to mention that The Church of Jesus Christ of Latter-day Saints became in 1913 the first church to sponsor Scouting in the USA, and for over 100 years it sponsored more Boy Scout troops and other Scout units than any other organization in America. The percentage of Latter-day Saint Scouts who have earned the Eagle Scout rank is <u>double</u> that of the national average in the Boy Scouts of America.

Lest you doubt me about the accomplishments of Latter-day Saints, let me insert here the results of some studies by respected non-Mormon news and research organizations: (okay, I've emphasized some of the more juicy parts)

"Protestants, Catholics and Mormons Reflect Diverse Levels of Religious Activity"
July 9, 2001 study released by the Barna Research Group of Ventura, California. The study found that <u>Mormons are more likely to read the Bible during a week than are Protestants.</u> The Barna institute for religious studies identified that outside of Sunday church sermons Mormons were more likely to have read the bible (not the Book of Mormon, — the Bible) than any other religion polled.

National Study of Youth and Religion, 2005
UNC, Chapel Hill (U.S. Adolescents Ages 13-17) — The Study found that Church of Jesus Christ of Latter-day Saints <u>(LDS) youth were more likely to exhibit Christian characteristics than Evangelicals (</u>the next most observant group)

A national 2010 Pew Forum on Religion & Public Life survey This study aimed to test a broad range of religious knowledge, including understanding of the Bible, core teachings of different faiths and major figures in religious history: <u>on questions about Christianity and the Bible, Mormons scored the highest.</u> They also scored second only to Jews in knowledge of Judaism. [Overall, Mormons understand their own doctrines and the Bible better than other Christian denominations.]

City Journal - Autumn 2012 vol. 22 no. 4

Today, some religious fundamentalists continue to rail against Mormons, while coastal sophisticates scoff at their earnest approach to life, religion, and family. Yet the methodical Mormon way, which stresses education, ambition, and charitable giving, <u>has succeeded in ways equaled by few religious groups. Mormons enjoy levels of education and wealth higher than the national average,</u> for example. Some 54 percent of LDS men and 44 percent of women have secured postsecondary education; the numbers for the general American population are 37 percent and 28 percent, respectively. <u>Mormons also enjoy the nation's highest rate of charitable giving.</u>

And while many religious groups in the United States—including the Catholic and mainline Protestant churches, along with most non-Orthodox Jewish denominations—are struggling with declining numbers, <u>The Church of Jesus Christ of Latter-day Saintsis one of the nation's fastest-growing.</u> Its American membership jumped from 4 million to 6 million between 2000 and 2010. Its global growth over the same period was 45.5 percent, and today, most of its total membership of 16 million resides outside North America. The fastest growth is occurring in Brazil, the South Pacific, and Central America.

<u>The best advertisement for Mormonism, though, is the kind of society that it seems able to create.</u> In Utah, 60 percent of whose population belongs to the LDS Church, this state has enjoyed one of the fastest job-growth rates in the nation over the past decade, taking a strong lead in a host of industries, from energy and software to composite manufacturing. It has also seen the highest population growth rate of any state in the US, aside from neighboring Arizona and Nevada — and unlike those "bubble" states, Utah survived the housing bust in strong shape.[2]

– University of Pennsylvania's School of Social Policy and Practice Latter-day Saints <u>"volunteer and donate significantly more</u> than the average American and are even more generous in time and money than the upper quintile of religious people in America... When it comes to the time they spend volunteering, <u>the average adult American LDS member contributes as much as **seven times** more than that of the average American...</u> "Self-interest in this group didn't apply, which goes against all economics principles." The published findings further indicate that these "pro-social behaviors" are reflective of Latter-day Saint teachings, which emphasize Christian service and charity to others.

Pew Research Center – Forum on Religion and Public Life
THURSDAY, JANUARY 12, 2012 - Mormons in America

Certain in Their Beliefs, Uncertain of Their Place in Society The Pew Research Center is a nonpartisan think tank that provides information on the issues, attitudes and trends shaping America and the world. The center conducts public opinion polling, demographic studies, content analysis and other empirical social science research.

FINDINGS

Mormons exhibit <u>higher levels of religious commitment</u> than many other religious groups, including white evangelical Protestants. Three quarters of Mormons (77%) say they attend church at least once a week, 79% say they donate 10% of their earnings to the church, 83% say they pray every day and fully 98% say they believe in the resurrection of Jesus.

The survey finds that Mormons place <u>a high priority on family life</u>. Large majorities say that being a good parent (81%) and having a successful marriage (73%) are among their most important goals in life, <u>far surpassing the numbers in the general public</u> who say the same.

Okay, I could go on and on citing the almost-universal praises of the Mormon people as a whole, but you get the picture, right?

THE FRUITS OF LATTER-DAY CHRISTIANITY IN THE LIVES OF INDIVIDUALS

The Latter-day Saints are also a "peculiar people" in that they have achieved individual success and acclaim in disproportionate numbers to their percentage of the population. Latter-day Saints are less than 2 per cent of the US population (and less than that worldwide) but I'm sure you've heard of some of us, even though you may not have know it. I've broken down just a few of my Latter-day Saint brothers and sisters into different fields of achievement. This is not an exhaustive list by any means. It is just a sampling:

BUSINESS, INDUSTRY AND SCIENCE -- FOUNDER AND/OR CEO
Kay R. Whitmore, Kodak
Mark H. Willes – General Mills
Bruce Christensen – PBS
David Neeleman – Jet Blue
J. Ralph Atkin – Skywest
Gary Crittenden – American Express
Gary S. Baughman – Fisher-Price toys

Robert Boplingborke – Clorox

George W. Romney – American Motors

Mitt Romney – Bain Capital

J. Willard Marriott – Marriott Hotels

Nolan Archibald - Black and Decker

Jon Huntsman – Huntsman Chemicals

Alan Ashton and Bruce Bastain – WordPerfect Corporation

Stephen R. Covey – Franklin Covey

Ron Dittemore - director of NASA Space Shuttle program

Don Lind – astronaut

Richard Searfoss – astronaut

Jake Garn – U.S. Senator also astronaut

Henry Eyring – chemist - former president American Chemical Society

EDUCATION

Kim Clark – President, BYU Idaho, former Dean Harvard Business School Clayton Christensen – Harvard Business School professor Richard Lyman Bushman, Professor of History emeritus at Columbia University Gordon Gee President of Ohio State University, former Chancellor, Vanderbilt Dr. V. Lane Rawlins - President, Washington State University Steven Charles Wheelwright - Pres. BYU Hawaii, Sr associate dean, Harvard University David Ulrich - Professor of business administration, University of Michigan (many more)

GOVERNMENT

Reed Smoot, US Senator (first Latter-day Saint in Congress)

Sen. Orrin Hatch – served as chairman of U.S. Senate Judiciary Committee 17 members of Congress (1999-2000) incl Senate Majority Leader

Harry Reid – Senator from Nevada

Paula Hawkins, first elected woman US Senator (FL) 1980

Jean Westwood, first woman National chairman of Democratic Party 1972

Richard Richards, Nat. Chairman of Republican Party 1981

Richard P. Cowley – FBI agent who brought to justice John Dillinger and Baby Face Nelson

James C. Fletcher – former head of NASA

Ezra Taft Benson - - Secretary of Agriculture under President Eisenhower

David Kennedy, Sec. of Treasury, Ambassador to NATO

Gregory Newell, Ambassador to Sweden (youngest ever)

Keith Foote Nyborg, Reagan, Ambassador to Finland

Ivy Baker Priest, Eisenhower, U.S. Treasurer
Bay Buchanan, Reagan, U.S. Treasurer
Stewart Udall, Kennedy/Johnson, Sec. of Interior
N. Eldon Tanner, Canada, cabinet minister
Roberto A. Cruz, Buenos Aires, Argentine Parliament
Moroni Bing Torgan, Brazilian congressman
Kresimir Cosic, Croatian Ambassador to U.S. (BYU basketball star)
Terry Rooney, British MP (Member of Parliament)

INVENTIONS

Philo T. Farnsworth – the "Father of Television" - invented our current form of TV
Harvey Fletcher – invented stereophonic sound
Robert Ingebretsen – developed the process to digitize sound for making CD's
John Browning – repeating rifle – BAR – machine gun (helping the US win WWII)
Carlyle Harmon – disposable diapers
H. Tracy Hall – man-made diamonds
Nolan Bushnell – first computer games (Pong)
Andrew K. Watt – anti-lock automobile brakes
Dr. Robert K. Jarvik – artificial heart
Jim Jensen – paleontologist who found world's largest dinosaur

ENTERTAINMENT
-MUSIC

The Mormon Tabernacle Choir ("America's Choir")
The Osmonds, Donny and Marie Osmond, Jimmy Osmond
The Lettermen (Jim Pike, Bob Engemann) – many gold records
David Archuleta – top "American Idol" TV performer and pop singer Gladys Knight – top Grammy-winning pop star
SheDaisy – country singers
The Jets – teen music sensations
Arial Bybee – mezzo-soprano New York Metropolitan Opera – 450 performances
Sandra Turley - lead role of Cossette in *Les Misérables* on Broadway
Liriel Domiciano – world-renowned Brazilian soprano
The King Sisters/ The King Family 1940's Big Band singers, ABC –TV network series

Robert Starling

-FILM/TV

Derek and Julianne Hough – lead pro dancers ABC-TV "Dancing with the Stars"

Larraine Day – actress – 45 movies opposite John Wayne, Kirk Douglas, many stars

Dean Jagger – actor – "Brigham Young", "12 O'Clock High" (Academy Award)

Billy Barty – actor – 200 movies and many TV shows – "Willow", "Rumpelstiltskin"

Gerald Molen – producer – "Schindler's List" (Academy Award), "Jurassic Park", more

Arnold Friberg – artist and designer – "The Ten Commandments", NFL art series, more

Samuel W. Taylor – screenwriter – "The Absent Minded Professor", "Son of Flubber"

Leigh Harline – composer – (2 Academy Awards) "It's a Wonderful Life", Disney Theme

Delos Jewkes – voice of God in "The Ten Commandments", appeared in 300 movies

Glen Larson – TV Producer – "Battlestar Galactica", "Knight Rider", "Magnum P.I."

Johnny Whitaker – actor – "A Family Affair"

Rhonda Fleming – actress – 40 movies, many TV shows

Merlin Olsen – actor – "Little House on the Prairie", "Father Murphy"

Robert Clarke – actor - king of "B" movies plus TV roles "Dragnet", "Adam 12" etc.

Tina Cole actress - TV series "My Three Sons"

Ken Jennings – top winner on "Jeopardy"

Ray Coombs – TV host "Family Feud"

Bob Hilton – announcer for many TV game shows

Gordon Jump – actor – lead in "WKRP in Cincinnati", "Soap", Maytag Repairman

Don Bluth – animation producer – "All Dogs Go To Heaven", "American Tail", more

Kieth Merrill – Academy Award winning film director

Edwin Catmull – founder of Pixar – "Toy Story", "Finding Nemo", "Brave", more

Ricky Schroeder – NBC's "Silver Spoons" and more

AUTHORS, also NEWS AND INFORMATION

Stephanie Meyers – author ("Twilight" novel and movie series) Orson Scott Card – science fiction author - Hugo and Nebula awards – "Ender's Game",

Anne Perry – a top British mystery writer – over 70 books

Jane Clayson – co-host CBS "The Early Show"– also on ABC "Good Morning America"

Jack Anderson - Pulitzer Prize winner - Washington DC syndicated columnist

Dale Van Atta - Washington DC syndicated columnist

Dian Thomas – author, speaker, TV personality – "Roughing It Easy"

Glenn Beck – 3rd most popular radio talk show host in US – Fox TV, BLAZE TV, author

W. Cleon Skousen – author – FBI Agent – founder, Center for Constitutional Studies
Raymond F. Jones – sci fi author "This Island Earth", many more books and mag stories
Tracy Hickman – author - Dragonlance book series
Richard Paul Evans – author – "The Christmas Box" book, movie, 8 million sold
Merlo J. Pusey – Pulitzer Prize- biography of Charles Evans Hughes, Chief Justice

OLYMPIC CHAMPIONS
Peter Vidmar 1980 Gold and Silver, gymnastics
Rulon Gardner 2000 Gold, Greco-Roman Wrestling
Alma Richards 1912 gold, high jump
Paula Meyers Pope 1952 & 1960 silver, 1956 silver and bronze, diving
Jane Sears 1952, bronze, swimming
Troy Dalbey 1988 gold, (2) swimming
Kresimir Cosic gold 1980, silver 1968 and 1976, bronze 1972, basketball
Noelle Pikus-Pace, Torah Bright, and Chris Fogt,
- 2 silver and a bronze in the 2014 Winter Olympics

NATIONAL FOOTBALL LEAGUE (NFL)
Mike Holmgren – head coach of Green Bay Packers
Andy Reid – head coach of Philadelphia Eagles
Steve Young – MVP of NFL (1992, 1994) and Superbowl (1994) San Francisco 49ers
Danny White – quarterback Dallas Cowboys
Hal Mitchell – tackle, New York Giants
(many more)

NATIONAL BASKETBALL ASSOCIATION (NBA)
Boston Celtics – Danny Ainge, Greg Kite, Fred Roberts
Jimmer Fredette – Sacramento Kings
Shawn Bradley – Philadelphia 76ers, New Jersey Nets, Dallas Mavericks
Casey Jacobsen – Phoenix Suns
Travis Hansen – Atlanta Hawks
Travis Knight - LA Lakers, Boston Celtics, New York Knicks
Mark Madsen - LA Lakers, Minnesota Timberwolves
Scot Pollard – Indiana Pacers
Thurl Bailey – Utah Jazz

BASEBALL
Harmon Killebrew – Minnesota Twins, Am League MVP 1969, 5th in all-time home runs
Dale Murphy – Atlanta Braves
Wally Joyner – California Angels
Vernon Law – Pittsburg Pirates
Jack Morris – Detroit Tigers
(many more)

NCAA FOOTBALL
Lavelle Edwards – BYU coach – 6th most wins in NCAA history, Coach of the Year,
— 1984 National NCAA Football Champions
Ty Detmer – Heisman Trophy Winner 1990
Outland Trophy - Merlin Olsen, Jason Buck
(many more)

OTHER SPORTS
Rugby – Sid Going- considered the greatest player in New Zealand
Ed Parker - karate champion – taught Karate to Elvis
Vanik (Russia) world champion in Karate in July 2011
Billy Casper - Masters Golf champion
Johnny Miller – PGA Tour Hall of Fame
Gene Fullmer - boxing champion
Jack Dempsey – world heavyweight boxing champion 1919-1926
(many more)

ART
Brian Crane – *Pickles* comic strip
Gutzon Borglum – sculptor of Mt. Rushmore (came from a Mormon family)
Arnold Friberg - NFL art series, Book of Mormon series, Canadian Mounties series, more
James Christensen – illustrator, fantasy painter
Avard Fairbanks – sculptor
Michael Allred – comic artist – Marvel, "The Atomics", "Madman"
Earl Bascom – sculptor, western art
Richard Comley – Canadian comic artist – creator "Captain Canuck" comics
Ed "Big Daddy" Roth – comic artist ("Rat Fink" creator) and car designer (more)

BEAUTY QUEENS

Miss America

Colleen Kay Hutchins

Charlene Wells Hawks

Mrs. America

Joan Fisher, Salt Lake City, Utah

Alice Beuhner, Salt Lake City, Utah

Deborah Wolfe, Huntington, WV

Miss Teenage America

Laura Baxter, Danville, CA

Miss Universe

Linda Bement, SLC

Porntip Nakhirunkanok, Thailand

(whew! – I gotta stop now – if you want more go to www.famousmormons.net)

Bottom Line:

Is the world blessed by Latter-day Saints? Is it a better place for the Latter-day Saints who are in it? Would the world be a poorer place without Latter-day Christianity?

Does Latter-day Christianity bear good fruit? You decide.

ENDNOTES FOR CHAPTER 12

1   Matt 7: 17-20

2   http://www.city-journal.org/2012/22_4_snd-mormons.html

EVIDENCE 13

PECULIAR BELIEFS FOR A
"PECULIAR" PEOPLE

(A reminder: As I said before, in 1 Peter 2:9 the New Testament saints were told "ye are a chosen generation, a royal priesthood, an holy nation, a <u>peculiar people"</u>. But more accurate Bible translations render the KJV "peculiar" as <u>"God's own possession", or "treasured"</u>.)

I confess that "Mormonism" has some beliefs and practices that may seem "peculiar" (in the modern sense) to those not familiar with them. But then, so does almost any religion. Protestants find it "peculiar" that Catholics believe in Transubstantiation – the doctrine that the bread and wine of Communion actually become the literal flesh and blood of Christ at the moment they are consumed. Jews wear unique religious clothing and don't eat pork. Mainline Protestants and Catholics find it "peculiar" that Pentecostals speak in unknown tongues. Many Evangelicals appear to be "slain in the spirit" during their services. The Shakers or "shaking Quakers" were given to ecstatic dancing in their worship. And so on.

Unfortunately those who don't share someone else's beliefs often ridicule them. I try to respect the beliefs of others and I hope they would do the same, but that is not always human nature. Atheists and other secular folks often make fun of all religious people. I guess we're fortunate that we live in an age where people of different beliefs are not called "heretics" and burned at the stake rather than just ridiculed in a Broadway play or on Saturday Night Live.

I will attempt to show that some of the most scoffed-at LDS beliefs are actually firmly rooted in Christian history and doctrine, even though they may have been lost in the past and are unknown to most modern Christians. But before we get into the "peculiar" beliefs, what about the ones we share with other Christians? Let's take a look:

BELIEFS WE SHARE WITH OTHER CHRISTIANS

1. God is our Heavenly Father. He is a real person who hears and answers prayers.

2. Jesus is the Only Begotten Son of God. He is a different person, but he is Deity just like his Father.

3. The Holy Ghost is also God. He is also a different person but he also is Deity.

4. Jesus became "fully man" in his incarnation but remained "fully God".

5. Jesus died as a sinless sacrifice so we can be resurrected and forgiven of our sins.

OK, now on to the "peculiar" doctrines which are unique to Mormonism:

BAPTISM (AND OTHER ORDINANCES) FOR THE DEAD

Many (most?) Christians believe that water baptism is essential for salvation. And yet many good people who lived before the time of Christ (and since that time) never had the opportunity to receive a Christian baptism, through no fault of their own. Will they be damned to hell? This is a question that plagued Christian converts in the New Testament whose parents and grandparents died without baptism. And it has continued to be debated for centuries.

Hugh Nibley writes: "One of the first questions that Clement, an early church Father, puts to Peter upon meeting him is, *shall those be wholly deprived of the kingdom of heaven who died before Christ's coming?"* To this the apostle gives a most significant answer: he assures Clement that the people in question are not damned and never will be, and explains that provision has been made for their salvation, but this, he says, is *"as far as we are allowed to declare these things,"* excusing himself from telling more: *"you compel me, O Clement, to touch upon things which we are forbidden to discuss."*[1]

We know that during the three days that Christ's body was in the tomb, his spirit went to preach to the spirits in prison. (1 Peter 3:19) But why would he teach them the Gospel if there were no way for them to receive the saving ordinance of baptism? Only one church today has the answer.

One of the ordinances performed in LDS temples is the vicarious or proxy baptisms for the dead.

Since we believe that water baptism by immersion is essential for salvation, Latter-day Saints spend a lot of time and resources identifying our deceased ancestors through research in family history or genealogy. We then take the names of these people to our temples, where we are baptized and receive other ordinances on their behalf. We also perform this selfless services for others to whom we are not directly related.

Special baptismal fonts are constructed in our temples that are similar to those used in the temple of Solomon. (2 Chronicles 4:1-5) The water basin is built on the backs of twelve oxen, symbolizing the twelve tribes of Israel.

The officiator and the person being baptized for the deceased stand in the water just as in a regular baptism for a living person. The only difference is that the individual is baptized "for and in behalf of" the named person who is dead.

In the Catholic Church today candles are lighted and prayers are said for the dead. Before the Reformation, the Catholic Church sold indulgences to living people to buy freedom from Purgatory for their dead relatives. The question is, is baptism for the dead really "peculiar" or is it a "treasured" and valid restoration of a lost practice of New Testament Christians?

The Apostle Paul made reference to this doctrine in his teaching to the Corinthian saints about resurrection:

Else what shall they do which are baptized for the dead, if the dead rise not at all? why are they then baptized for the dead?

— *1 Cor 15:29*

Paul is clearly referring to a Christian practice that some of the Corinthian saints are participating in but they've forgotten WHY they are doing it. He is referring to that practice in this verse to remind them of the reality of the resurrection.

Some of the critics of Mormonism have engaged in exegetical and logical gymnastics to try and deny that this was a Christian practice. They point out that Paul uses the word "they" instead of "we" to describe those *"which are baptized for the dead"*. They claim that "they" refers to some other heretical group, not to the Christians to whom Paul is writing. But that argument doesn't make any sense. Why would Paul refer to an errant practice that someone else is doing to prove his point that true Christians should believe in the resurrection? His argument only makes sense if the Christians are being baptized for the dead. Of course he is obviously writing to those Corinthians who are "backsliding" as seen in other verses. Perhaps the "they" he is referring to are the more righteous members of the church there.

Hugh Nibley writes:

Most biblical scholars today admit that (Christian proxy baptisms) is exactly what Paul had reference to, although most will say that they don't know much about it. The Lutheran scholar and Bishop Krister Stendahl states *that "the text seems to speak plainly enough about a practice within the Church of vicarious baptism for the dead. This is the view of most contemporary exegetes."*[2]

"The normal reading of the text," writes Gordon Fee, *"is that some Corinthians are being baptized, apparently vicariously, in behalf of some people who have already died".*[3]

"It seems that in Corinth," writes Raymond E. Brown, *"some Christians would undergo baptism in the name of their deceased nonChristian relatives and friends, hoping this vicarious baptism might assure them a share in the redemption of Christ."*[4]

John Hurd, Jr. writes in the Mercer University Press:

"The most common opinion among critical scholars is that Paul was referring to the practice of vicarious baptism on behalf of dead persons. "[5]

An article in Christianity Today states:

"The most plausible interpretation is that some in Corinth were getting baptized vicariously for the dead."[6]

Fortunately we also have historic evidence that baptism for the dead was a Christian practice in the dominant church until it was abandoned by the sixth canon of the Council of Carthage in A.D. 397. Some of the smaller sects (often called heretics by the larger church) continued the practice, and elements of the Syrian and Coptic Christian church in Egypt still teach it. Epiphanius wrote of the Marcionites of the fourth century, *when any of them had died without baptism, they used to baptize others in their name, lest in the resurrection they should suffer punishment as unbaptized."*

—(Heresies, 8:7.)

Tertullian acknowledged that the Corinthians practiced proxy baptism

—(On the Resurrection of the Flesh, 48).

WHY IS THERE NOT MORE IN THE BIBLE ABOUT BAPTISM FOR THE DEAD?

If this is a valid Christian doctrine, why don't we hear more about it in the Bible? Actually, the version of the scriptures used by the earliest Christians did.

One of the most popular books among Christian congregations in the first few centuries was the *Shepherd of Hermas*. It was included in several early lists of canonical books. Had it been retained as part of the canon there would have been more references to baptism for the dead in the scriptures.

Clement, the Bishop of Alexandria (150 AD) quoted Hermas in his teachings:

And the Shepherd, speaking plainly of those who had fallen asleep, recognizes certain righteous among Gentiles and Jews, not only before the appearance of Christ, but before the law ... He says accordingly that ... they descended, therefore, with them into the water, and again ascended. ... (for) those who had fallen asleep before ... know the name of the son of God. Wherefore, they also ascended with them.[7]

So .... does baptism for the dead still seem such a "peculiar" doctrine? Not to early Christians. What seems more "peculiar" to me is to preach that a loving, merciful and just God would condemn to eternal punishment billions of his children just because they did not have the good fortune to hear about Christ and have the opportunity in mortality to accept him as their savior. Yet that is exactly what many "Christian" churches teach today.

MARRIAGE FOR TIME AND ALL ETERNITY

Another doctrine or belief and practice that is "peculiar" to the LDS church is marriage "for time and all eternity". We believe that families are meant to last beyond mortality. One of the favorite bumper stickers you might see on a Mormon car says "Families are Forever".

Many Christians and people of other faiths also seem to have an innate belief that they will be with their loved ones in the Hereafter. But when a couple is married in a civil ceremony or in any church that I know of, they are joined only "until death do you part" or "for the period of your mortal lives". That is the length of the marital contract into which they are entering. Neither a Justice of the Peace nor a rabbi, priest nor pastor can offer them anything longer lasting than that.

And yet when Jesus gave to Peter the "keys of the kingdom" he said:

"Whatsoever ye shall bind on earth shall be bound in heaven: and whatsoever ye shall loose on earth shall be loosed in heaven."

—Matt 18:18

As I explained back in chapter 5, the priesthood authority that Jesus gave to his apostles (including the binding/loosing power just mentioned) was lost from the earth when the apostles died, but it has been restored to the earth by heavenly messengers in these latter days. Like baptisms for the dead, these marriages and the sealing together of families that last forever are sacred ordinances that were lost to historic Christianity but are now performed in Mormon temples.

Do you really feel that you could be happy in heaven without the companionship of the person that you've loved and cherished all your life here on earth? I can't imagine that. As I said, many (most?) people have a personal belief that they will have the same familial relationship in heaven with their parents, spouses, and children that they enjoy here on earth, but their religion cannot promise them that will be the case.

MARRIAGE FOR ETERNITY IN ANCIENT CHRISTIANITY

But is all this "eternal marriage" stuff just something that Joseph Smith invented to make his followers feel better? In a word, NO. Although the practice is not found in "traditional" or "historic" or "orthodox" Christianity at present, recent discoveries have brought to light documentation that it was practiced among pre-Nicene Christian believers.

Around 1947 an Egyptian camel driver discovered a group of early Christian texts in Upper Egypt that is now known as the Nag Hammadi Library. This was about the same time that the Dead Sea Scrolls came to light in Israel. The Nag Hammadi texts were written in Coptic on papyrus pages that were originally bound in 12 or 13 leather books or "codices". These were the scriptures of early Christians in Egypt from about the third century A.D.

Among the writings we find reference to a temple with a "bridal chamber" at its center where Christians were joined in marriage "never to be separated". This bridal chamber was even described as having mirrors on opposite walls so that couples could see their images reflected into infinity, just as we find in the LDS temples today.[8]

Among the Christians at Nag Hammadi it was taught that when God took a rib from Adam and created Eve, the two were separated. The Bible describes marriage as man and wife becoming "one flesh" again. But when God performed the first marriage in the Garden of Eden to re-unite them there was no death on earth. They could not have been married "till death to you part" so theirs would have to have been an eternal union. In the temple ordinances at Nag Hammadi;

"the woman is united to her husband in the bridal chamber. Indeed those who have united in the bridal chamber will no longer be separated...."[9]

Boy, that Joseph Smith was a lucky guesser wasn't he? The doctrine of eternal marriage that he revealed to the Latter-day Saints was not discovered by the rest of the world until over a hundred years later!

IF I AM A FAITHFUL LATTER-DAY SAINT, WILL I BECOME THE GOD OF MY OWN PLANET?

Here's another "peculiar" LDS doctrine:

In a popular Broadway play called "The Book of Mormon Musical", one of the characters sings in a song called "I Believe":

"I believe that God has a plan for all of us. I believe that plan involves me getting my own planet."

This is a light-hearted jab at one of the more "peculiar" (AKA"treasured") LDS doctrines that we call the doctrine of "Eternal Progression". That is, as children of our Father in Heaven our ultimate goal goes beyond "salvation" to obtain the "rewards" or the "things that accompany salvation" (Heb. 6:9). That includes becoming like our Father and Christ and inheriting all that God has for us. I've already shown in Chapter 9 that this doctrine of "divinization" or "theosis" was taught extensively in first century Christianity before it was lost in the Dark Ages.

So, if God our Father has created worlds without number and we are to inherit all that he has as joint heirs with Christ (Rev. 21:7 and Rom 8:16-17), then if I "endure to the end" and "overcome", what will I get?

To him that overcometh will I grant to <u>sit with me in my throne</u>, even as I also overcame, and am set down with my Father in his throne.

—(Rev. 3:21)

Will I get my own planet like the song says? No. I'll become the god of my own <u>galaxy</u>. Or maybe my own universe! It makes sense, doesn't it? We may not understand it all now, but Paul promised us that someday we will.

For we know in part, and we prophesy in part. But when that which is perfect is come, then that which is in part shall be done away. When I was a child, I spake as a child, I understood as a child, I thought as a child: but when I became a man, I put away childish things. For now we see through a glass, darkly; but then face to face: now I know in part; but then shall I know even as also I am known.

—1Cor. 13:9-12

Indeed we do now "see through a glass darkly" and we "know in part". But because the "restitution of all things" has taken place and God has called modern-day prophets again on the earth, we now know a lot more about the "plain and precious things" of Christianity that were lost during the Dark Ages. Perhaps it's time to "put away childish things" of "Kindergarten Christianity" and get on to the meat of the Gospel. Even if it does seem a bit "peculiar".

As the author of Hebrews wrote:

Therefore (not) leaving the principles of the doctrine of Christ, <u>let us go on unto perfection</u>; not laying again the foundation of repentance from dead works, and of faith toward God, Of the doctrine of baptisms, and of laying on of hands, and of resurrection of the dead, and of eternal judgment. And this will we do, if God permit.

—(Hebrews 6:1-3)

Therefore if you will permit, let's "go on" to another "peculiar" Latter-day Saint doctrine:

WAS JESUS THE SPIRIT BROTHER OF LUCIFER?

Oh yes, this is a favorite item of the anti-Mormons. They love to spit this one out like it is a nail to drive into the coffin of "Mormonism". But once again, they are in ignorance of the facts.

First of all, the Bible teaches us that God is the father of our spirits:

Furthermore we have had fathers of our flesh which corrected us, and we gave them reverence: shall we not much rather be in subjection unto <u>*the Father of spirits,*</u> *and live?*

—Heb. 12:9

<u>*Forasmuch then as we are the offspring of God ...*</u>

—Acts 17:29

Paul says that in addition to being Lord and Savior, Jesus is also the firstborn of God's spirit children: *For whom he did foreknow, he also did predestinate to be conformed to the image of his Son,* <u>that he might be the firstborn among many brethren</u>.

— Romans 8:29

The Bible also says that Lucifer (who became Satan) is one of the sons of God.

Now there was a day when <u>*the sons of God*</u> *came to present themselves before the Lord, and* <u>*Satan came also among them*</u>.

—Job 1:6

The writer of Job repeated again:

Again there was a day when the <u>*sons of God*</u> *came to present themselves before the Lord, and* <u>*Satan came also among them*</u> *to present himself before the Lord.*

— Job 2:1

So let's check our logic, okay?

1. We are all (including Lucifer/Satan) spirit sons and daughters of God the Father.

2. Jesus Christ is the firstborn of Father's spirit children

3. We're all related.

Therefore:

Lucifer/Satan is the younger brother of Jesus.

Hitler and Mother Teresa are also siblings. As are you and I. It's true.

What? You don't agree with my interpretation of scripture? Well, the 2nd century Church Father Lactantius does. Who do you think we should believe? Who has the greater knowledge?

"...He (God) produced a spirit like unto Himself...then He made another being, in whom the disposition of the divine origin did not remain. Therefore, he [the second being] was infected with his own envy as with poison, and passed from good to evil... for he envied his predecessor, who through his steadfastness is acceptable and dear to God the Father. This being, who from good became evil by his own act, is called by the Greeks Diabolus..." [10]

Matthew Roper commented on it this way:

> A rather similar doctrine to that of the Mormons was taught by the Latin father, Lactantius (d. A.D. 320), whom all affirm to be Christian. "According to Lactantius," as Giovanni Papini summarizes his position, "***Lucifer would have been nothing less than the brother of the Logos***... The elder spirit, filled with every divine virtue and beloved by God above all other spirits, can easily be recognized as the Word, that is, the Son. But Lactantius's story leads one to think that the other spirit, also endowed with every grace, was the second son of the Father: **the future Satan would be, no less, the younger brother of the future Christ.**" If Lactantius could hold such a belief and still be a Christian, how can The Church of Jesus Christ of Latter-day Saints be driven from Christendom for teaching a similar doctrine?[11]

WAS JESUS MARRIED?
OUTSIDE LATTER-DAY CHRISTIANITY

Some critics of The Church of Jesus Christ of Latter-day Saints indicate that since "Mormonism" teaches that Jesus was married, we have a "different Jesus" from the Jesus of the Bible and of traditional Christianity. They write:

The unmistakable conclusion is that the LDS god was a mortal man who was married and his marriage qualified him for being exalted to godhood. The god of the Mormons is a man-god who once was a man like any other man, who by his good works was exalted to *godhood. That is what the Mormons are working for.... not salvation... but godhood. (See Genesis 3:5, Godhood is what Satan promised Eve if she disobeyed God and ate the fruit of the tree of the knowledge of good and evil) The Jesus, the Mormons proclaim to love so dearly, is <u>absolutely not</u> the Jesus Christ of the Bible, but according to their teaching the sexual offspring of their god and one of his many wives in heaven. In fact Jesus, Satan and all men are the actual offspring of their god of flesh and bone.*[12]

(Note: Those who quote Genesis 3:5 and say that Satan was lying to Eve conveniently omit reading Genesis 3:22 where God said that Satan was NOT lying in this particular instance: *And the LORD God said, Behold, <u>the man is become as one of us, to know good and evil:</u>)* But let's get back to the question of Jesus' martial status.

INSIDE LATTER-DAY CHRISTIANITY
DOES "MORMONISM" TEACH THAT JESUS WAS MARRIED?

Officially? No. And does it matter? To Jesus it does, of course. But as far as our salvation is concerned? Not really. But since I've studied the matter a bit and I have some opinions on it, I'll share with you some knowledge that just may blow your mind.

Although not an official tenet of church doctrine, certain leaders of The Church of Jesus Christ of Latter-day Saints have in the past taught at least the possibility that Jesus may have been married while in mortality. Latter-day Saint Apostle Orson Hyde made these statements:

"It will be borne in mind that once on a time, there was a marriage in Cana of Galilee; <u>... no less a person than Jesus Christ was married on that occasion.</u> If he was never married, his intimacy with Mary and Martha, and the other Mary also whom Jesus loved, must have been highly unbecoming and improper to say the least of it."

"I will venture to say that if Jesus Christ were now to pass thought the most pious countries in Christendom with a train of women, such as used to follow him, ... he would be mobbed, tarred, and feathered, and rode, not on as ass, but on a rail."[13]

I personally believe there's a good indication that Jesus was married, although the issue is not important to my (or any one else's) salvation, but it is one which may lead to a better understanding of our relationship to Christ and of his relationship to us and to the Father. If anything, he was our example in all things, even so far as to going to be baptized of John to "fulfill all righteousness" even though as the only sinless person to live on the earth, he had no need of baptism for remission of sins.

Apparently I'm far from being alone. In a survey conducted by the online religious website Beliefnet, thanks to the novel and movie "*The DaVinci Code*" 19% of respondents said they believe that Mary Magdalene was in fact the wife of Jesus.[14]

The Bible story of the life of Jesus has a gaping hole of 18 missing years from the time he was 12 until the time he began his ministry at age 30, during which time the usual pattern for a boy growing up in a Jewish household would be to marry and have children. The Essene community that produced the Dead Sea scrolls was thought by archaeologists to be a group of celibate individuals until they discovered the graves of woman and children as part of the community. It is now understood that among the Essenes custom dictated that a young man would marry and have children and then later become celibate upon entering into the ministry where he could devote full time to that enterprise. I don't know if that's the pattern that Jesus followed, but it does indicate a possible variation of a theme.

DID ISAIAH FORETELL THE MARRIAGE OF CHRIST AND HIS HAVING CHILDREN?
Some scholars have looked at certain passages in Isaiah where it speaks of the Messiah being crucified and it says "and he shall see his seed." They have deduced from these that the Messiah was prophesied to have children or "seed." Others have a different interpretation of these passages. (Isaiah 53:10)

WHO WAS THE GROOM AT THE WEDDING OF CANA?
As the apostle Orson Pratt/Hyde indicated, there is enough evidence to at least establish a plausibility that Jesus was the bridegroom at the wedding of Cana. Why else would his mother be concerned about the wine to feed the guests and why would she come to him in regard to it?

COULD JESUS HAVE BEEN MARRIED TO MORE THAN ONE WIFE?
In the account of Jesus' visit to the home of Lazarus in Bethany, we find that Mary sat at the Lord's feet to hear his teachings while Martha busied herself with preparation of the meal.

She chided Jesus for letting her sister get away with not helping with the housework. This, according to some scholars, has indicated a familiarity with Jesus in their household far beyond that of an ordinary guest. It has lead to speculation that Jesus may have been married to one or both of these young Jewish women and that Lazarus was indeed the Savior's brother-in-law.

INSIDE CHRISTIANITY
A PRESBYTERIAN MINISTER THINKS JESUS WAS MARRIED

In 1970 a Presbyterian minister in West Virginia named William E. Phipps published a book titled *Was Jesus Married?* I had the opportunity to film an interview with Pastor Phipps in 1979 for the movie *"In Search of Historic Jesus"*. Unfortunately the interview was left on the cutting room floor by the producers. In his book he set forth several reasons for his belief that Jesus might have been married:

1. The argument of silence (that is the lack of any comment in the bible as to whether Jesus was married or not) if anything shows that he was following of a normal custom, which was to be married.

   It is the <u>unusual</u> that draws attention and merits notice in the written record, such as the unusual garb and diet of John the Baptist when he lived in the wilderness. We would not know that he wore garments of camel hair and ate honey and wild locusts if that were the norm.

2. It was the law in Israel at the time of Jesus that in order to be a teacher or a rabbi a person over the age of 18 must be married. The detractors of Jesus tried to find every reason to criticize him that they could, but none ever said that he wasn't married.

3. The argument of silence could likewise be applied to the apostles with the one exception of Peter. In the words of Pastor Phipps, "if it hadn't been for Peter's wife's mother getting sick we would have never known that Peter was married." (see Matt. 8:14)

4. Another reason for understanding that Jesus might have been married is found in the Latter-day Saint doctrine of eternal progression. If indeed Jesus was to be our example in all things "to fulfill all righteousness" as he was in baptism, it is logical that he would participate in the "new and everlasting covenant" of eternal marriage. Latter-day Saints believe that males and females do not progress to godhood singly, but together as an eternal family unit. It is logical that our Savior should have set the example for us in this aspect as well and that indeed he could not achieve a fullness of his godhood without participating in that everlasting covenant himself.

A MOTHER IN HEAVEN?

Okay, here's one last "peculiar" Latter-day Saint teaching. Again, this is not an official doctrine of the church and it is not really pertinent to our salvation, but critics of "Mormonism" bring it up from time to time so perhaps I should say a little about it.

All of God's living creations, including *homo sapiens* includes male and female. And if we truly are created in the image and likeness of God (meaning we are <u>like</u> him), would that not indicate that God our Father also has a female counterpart? (I reject the philosophical speculation by some that God is some sort of celestial hermaphrodite that is both male and female.) In fact it was a common belief in Canaan and Israel before the Babylonian captivity that the supreme Hebrew god *El (*or sometimes *Jehovah)* had a wife or "consort" named *Asherah.*

In one of my favorite LDS hymns we read:
In the heav'ns are parents single?
No, the thought makes reason stare!
Truth is reason; truth eternal,
Tells me I've a mother there.[15]

Now before you get all excited and yell "Heretic!" at me, let me say that among Latter-day Saints there is rarely any discussion about a Heavenly Mother. It's not an official doctrine of the Church. But when you think of it, it just kinda makes sense, doesn't it? (And it sure is a kick in the teeth to those anti-Mormons who say that we believe our sisters/ daughters/ wives are second-class citizens in the kingdom of God, huh?)

Okay, I could go on with some of the other "peculiar" Mormon teachings that critics of my faith like to ridicule, but I think you get the point. In each case what seems at first to be heretical or downright silly turns out upon closer inspection and careful study to be a legitimate Christian doctrine. I would encourage you to remember that the next time you hear something "peculiar" about the Latter-day Saints. As I said at the beginning of this chapter, more accurate Bible translations render the KJV "peculiar" as "God's own possession", or "treasured".

ENDNOTES TO CHAPTER 13

1 *Collected Works of Hugh Nibley, Vol.4, Ch.4, p.103*

2 Hugh Nibley, *Mormonism and Early Christianity*, vol. 4 in *The Collected Works of Hugh Nibley,* Salt Lake City: Deseret Book and F.A.R.M.S., 1987, 100 167

3 Gordon Fee, *The First Epistle to the Corinthians*, Grand Rapids: Eerdmans, 1989, 76364

4 (Raymond E. Brown, Joseph A. Fitzmyer, and Roland E. Murphy, *The Jerome Biblical Commentary*, 2 vols, Englewood Cliffs, NJ: Prentice Hall, 1968, 2:273.)

5 John Coolidge Hurd Jr.*, The Origin of I Corinthians.* Macon, Georgia: Mercer University Press, 1983, 136.

6 D. A. Carson, research professor of New Testament at Trinity Evangelical Divinity School, Deerfield, Illinois. *Christianity Today* magazine. August 10, 1998 Vol. 42, No. 9, Page 63

7 Clement of Alexandria, *Stromata III*, 6, in PG 9:268; *Stromata II,9*, in PG 8:980, *Hermas*, Sim. 9.16

8 Jorunn Jacobsen Buckley's important study, "A Cult-Mystery in the Gospel of Philip" (*Journal of Biblical Literature* 99 [1980]: 569–81), argues both for the literalness of the ordinance performed in the bridal chamber and for its absolute centrality.

9 Gospel of Philip 118:17-29, James M. Robinson's *Nag Hammadi Library in English*, Harper and Row Publishers, 1988. pp. 148-159

10 Lactantius, *Divine Institutions*, Book 2, chap. 9, *The AnteNicene Fathers*, 7 Grand Rapids: Wm. B.Eerdmans Publishers, 1978, p.52

11 *Matthew Roper, Review of Books on the Book of Mormon, p.84*

12 http://bible-truth.org/LDSpolygamy.html

13 *Journal of Discourses*, Vol. 4, pages 259-260

14 www:patheos.com

15 *"O My Father," Hymns of The Church of Jesus Christ of Latter-day Saints, no. 292*

APPENDIX 1

WHAT IS A CHRISTIAN?

If you and I were meeting on a Sunday morning in Tehran, Iran as the only "Christians" in that hostile Moslem city, would we be so finicky about definitions of what a Christian really is or could we sit and have a Bible study and fellowship together and enjoy our common heritage on that Sunday morning, and our common faith in Jesus Christ?

As I and other Latter-day Saints listen on Christian radio to people like James Dobson or J. Vernan McGee, Chuck Swindal, John McArthur, etc. I find that 98 per cent of what I hear I can say a hearty "amen" to and I'm nourished by it. Does that surprise you? Is it not true that we both believe in a Godhead consisting of three persons; the Father, the Son and the Holy Ghost? Read our Articles of Faith, that every young Latter-day saint has to memorize to graduate from primary and see how much of it you can say "amen" to. (see Appendix 5)

Of course there are some "nooks and crannies" of theology in every faith on which I'm sure we won't agree, but that's also true internally among members of our respective faiths. One of my Baptist friends once told me that if you get three Baptists together you'll have at least five doctrinal opinions!

But what are the essential elements of belief that form the everyday life and practice of each religions' adherents? Does that constitute what makes a Christian? If we have different understandings of what those three persons of the Godhead are, perhaps we could learn from what Rich Beuhler, a personality on the largest Christian radio station in the U.S. said - *"I hesitate to call a person a non-Christian just because his fuzzy understanding of the trinity is different from my fuzzy understanding of it."*

I am wounded in my soul whenever someone refers to those of my faith as members of a "nonChristian cult." I think to myself, what is it in their minds that makes a Christian?

Certainly I would agree in order to be a Christian a person has to believe that Jesus Christ is the literal Son of God and that He is indeed God incarnate and that he died for our sins and is the only means by which we can be saved. I would think that a person who is a Christian would need to believe that the Bible as it is transmitted and translated correctly is literally God's word.

But there are those who seem to put other requirements on being a Christian and I ask, for example, to be a Christian do I have to believe in a pre, mid, or post-tribulation Rapture?

Do I have to be able to read the Bible in Greek and Hebrew?
Do I have to be able to read at all to be a Christian?
Must I have come forward at an altar call and sign a decision slip to be Christian?
Can I be a Christian and not believe that every single word of the Bible in any given translation is exactly as it came from the mouth of God?
Can I be a Christian and not be certain that all of the Bible is God's word or that the Bible is all of God's word?
Can I be a Christian and not wear a cross or not have a fish on the back of my car?
Can I be a Christian and not listen to Christian radio or television?
Can I be a Christian and not be a Baptist?
Can I be a Christian and not be a Catholic?
Can I be a Christian and not be a Fundamentalist or Evangelical?
Can I be a Christian and not speak in tongues?
Can I be a Christian and not know the four spiritual laws?
Can I be a Christian and not believe that once saved I'm always saved?
In other words who's definition of what it takes to be a Christian must I live by, or shall I just do as Jesus Christ himself said, and follow him?
If I do try to follow him, am I not a Christian?

APPENDIX 2

THE DOCTRINE OF THE TRINITY
IS NOT FOUND IN THE BIBLE

Although critics of "Mormonism" constantly use their "orthodox" belief in the Trinitarian creeds as a litmus test to exclude The Church of Jesus Christ of Latter-day Saints from their definition of a "Christian" faith, numerous Christian scholars and theologians have stated that the doctrine of the Trinity is not found in the Bible. Thus the believers of the Trinitarian creeds do not pass their own test of "sola scriptura". Here are a few examples: (emphasis mine)

- **In the New Testament we do not find the doctrine of the Trinity** in anything like its developed form, not even in the Pauline and Johannine theology
    —(*Encyclopædia of Religion and Ethics*, James Hastings, Trinity, p 458)

- In the immediate post New Testament period of the Apostolic Fathers no attempt was made to work out the God-Christ (Father-Son) relationship in ontological terms. **By the end of the fourth century**, and owing mainly to the challenge posed by various heresies, **theologians went beyond the immediate testimony of the Bible** and also beyond liturgical and creedal expressions of Trinitarian faith to the ontological trinity of coequal persons "within" God. The shift is from function to ontology, from the "economic trinity" (Father, Son, and Spirit in relation to us) to the "immanent" or "essential Trinity" (Father, Son, and Spirit in relation to each other). ... By the close of the fourth century the orthodox teaching was in place: God is one nature, three persons (*mia ousia, treis hupostaseis*).

— (*The Encyclopedia of Religion*, Mircea Eliade, Trinity, Vol 15, p 53-57)

- **"Of a doctrine of the Trinity in the strict sense there is of course no sign**, although the Church's triadic formula left its mark everywhere."

– (Early Christian Doctrines, J.N.D. Kelly, p. 95)

The doctrine of the Triune God has had an amazing history. Convinced that this doctrine is a Christian doctrine that did and could originate only from divine revelation, I start the study from the authentic record of divine revelation that is found in the sacred writings of the Old and New Testaments.

What does the Old Testament tell us of God? It tells us there is one God, a wonderful God of life and love and righteousness and power and glory and mystery, who is the creator and lord of the whole universe, who is intensely concerned with the tiny people of Israel. It tells us of His Word, Wisdom, Spirit, of the Messiah He will send, of a Son of Man and a Suffering Servant to come.

But it tells us nothing explicitly or by necessary implication of a Triune God who is Father, Son and Holy Spirit. If we take the New Testament writers together they tell us there is only one God, the creator and lord of the universe, who is the Father of Jesus. They call Jesus the Son of God, Messiah, Lord, Savior, Word, and Wisdom. They assign Him the divine functions of creation, salvation, and judgment.

Sometimes they call Him God explicitly. They do not speak as fully and clearly of the Holy Spirit as they do of the Son, but at times they coordinate Him with the Father and the Son and put Him on a level with them as far as divinity and personality are concerned. They give us in their writings a triadic ground plan and triadic formulas. They do not speak in abstract terms of nature, substance, person, relation, circumcision, and mission, but they present in their own ways the ideas that are behind these terms. **They give us no formal or formulated doctrine of the Trinity, no explicit teaching that in one God there are three co-equal divine persons**. But they do give us an elemental Trinitarianism, the data from which such a formal doctrine of the Triune God may be **formulated**. To study **the gradual transition from an unformulated Biblical witness to the Father, Son and Holy Spirit to a dogmatic formulation of a doctrine of the Triune God, we look first to the Eastern Church where most of this development took place**.

The **Apostolic Fathers** were witnesses to the Biblical data and the traditional faith rather than theologians, but they furnished useful insights into the lines along which the Church's unconscious theology was developing. Most of them indicated quite clearly a belief in the divinity of Christ, less clearly a belief in the distinct personality and divinity of the Holy Spirit. They gave solid evidence of a belief in three pre-existent 'beings,' but **they furnished no Trinitarian doctrine, no awareness of a Trinitarian problem.**

—(*The Triune God*, Edmund Fortman, p 6)

- "Question of Continuity and Elemental Trinitarianism: From what has been seen thus far, the impression could arise **that the Trinitarian dogma is in the last analysis a late 4th-century invention.** In a sense, this is true; but it implies an extremely strict interpretation of the key words Trinitarian and dogma. **The formulation "one God in three Persons" was not solidly established**, certainly not fully assimilated into Christian life and its profession of faith, **prior to the end of the 4th century**. But it is precisely this formulation that has first claim to the title the Trinitarian dogma.

Among the Apostolic Fathers, there had been nothing even remotely approaching such a mentality or perspective; among the 2nd-century Apologists, little more than a focusing of the problem as that of plurality within the unique Godhead. ... From the vocabulary and grammar of the Greek original, the intention of the hagiographer to communicate singleness of essence in three distinct Persons was easily derived. ... If it is clear on one side that **the dogma of the Trinity in the stricter sense of the word was a late arrival, product of 3 centuries' reflection and debate**, it is just as clear on the opposite side that confession of Father, Son, and Holy Spirit-and hence an elemental Trinitarianism-went back to the period of Christian origins. —(New Catholic Encyclopedia, 1965, Trinity, p. 299-300)

- THE DOGMA of the Trinity-The Trinity is the term employed to signify the central doctrine of the Christian religion-the truth that in the unity of the Godhead there are Three Persons the Father the Son, and the Holy Spirit, these three Persons being truly distinct one from another. ... In Scripture there is as yet no single term by which the Three Divine Persons are denoted together. **The word [tri'as] (of which the Latin trinitas is a translation) is first found in Theophilus of Antioch about A. D. 180.**

He speaks of "the Trinity of God [the Father], His Word and His Wisdom" ("*Ad. Autol.*", 11, 15, P. G., VI, 1078). The term may, of course, have been in use before his time. **Shortly**

afterwards it appears in its Latin form of trinitas in Tertullian. ... it has no place in the Liberal Protestantism of today.

The writers of this school contend that the doctrine of the Trinity, as professed by the Church, is not contained in the New Testament, but that it was first formulated in the second century and received final approbation in the fourth, as the result of the Arian and Macedonian controversies.

— (*The Catholic Encyclopedia*, 1912, Vol. 15, p 47-49)

- The greatest and most influential of the Christian Fathers, Origen, Athanasius, Basil and the Gregories, and Augustine, all acknowledged that, for all the light thrown upon it in the Biblical revelation, the divine Nature remained for them a mystery transcending reason.

— (*Encyclopædia of Religion and Ethics*, James Hastings, Trinity, p 461)

- "The doctrine of the Trinity did not form part of the apostles' preaching, as this is reported in the New Testament."

—(*Encyclopedia International*, Ian Henderson, University of Glasgow, 1969, page 226)

- **"The word Trinity is not found in the Bible, and, though used by Tertullian in the last decade of the 2nd century, it did not find a place formally in the theology of the Church till the 4th century**.

— (*New Bible Dictionary*, J. D. Douglas & F. F. Bruce, Trinity, p. 1298)

- It was the custom in former times for **theologians to blend their own speculations** and those of others with the statement of the Bible doctrine.

— (McClintock and Strong: *Cyclopedia of Biblical, Theological, and Ecclesiastical Literature*, vol x, Trinity, p. 551-553)

- The trinity of God is defined by the Church as the belief that in God are three persons who subsist in one nature. **The belief as so defined was reached only in the 4th and 5th centuries AD and hence is not explicitly and formally a biblical belief.** The trinity of persons within the unity of nature is defined in terms of "person" and "nature" which are Greek philosophical terms; actually **the terms do not appear in the Bible.** The

trinitarian definitions arose as the result of long controversies in which these terms and others such as "essence" and "substance" were erroneously applied to God by some theologians.

— (Dictionary of the Bible, John L. McKenzie, Trinity, p. 899)

- The NT does not contain the developed doctrine of the Trinity.... All this underlines the point that **primitive Christianity did not have an explicit doctrine of the Trinity** such as was subsequently elaborated in the creeds of the early church."

— (*New International Dictionary of New Testament Theology*, Brown, Colin, 1932, God, vol 2, p. 84, J. Schneider)

- "Because the Trinity is such an important part of later Christian doctrine, it is striking that the term does not appear in the New Testament. Likewise, the developed concept of three coequal partners in the Godhead found in later creedal formulations cannot be clearly detected within the confines of the canon. While there are other New Testament texts where God, Jesus, and the Spirit are referred to in the same passage (e.g., Jude 20-21), it is important to avoid reading the Trinity into places where it does not appear.

— (*Oxford Companion to the Bible*, Bruce M. Metzger and Michael D. Coogan, Trinity, p. 782)

APPENDIX 3

"SOLA FIDE" (FAITH ALONE) AND THE BIBLE

Many Christians today place a great emphasis on the idea that grace alone or faith alone is the only thing required by Christ for their salvation. They claim that Mormons believe we can "work our way to heaven" because we believe that doing good works is a necessary evidence of our faith. We believe we're saved by faith, but not by faith **alone**.

As I mentioned in my chapter on salvation, Martin Luther first introduced the doctrine of *sola fide* (faith alone) over a thousand years after the books of the Bible were written. He did so in rebellion against the millennia-old Roman Catholic dogma that participation in certain church sacraments was necessary to be saved.

I thought it would be useful to my readers to provide the Biblical passages used by both those who defend and those who oppose this Reformation doctrine. I'm fairly certain that most modern Christians are quite familiar with the first group of verses, but not so much with the second group.

- Enjoy.

PASSAGES USED TO DEFEND *SOLA FIDE* (salvation by faith alone)
- Luke 23:40-43: "But the other criminal rebuked him. 'Don't you fear God,' he said, 'since you are under the same sentence? We are punished justly, for we are getting what our deeds deserve. But this man has done nothing wrong.' Then he said, 'Jesus, remember

me when you come into your kingdom.' Jesus answered him, 'I tell you the truth, **today you will be with me in paradise.'"**

- John 3:16: "For God so loved the world, that He gave His only begotten Son, so that **whoever believeth in Him shall not perish, but shall have everlasting life**."

- John 3:18: "**Whoever believes in him is not condemned**, but whoever does not believe stands condemned already because he has not believed in the name of God's one and only Son."

- John 6:28-29: "Then they said unto him, 'What shall we do, that we might work the works of God?' Jesus answered and said unto them, '**This is the work of God, that ye believe on him whom he hath sent.'"**

- John 5:24: "Verily, verily, I say unto you, He that heareth my word, and **believeth** him that sent me, hath everlasting life, and shall not come into condemnation; but is passed from death unto life."

- John 6:40: "And this is the will of him that sent me, that every one which seeth the Son, and **believeth** on him, may have everlasting life, and I will raise him up at the last day."

- John 6:47: "Verily, verily, I say unto you, He that **believeth** on me hath everlasting life."

- Acts 10:43: "Of Him all the prophets bear witness that through His name everyone who **believes** in Him receives forgiveness of sins."

- Acts 16:31: "**Believe** on the Lord Jesus Christ, and you shall be saved."

- John 14:6: "Jesus saith unto him, I am the way, the truth, and the life: no man cometh to the Father, but by me."

- Acts 26:18: "...that they may receive forgiveness of sins and an inheritance among those who are sanctified by faith in me..."

- Romans 1:17-18: "**Therefore the just shall live by faith**. The wrath of God is indeed being revealed from heaven against every impiety and wickedness of those who suppress the truth by their wickedness."

- Romans 3:28: "Therefore we conclude that **a man is justified by faith** without the deeds of the law."

- Romans 4:5: "But to him that worketh not, but **believeth** on him that justifieth the ungodly, his **faith is counted for righteousness**."

- Romans 5:1: "Therefore **being justified by faith**, we have peace with God through our Lord Jesus Christ."

- Romans 6:23 "For the wages of sin is death; but the gift of God is eternal life through Jesus Christ our Lord."

- Romans 10:9: "That if thou shalt **confess with thy mouth** the Lord Jesus, and shalt **believe** in thine heart that God hath raised him from the dead, thou shalt be saved."

- Romans 11:6: "And **if by grace, then is it no more of works:** otherwise grace is no more grace. But if it be of works, then is it no more grace: otherwise work is no more work."

- Galatians 2:16: "Knowing that **a man is not justified by the works of the law, but by the faith of Jesus Christ**, even we have believed in Jesus Christ, that we might be justified by the faith of Christ, and not by the works of the law: for by the works of the law shall no flesh be justified."

- Galatians 2:21: "I do not frustrate the grace of God: for if righteousness come by the law, then Christ is dead in vain."

- Galatians 5:4,5: "Christ is become of no effect unto you, **whosoever of you are justified by the law; ye are fallen from grace.** For we through the Spirit wait for the hope of righteousness by faith."

- Ephesians 2:8-10: "**For by grace are ye saved through faith; and that not of yourselves**: it is the gift of God: **Not of works, lest any man should boast**. For we are his workmanship, created in Christ Jesus unto good works, which God hath before ordained that we should walk in them."

- Philippians 3:9: "And be found in him, not having mine own righteousness, which is of the law, but that which is through the faith of Christ, **the righteousness which is of God by faith."**

- Galatians 3:8: "The Scripture foresaw that God would justify the Gentiles by faith..."

- 1Timothy 1:16: "However, for this reason I obtained mercy, that in me first Jesus Christ might show all long suffering, as a pattern to those who are going to believe on Him for everlasting life."

- **Titus 3:5: "Not by works of righteousness** which we have done, but according to his mercy he saved us, by the washing of regeneration, and renewing of the Holy Ghost."

PASSAGES USED TO ARGUE AGAINST *SOLA FIDE*

- Matthew 5:16: "Let your light so shine before men, **that they may see your good works**, and glorify your Father which is in heaven."

- Matthew 5:48 (part of the Expounding of the Law within the Sermon on the Mount): "**Be perfect, therefore**, as your heavenly Father is perfect." (Compare Imitatio dei)

- Matthew 7:21 (part of the Sermon on the Mount): "Not everyone who says to me, 'Lord, Lord,' will enter the kingdom of heaven, but **only he who does the will of my Father who is in heaven**."

- Matthew 7:24-27 (part of the Sermon on the Mount): "Therefore everyone who hears these words of mine **and puts them into practice** is like a wise man who built his house on the rock. The rain came down, the streams rose, and the winds blew and beat against that house; yet it did not fall, because it had its foundation on the rock. But everyone who hears these words of mine and **does not put them into practice** is like a foolish man who built his house on sand. The rain came down, the streams rose, and the winds blew and beat against that house, and it fell with a great crash."

- Matthew 16:27: "For the Son of Man is going to come in his Father's glory with his angels, and then **he will reward each person according to what he has done**."

- Matthew 19:17: "'Why do you ask me about what is good?' Jesus replied. 'There is only One who is good. **If you want to enter life, obey the commandments.**'"

- Matthew 24:10-20 (part of the Olivet discourse): "Then many will fall away, and they will betray one another and hate one another. And many false prophets will arise and lead many astray. And because of the increase of lawlessness, the love of many will grow cold. But **the one who endures to the end will be saved**."

- Matthew 25:31-46 (part of The Sheep and the Goats): "When the Son of Man comes in his glory, and all the angels with him, he will sit on his throne in heavenly glory. All the nations will be gathered before him, and he will separate the people one from another as a shepherd separates the sheep from the goats. He will put the sheep on his right and the goats on his left. Then the King will say to those on his right, 'Come, you who are blessed by my Father; **take your inheritance**, the kingdom prepared for you since the creation of the world. **For I was hungry and you gave me something to eat**, I was thirsty and you gave me something to drink, I was a stranger and you invited me in, I needed clothes and you clothed me, I was sick and you looked after me, I was in prison and you came to visit me.'

Then the righteous will answer him, 'Lord, when did we see you hungry and feed you, or thirsty and give you something to drink? When did we see you a stranger and invite you in, or needing clothes and clothe you? When did we see you sick or in prison and go to visit you?' The King will reply, 'I tell you the truth, whatever you did for one of the least of these brothers of mine, you did for me.' Then he will say to those on his left, 'Depart from me, **you who are cursed**, into the eternal fire prepared for the devil and his angels. **For I was hungry and you gave me nothing to eat**, I was thirsty and you gave me nothing to drink, I was a stranger and you did not invite me in, I needed clothes and you did not clothe me, I was sick and in prison and you did not look after me.' They also will answer, 'Lord, when did we see you hungry or thirsty or a stranger or needing clothes or sick or in prison, and did not help you?' He will reply, 'I tell you the truth, whatever you did not do for one of the least of these, you did not do for me.' Then they will go away to eternal punishment, but the righteous to eternal life."

- Matthew 28:19-20a (part of the Great Commission): "Therefore go and make disciples of all nations, baptizing them in the name of the Father and of the Son and of the Holy Spirit, **and teaching them to obey everything I have commanded you**."

- Luke 8:21: "But He answered and said to them, 'My mother and My brothers are these who hear the word of God **and do it.'**"

- Luke 10:25-28: "On one occasion an expert in the law stood up to test Jesus. 'Teacher,' he asked, 'what must I **do** to inherit eternal life?' 'What is written in the Law?' he replied. 'How do you read it?' He answered: "'Love the Lord your God with all your heart and with all your soul and with all your strength and with all your mind"; and, "Love your neighbor as yourself." 'You have answered correctly,' Jesus replied. **'Do this and you will live.'**"

- John 5:29: "And will come out—**those who have done good, to the resurrection of life**, and those who have done evil, to the resurrection of condemnation."

- Acts 26:20: "First to those in Damascus, then to those in Jerusalem and in all Judea, and to the Gentiles also, I preached that they should repent and turn to God and **prove their repentance by their deeds.**"

- Romans 2:6,7; 13: "For he will repay **according to each one's deeds**. To those who by patiently doing good seek for glory and honor and immortality, he will give eternal life; for it is not those who hear the law who are just in the sight of God; rather, those who observe the law will be justified."

- Galatians 6:7b-9: "A man reaps what he sows. The one who sows to please his sinful nature, from that nature will reap destruction; the one who sows to please the Spirit, from the Spirit will reap eternal life. **Let us not become weary in doing good**, for at the proper time we will reap a harvest if we do not give up."

- Corinthians 7: 19: "Circumcision means nothing and uncircumicsion means nothing; **what matters is keeping God's commandments**."

- Corinthians 5:10: "For we must all appear before the judgment seat of Christ; that every one may receive the things done is his body, **according to that he hath done**, whether it be good or bad."

- Philippians 2:12b-13: "**Work out your salvation with fear and trembling**, For God is one who, for his good purpose, works in you both to desire and to work."

- Timothy 4:16: "Attend to yourself and to your teaching; persevere in both tasks, for by doing so you will save both yourself and those who listen to you."

- Timothy 6:18-19: "That they do good, **that they be rich in good works**, ready to distribute, willing to communicate; Laying up in store for themselves a good foundation against the time to come, **that they may lay hold on eternal life**."

- Hebrews 10:24: "And let us consider how we may spur one another on toward love and **good deeds**."

- James 1:22: "Do not merely listen to the word, and so deceive yourselves. **Do** what it says."

- James 2 (excerpts): "... What doth it profit, my brethren, though a man say he hath faith, and have not works? can faith save him? ... Thou believest that there is one God; thou doest well: the devils also believe, and tremble. But wilt thou know, O vain man, that **faith without works is dead**? Was not Abraham our father justified by works, when he had offered Isaac his son upon the altar? Seest thou how faith wrought with his works, and **by works was faith made perfect**? ... Ye see then how that **by works a man is justified**."

- James 2:24: "You see that a person is justified by works and **NOT** by faith **alone**." (Emphasis added) **(In fact, this is the only time the phrase "faith *alone*" appears in the Scriptures.)**

- Peter 1:17: "Now if you invoke as Father **him who judges impartially according to each one's works**, conduct yourselves with reverence during the time of your sojourning."

- Peter 2:12: "Having your conversation honest among the Gentiles: that, whereas they speak against you as evildoers, they may **by your good works**, which they shall behold, glorify God in the day of visitation."

- John 2:3-7: "We know that we have come to know him if we obey his commands. **The man who says, 'I know him,' but does not do what he commands is a liar, and the truth is not in him**. But if anyone **obeys** his word, God's love is truly made complete in him

- Revelation 2:23: "Then all the churches will know that I am he who searches hearts and minds, and I will repay each of you **according to your deeds**."

- Revelation 14:12-13: "Here is a call for the endurance of the saints, those who keep the commandments of God and hold fast to the faith of Jesus. And I heard a voice from heaven saying, 'Write this: Blessed are the dead who from now on die in the Lord.' 'Yes,' says the Spirit, 'they will rest from their labours, for **their deeds follow them.'**"

- Revelation 20:13: "All the dead were **judged according to their deeds**."

- Revelation 22:12: "Behold, I am coming soon. I bring with me the recompense I will give to each **according to his deeds**."

APPENDIX 4

A MORMON CHALLENGES "THE GODMAKERS" MOVIE

(formerly called "Errors, Distortions And Untruths In The Movie "The Godmakers")
-by Robert Starling Revised January 10, 1995

The movie "The Godmakers" is described by a multi denominational group, the National Conference of Christians and Jews, as "making extensive use of 'half truth', faulty generalizations, erroneous interpretations, and sensationalism. It is not reflective of the genuine spirit of the Mormon faith."

Unable to accept this assessment, the supporters of the film have demanded specific examples of the above mentioned faults. The following is a partial list of such specifics in the approximate order that they are found in the film.

1. LDS temple services are said to be "reserved for an elite few." In actuality, great efforts are made to assist all members to align their lives with the principles of the Gospel of Jesus Christ so that they may enter the temples. They are not "reserved" for the "elite." If not all members worship there, it is by their own choice, and represents a fulfillment of the Biblical truth, "many are called, but few are chosen," for "strait is the gate and narrow the way, and few there be that find it."

2. After LDS mission president Harold R. Goodman described the interview for receiving a temple recommend, a misleading film edit was made so that he seemed to say, "that is the only way we can be with our Heavenly Father." While it is true that certain of the highest heavenly rewards are contingent on making covenants with God in the temple (and living up to them), this is not required for salvation and entrance into the Celestial Kingdom where we will be in the presence of our Heavenly Father.

   Anyone familiar with LDS doctrine knows this, and the film was edited in such a way as to create a deliberate deception.

3. It was said that "many Mormons came thousands of miles and stood in the rain" to tour the Seattle temple before its dedication because "this may be the only time they may be allowed to enter a Mormon temple" as one of the "select few." In view of #1 above, any LDS member who cared enough about the temple to make that kind of a journey would certainly find it easier to obtain a recommend and attend a temple nearer home. The statement was absurd and unfounded.

4. The Mormon "gods" were said to have "worked their way up" to become gods. This is alien to LDS theology. While we believe that we are the "offspring of God," (Heb. 12:9, Acts 17:29, Ps. 82:6) and "joint heirs with Christ," (Rom. 8:17, 1 Jn. 3:2, Rev. 3:21) we can no more "work ourselves up" to godhood than a piece of coal can "work itself up" to become a diamond or a caterpillar can "work itself up" to be a butterfly. In each case the potential is there, but it is God who must work the miracle. He is the only "Godmaker"!

   LDS strive to follow the Savior's admonition to "Be ye perfect even as your Father in Heaven is perfect."(Matt. 5:48) And yet we know that "we have all sinned and come short" of that perfection. In fact, we know that we won't achieve it in this life, and that we must all rely on the Grace of Christ to return to the presence of our Heavenly Father. But "we know that when he shall appear, we shall be like him"(1 John 3:2).

   Following the admonition of Paul, we as Latter-day Saints "let this mind be in (us) which was also in Christ Jesus: Who, being in the form of God, thought it not robbery to be equal with God."

   (Philippians 2:5,6) We do not apologize for believing the Bible. Most Christians consider themselves "a child of the King," yet they don't know what that really means. Latter-day

Saints believe the Bible when it says the faithful children of our Heavenly Father are to inherit the kingdom, receive a throne, and sit at the right hand of God. (Rev. 3:21)

5. The quote "As man is, God once was, and as God is, man may become" was credited to James E. Talmadge. It was Lorenzo Snow who said this. This is a small thing, but it's evidence of poor research and a disregard for accuracy. Almost any LDS high school seminary student could give the correct attribution for this quote.

6. To demean God's Biblical command to "be fruitful and multiply" by referring to "endless Celestial sex" is an example of the tasteless sensationalism decried by the National Council of Christians and Jews in their report which totally discredited this film.

7. The principles of Celestial Marriage and Eternal Progression were said to be "secrets" that "Mormons don't talk about." This is untrue. While the principle of man's becoming like our Heavenly Father is not discussed in our church meetings nearly as much as one would believe from reading anti-Mormon literature, it is certainly not a secret.

8. Mormonism is described as being far removed from "orthodox" Christianity. It must be remembered that orthodoxy is often subjective in its definition. Christ himself flew in the face of the religious "orthodoxy" of His time. But who was right? Our Lord, or the Scribes and Pharisees? In reality the LDS church is much closer to the "orthodoxy" of the original first century Christians than other churches in the world today. (The popular Protestant doctrine of salvation by faith alone is itself far removed from the historic Catholic theology by which "orthodoxy" was defined for over 1,000 years!)

9. A story is shown in animation of Elohim growing up as a mortal on a planet and later becoming God, our Heavenly Father. Somehow this is implied to be a fantastic and un-Christian doctrine. Yet this is exactly like the story told in the four Gospels of the mortal existence of our Lord Jesus Christ, who later rose from the dead and received the fullness of His glory as God the Son, equal in power and dominion with His Father. Jesus said that he did nothing that he had not seen the Father do. (John 5:19) If Jesus is God, yet lived as a mortal, then why could not His Father have done the same?

10. Blacks are described as being "neutral" in the war that was fought in heaven against Lucifer and the spirits who followed him. This is incorrect. LDS are taught that there were no neutrals in that conflict. The implication in the film that the LDS church is racist is unjustified. Many blacks and other minorities hold responsible positions of

leadership in our Church, and our Indian Placement Program (where LDS members open their homes to assist in the education of Native American children) is unequaled by any other Christian denomination.

11. God the Father (Elohim) is pictured "returning to Earth in human form from the 'starbase Kolob' to have sex with the Virgin Mary in order to provide Jesus with a physical body." The caricature of the Lord of the Universe knocking on the door of a home in Nazareth in the middle of the night is a total perversion of LDS beliefs and has rightly been called "religious pornography" by many Christians who have more taste than the people who produced this film.

   Two marvelous events happened on that wondrous night (or day) when Jesus was conceived in Mary's womb. According to the Bible, (1) the Holy Ghost came upon her, and (2) the power of the Highest "overshadowed" her. The first was necessary because no mortal can endure the presence of God the Father without the protection of the Holy Ghost. But Jesus is not the son of the Holy Ghost.

   God the Father is "the Highest," and it is He who is the father of Jesus. To say otherwise is to "wrest the scriptures."

12. A few speculative remarks from early LDS leaders regarding Jesus having married and fathered children is implied to be official Church doctrine, which it is not. However such a doctrine would not be un-Christian, since the Bible is silent on the subject. (In fact a Presbyterian minister in West Virginia has written a book giving Biblical reasons why he believes that Jesus was indeed married!)

13. Joseph Smith is described as "a young treasure seeker." Although he did once hire out as a laborer for a man looking for treasure, this derogatory term is a definite "half truth" and in no way accurately describes his usual occupation or character.

   It is also highly questionable whether it can be substantiated that he was "known for his tall tales," or if this is merely an invention of the film's authors. His mother said he shared stories from The Book of Mormon history with family members, but these are no more "tall tales" than telling about Moses parting the Red Sea.

14. Statement from the film: "The Mormons thank God for Joseph Smith, who claimed that he had done more for us than any other man, including Jesus Christ." This is patently

false. The original quote from D & C 135:3 said Joseph Smith had done more for the salvation of men" save Jesus only" than any other man who had lived in the world. There is a world of difference in the two statements, and difference is the truth of what was said versus the deception of those who have deliberately misquoted Joseph Smith. Defenders of the film have confused this misquote with another reference in LDS

Church history (taken from the book also titled The God Makers, not the movie, which is what I am dealing with here) where Joseph Smith said of "keeping a whole church together" that "neither Paul, John, nor Jesus ever did it. I boast that no man ever did such a work as I!" (Let the reader compare the three quotes to see where the deception lies!) Here, Joseph did not say that he was greater than Jesus as the anti-Mormons have claimed, but rather that he had done a greater work than Jesus. Was this blasphemy? Or fulfillment of a prophecy made by Jesus himself? In John 14:12, the Lord said of whoever believed on Him; "the works that I do shall he do also; and greater works than these shall he do..."

Perhaps Joseph did get a little carried away in his boasting of what happened to be a true fact of history. But this is a human fallibility that Joseph shared with many other Biblical prophets (see Paul in 2 Cor. 11:16-33). In no way does this negate his prophetic calling nor invalidate the truthfulness of the church he restored. To even mention it shows how desperately the critics of the LDS church are grasping at straws. A quick reading of Joseph's speeches or writings would show immediately that neither he nor his followers have ever considered him to be greater than Jesus Christ.

15. It is stated that "the Mormon church pressures individuals into divorcing their spouses when they are not measuring up to the Church's standards." This is totally untrue. Several ex-Mormons interviewed in the film said they were counseled by their Bishops to divorce. A quick look at handbooks for Bishops will reveal that the official Church policy is quite the contrary. LDS couples are counseled to make every effort to strengthen and preserve their marriages and families. If Ed Decker knows "literally hundreds of families with stories like this" (being advised to divorce), then why did he have to hire actors to portray 2 of the "estranged husbands" in the film? (These were in addition to two other actors playing attorneys.)

16. One of the major allegations of the film is that "there is a whole area of psychiatric care dealing with depression in the Mormon woman." Much has been made of a 1983 TV

documentary produced by KSL television in Salt Lake City called "Mormon Women and Depression." (I watched it and have it on videocassette.) It is never mentioned, however, that this was only one part of a series of programs on depression in various segments of the Utah population. Its importance has been blown out of proportion... another example of the "half truths" in this film which were condemned by the investigators from the NCCJ.

It should also be noted that in the last few years there has been a rise in the awareness of depression in women in general (some think it's brought on by the feminist movement), and a recognition of illnesses like Pre-Menstrual Syndrome, etc. If one is to believe the multitude of commercials heard on Christian radio stations (at least in the LA area) which advertise counseling and PMS treatment centers, it could more legitimately be said that "there is a whole area of psychiatric care dealing with depression in CHRISTIAN women." To single out Mormonism as a cause of depression is at best false and misleading. I have no doubt that virtually 100 percent of LDS women who feel depressed would say if asked that their faith in Christ which they're taught in the Mormon church is their greatest help in OVERCOMING that depression.

17. According to Ed Decker in the film, "Heaven to the Mormon woman is being pregnant for all eternity, one spirit baby after the next." A mental picture is thus drawn which is supposed to be repugnant to today's "liberated" women and somehow un-Christian. In reality, God has not yet completely revealed the process by which spirit children are added to His eternal family (of which we are all a part). But surely the process is more sophisticated than the nine month gestation period and pregnancy through which mortal women suffer to give birth. It was only after the Fall that God said to the woman Eve, "I will greatly multiply thy sorrow and thy conception; in sorrow thou shalt bring forth children." Therefore "pregnant" is a term which in all likelihood is applicable only to the post-Fall mortal condition.

18. Sandra Tanner is described as "considered to be one of the greatest living authorities on Mormonism." Considered by whom? Anti-Mormons? Being an "expert" on only one side of an issue doesn't make one an "authority." Dr. Jan Shipps, a non Mormon professor at Indiana University At Indianapolis is a much more believable "expert." Her book entitled *Mormonism, A New Religious Tradition* is acclaimed as an objective alternative to Tanner's polemic tome.

19. Mrs. Tanner says Utah (67% LDS) has a higher rate of divorce and suicide than the national average. Teen suicide is supposedly much higher than nationally. "This is partly due to the fact the Mormons emphasize perfection," she says. (For more details on the questionable statistics, see #44 below) Is it un-Christian to strive for perfection? Was it not Christ himself who said "Be ye therefore perfect, even as your Father in Heaven is perfect"? (Matt. 5:48) And though we, like Paul, have not "already attained" perfection, but "follow after" as we "press toward the mark" (Philip 3:12), is not the purpose of the church "for the perfecting of the saints" (Eph. 4:12)?

A truly heart rending and tragic case is presented of 16 year old Kip Eliason who committed suicide in 1982. When he approached LDS counselors regarding his "sexual feelings that were in direct conflict with the teachings of the Church," they lovingly reinforced those teachings and standards. This is implied to have led to the boy's death, and therefore is supposedly another proof that the LDS Church is not Christian.

Ironically, an almost identical case of a teen's suicide after receiving counseling from a religious leader has led to a landmark lawsuit filed by the second boy's parents. Except in this case the defendant is not a Mormon but a leading figure in the Evangelical Christian community who is also an ardent supporter of "The Godmakers." Did not Jesus say that we should cast out the beam in our own eye before worrying about the mote in the eye of our neighbor? Clearly, this kind of tragedy can happen in any church. Such exploitation of the Eliason family's grief by the filmmakers is unforgivable!

20. Ed Decker charges that The Book of Mormon calls the "Christian body" the "whore of Babylon." Actually two churches are mentioned in 1 Nephi 14:10 the "church of the Lamb of God" and the "church of the devil." It is the latter which is described as "whore of all the earth." However this church is further described in 1 Nephi 22:23 as actually a collection of "all churches which are built up to get gain, and all those who are built up to get power over the flesh, and those who are built up to become popular in the eyes of the world."..etc. Only those churches which fit this description need worry (and according to the complaints of many Christians, there unfortunately seems to be quite a few of them).

21. Ed Decker also charges in the film that the LDS temple ceremony "mocks the Christian pastor and calls him a hireling of Satan." The depicting of a nameless clergyman in the temple instruction is simply a teaching device where he recites the traditional creeds regarding the nature of God, which we believe to be in error. No disrespect or "mocking"

of any Christian pastor or any denomination is intended. In fact, the minister's integrity is demonstrated when he repents and changes his ways after he learns the truth from the apostles Peter, James, and John. (Note: Recent changes in the temple films have deleted the above portion of the instruction altogether.)

22. The film's narrator states that: "Mormons are instructed to use Christian terminology when talking to potential converts. Words such as 'God', 'Jesus', and 'salvation' all have different Mormon meanings which the outsider may not be aware of..."

LDS members use no different terminology when talking to non LDS than when talking to each other.

The sort of sinister deception that is implied simply does not exist. Any deviation from the Biblical usage and definition of the above words lies with the film's authors, not with the Latter day Saints.

23. Reference is made to "nine versions" told of Joseph Smith's First Vision, "each of which contradicts the other." These "unpublished" accounts are supposedly "deliberately kept from you by Mormon leaders" to conceal the truth. As a point of fact, the different versions were published in a feature article by James B. Allen in the official LDS church magazine The Improvement Era (April 1970) with the express approval of the "Mormon leaders," for all to see. An in depth article on this subject by Dean Jesse was also published in BYU Studies (Spring 1969).

A careful comparison will show that there is no more "contradiction" among the accounts than one will find in comparing the four descriptions of the life of Jesus found in Matthew, Mark, Luke, and John. In each case, different aspects of the events were emphasized or highlighted according to the needs of the intended audience at the time of the writing.

Similarly in Acts 9, 22, & 26 we find three different accounts of Saul's "first vision," with discrepancies as to who fell down and whether those with Saul saw the light or heard the voice, etc.

Yet both Saul's and Joseph's visions did take place. (They are actually quite similar.)

24. The film points out that there have been many changes in the LDS scriptures in their various editions. This is implied to be a fatal flaw. If so, then the rest of Christianity must share the same deficiency considering the thousands of changes made in the Bible in the hundreds of translations and editions that have been printed. Usually changes in LDS scripture have been made to correct typographical or punctuation errors, or to make the text either (1) agree more closely with the earliest editions, (2) seem more grammatically palatable to the modern reader, or (3) express under inspiration a clearer meaning of the original intent. (see #28 below)

25. Statements said to be made by Joseph Smith and Brigham Young regarding the possible inhabitants of the sun and moon were reported from journal entries or from third hand memory, and are suspect.

To imply that those quotes really represent LDS doctrine is another in a long list of distortions in this propaganda film.

But the real issue is, can a prophet believe something which is found to be in error by the science of a later age? If the Bible is true, the answer is yes. Leviticus 11 and Deut. 14 list the hare as an animal that chews the cud, which science has disproved. And Gen. 30:35-43 says that placing striped sticks in view of mating animals results in striped offspring. ...Moon men? These examples sound equally absurd in light of modern day scientific knowledge. The Rev. J. R. Dummelow in his One Volume Bible Commentary said something about the author of Genesis which could equally be applied to Joseph Smith or Brigham Young: "His scientific knowledge may be bounded by the horizon of the age in which he lived, but the religious truths he teaches are irrefutable and eternal."

26. Decker says: "The true doctrine (of the LDS church) teaches that there is no eternal life without a polygamous relationship." This is blatantly untrue. The church teaches that the highest heavenly rewards are reserved for those who enter the "new and everlasting covenant" of eternal marriage, but they can be married to just one person and receive the same rewards as anyone in a "polygamous relationship."

On polygamy: (the practice of which was officially ended by the LDS church in 1890) —if Joseph Smith seemed reticent to tell his wife Emma about this law of God at first, it is an understandable human foible. (Especially if you knew Emma!) But this no more disqualifies him from the office of prophet than the similar frailties seen in Abraham's lie to Pharaoh about Sara being his sister, or in Moses' boast to the Children of Israel that he would give them water from a rock in the desert. (Num. 20:7-12. His failure to acknowledge God on that occasion kept him out of the Promised Land as punishment, but did not negate his prophetic calling or nullify the scriptures he wrote.) In addition, it should be noted that these same ancient prophets and their followers also practiced polygamy... with the approval and sanction of God.

27. Sandra Tanner charges that LDS church historical records are hidden from the members in some sort of dark cover-up. Obviously the rare and valuable documents must be protected from public access, just like the closed stacks in many libraries and museums. Nor would the Church see the need to admit a known anti Mormon like Mrs. Tanner.

Incidentally, Mrs. Tanner and her husband have made a substantial business of publishing those same LDS church historical records that are supposedly "hidden." They must not be too hard to get hold of!

28. Decker says that Christian scholars are "always refining" the scriptures in the quest to "improve and validate the authenticity of the Holy Scripture." Then he says, "In Mormonism it's completely opposite." And yet when LDS efforts are made to "refine" scripture, resulting in changes, he decries these changes as proof of the non validity of LDS scriptures. (see #24 above) Come on, Ed... you can't have it both ways!

29. Dr. Charles Crane is presented as an "expert on Mormon archaeology." He is actually a Church of Christ minister with advanced degrees in "Ministry," "Divinity" and Psychology, (not archaeology) who in correspondence with me says he has "sought to study the archaeology of The Book of Mormon." He revealed no details on the extent of his study, so I must question his "expert" status.

30. Both Crane and Tanner claim that because the cities of The Book of Mormon are not found on modern maps, "there is no evidence for the book, any yet it's supposed to be a historical record." Dr. Richard Fales ("author, lecturer, archaeologist" what are his credentials?) says "not one single artifact has been found that even remotely relates to the (Book of Mormon) civilizations." He calls the book a "fairy tale."

Point of fact: Many books have been written detailing dozens of archaeological parallels between The Book of Mormon and the history of ancient America. The Book of Mormon's claims regarding wheeled vehicles, great walled cities with prayer towers, baptismal fonts, the use of cement, the presence of horses and elephants, etc. seemed absurd in 1830 when it was published. Yet these claims have been vindicated by archaeological discoveries since that time.

In addition, one particular artifact (Stela 5 Izapa from Chiapas, Mexico) contains a large and detailed drawing of the Tree of Life which appears to be a direct connection with The Book of Mormon. Competent scholars have found over 50 elements in Stela 5 which correspond to parts of a long and involved vision given by God to the prophet Lehi in the 8th chapter of 1st Nephi. This artifact was discovered by a Smithsonian dig in 1941, and to date no non-LDS scholar has offered a viable alternative interpretation of the inscription. Not bad for a "fairy tale"! (see the Ensign June 1985 pp. 54, 55.)

A note on the film's statement that "archaeology has been able to prove the existence of all great civilizations": It was only in the late1800's after many years of struggle against the archaeological "establishment" that the explorer Heinrich Schliemann finally found proof that unearthed the ancient city of Troy described in Homer's epic poems. Until that time they were considered to be in the realm of "fairy tales." Who's to say that in a year or two the great Book of Mormon cities of Bountiful or Zarahemla will not be uncovered and make news around the world? What will the anti Mormons say then?

Anyone sincerely wishing to study scientific evidences of The Book of Mormon should contact the Foundation for Ancient Research and Mormon Studies (FARMS) for a catalog of scholarly papers on a wide range of topics. (Update: Contact www. bookofmormoncentral.org)

(see also www.BMAF.org)

31. The film states that: "Mormon missionaries are converting people throughout the world by explaining to them that archaeology has "proven" The Book of Mormon to be true." This is false.

Sometimes archaeological evidences are shared with people to pique their interest and get them to seriously consider the book, but LDS missionaries are trained to teach people that the ultimate test of the truthfulness of The Book of Mormon is through an answer to prayer and a personal witness from the Holy Ghost, as described in James 1:5, 6. It is only through the Spirit of God that true conversion takes place.

32. Regarding the Book of Abraham in The Pearl of Great Price, which was revealed to Joseph Smith through the gift and power of God: The film says, "Several famous Egyptologists have now translated it (the Egyptian Papyri associated with the Book of Abraham) and have found that it doesn't have anything to do with the time of Abraham at all."

At least one of these "famous Egyptologists" Dee Jay Nelson made false claims about his academic background and his alleged employment as a translator for the LDS church. How many other holes are there in "The Godmakers" story?

The sincere investigator on this topic will find a wealth of information in Dr. Hugh Nibley's articles in BYU Studies (1968 and 1971) as well as those in the Improvement Era almost every issue from Jan. 1968 to May 1970, plus one in the *Ensign*, March 1976. Also see Michael Rhodes's study in BYU Studies 17 (1977). Also Nibley's book, The Message of the Joseph Smith Papyri (1975)

33. The 1978 revelation to President Kimball to give the LDS priesthood to blacks was said to have come because of "social pressure." This is wrong. The greatest period of pressure of this nature came in 1971. By 1978 it was hardly an issue because the civil rights movement was at a comparative ebb.

The revelation came as an answer to prayer from God's prophet and mouthpiece on Earth, at a time when increasing numbers of blacks were beginning to join the LDS Church. Church leaders desired to extend all blessings of membership to these people, and after much supplication God heard their prayers.

34. The film says that "the finality of Mormon theology is not based on evaluation by scriptural evidence," and that LDS missionaries do not encourage the people they're teaching to read from the Bible, only The Book of Mormon. This is untrue. In the Uniform System for Teaching Families, (the basic lessons that LDS missionaries use all over the world) they are expressly instructed to: "use only Biblical references with investigators." Nothing is taught in LDS doctrine that is in conflict with the Bible, and every opportunity is taken to point this out by studying the relevant Bible verses. (LDS prefer to use the King James Version)

35. The witness of truth by the Holy Ghost in the heart of the individual person described as a "burning in the bosom" is said to be a "totally subjective" process. This is incorrect, as

many Christians will testify. There are many times when one is walking in the Spirit that "the heart will be told what the mind cannot know." And yet the reliance by LDS on the Spirit for guidance and inspiration is implied to be somehow un-Christian! The makers of "The Godmakers" would prefer to gamble their Eternal Salvation on someone's (usually theirs) subjective interpretation of this Bible verse or that. (My Baptist friends tell me that when you get any three Baptists together on a Bible verse you'll get at least five opinions!)

Latter day Saints rely heavily on the Scriptures, including the Bible. But we believe that "no prophecy of the scripture is of private interpretation"(2 Pet. 1:20) "But God hath revealed them unto us by his Spirit: for the Spirit searcheth all things, yea the deep things of God.... Which things also we speak, not in the words which man's wisdom teacheth, but which the Holy Ghost teacheth: comparing spiritual things with spiritual."(1 Cor.2:10-13) This is the real test.

The Saints in the days of Paul relied on the witness of the Spirit instead of hermeneutics. The Saints of these latter days believe that true Christians must still do the same. It is the "rock" of revelation from God to man (as the Christian singer Sandi Patti so eloquently puts it in her wonderful song) on which the true church of Jesus Christ is built; not someone's Biblical interpretation, however learned. The "Born Again" experience itself necessitates the Holy Spirit witnessing to a person that Jesus is indeed their personal Savior, Lord, and Christ. It cannot come by Bible study alone.

36. The "reenactment" (so called) of LDS temple ceremonies is perhaps the most disappointing and offensive part of this film. An utter disregard is shown by the filmmakers for the sensitivities of other human beings. Ceremonies that are considered sacred by millions of people are trampled upon, ridiculed, and distorted, with definite purpose and malice aforethought. A great many right thinking Christians have expressed revulsion at this kind of propagandistic approach.

The producers of the film have admitted their use of deception to obtain stock footage of temple interiors from the LDS church information services, and to arrange interviews with church officials who appear in the film. These despicable tactics speak for themselves.

The LDS temple ceremonies are said to be "Mason like" and "occultic." There is nothing "occultic" about the covenants that LDS people make with our Heavenly Father in the temples, nor about the work done there for the dead. In fact one of these ceremonies baptisms for the dead was mentioned as a practice of the early Christians by the apostle Paul in 1 Cor.15:29. This is merely a way in which these necessary ordinances can be performed as a vicarious service for those who have died without the opportunity to hear the Gospel of Jesus Christ and accept Him as their Savior through baptism.

(Most Christian denominations have a hard time explaining what happens to these people.) What is described as a "fanatical program to evangelize the dead" is simply the fulfillment of prophecy in the last verse of the Old Testament (Malachi 4:6) that in the last days God will "turn the hearts of the children to their fathers." What is so "fanatical" or sinister or "occultic" about that?

If there is anything "Mason like" about the LDS temple ordinances, it might be explained by the fact that the Masonic order began among workers on the great Temple of Solomon. If God is "the same yesterday, today and forever," then the same ceremonies were performed by God's righteous believers in the Temple of their day. If God then revealed the ordinances to the prophet Joseph Smith in our day, a corrupted version handed down through the centuries by the Masons might still bear some resemblance to the original.

37. The sacred undergarment worn by LDS who have made special covenants with God in the temples is said to be "unattractive" and "de-humanizing." (Why should it be attractive since it is not meant to be seen? It's an undergarment!) These garments are patterned after the garments of skins that God made for Adam and Eve when He cast them out of the Garden of Eden. (Gen.3:21) Perhaps the filmmakers should take up their complaints with the original Tailor!

A parallel to the LDS temple garment can be seen in a similar item of under apparel worn by the most orthodox Jewish sects a holdover from Israel's righteous days when they performed temple worship thousands of years ago. It should also be noted that a similar item is mentioned in the earliest Jewish and Christian writings such as the Dead Sea Scrolls and the Nag Hammadi codices.

The extreme measures referred to in the film that are supposedly taken by LDS to avoid ever losing physical contact with the temple garment are totally incorrect. There are many occasions such as visits to a doctor, swimming, playing basketball, etc. when "temple Mormons" rightly do not wear the garment. The film portrayed a caricature that does not exist.

38. Another caricature is built up of Joseph Smith as a "treasure seeker" who was "involved in the occult." This description does not fit the man as all, as revealed in many accounts regarding him written by his contemporaries. (See #13 above) The mistake is also made of trying to judge Joseph, who lived in the mid 1800's, by the culture and practices of the 1980's. Similarly a person in the next century might say that having a Jack o'lantern on Halloween is a sure sign of being "involved in the occult," and the hobbyist with a metal detector is a "treasure seeker"!

39. An avowed Satanist's book is used as an authoritative source to come up with a mythical god "Mormo" whose followers are allegedly called "Mormons." Obviously if the same book were to have reference to a god "Metho" whose followers were called "Methodists," they would give it no credence or notice, except perhaps for a good horse laugh. To stoop to such antics in a supposedly serious "documentary" is inexcusable.

40. Likewise, the claim that the Chinese word "Mormon" means "gates of Hell" relies on an extremely tortured translation and is meaningless. It's just another example of sensationalism. The National Enquirer would win a Pulitzer Prize in comparison to the writers of this film!

41. Some sort of sinister implication (complete with evil sounding music to match) is made in speaking of the "wealth" of the LDS church and great landholdings. The narrator fails to mention that virtually all of the Church's real estate is identified as meetinghouses for LDS members (built with as little as 4% of the cost paid by the local congregations in recent years even this requirement has been removed), schools, and farms where food is raised to feed the needy in the model LDS welfare program.

The LDS church does have some stock in the parent corporation that owns the LA Times, but can hardly be considered a "major stockholder" (especially in view of some of the articles unfavorable to the Church which have appeared in that paper and its sister publication in Denver).

42. Money is said to be "extracted" from LDS church members in a "mandatory" tithing program.

These buzz words are by now quite tiresome, and again they are totally false! Tithes and offerings are no more "mandatory" for Mormons than for other Christians. As with any principle of the Gospel there are certain rewards (both temporally and spiritually) for obedience. But to show the picture of the young Deacon gathering Fast Offerings and imply that he was "shaking down" the Mormon mother for tithing... come on now! (The Fast offering is a separate contribution where members fast for two meals on the first Sunday of every month and give the cost of the meals into a special fund to feed the needy. This practice is now being picked up by some other Christian churches.)

43. Mormons are said to "own a substantial portion of Hawaii." It is not indicated whether they are referring to individual LDS members or to the Church. In either case the truth is stretched quite a bit.

44. Utah (identified as 75% Mormon actually it's closer to 50%) is said to "rank among the highest" of the states in divorce, suicide, child abuse, teenage pregnancy, venereal disease, and bigamy.

Utah (according to Atlanta's Communicable Disease Center) is 47th among the states in venereal disease. This is hardly "among the highest." In view of this kind of error, the rest of the statistics cited are highly suspect. The following, however, might explain any unexpectedly high figures for the state of Utah if they proved to be correct:

Utah is among the lowest states in abortions, which accounts for more teenage pregnancies carried to term. And since most young LDS people don't plan to be "sexually active" as do teens in other states, they are more likely to become pregnant when they do make mistakes. And since they try harder to "do the right thing" by getting married when they get pregnant, there are more teen marriages and hence more divorces.

And since Utah has some of the most strict child abuse reporting laws in the nation, (you must legally report even any SUSPECTED abuse) there is perhaps more reported child abuse than in other states. (Not necessarily more abuse.)

Therefore it can be seen that the supposedly damning statistics reveal in actuality the good "fruits" of the LDS church. The filmmakers failed to mention that of active LDS church members married in the temple, the number of divorces is only ONE FIFTH the national average.

45. The film says that "Mormonism undercuts the Bible," which is definitely false. Our 8th Article of Faith states, "We believe the Bible to be the word of God, as far as it is translated correctly." We believe it to be "verbally inspired" as do other Christians. That is, that it was "inerrant" as it flowed from the mind of God through the pens of the original writers. However we believe (along with most Christians) that copying and translation errors do occur. No Christian would accept as God's word any verse of the Bible which scholarship proves to be mistranslated, and neither do Mormons.

The film also says that Mormonism "undercuts all the other churches," which is misleading. Although we believe that the complete fullness of the Gospel of Jesus Christ is found only in our church, we believe that almost all religions contain some of God's truth and are beneficial to mankind.

It is not the Latter day Saints who brand another faith as a "cult" and seek to exclude its members from fellowship with other Christians. We leave that activity to the anti-Mormons.

46. It is said in the film that many LDS church members only remain in the church because

"Mormonism is a nice place to raise your family...it's the easy road." That description may be true in Utah, but it does not account for the rapid growth of the LDS church in other parts of the world like Latin America and Japan, where becoming a "Mormon" is anything but "the easy road." Many millions of people have decided to follow Christ as the Holy Ghost has led them by joining the LDS church, and in doing so have lost their jobs, families, everything. Sometimes even their lives.

47. "I learned that the God of Mormonism was not the God of the Bible." This statement near the end of the film shows that the person who uttered it has an incomplete knowledge of both Mormonism and the Bible. The God of Mormonism is not the God of the Nicene Creed, but He definitely IS the God of the Bible.

48. "But there's fraud...deliberate misrepresentation." This quote from Dick Baer aimed at the LDS church applies more aptly to his propaganda film "The Godmakers," as has been pointed out herein.

The foregoing <u>48 specific points</u> constitutes a partial list of the errors, distortions, and untruths in the film. These comments will also apply equally to the same problems found in the book of the same name, written by Ed Decker and Dave Hunt. A more complete response to the book has been written, but the major points of emphasis will probably not vary a great deal from those of the film which have been dealt with here. The book is called *The Truth About The Godmakers*, and is available at most LDS bookstores. More information on the book response may be obtained from the author, Gilbert Scharffs, 2898 Mill Creek Road, Salt Lake City, Utah 84109.

It is unfortunate that the authors and producers of the "Godmakers" film and book have felt it necessary to expend such great amounts of money, time and energy to persecute the Church of Jesus Christ of Latter day Saints. It is equally unfortunate that so many good Christians and pastors have unknowingly "aided and abetted" in this persecution by opening their churches and their pulpits to those who have been perpetuating it. Hopefully, this response will shed some light and lead to a better understanding between Latter day Saints and their fellow disciples in the Body of Christ.

In his brilliant essay on "What it Means to Be a Mormon Christian," BYU English professor Eugene England shared a quote from the great reformer Martin Luther: "The kingdom of God is like a besieged city surrounded on all sides by death. Each man has his place on the wall to defend and no one can stand where another stands, but nothing prevents us from calling encouragement to one another." England then goes on to say, "It would be tragic if we Christians, standing each in our different places, were to desert our place on the wall... to turn on each other."

Intolerance has no place among Christians. Jesus himself taught that lesson when his apostles came to him saying they had forbidden one casting out devils in His name because "he followeth not with us."

The Savior said: "Forbid him not: for he that is not against us is for us" (Luke 50:49). Likewise in Acts 5:27-39 we find: "Refrain from these men, and let them alone: for if this counsel or this work be of men, it will come to naught: But if it be of God, ye cannot overthrow it; lest haply ye be found even to fight against God."

This is a commandment from Jesus that the producers of "The Godmakers" and those who assist them need to learn and obey.

The foregoing is my own work and does not represent any official statement of The Church of Jesus Christ of Latter day Saints.

Robert D. Starling

S. 1740 W.

Riverton, UT 84065

starlingrd@msn.com

I especially welcome the opportunity for clarification or dialogue with non LDS readers.

APPENDIX 5

The LDS Articles of Faith

(from www.mormon.org)

One of the first things Mormons are taught as children are the Articles of Faith — 13 statements that summarize our fundamental beliefs.

Two years before he died, the Prophet Joseph Smith wrote them in a letter to a newspaper editor named John Wentworth who had asked for information about the Church.

Ever since the Articles of Faith were written, they've inspired and directed us in the basic principles of our religion. They enhance our understanding of certain doctrines and help us commit to living them. They invite further thought. And they're a good tool for explaining our beliefs to people unfamiliar with them.

Articles of Faith
1. We believe in God, the Eternal Father, and in His Son, Jesus Christ, and in the Holy Ghost.

2. We believe that men will be punished for their own sins, and not for Adam's transgression.

3. We believe that through the Atonement of Christ, all mankind may be saved, by obedience to the laws and ordinances of the Gospel.

4. We believe that the first principles and ordinances of the Gospel are: first, Faith in the Lord Jesus Christ; second, Repentance; third, Baptism by immersion for the remission of sins; fourth, Laying on of hands for the gift of the Holy Ghost.

5. We believe that a man must be called of God, by prophecy, and by the laying on of hands by those who are in authority, to preach the Gospel and administer in the ordinances thereof.

6. We believe in the same organization that existed in the Primitive Church, namely, apostles, prophets, pastors, teachers, evangelists, and so forth.

7. We believe in the gift of tongues, prophecy, revelation, visions, healing, interpretation of tongues, and so forth.

8. We believe the Bible to be the word of God as far as it is translated correctly; we also believe the Book of Mormon to be the word of God.

9. We believe all that God has revealed, all that He does now reveal, and we believe that He will yet reveal many great and important things pertaining to the Kingdom of God.

10. We believe in the literal gathering of Israel and in the restoration of the Ten Tribes; that Zion (the New Jerusalem) will be built upon the American continent; that Christ will reign personally upon the earth; and, that the earth will be renewed and receive its paradisiacal glory.

11. We claim the privilege of worshiping Almighty God according to the dictates of our own conscience, and allow all men the same privilege, let them worship how, where, or what they may.

12. We believe in being subject to kings, presidents, rulers, and magistrates, in obeying, honoring, and sustaining the law.

13. We believe in being honest, true, chaste, benevolent, virtuous, and in doing good to all men; indeed, we may say that we follow the admonition of Paul-We believe all things, we hope all things, we have endured many things, and hope to be able to endure all things. If there is anything virtuous, lovely, or of good report or praiseworthy, we seek after these things.

APPENDIX 6

THE GIFT OF TONGUES AMONG THE LATTER-DAY SAINTS

I originally wrote the following paper for a presentation at a Sunstone conference in Los Angeles in the 1980's. Much of what is written here is unknown even to most Latter-day Saints.

"AND THESE SIGNS SHALL FOLLOW THEM THAT BELIEVE:
- LDS GLOSSOLALIA"
by Robert D. Starling December 5, 1987

As members of the Church of Jesus Christ of Latter-day Saints, our Seventh Article of Faith states:

"We believe in the gift of tongues, prophecy, revelation, visions, healing, interpretation of tongues, and so forth."

Prophecy, revelation, visions, and healing are almost second nature to us. As a people and as a Church, we believe explicitly in miracles in these latter days. Even if our own **personal** experience with the miraculous is limited, we are surrounded each week with many brothers and sisters who can attest to God's power in these areas.

But what about these gifts of "tongues", and "interpretation of tongues"? For most of us, that's a little different, isn't it?

A GIFT PROMISED BY CHRIST

These were among the gifts promised by Jesus to those that believed on Him in Mark 16:17. After giving His apostles the Great Commission to "preach the gospel to every creature", the Savior said

"And these signs shall follow them that 'believe; in my name shall they cast out devils; they shall speak with new tongues..." ... and so forth.

TONGUES IN THE NEW TESTAMENT AND BOOK OF MORMON

The fulfillment of our Lord's promise was not long in coming. As the disciples met "with one accord in one place" on the day of Pentecost, we read that "suddenly there came a sound from heaven as of a rushing mighty wind, and it filled all the house where they were sitting. And there appeared unto them cloven tongues like as of fire, and it sat upon each of them. And they were all filled with the Holy Ghost, and began to speak with other tongues, as the Spirit gave them utterance." (Acts 2:1-4) The experience apparently caused a commotion in the neighborhood, causing a "multitude" to come together. (v.6)

It seems that several aspects of the gift of tongues were in evidence that day: (1) The speech of the disciples was incoherent babbling to those present who came to "mock" and who were unresponsive to the Spirit. They accused Peter and the others of being drunken and "full of new wine". And yet, (2) The gift of interpretation of tongues was obviously present, as the people who understood fifteen or more dialects each heard the speakers "in our own tongue, wherein we were born." (v.8)

Later when Peter preached the Gospel to Cornelius and his family, the Holy Ghost was poured out upon them. Peter and others "heard them speak with tongues", thus providing evidence that these first Gentile converts to Christianity were accepted by God as candidates for baptism. (Acts 10:46) Later Paul re-baptized certain believers who had not been previously taught about the Holy Spirit.

When he laid his hands on them and the Holy Ghost came upon them, "they spake with tongues, and prophesied" (Acts 19:6).

In the Book of Mormon, the prophet Amaleki exhorted all men to believe "in the gift of speaking with tongues, and in the gift of interpreting languages, and in all things which are good". (Omni v.25) This gift is also enumerated with other spiritual gifts in Alma 9:21

TONGUES IN THE DOCTRINE AND COVENANTS

When the Gospel was restored in this dispensation, a "restitution of all things" took place as prophesied in the New Testament (Acts 3:20-21). The gift of tongues was brought back to the earth along with other spiritual gifts.

In a listing of the gifts in the Restored Church found in D&C Section 46, we see that "it is given to some to speak with tongues; And to another is given the interpretation of tongues. And all these gifts come from God, for the benefit of the children of God." (v. 24-26) On March 27, 1836, in the dedicatory prayer for the Kirtland Temple recorded in D&C 109:35-37, the prophet Joseph asked of God,

"Let the anointing of thy ministers be sealed upon them with power from on high. Let it be fulfilled upon them as upon those on the day of Pentecost; let the gift of tongues be poured out upon thy people, even cloven tongues as of fire, and the interpretation thereof. And let thy house be filled as with a rushing mighty wind, with thy glory."

Later that same day, that prayer was answered fully in a meeting of 416 members of the priesthood quorums, as Joseph Smith himself described in the History of the Church, Vol. 2, Page 428.

"Brother George A. Smith arose and began to prophesy, when a noise was heard like the sound of a rushing mighty wind, which filled the Temple, and all the congregation simultaneously arose, being moved upon by an invisible power; many began to speak in tongues and prophesy; others saw glorious visions; and I beheld the Temple was filled with angels, which fact I declared to the congregation.

The people of the neighborhood came running together (hearing an unusual sound within, and seeing a bright light like a pillar of fire resting upon the Temple), and were astonished at what was taking place."

Thus the apostles of this Dispensation experienced almost an exact repetition of the Pentecost experience of their spiritual counterparts at the time of the Savior.

KNOWN AND UNKNOWN TONGUES

Throughout God's dealings with mankind, the expression of the gift of tongues has been manifested in at least two different ways. Paul told in 1 Corinthians 13:8 of speaking with both "the tongues of men and of angels". Thus this gift can be seen both as: (1) speaking or interpreting by the Spirit in an earthly language or dialect of "men", which is not known by the speaker(s) or hearer(s), and (2) speaking or interpreting in a "new" or "unknown" tongue, which Paul described as the tongues "of angels".

Let's consider them in order.

"KNOWN TONGUES"

This form of the gift is most familiar to modern Latter-day Saints. Countless missionaries have testified regarding the help they've received from the Holy Ghost in learning a foreign language so they could teach the Gospel. In fact most members of the Church when asked about "tongues" today will refer **only** to this expression of the gift.

And indeed this does seem to be its primary purpose. In 1839 the Prophet Joseph Smith taught a conference of the Twelve that, "Tongues were given for the purpose of preaching among those whose language is not understood; as on the day of Pentecost, etc."

—(History of the Church, V.3 p. 379. See also V.2 p. 162.)

Joseph F. Smith as a teenaged missionary in Hawaii was blessed by the Spirit so that after only 100 days of prayer and study he was able to preach the Gospel to the Hawaiians in their native language as if it were his own. Later he said,

"So far as I'm concerned, if the Lord will give me the ability to teach the people in my native tongue, or in their own language to the understanding of those who will hear me, that will be sufficient gift of tongues to me."

—Doctrines of Salvation p. 201

One of the favorite inspirational stories of the pioneers on their westward trek related how a young Jane Grover saved her family from Indians at Council Bluffs Iowa by miraculously speaking to them in their own language.

— Childrens Friend, July 1961, p.41

Among the best-known incidents of the gift of modern times occurred in Huntley, New Zealand, when Elder David O. McKay spoke in English to an assembly of a thousand Maori native Church members.

The congregation was blessed with the gift of interpretation, so that they understood him perfectly in their own language. When an interpreter began to give a summary of the talk in Maori, some of the non-English speaking members of the congregation stood up and corrected his interpretation!

— Gospel Ideals, p. 552

One of the most recent manifestations of speaking in known languages through the Spirit involves Elder Yoshihito Kikuchi of the First Quorum of 70. He relates that while serving as a young missionary in his native Japan, he attended a conference conducted in English. He had prayed that he might be able to understand the talks, though he spoke only Japanese. Near the end of the conference he himself was unexpectedly called upon to speak. After a few words in Japanese he began to give a beautiful testimony in perfect English.

— Church News 10/29/77

THE GIFT OF LANGUAGES IN OTHER CHURCHES

But what about the gift of tongues in other churches? The Bible says that the "fervent prayer of a righteous man availeth much" (James 5:16) even without the power of the Priesthood.

Apparently on occasion the gifts of the Spirit may be manifested among "them that believe" in Christ who are not members of our Church.

In his book, *With Other Tongues* (pp. 96-99), former *Guideposts* editor John Sherrill tells of a Christian missionary named Mr. Garlock who was captured by a tribe of cannibals called the Pahns.

Much like the young pioneer girl at Council Bluffs, Garlock's life was preserved when he was miraculously able to speak to them in their own language. Other similar instances have also been recorded.

"UNKNOWN" TONGUES

Let's look now at the second expression of the gift of tongues. Perhaps few aspects of Christianity are more controversial or misunderstood than the phenomenon of speaking in "unknown" tongues, sometimes referred to by the scientific term "glossolalia".

In the Protestant and Catholic worlds there are wide variations in belief regarding glossolalia, with strong feelings on each side of the issue. Many books, articles, and papers have been written to either defend or condemn these "ecstatic utterings", which by definition consist of incoherent babblings and resemble no known language on earth.

Views on the practice range from those who think it is being faked' or is of Satanic origin, to the other extreme of those who believe a person is not really "saved" unless he receives the "baptism of the spirit" as evidenced by speaking in unknown tongues.

A HISTORY OF THE "TONGUES" MOVEMENT IN THE 20TH CENTURY

Although glossolalia is specifically mentioned in the Bible as a legitimate spiritual gift, its common usage in Christianity is a fairly recent development. Historians trace the modern movement to New Year's Eve 1900 in a small church near Topeka, Kansas, where it began with a young girl named Agnes Ozman and her pastor, Charles Parham.

It quickly spread to the West Coast and found fertile soil in 1906 in the Azusa Street congregation of Los Angeles. This was the beginning of what came to be known as the "Pentecostal" movement, and by 1936 there were more than 2 million adherents in many countries around the world.

For the most part those who "spoke in tongues" were initially in congregations of relatively poor and uneducated people, and often they were looked down upon and called "Holy Rollers" by those in mainstream Christian denominations. (That term relates to the frequent occurrence of tongue-speakers'

falling down and rolling on the floor in apparent "spiritual ecstasy".) There were times when so-called "Pentecostals" faced persecution of a more violent nature, and in Camp Creek, North Carolina a church was burned to the ground by a mob of other alleged "Christians", similar to the anti-Mormons mobs who attacked the Saints in Missouri and Illinois.

THE "CHARISMATICS"

In 1960 the "tongues" movement entered a new era of respectability when a minister named Father Dennis Bennett of St. Mark's Episcopal church in Van Nuys, California claimed to have received the "gift". Although he was asked to resign by his church, his experience marked the beginning of a migration of glossolalia into groups of so-called "charismatics" within mainstream Protestant and even Catholic congregations. By the mid-sixties it was not uncommon to find Charismatic groups in many (if not most) Christian denominations.

SCIENTIFIC STUDIES

As "speaking in tongues" became more widespread and the subject of a great deal of media attention, scientific studies were undertaken to investigate the practice. It was discovered that in some cases tongue-speakers frequently repeated certain patterns of nonsense phrases over and over. And over a period of time they seemed to "learn" the "technique" of glossolalic speech. In other cases however, researchers using tape-recorded glossolalia were mystified and could find no non-supernatural explanation for the phenomenon. But even among those whose first experience with tongues seemed a genuine product of spiritual outpouring, after a time some of them seemed to slip in and out of glossolalic speech with a suspicious ease and voluntude.

NON-CHRISTIAN GLOSSOLALIA

Much to the surprise of many charismatic Christians, researchers have also discovered glossolalia in several non Christian cultures. The Eskimos of Greenland have been observed to speak in tongues at the height of frenzied rites, the shaman of North Borneo speaks to celestial spirits in their own language, and in East Africa many persons possessed by demons speak fluently in Swahili or English although under normal circumstances they do not understand either language.

— Tongues: To Speak or Not to Speak, Donald Burdick, p. 66

CONCLUSIONS REGARDING NON-MORMON GLOSSOLALIA

It's difficult with such wide-ranging data to draw any firm conclusions that would account for all instances of "speaking in unknown tongues". And although there might be a temptation for Latter-day Saints unfamiliar with the practice to scoff at it or condemn it, we must remember the scriptural admonition to "forbid not to speak in tongues" (1 Cor. 14:39) and to "desire spiritual gifts" (1 Cor. 14:1) This is particularly true when we look at the experiences with "unknown tongues" in our own LDS history.

GLOSSOLALIA AMONG THE LATTER-DAY SAINTS

Brigham Young is thought to be the first person in the Restored Church to speak in "unknown" tongues. According to his own history, in September 1832 he traveled from Mendon, N.Y. to Kirtland, Ohio in company with Heber C. Kimball and Joseph Young to meet the Prophet Joseph Smith. He writes,

"We visited with many friends along the way, and some branches of the Church. We exhorted them and prayed with them, and I spoke in tongues. Some pronounced it genuine and from the Lord, and others pronounced it of the devil."

Upon arriving in Kirtland and meeting the Prophet, Brigham continued: In the evening, a few of the brethren came in, and we conversed upon the things of the kingdom. He (Joseph) called upon me to pray; in my prayer I spoke in tongues. As soon as we arose from our knees, the brethren flocked around him, and asked his opinion concerning the gift of tongues that was upon me. He told them it was the pure Adamic language.. Some said to him they expected he would condemn the gift Brother Brigham had, but he said "No, it is of God." [1]

Joseph Smith also recorded Brigham's visit in his official history of the Church: "At one of our interviews, Brother Brigham Young and John P. Greene spoke in tongues, which was the first time I had heard this gift among the brethren; others also spoke, and I received the gift myself." (HC vol. 1 p. 296-297) In a priesthood conference the following January, President Smith again spoke in tongues, along with many others. (HC v. 1 p. 323)

The gift apparently became fairly common in the early days of the Restoration:

- On September 11, 1833, W.W. Phelps sung a hymn in tongues that was interpreted by Elder Lyman Wight. (HC v. 1 p.409)

- At a meeting in Kirtland of High Councilors and General Authorities on January 22, 1836, the Prophet relates: *"the gift of tongues fell upon us in mighty power, angels mingled their voices with ours, while their presence was in our midst, and unceasing praises swelled our bosoms for the space of half an hour."* ' (HC v.II p.383) (He also records that the brethren returned home from that meeting at two o'clock in the morning!)

- On the evening of December 30, 1845 a Sister Whitney sang a beautiful song of Zion in tongues in the Navoo Temple. It was interpreted by both her husband and Brigham Young. (HC v.7 p.557)

- When George Q. Cannon and the first LDS missionaries dedicated Hawaii for the preaching of the Gospel in December 1850, one of the elders spoke in tongues and another interpreted. (*The Instructor* Aug. 1964, centerfold)

- When Heber J. Grant was a little boy he was present with his mother at a Relief Society meeting in Salt Lake City. Eliza R. Snow pronounced a blessing on his head and prophesied through the gift of tongues that he would someday become an Apostle.

— *The Presidents of the Church, Preston Nibley, p.284*

And LDS glossolalia is not limited to the early days of the Restoration, either...

Sometime after World War I, Hildegard Hahl was a young girl in Germany when she heard a talk in sacrament meeting by a young American missionary who had not yet learned to speak German. On the way home she asked her parents what language he had spoken, because she had understood him perfectly although he had not talked in English or German. Her father replied that the elder had spoken in tongues.

— *Ensign*, Jan.1983, "Mormon Journal"

GUIDELINES FOR THE USE OF TONGUES

The exercise of the gift of tongues when it refers to known languages has many beneficial uses in preaching the Gospel, as we've already noted. But what of "unknown" tongues? Granted, we recognize it as a legitimate gift, but what is it for? Why do we have it? When (and why?) might it be used among the Saints?

Since we're admonished in 1 Cor. 12:31 to "covet earnestly the best gifts", should Latter-day Saints actively pursue glossolalic experiences? If tongues was a frequent gift in the early days of the Restoration, why is it not more evident in the Church today?

Paul spent the better part of 1st Corinthians 14 cautioning the Saints of his day against an over-emphasis of this gift, and gave some good counsel regarding it. Even though he "spake with tongues more than you all", (1 Cor 14:18) he said he "would rather speak five words of understanding than ten thousand in tongues" (v. 19). Paul said we should "seek rather to prophesy" (v. 1) or preach by the Spirit in known languages, so that we might not sound an "uncertain trumpet"(v.8), but rather a clear call to battle.

He also counseled, "If any man speak in an unknown tongue, let it be by two, or at the most by three, and that by course; and let one interpret. But if there be no interpreter, let him keep silence in the church; and let him speak to himself, and to God." — (1 Cor. 14:27-28) (Incidentally, the word "unknown" used referring to tongues was inserted several times in this chapter by the King James translators. The word is not found in the original Greek. The Joseph Smith Translation uses "another" tongue instead.)

The apostle Paul indicates that one reason for the gift of tongues is to be a "witness to the unbelievers"(v.22) — a demonstration of God's power. This might tend to explain why it was more frequently seen in the early days of the Latter-day church along with other miracles, to validate the Restoration of Apostolic Priesthood authority. He also said that tongues were to "edify the speaker, not the hearer" (v.4)

The prophet Joseph Smith also gave some cautions regarding tongues. He said that no revelation of Church doctrine or government was to be received via tongues, and Joseph said we should be on our guard because it's easy for Satan to deceive people via tongues. For example, on August 6, 1834 a part of the Church in Jackson and Clay counties known as the Hulet Branch was led astray through an incorrect application of the gift of tongues, and it was necessary for the High Council of Zion to send brethren to labor with them and set the truth in order before them.

—(HC v.II, pp. 139-141, 162-163)

SUMMARY

In summary then, to answer the original questions:

"Is there evidence of the gift of today?"

Yes, in great abundance regarding known languages, but less so with respect to "unknown tongues".

Still, we acknowledge that glossolalia is a legitimate spiritual gift for "them that believe" in Christ.

And we "forbid not to speak in tongues" (although it might cause quite a stir in most of our wards should it occur in our next Fast and Testimony meeting!).

"How can we interpret accounts of members of other churches speaking in tongues?"

We must do as the Bible says and "judge with righteous judgment" (John 7:24) (and at times with large grain of salt), all the while realizing that spiritual gifts were promised to "all them that believe", not just to members of the Church.

We might ask: Does the experience edify? (at least the speaker, if not the hearers) Does it follow Paul's guidelines regarding the number of speakers and the necessity of an interpreter?

Does it testify of Christ? Is it done "decently and in order"? (1 Cor. 14:40) Even if these scriptural criteria are met, we cannot be **certain** that any given experience of glossolalic speech is definitely of God, but it is possible.

CONCLUSION

Because glossolalia is a highly visible gift and definitely out of the ordinary, the temptation exists to seek after it. But the Savior said, *"it is a wicked generation that seeketh after a sign"*, and this is how people sometimes approach the gift of tongues.

President Joseph F. Smith wrote,

"I believe in the gifts of the Holy spirit unto men, but I do not want the gift of tongues, except when I need it. ... Yet if the Lord gives you the gift of tongues, do not despise it, do not reject it. For if it comes from the Spirit of God, it will come to those who are worthy to receive it, and it is all right.

But this idea of seeking it, desiring it, when you don't pay your tithing, when you don't pray in your families, when you don't pay your debts, when you desecrate the Sabbath day, and when you neglect other duties in the Church; I tell you the devil will take advantage of you by and by, if he does not at first".

—(Apr. C.R., 1900, p. 41)

Instead, we must remember that this is only **one** of the gifts of the Spirit, and we should "seek after the **best** gifts." (Perhaps it's significant that "tongues" is almost always mentioned **last** whenever Scripture lists the gifts.)

We should also remember that not all receive the **same** gifts. (1 Cor. 12) Paul said "do all speak with tongues? do all interpret?", implying that they do not. (1 Cor. 12:30) Instead, the better path is that we seek after the **source** of these spiritual gifts. Our goal should be to live our lives in such a way that we have a closer companionship with the Holy Ghost Himself, and with our Father in Heaven and His son Jesus Christ. Then, **when** and **if** Father sees that we need them, He will see that we receive our portion of the spiritual gifts —those signs that our Savior said would follow "them that believe".

END

ENDNOTES FOR APPENDIX 6

1   — *Millennial Star,* vol.xxv, p.439. (quoted in *History of the Church* [hereinafter HC] vol. 1 p.297)

APPENDIX 7

THE MORMONS, THE BLACKS, AND THE PRIESTHOOD

- WHY I BELIEVE — by Robert Starling
(PLEASE NOTE: THIS ESSAY WAS WRITTEN IN 1976, <u>TWO YEARS PRIOR</u> TO THE REVELATION GRANTING THE PRIESTHOOD TO ALL WORTHY MALES IN THE CHURCH OF JESUS CHRIST OF LATTER-DAY SAINTS.)

It seems that the Church of Jesus Christ of Latter-day Saints has always been under fire or persecution for one or another of its doctrines that doesn't agree with the prevailing thought of the religions and/or the general populace.

When Joseph Smith first reported in 1820 that our Heavenly Father and his Son Jesus Christ had appeared to him in a vision, it touched off a storm of controversy in the area. Then in the late 1800's, the Mormon Church came under tremendous persecution for its doctrine of plural marriage. And now, in modern times, the Latter-day Saints are under severe criticism for the Church's policy of not allowing Negro members to hold the Priesthood if they are worthy as other male members do.

How, it is asked, can any intelligent and right-thinking Mormon support the Church's supposedly racist position on this issue? As I feel myself to be a reasonably intelligent and right-thinking Mormon, and having been asked feelings about this on occasion, I feel constrained to —as the Apostle Peter put it — "give reason for the belief that is in (me)."

First, let's understand that this is a religious matter, based solely on what we Latter-day Saints believe to be a commandment of God, given through His Holy prophets. Therefore we can no more disregard God's mandate in this matter than we can disregard the Ten Commandments.

But how, it is asked, can a just God give such a commandment? This requires a better understanding of God and our relationship to Him. An important point to remember is that the only thing we can know about God is what He has revealed to mankind. All else is speculation. Mormonism is not a speculative religion, but is firmly based on what God has revealed to man through His chosen mouthpieces, the prophet (Amos 3:7). Since our human speculation about what is right and just is based on our finite knowledge and intelligence, we don't always understand the infinite wisdom of our Heavenly Father.

"My ways are not your ways, neither are my thoughts your thoughts, saith the Lord".
—(Isaiah 55:8)

Next, let it be remembered that except for the restriction on the Priesthood for Negro people, all the blessings and fruits of the Church are available to all its members. There are many Negro members of the Church who participate actively and are an asset to the Church, including at least one member of the Salt Lake Mormon Tabernacle Choir, and a recently elected vice president of the Brigham Young University student body.

I have used the term "Negro" rather than "black" for a reason. The restriction on holding the priesthood is not based on the color of a man's skin, but is a matter of lineage. For instance there are Church members who are Australian aborigines or some Polynesians that are blacker than many Negroes, and they hold the full rights of the Priesthood. The restriction is limited to the descendants of Cain, who first received the curse of a black skin as a mark from God after murdering his brother Abel. His lineage was preserved through the Flood by Egyptus, the wife of Noah's son Ham.

"All right", you may say, "if God has told the Mormons that the Negroes cannot hold the Priesthood, then where is it in their scripture?" The most explicit references concerning this are found in the Pearl of Great Price, in revelations that were first given to Moses and Abraham, and revealed to the prophet Joseph Smith either by direct inspiration or through translation of ancient papyrus scrolls from Egypt.

These can be found in the Book of Moses, (7:8,12,22), and the Book of Abraham (1:16-31).

To demonstrate that the restriction of certain of God's blessings to certain lineage has precedent and is consistent with other scripture let's do a little research, always remembering that the Priesthood cannot be taken upon himself by a man but must be given from God by prophecy, as Aaron was called.

—(Hebrews 5:4)

God gave many promises to Abraham, Isaac, and particularly Jacob (called Israel) that their posterity would be a "chosen people" and that He (Jehovah) would be their God, and they would be His people. But even though all of the twelve Tribes of Israel were of the "chosen people", the Priesthood was restricted to only those of one tribe, the tribe of Levi. And the higher priest's office was to be held only by Aaron and his sons. Anyone trying to usurp the Priesthood authority was dealt with directly by God, with great severity. (Judges 3:3-10, Numbers 18:1-7, & 21-23, Numbers 16:7-10, 21, 28, 30-35)

In the New Testament we find that the Savior Himself at first directed the Apostles to restrict their preaching to those of the House of Israel. On their first missionary journey they were told to "go not into the way of the Gentiles, and into any city of the Samaritans enter ye not: But go rather to the lost sheep of the house of Israel" (Matthew 10:5 & 6). It was not until after Christ's resurrection that He gave them the charge to "go ye unto all the world" with the Gospel message.

On one occasion a Gentile woman of Canaan came to Christ asking Him to heal her daughter. At first He refused to even recognize her presence, saying to his Apostles, "I am not sent but unto the lost sheep of the house of Israel ... It is not meet to take the children's bread, and to cast it to dogs."

Because of her persistence and great faith, however, he made an exception and healed her daughter (Matthew 15:21-28). This incident further illustrates that at that point in time, Christ's teachings and His blessings were meant to be restricted to a certain lineage - that of the twelve tribes of Israel (This is also found in Mark 7:26).

CONCLUSIONS:
(1) God restricts some blessings at certain times because of lineage. This is undeniable from scriptural evidence.

(2) According to latter-day scriptures, He has restricted the Negroes from holding the Priesthood at this time.*

(3) Although we may not know why, this is God's commandment to us and we must obey. If any change comes in this policy, it must come by revelation from God, or it would be in defiance of His law.

*NOTE: Brigham Young and other modern prophets have stated that the Negro lineage will receive the Priesthood at some future date, but we do not know when that will be.

Having given the scriptural reasons and references, let me add my personal testimony concerning these things. I have a witness from the Holy Ghost to my spirit that Joseph Smith and the prophets who have succeeded him in these latter days have spoken the will of the Lord. I know that our Heavenly Father loves all his children, and that He has wisdom beyond our finite knowledge. Therefore I have faith that His commandments are right and just. The Church of Jesus Christ of Latter-day Saints can do more for the eternal salvation of the Negro people than any other church on the face of the earth, because it is the only church that contains the fullness of the truth of the Gospel of Jesus Christ.

And it is in the name of Jesus Christ that I give this testimony, to anyone who may care enough to read it.

Robert D. Starling
August 10, 1976

APPENDIX 8

A LETTER TO PASTOR ROBERT JEFFRESS OF DALLAS FIRST BAPTIST CHURCH

Dear Staff Members at First Baptist Dallas, October 14, 2011

I've tried unsuccessfully to find an email address for Dr. Robert Jeffress, so I'm sending this to all of the members on the First Baptist Dallas staff that I found listed on your website. I hope that at least one of you will forward this on to Pastor Jeffress because I feel it's important that he have the opportunity to read and understand it.

(Note: I never received any response from anyone at Dallas First Baptist)

= = =

Dear Pastor Jeffress,

I'm just one of the millions of people who saw and heard on TV news shows your statements that "Mormonism is a cult" and "not a part of orthodox Christianity". As a faithful lifelong member of The Church of Jesus Christ of Latter-day Saints I felt a strong reaction to those statements, as you might imagine. My remarks here are only my personal thoughts, but I assure you they are heartfelt.

My reaction was twofold. First, I saw your remarks as an unfortunate "below-the-belt" swipe at Mitt Romney in the hopes of advancing your own favorite political candidate. While you certainly have the right to do that, I think many Americans join me in feeling that such a move was beneath a prominent religious leader such as yourself.

Second, as a devoted believer and follower of Jesus Christ I was saddened that you felt the need to speak out against my faith and beliefs. I'm sure there are those who think it was done with malice, but I'll try to do the Christ-like thing and give you the benefit of the doubt. Perhaps you've just been misinformed about "Mormonism" as many others have been.

But it might surprise you to learn that I actually agree with part of what you said, although perhaps for different reasons than you might imagine.

You said that Mitt Romney is "not a Christian" (and by association myself and the other six million-plus Americans who are Latter-day Saints). But I believe you need to be more specific. There are many different kinds or "flavors" of Christians. I agree that the LDS people are not Baptist Christians or Evangelical Christians or Catholic Christians, etc. I will even agree that we're not part of "orthodox" or "traditional" flavor of Christianity, if by that you mean the post-Nicene church that became the "universal" or "catholic" version of Christendom.

I believe my faith to be the original church of the Corinthians, the Ephesians, and yes, those who were first called Christians in Antioch, - that same church now restored in these latter days. So I call myself a "latter-day Christian", with theological roots that precede the "historical" or "orthodox" version that was the product of the various councils and creeds. That "orthodoxy" eventually became so corrupt and so apostate that the Reformers broke away from it in protest of its having "fallen away" from Biblical truths (2 Thess. 2) and "changed the ordinances" (Isa. 24:5) so that the "faith once delivered to the saints" (Jude 1:3) was no longer recognizable as the church that Jesus organized.

There were many enlightened Christian thinkers and theologians in history who, like Joseph Smith, believed that Christianity had become apostate and that a restoration of the New Testament church of Christ was necessary. John Wesley the founder of Methodism wrote:

It does not appear that these extraordinary gifts of the Holy Ghost were common in the Church for more than two or three centuries. We seldom hear of them after that fatal period when the Emperor Constantine called himself a Christian; . . . From this time they almost totally ceased; . . . The Christians had no more of the Spirit of Christ than the other Heathens . . . . This was the real cause why the extraordinary gifts of the Holy Ghost were *no longer to be found in the Christian Church; because <u>the Christians were turned Heathens</u>* <u>*again, and had only a dead form left.*</u>

The Works of John Wesley, vol. 7, pp.26-27

As I'm sure you well know, John Smythe the founder of the Baptists first left his position as a Church of England minister and joined the Separatists, but then dissolved his congregation to re-form it as the first General Baptist church among English expatriates in Amsterdam in 1609. He felt that the "historic" or "orthodox" Christianity of his time had wandered astray, especially with regard to the apostate doctrine of infant baptism. Those first Baptists were considered a "cult" by many Protestants in the "traditional" Christian denominations that persecuted them unmercifully.

Around 1640, Roger Williams of Providence, Rhode Island, founder of the first Baptist church in America refused to continue as pastor on the grounds that there was:

... <u>no regularly-constituted church on earth</u>, nor any person authorized to administer any Church ordinance: nor could there be <u>until new apostles are sent</u> by the great Head of the Church, for whose coming, I am seeking.

(Picturesque America, or the Land We Live In, ed. William Cullen Bryant, New York: D. Appleton and Co., 1872, vol. 1, p. 502.)

If I understand your words correctly your definition of a Christian (and that of most Evangelicals) is a pretty narrow one, far different from the standard meaning found in most dictionaries. Personally I think anyone who accepts Jesus Christ as the Only Begotten Son of God and as his/her personal Savior who died for our sins and was bodily resurrected on the third day is a Christian. C.S. Lewis described such people as "mere" Christians.

But your narrow definition would exclude anyone who:

1. Does not believe in a closed canon of the 66 books of the Protestant Bible.

2. Does not accept the Nicene Creed as an accurate description of the nature of God the Father, His Son Jesus Christ, and the Holy Ghost.

3. Believes in living prophets and apostles as the "foundation" of Christ's earthly church.

4. Believes in continuing revelation from God to man.

I could go on. I'm very familiar with the standard arguments against "Mormonism".

But the Bible says that believers in Christ were first called Christians at Antioch (Acts 11:26). I would respectfully submit that those Christians:

1. Did not believe in a closed canon of scripture. (some of the New Testament had not yet been written.)

2. Did not accept the Nicene Creed as an accurate description of the nature of God the Father, His Son Jesus Christ, and the Holy Ghost. (it would not be written for 300 years)

3. Believed in living apostles and prophets as the "foundation" of Christ's earthly church.

4. Believed in continuing revelation from God to man.

So if you're going to say that Mitt and I are not Christians based on those reasons, you'll have to say that the believers in Antioch were not Christians either according to your definition.

You said in your Hardball television interview that "Mormonism" is a "cult" because:

1. "Mormonism came 1800 years after Jesus Christ"

2. "Mormonism has its own human leader, Joseph Smith"

3. "it has its own set of doctrines"

4. "it has its own religious book, The Book of Mormon, in addition to the Bible"

Your exact following words were: "and so by that definition it is a theological cult". You made a weak distinction between a theological cult and a sociological one, but most people will not even notice that fine differentiation. It was obvious to any sophisticated viewer that your main goal was to keep repeating the word "cult". It's such an inflammatory buzz word that I'm sure your goal is to use it as often as you can to scare people away from "Mormonism" without seriously considering our theology and our beliefs. It's a word used to end or avoid discussion, not to foster it.

As a Latter-day Saint I welcome the opportunity to "stand ready to give a reason for the faith that is in me", but those who sling around the word "cult" with respect to The Church of Jesus Christ of Latter-day Saints seek to cut off debate rather than to encourage dialog. It's as though they are afraid of an open and honest discussion.

But following your own definition of "cult" for a moment, I'd like to respectfully submit that:

1. Roman Catholicism came 300 years after Jesus Christ.

2. Roman Catholicism has its own human leader, the Pope (or Peter if you accept the Catholic claims that he was the first Pope)

3. Roman Catholicism has its own set of doctrines (Mariology, transubstantiation, priestly celibacy, veneration of "saints", indulgences, etc.)

4. Roman Catholicism has its own religious books (9 *deuterocanonical* more than those found in the Protestant Bible – also used in Eastern Orthodox churches)

And even your own Baptist flavor of Christianity in some ways fits your definition of what makes a cult;

1. "Baptistism" came 1609 years after Jesus Christ

2. "Baptistism" had its own human leader John Smythe – a Church of England minister (see footnote below from the website of the Baptist History and Heritage Society)

3. "Baptistism" had its own unique doctrines, including the "believer's baptism" of adults.

4. "Baptistism" was considered a cult by the "orthodox" or "traditional" or "historic" Christian denominations of the time. In fact Baptists suffered severe persecution from other Christians who believed in the "mainline" doctrine of infant baptism prevalent in that era. Thousands of Baptists were martyred for baptizing adults.

One of the dictionary definitions of a cult is that is a small isolated group that is out of the mainstream. That certainly does not apply to my church. The Church of Jesus Christ of Latter-day Saints is the fourth largest religion in America, and the second largest Christian church in Washington, Oregon, and California (after Catholicism). You mentioned that there are 15 million Southern Baptists. By 2012 at the present rate of growth there will be more Latter-day Saints than that.

Pastor Jeffress, in order to be consistent and truthful you would have to admit that the same definition you've used to brand "Mormonism" a cult applies at least in part to Roman Catholicism and "Baptistism" as well. Are you willing to say that on national television? I would hope so. I would hope that you'd want to be totally consistent and truthful.

Thank you for your time. I'm attaching a summary I wrote of what I believe happened to "the faith once delivered to the saints". There was a great apostasy that fundamentally changed the New Testament church of Jesus Christ into something so different that those Christians at Antioch or Peter or Paul would not have recognized it in the Dark Ages that came upon the earth. (Amos 8:12) That apostasy required the "restitution of all things" prophesied in Acts 3:21 to occur before Christ's return. That restitution or restoration of original Biblical Christianity was what was looked forward to by Roger Williams.

I testify to you that that restoration has come, and the original Christianity is back on the earth in its fullness as The Church of Jesus Christ of Latter-day Saints. If you would like to investigate these claims I'll be happy to "bring forth my strong reasons" for "the faith that is in me." I would welcome a thoughtful dialog.

Cordially yours,

Robert Starling
A Latter-day Christian.
S. 1740 W. Riverton, UT 84065
starlingrd@msn.com

(footnote re: above reference to John Smyth)
BHHS -- Baptist Beginnings http://www.baptisthistory.org/baptistbeginnings.htm
The first General Baptist church, led by John Smyth, was founded in Amsterdam, Holland, in 1608/09. Its members were English refugees who had fled England to escape religious persecution. John Smyth was a minister in the Church of England. As a student and later as a pastor and teacher. ... By 1608/09, Smyth was convinced his Separatist church was not valid. Most of the members had only infant baptism, and the church was formed on the basis of a "covenant," rather than a confession of faith in Christ. Smyth therefore led the church to disband in 1608/09 and re-form on a new basis–a personal

confession of faith in Christ, followed by believer's baptism. Since none of the members had been baptized as believers, Smyth had to make a new beginning. He baptized himself and then baptized the others. His baptism was by sprinkling or pouring, but it was for believers only.

Printed in the United States
By Bookmasters